The Masorah of the Former Prophets in the Leningrad Codex

Texts and Studies

14

Series Editor

H. A. G. Houghton

Editorial Board

Jeff W. Childers

Viktor Golinets

Christina M. Kreinecker

Alison G. Salvesen

Peter J. Williams

Texts and Studies is a series of monographs devoted to the study of Biblical and Patristic texts. Maintaining the highest scholarly standards, the series includes critical editions, studies of primary sources, and analyses of textual traditions.

The Masorah of the Former Prophets in the Leningrad Codex

Volume 6
2 Kings

David Marcus

2022

Gorgias Press LLC, 954 River Road, Piscataway, NJ, 08854, USA

www.gorgiaspress.com

Copyright © 2022 by Gorgias Press LLC

All rights reserved under International and Pan-American Copyright Conventions. No part of this publication may be reproduced, stored in a retrieval system or transmitted in any form or by any means, electronic, mechanical, photocopying, recording, scanning or otherwise without the prior written permission of Gorgias Press LLC.

2022

ISBN 978-1-4632-0604-8 **ISSN 1935-6927**

Library of Congress Cataloging-in-Publication Data

A Cataloging-in-Publication Record is available from the Library of Congress.

Printed in the United States of America

TABLE OF CONTENTS

Table of Contents v
Abbreviations vii
Preface ix
How the Corpus is Arranged xi
    Textual notes concerning the Mp xvi
    Textual notes concerning the Mm xviii
2 Kings 1

ABBREVIATIONS

absol	absolute	M^A	Aleppo Codex
adj	adjective	M^C	Cairo Codex
cj	conjunction	M^L	Leningrad Codex
consec	consecutive	Mf	Masorah finalis
cstr	construct	Mm	Masorah magna
def	definite	Mp	Masorah parva
etc	et cetra "and others"	ms(s)	manuscript(s)
fem	feminine	n	note
fol	folio	neg	negative
gen	genitive	perf	perfect
imper	imperative	pers	person
impf	imperfect	pl	plural
indef	indefinite	prep	preposition
infin	infinitive	pron	pronoun
interrog	interrogative	ptcp	participle
lit	literally	rel	relative
masc	masculine	sfx(s)	suffix(es)
M	The Accepted Masoretic text	sg	singular
		v(v)	verse(s)

PREFACE

This volume is the final volume of a six-volume set on the *Masorah of the Former Prophets in the Leningrad Codex*. It transcribes, translates and annotates every masoretic note in the Leningrad Codex that accompanies the text of *2 Kings*. This corpus of notes is preceded by a chapter, originally published in the volume on *Joshua*, detailing how the entries are arranged. Other introductory material, such as essays on the transmission of the masorah of Leningrad, on its relationship with other masorahs, and on the reason for the masoretic notes, may be found in the *Introduction* to the *Joshua* volume.

HOW THE CORPUS IS ARRANGED

This corpus transcribes, translates and annotates every masoretic note in the Leningrad Codex that accompanies the text of the six books of the Former Prophets (Joshua, Judges, 1 Samuel, 2 Samuel, 1 Kings, and 2 Kings). The following sample entry of the lemma וַיְבִיאֻהוּ (Judg 1:7) will serve to illustrate how the corpus is arranged. First we present the entry as it occurs in the corpus, and then describe each section of this entry in more detail.

> **Judges 1:7**
> וַיֹּאמֶר אֲדֹנִי־בֶ֗זֶק שִׁבְעִ֣ים מְלָכִ֡ים בְּהֹנוֹת֩ יְדֵיהֶ֨ם וְרַגְלֵיהֶ֜ם מְקֻצָּצִ֗ים הָי֤וּ מְלַקְּטִים֙ תַּ֣חַת שֻׁלְחָנִ֔י כַּאֲשֶׁ֣ר עָשִׂ֔יתִי כֵּ֥ן שִׁלַּם־לִ֖י אֱלֹהִ֑ים וַיְבִיאֻ֥הוּ יְרוּשָׁלַ֖͏ִם וַיָּ֥מָת שָֽׁם׃ פ

1:7   וַיְבִיאֻהוּ

Seven times   ז̇   Mp

1–5 **Judg 1:7**; **1 Sam 5:1** (וַיְבִאֻהוּ); 2 Kgs 23:30 (וַיְבִיאֻהוּ); **Jer 26:23** (וַיְבִיאֻהוּ); **Ezek 19:4** (וַיְבִאֻהוּ)

6–7 **Ezek 19:9** (וַיְבִאֻהוּ); 2 Chr 22:9 (וַיְבִיאֻהוּ)

וַיְבִיאֻהוּ *seven times*   ז̇ [ויביאהו] (ויבאהו)   Mm

1–5 Judg 1:7   אדני בזק
     1 Sam 5:1   ופלשתים
     <Ezek 19:4>
     Ezek 19:9   בסוגר
     {Ezek 19:8}   {ממדינות}
     2 Kgs 23:30   וירכבהו
6–7 2 Chr 22:9   אחזיהו
     Jer 26:23   אוריהו

xi

Com.: The Masorah notes the *seven* occurrences of this lemma, written plene and defective second י (וַיְבִיאֻהוּ/וַיְבִאֻהוּ), in the pl., to distinguish them from its more numerous occurrences (13x), written plene and defective second י, in the sg. (וַיְבִיאֵהוּ/וַיְבִאֵהוּ); see Ognibeni, *'Oklah*, §1K.

All the highlighted Mp notes read *seven times* except for the one at **1 Sam 5:1**, which reads *six times defective* (second י) because it does not include the form here at Judg 1:7 that is written plene second י (וַיְבִיאֻהוּ).

In the Mm, in place of a catchword for the Ezek 19:4 reference, a catchword מְמְדִינוֹת from Ezek 19:8 has mistakenly been written.

Depending on what is in the ms., each entry may consist of the following: (1) its lemma (2) a Masorah parva (Mp) note; (3) references for the Mp note; (4) a Masorah magna (Mm) note; (5) catchwords and references for the Mm note; (6) a commentary; and (7) textual notes.

1. **The lemma**. The lemma entry consists of the chapter and verse number (here, 1:7) of the respective book and the form of the word or words (= the lemma) as it appears in the text of M^L.

      Judg 1:7   וַיְבִיאֻהוּ

The verse numbers correspond to the standard enumeration of the various chapters as presented in the editions of *BHS* or *BHL*.[1] The lemma is always presented with its vowels, as it is written in the text of M^L and, where germane for the understanding of a note, the lemma is provided with accentuation.[2]

2. **The Masorah parva (Mp) note**. The Masorah parva note consists of three elements. Firstly, on the right hand side is an indication that the note is a Masorah parva (Mp) one, and not a Masorah magna note (Mm).

    Seven times   ז̇   Mp

Secondly, this Mp indication is followed by the masoretic note as it appears in the ms. (here ז̇). Thirdly, in the left hand margin is the translation of the note (here "seven times").

3. **The references for the Mp note**. The references for the Mp note are arranged chronologically according to the order of the traditional canonical books (e.g., To-

---

[1] Occasionally the verse numbers will vary in different printed editions. For example, at Joshua 21 the enumeration in *BHS* includes two verses (36 and 37), which are not in the editions of *Mikra'ot Gedolot 'Haketer'* or Breuer, *Torah Neviim Ketuvim*.

[2] Especially in cases where the note is concerned with words accented *mil'êl* (on the penultimate) or *milra'* (the ultimate).

rah, Prophets, and Writings). The main difference between this traditional order and that of M^L is in the order of the Writings. The traditional order lists Psalms, Proverbs, Job, etc. with Chronicles at the end, whereas the Codex places Job before Proverbs, and Chronicles before Psalms.

1–5 **Judg 1:7**; **1 Sam 5:1** (וַיְבִאֻהוּ); 2 Kgs 23:30 (וַיְבִאֻהוּ); **Jer 26:23** (וַיְבִאֻהוּ); **Ezek 19:4** (וַיְבִאֻהוּ)

6–7 **Ezek 19:9** (וַיְבִאֻהוּ); 2 Chr 22:9 (וַיְבִאֻהוּ)

Where the lemma has Mp notes elsewhere in the ms, those references are indicated in bold type. In the above example, in addition to Judg 1:7, the references that are indicated in bold type are 1 Sam 5:1; Jer 26:23; Ezek 19:4 and 19:9, and all these have Mp notes at their respective occurrences in M^L.

Unless it is so indicated in the commentary, it can be assumed that the notes at these occurrences are exactly the same as the note in the lemma under discussion. In this case, all the highlighted Mp notes read "seven times" except that at 1 Sam 5:1, which reads "six times defective." The difference between the note headings is explained in the commentary.

Where the form of the lemma varies in the other references, the vocalization of those other references is given in parentheses. Here the vocalization of all the forms other than that at Judg 1:7 differs, so the vocalization of these forms is given in parentheses following their specific references. It will be seen that all forms, other than the lemma at Judg 1:7, which reads וַיְבִיאָהוּ (plene second י), are vocalized as וַיְבִאֻהוּ (defective second י).

Where a Mp also has a Mm note, that fact is indicated by underlining. In the above example, the only Mp that has a Mm note is the one at Judg 1:7 and so that reference is indicated both by bold type (because it has a Mp note), and by underlining (because it has a Mm note).

For clarity of reading the references are bunched in groups of five, and preceded by Arabic numerals (1–5).

4. **The Masorah magna (Mm) note**. The lemma heading is always introduced by the siglum Mm on the right hand side to indicate that the note is a Masorah magna note (Mm) rather than a Masorah parva note (Mp):

וַיְבִיאָהוּ seven times ז֔ [ויביאהו] (ויבאהו)   Mm

The Mm heading is reproduced exactly as it is written in the ms. Where a lemma heading differs from the text of M^L lemma that heading is placed in parentheses and is followed by the text of the ms. in square brackets.[3] In this example from Judg 7:1

---

[3] This method will allow future researchers to investigate whether or not the text of the Masorah represents a different source. Examples of possible preservations of alternate textual readings in a Masorah note are (1) at Judg 9:6 (אֵלוֹן) in the catchwords given for 1

the lemma וַיְבִיאֻהוּ (plene second י) is written in the Mm heading as ויבאהו (defective second י). Since the lemma heading differs from the text of M^L, which is וַיְבִיאֻהוּ, the heading is placed in parentheses (ויבאהו), and the form that occurs in the text of M^L is placed immediately afterwards in square brackets [ויביאהו]. The Mm form is presented unpointed since all Hebrew words in the Mm are unpointed. Only in exceptional cases are vowels or accents given in the Mm.[4]

The lemma heading is immediately followed by the masoretic note as it appears in the ms. (here ז̇). On the left hand side the lemma, that is given in the Mm unvocalized (ויביאהו), is vocalized (וַיְבִיאֻהוּ) together with a translation of the note ("seven times").

5. **The catchwords and references for the Mm note.** The Mm gives the references to the biblical verses by means of *sîmanîm* or catchwords. These catchwords represent one or more words from the verse that is being referred to. There is no fixed formula for the selection of catchwords from a verse although there is a tendency for catchwords to be either at the beginning of a verse or close to the lemma that is in the verse.[5] When Mm notes are repeated, catchwords from different parts of a verse are often used.[6]

The Mm catchwords and their references are both lined up vertically so that one can immediately match the catchwords with their appropriate verse listed in the same horizontal line.

Sam 10:3, where the form והלכת is written instead of וחלפת (וְחָלְפָתְ); see *BHK ad loc.*; (2) at 1 Kgs 11:2 (אָכֵן) in the catchwords given for Ps 31:23, where the form נגרתי (cf. Lam 3:54) is written instead of נגרזתי (נִגְרַזְתִּי) that occurs in M. In his *Massorah Gedolah*, Weil changes all these differences to the reading of M^L by means of asterisks so there there is no way that a reader can tell what was in the orginal note. On this point, see also Loewinger, "Review," 603–04.

[4] For example at Josh 18:13 (ועטן כבד), 22:3 (מצות), 1 Sam 16:1 (וְלֵךְ), 23:11 (עבדך), 1 Kgs 13:2 (נולד), 22:34 (הפך ידך), 2 Kgs 8:5 (הוא מספר למלך), and 14:13 (ואת אמציהו מלך יהודה).

[5] In our study of doublet catchwords we found that these catchwords tend to be contiguous, and either follow or precede the doublet they illustrate; see Marcus, "Doublet Catchwords," §6.

[6] See for example the different catchwords in the two Mm notes at Judg 5:30 (רַחַם), at 2 Sam 15:27 (הֲרוֹאֶה); etc.

	The References	**The Catchwords**
1–5	Judg 1:7	אדני בזק
	1 Sam 5:1	ופלשתים
	<Ezek 19:4>	
	Ezek 19:9	בסוגר
	{Ezek 19:8}	{ממדינות}
	2 Kgs 23:30	וירכבהו
6–7	2 Chr 22:9	אחזיהו
	Jer 26:23	אוריהו

The catchwords generally conform to the way the catchwords appear in their appropriate passages in M^L. However, occasionally catchwords are written incorrectly, abbreviated, or omitted altogether, and sometimes extraneous words appear which do not belong to the context.

Where the catchwords differ from the text of M^L or are written in an abbreviated fashion, the form found in the Masorah is placed in parentheses and the form that appears in the text of M^L follows in square brackets. Where a catchword has been omitted from the list the reference is included in angle brackets. In the example above no catchword has been included in the Mm list for Ezek 19:4 so the reference is supplied in angle brackets (<Ezek 19:4>). Where extraneous material appears in a reference this extraneous material is highlighted *in situ* by means of curly brackets or braces {...}. Thus in the example above, the catchword מִמְּדִינוֹת from Ezek 19:8, which has mistakenly been written in this Mm note is placed in curly brackets.

This work always replicates the catchwords in the order in which they appear in the masoretic note. It will be noticed in this example that the references are not in the standard chronological biblical order. Here the references for both sets of catchwords from Ezekiel have been placed before the catchwords for 2 Kgs 23:30, and the catchword for 2 Chr 22:9 has been placed before that of Jer 26:23.

All references that have Mm entries are indicated by being underlined. In the above example the only reference that is underlined is the one at Judg 1:7 but it is not uncommon, as will be seen throughout the work, for numerous references to have Mm notes.

6. **The commentary**. The commentary, which is always introduced by the designation *Com.*: in the left hand margin, offers a possible explanation for the note, indicates any problems with the note, or may simply refer the reader to the first time that this note was encountered. The commentary will usually observe that occurrences of the lemma are to be distinguished from occurrences of another similar or contrasting form. If the number of those other occurrences are two or just one, the actual biblical references are indicated. But when the number of the other occurrences are three or more, then the biblical references are not given, only an indication of the number of such occurrences in Arabic numerals followed by an x. (e.g., 6x = six times). Very large numbers in the hundreds are simply indicated by 100+ or 200+ etc.

Com.: The Masorah notes the seven occurrences of this lemma, written plene and defective second י (וַיְבִיאֻהוּ/וַיְבִאֻהוּ), to distinguish them from its more numerous occurrences (13x), written plene and defective second י, in the sg. (וַיְבִיאֵהוּ/וַיְבִאֵהוּ); see Ognibeni, *'Oklah*, §1K.

All the highlighted Mp notes read *seven times* except for the one at **1 Sam 5:1**, which reads *six times defective* (second י) because it does not include the form here at Judg 1:7 that is written plene second י (וַיְבִיאֻהוּ).

In the Mm, in place of a catchword for the Ezek 19:4 reference, a catchword מִמְּדִינוֹת from Ezek 19:8 has mistakenly been written.

In the above example from Judg 1:7, the Masorah notes the seven occurrences of the lemma וַיְבִיאֻהוּ in the plural with a masc. sfx., written plene and defective second י (וַיְבִיאֻהוּ/וַיְבִאֻהוּ), to distinguish them from the more numerous occurrences (13x) of this lemma, written plene and defective second י, in the sg. with masc. sfx. (וַיְבִיאֵהוּ/וַיְבִאֵהוּ). The thirteen occurrences are not given because they are readily available in standard printed concordances or electronic search programs.

The commentary is the place where divergent Mp headings are noted. In the above example, the Mp heading at 1 Sam 5:1 reads "six times defective," whereas all the other Mp notes highlighted in the note read "seven times." The commentary observes that the 1 Sam 5:1 heading can be explained because that heading "six times defective" is only taking into account forms of this lemma that occurs written defective second י (וַיְבִאֻהוּ) and not taking into account the form that occurs at Judg 1:7, which is written plene second י (וַיְבִיאֻהוּ). However, all the other headings, including the one at Judg 1:7, that read "seven times" are taking into account forms that are written both defective and plene second י (וַיְבִיאֻהוּ/וַיְבִאֻהוּ).

The commentary is also the place where any problem with the catchwords or references are noted. Thus in the above example, a note is made about the fact that in place of the proper catchword for the Ezek 19:4 reference, a catchword מִמְּדִינוֹת from Ezek 19:8 has mistakenly been written.

7. Textual notes. The textual notes appearing after the commentary section deal with matters pertaining to the text of the manuscript as far as the masoretic notes are concerned. Thus they deal with the circelli, the small circles that are on top of a word or phrase, and comment on their absence or misplacement particularly whether a lemma needs to be shortened or lengthened. These notes also deal with the placement of the Mm notes if they do not occur on the same folio as the text of the lemma, and notes whether they occur on the preceding or following folio.

Textual notes concerning the Mp

The types of notes given in these textual notes concerning the Mp are indicated below.

- *Circellus but no note.* These are cases where a lemma has a circellus placed over the word or phrase, but there is no corresponding note; see at Judg 6:12 (וַיֵּרָא) and 1 Kgs 8:26 (וְעַתָּה אֱלֹהֵי יִשְׂרָאֵל). In all these cases the correct note can be correctly surmised.

- *Note but no circellus.* These are cases where a lemma has a note, but there is no circellus placed over the accompanying word or phrase; see at Josh 10:26 (וַיְמִיתֵם) and 1 Sam 2:4 (אָזְרוּ חָיִל). This feature is common in *kətîb/qərê* cases, and in many cumulative notes (see at 2 Sam 13:37, עַמִּיחוּר and 2 Kgs 6:11, עַל).

- *One circellus but two notes.* These are cases where only one circellus has been placed on a lemma, but two notes are given. This occurs most frequently with *kətîb/qərê* notes (see at 2 Sam 22:15 (וַיְהֻמֵּם) and 1 Kgs 22:13 (דְּבָרֶיךָ), and many times in these cases one note is placed on the left side of the column and the second Mp note is placed on the right side.

- *Two circelli on one word.* These are cases where two circelli have been placed on a lemma but only one note is given; see at Josh 2:3 (הוֹצִיאִי) and Judg 11:25 (נִלְחֹם).

- *Circellus placed on first word in verse.* This feature is particularly common with cumulative or collative type notes such as sequences of prepositions (אֶל...עַל...עַל) or (שָׁם...שָׁמָּה). In these cases the circellus is placed not on אֶל or שָׁם, but on the first word in the verse in which these sequences occur; see 1 Sam 15:1 (אֶל) and 2 Kgs 4:10 (שָׁם).

- *Only two circelli given for large phrases.* With *four- five- or six-word* phrases it is not unusual for only *two* circelli to be given. For example, on the phrase אֲשֶׁר־נִשְׁבַּעְתִּי לַאֲבוֹתָם לָתֵת לָהֶם (Josh 1:6) there are only two circelli: one on אֲשֶׁר־נִשְׁבַּעְתִּי and one on לַאֲבוֹתָם לָתֵת; see also at Judg 1:17 (וַיִּקְרָא אֶת־שֵׁם־הָעִיר) and 1 Kgs 17:14 (כִּי כֹה אָמַר יְהוָה אֱלֹהֵי יִשְׂרָאֵל), and *passim*.

- *Misplaced circellus.* Occasionally the circellus has been misplaced in the manuscript. Instead of being on the lemma appropriate to the accompanying note, it has been placed on the preceding or following word. For example, at Judg 17:1 the circellus has mistakenly been placed on the word וּשְׁמוֹ, but it belongs on the following word מִיכָיְהוּ. On the other hand, at Judg 19:22, the circellus has been placed on the word מֵיטִיבִים instead of on the preceding one הֵמָּה.

- *Notes on the wrong side of the column.* Normally the Mp note is placed either in the left or right side of the column directly adjacent to its text. However, occasionally the note is placed in the wrong margin. Thus at 2 Sam 12:12, the note for נֶגֶד כָּל־יִשְׂרָאֵל has mistakenly been placed in the left column instead of the right column and, similarly, the note for וְנֶגֶד has mistakenly been placed in the right column instead of in the left one.

- *Lemma needs to be extended.* Occasionally, as is clear from parallel occurrences in M^L or from other mss., a lemma needs to be extended because it does not meet the requirements of the note. At Josh 1:14 there is a circellus on the word הַחַיִל, and a note that states "five times with a *pataḥ*." But the form הַחַיִל occurs fourteen times, so it is most likely, as is correctly indicated in M^A and in the Mp notes of M^L elsewhere, that the note should also include the preceding word גִּבּוֹרֵי, since the extended lemma גִּבּוֹרֵי הַחַיִל meets the requirements of the note occuring five times with a *pataḥ*. Similarly, at 1 Sam

1:1, only one circellus has been placed over וַיְהִי אִישׁ with a note that reads "twice." But that phrase occurs eight times so it is most likely that, with M^C and M^A, the note belongs to the three-word phrase וַיְהִי אִישׁ אֶחָד, that only occurs twice.

- *Lemma needs to be shortened.* A similar situation involves cases where the lemma needs to be shortened. At Judg 19:9 a circellus has been placed on the two words לַעֲרֹב לִינוּ with a corresponding note of "twice." But, since this phrase only occurs once, it is most likely that, with M^A, the note should just be only on לַעֲרֹב, that does occur twice. At 1 Sam 2:15 a circellus has been placed on the words וְאָמַר לָאִישׁ with a corresponding note of "thirty-two times." But, since the phrase וְאָמַר לָאִישׁ only occurs once, it is most likely that the note refers just to לָאִישׁ, which does occur thirty-two times.

- *Extra notes in the ms.* On some occasions one finds extra Mp notes which do not correspond to any word which is in the adjacent line. At Josh 19:25 (וְאַבְשָׁן), there are four Mp notes for one line of text, which only contains three words in the line. The fourth Mp note of ב does not match any parallel word in either column. At Judg 11:5 (מֵאֶרֶץ טוֹב), there is a Mp note of י, which has no associated circellus and which does not match any of the immediate words in its vicinity.

TEXTUAL NOTES CONCERNING THE M$_M$

The types of textual note concerning the Mm primarily have to do with the placement of the Mm note. Usually the Mm notes in M^L are placed on the upper and lower margins, and usually correspond to the occurrence of lemmas on that particular folio. However there are many occasions when a Mm note occurs on the following or preceding folio. For example, at 2 Kgs 21:12 the lemma תִּצַּלְנָה occurs in the ms. in folio 217r, but the Mm note on this lemma appears on the top right of the following folio 217v. The opposite is the case at 2 Kgs 3:17 where the lemma יִמָּלֵא occurs in the ms. in folio 204r, but the Mm note on this lemma appears on the bottom right of the preceding folio 203v.

There are some cases where the same note appear both in the preceding and following folio. Thus the lemma עַד־עֶצֶם הַיּוֹם הַזֶּה (Josh 10: 27) occurs in the ms. on folio 127v, but its Mm note appears once on the preceding page on the bottom left of fol. 127r, and once on the following page on the bottom left of fol. 128r. It is also possible for more than one note to be on the preceding or following folio. In fact, there is one case of six Mm notes occurring on a following folio! The lemmas יְדָעוּן (Josh 3:7), וְאַתָּה תְּצַוֶּה (Josh 3:8), כְּבֹאֲכֶם (Josh 3:9), גֹּשׁוּ (Josh 3:9), תֵּדְעוּן (Josh 3:10), and שְׁנֵי עָשָׂר (Josh 3:12) all occur in the ms. in folio 122v, but their Mm notes are written on the bottom right of the following folio 123r.

2 Kings

> **2 KINGS 1:2**
> וַיִּפֹּ֨ל אֲחַזְיָ֜ה בְּעַ֣ד הַשְּׂבָכָ֗ה בַּעֲלִיָּת֛וֹ אֲשֶׁ֥ר בְּשֹׁמְר֖וֹן וַיָּ֑חַל וַיִּשְׁלַ֣ח מַלְאָכִ֔ים וַיֹּ֤אמֶר אֲלֵהֶם֙ לְכ֣וּ דִרְשׁ֗וּ בְּבַ֙עַל֙ זְב֣וּב אֱלֹהֵ֣י עֶקְר֔וֹן אִם־אֶחְיֶ֖ה מֵחֳלִ֥י זֶֽה׃ ס

1:2   אֲחַזְיָה

Seven times   ז̇   Mp

1–5   2 Kgs 1:2; <u>9:16</u> (וַאֲחַזְיָה); 9:23ᵇ; 9:27 (וַאֲחַזְיָה); 9:29
6–7   2 Kgs 11:2ᵇ; <u>2 Chr 20:35</u>

Com.: The Masorah notes the *seven* occurrences of this lemma in various forms ending in ה, to distinguish them from its more numerous occurrences (30x) in various forms ending in הו (e.g., אֲחַזְיָהוּ).

This distinction is implied in the addition in the Mm at <u>2 Kgs 9:16</u> and <u>2 Chr 20:35</u> of the notation *second* (form of אֲחַזְיָה) *in the verse* to the 2 Kgs 9:23ᵇ reference, because the *first form* of Ahaziah's name in this verse is written אֲחַזְיָהוּ.

Similarly, there is an addition in the Mm at <u>2 Kgs 9:16</u> of the notation *second* (form of אֲחַזְיָה) *in the verse* to the 2 Kgs 11:2ᵇ reference, because the *first form* of Ahaziah's name in this verse is written אֲחַזְיָהוּ.

All the Mp and Mm headings for this lemma highlighted above read *seven times* apart from the Mp at 2 Kgs 9:16 (וַאֲחַזְיָה), which mistakenly reads *three times*. The latter number may originally have been intended for וַאֲחַזְיָהוּ, which does occur *three times* (at 2 Kgs 8:29, 9:21, and 12:19).

1:2   בַּעֲלִיָּתוֹ

Unique   ל̇   Mp

Com.: The Masorah notes the *sole* occurrence of this lemma with the prep. בּ, to distinguish it from its *sole* occurrence with a ו cj. (וְעֲלִיָּתוֹ) at 2 Chr 9:4.

1:2   וַיָּחַל

Unique   ל̇   Mp

Com.: The Masorah notes the *sole* occurrence of this lemma with a *pataḥ* under the ח, to distinguish it from its more numerous occurrences (9x) with a *sĕgōl* (וַיֶּחֱל); see the Mm at <u>1 Chr 10:3</u> *sub* וַיָּחֶל, and **1 Sam 31:3**.

1:2   אֶחְיֶה

Four times   דֿ   Mp

2 Kgs 1:2; **Ps 118:17**; **119:17**; Job 7:16

אֶחְיֶה *four times*   אחיה דֿ   Mm

2 Kgs 1:2	ויפל אחזיה בעד חשבכה
Ps 118:17	לא אמות כי אחיה
Ps 119:17	גמל על עבדך
Job 7:16	מאסתי לא (לעולם) [לעלם] אחיה

Com.: The Masorah notes the *four* occurrences of this lemma with a ח, to distinguish them from its more numerous occurrences (43x) written with a ה (אֶהְיֶה).

The Mp heading at Ps 119:17, just like the Mp heading here, reads *four times* however, the Mp at Ps 118:17 reads *four times ma'rik* (מאריך), that is, with *gaʿyâ* = *meteḡ*; see Wickes *Accentuation*, 24; and Dotan/Reich, *Masora Thesaurus*, ad loc.

But in M^L only *three* of the *four* forms listed above have a *gaʿyâ* (Ps 118:17 [אֶחְיֶה], 119:17 [אֶחְיֶה] and Job 7:16 [אֶחְיֶה]), but the form here does not (אֶחְיֶה).

This *gaʿyâ* does not appear either in the Ms of M^A nor in the printed editions of Cohen, *Miqraot Gedolot 'Haketer'* or Castro, *El codice*, but it is inserted in the editions of Breuer, *Torah Neviim Ketuvim*, and in the *Jerusalem Crown*.

---

2 KINGS 1:3

וּמַלְאַךְ יְהוָה דִּבֶּר אֶל־אֵלִיָּה הַתִּשְׁבִּי קוּם עֲלֵה לִקְרַאת מַלְאֲכֵי מֶלֶךְ־שֹׁמְרוֹן וְדַבֵּר אֲלֵהֶם הַמִבְּלִי אֵין־אֱלֹהִים בְּיִשְׂרָאֵל אַתֶּם הֹלְכִים לִדְרֹשׁ בְּבַעַל זְבוּב אֱלֹהֵי עֶקְרוֹן׃

1:3   לִדְרֹשׁ בְּבַעַל זְבוּב

Three verses in which one is liable to err   גֿ פסוק מטע   Mp

2 Kgs 1:3; 1:6; 1:16

Mm   ג׳ פסוקין דמטעין בעיניה   *Three* verses in this section in which one is liable to err

ומלאך יהוה דבר   2 Kgs 1:3
ויאמרו אליו (ואיש) [איש] עלה לקראתנו   2 Kgs 1:6
וידבר אליו   2 Kgs 1:16

קדמייה אתם הלכים לדרש   אַתֶּם הֹלְכִים לִדְרֹשׁ (2 Kgs 1:3)   The *first*:
תינינה אתה שלח (לדרוש) [לדרש]   אַתָּה שֹׁלֵחַ לִדְרֹשׁ (2 Kgs 1:6)   The *second*:
בתרי בישראל (לדרוש) [לדרש] בדברו   בְּיִשְׂרָאֵל לִדְרֹשׁ בִּדְבָרוֹ (2 Kgs 1:16)   The *last*:

Com.: The Masorah notes *three* verses containing the phrase לִדְרֹשׁ בְּבַעַל זְבוּב *to inquire of Baal-zebub*, where errors could be made because of the similar phraseology.

The circellus has been placed on וּמַלְאַךְ יְהוָה because it is the first phrase in the verse.

1:3   אֵלִיָּה

Five times   ה׳   Mp

1–5   **2 Kgs 1:3**; 1:4; 1:8; 1:12; **Mal 3:23**

Com.: The Masorah notes the *five* occurrences, apart from the Writings, of this lemma written with a final ה, to distinguish them from its more numerous occurrences (60x) written with the ending יָהוּ (אֵלִיָּהוּ).

This distinction is implied in the additional note at the end of the Mm to Mal 3:23 that reads *and similarly all the Writings apart from one*. The *one* exception in the Writings is מֵאֵלִיָּהוּ at 2 Chr 21:12.

1:3   וְדַבֵּר

Eleven times   יא׳   Mp

1–5   **2 Sam 19:8**; **2 Kgs 1:3**; 2:11; Isa 58:9; 58:13
6–10   Isa 59:4; **Jer 7:13**; 25:3; **35:14**; **Ezek 37:21**
11   **Neh 9:13**

| וְדַבֵּר *eleven times*, and their references | ודבר יא וסימנהון | Mm |

1–5	2 Kgs 1:3	ומלאך יהוה דבר
	2 Kgs 2:11	ויהי המה הלכים
	2 Sam 19:8	ועתה קום צא ודבר
	Isa 58:13	אם תשיב משבת רגלך
	Isa 58:9	אז תקרא ויהוה יענה
6–10	Isa 59:4	אין (קורא) [קרא] בצדק
	Jer 7:13	השכם ודבר
	Jer 25:3	מן שלש עשרה שנה
	Jer 35:14	הוקם את דברי יהונדב
	Ezek 37:21	ודבר (אלהם) [אליהם]
11	Neh 9:13	ועל הר סיני ירדת

Com.: The Masorah notes the *eleven* occurrences of this lemma with a ו cj., to distinguish them from its more numerous occurrences (77x) written without a cj.

1:3 וְדַבֵּר אֲלֵהֶם

| וְדַבֵּר אֲלֵהֶם *twice* | ודבר אלהם ב | Mm |

2 Kgs 1:3	המבלי אין אלהים
The *second occurrence* of לָקַח הִנֵּה אֲנִי לֹקֵחַ (Ezek 37:21)	הנה (אנכי) [אני] לקח בתריה

Com.: The Masorah notes the *two* occurrences of this lemma with a ו cj., to distinguish them from its *three* occurrences without a cj.

This distinction is implied in the addition of *the second occurrence* to the phrase הִנֵּה אֲנִי לֹקֵחַ in the Ezek 37:21 reference because, in the *first* occurence of this phrase in v. 19, the lemma appears without a ו cj. (דִּבֶּר אֲלֵהֶם)

---

2 KINGS 1:4

וְלָכֵן כֹּה־אָמַר יְהוָה הַמִּטָּה אֲשֶׁר־עָלִיתָ שָּׁם לֹא־תֵרֵד מִמֶּנָּה כִּי מוֹת תָּמוּת וַיֵּלֶךְ אֵלִיָּה׃

1:4 וְלָכֵן כֹּה־אָמַר יְהוָה

| *Twenty-one times* | כא | Mp |

1–5	**2 Kgs 1:4**; <u>19:32</u>; Isa 29:22; 37:33; Jer 6:21
6–10	Jer 11:11; 11:21; 14:15; 15:19; 18:13
11–15	Jer 22:18; **23:38**; 28:16; 29:32; 32:28
16–20	Jer 34:17; 36:30; 51:36; Amos 7:17; Mic 2:3
21	Zech 1:16

Com.: The Masorah here, and in the Mp heading at Jer 23:38, notes the *twenty-one* occurrences of this phrase, with and without a ו cj., to distinguish it from similar phrases that occur where the Tetragrammaton is followed by אֱלֹהֵי יִשְׂרָאֵל or צְבָאוֹת, אֱלֹהִים אֱלֹהֵי יִשְׂרָאֵל צְבָאוֹת.

The Mp and the Mm headings at 2 Kgs 19:32 read only *twenty*, thereby not including the *sole* occurrence (here) of this lemma with a ו cj.

In M^L there are only *two* circelli on this *four-word* phrase: one on וְלָכֵן כֹּה and one on אָמַר יְהוָה. With *four-* or *five-word* phrases it is not unusual for only *two* circelli to be given; see **Josh 1:6**, and *passim*.

1:4 אֵלִיָּה

Five times   הֹ   Mp

Com.: See directly above at **2 Kgs 1:3**.

> ### 2 KINGS 1:6
> וַיֹּאמְרוּ אֵלָיו אִישׁ ׀ עָלָה לִקְרָאתֵנוּ וַיֹּאמֶר אֵלֵינוּ לְכוּ שׁוּבוּ אֶל־הַמֶּלֶךְ אֲשֶׁר־שָׁלַח אֶתְכֶם וְדִבַּרְתֶּם אֵלָיו כֹּה אָמַר יְהוָה הַמִבְּלִי אֵין־אֱלֹהִים בְּיִשְׂרָאֵל אַתָּה שֹׁלֵחַ לִדְרֹשׁ בְּבַעַל זְבוּב אֱלֹהֵי עֶקְרוֹן לָכֵן הַמִּטָּה אֲשֶׁר־עָלִיתָ שָּׁם לֹא־תֵרֵד מִמֶּנָּה כִּי־מוֹת תָּמוּת׃

1:6   וְדִבַּרְתֶּם אֵלָיו

Unique   ל   Mp

Com.: The Masorah notes the *sole* occurrence of אֵלָיו with וְדִבַּרְתֶּם, to distinguish it from its *two* occurrences with וַאֲמַרְתֶּם אֵלָיו) וַאֲמַרְתֶּם) at Gen 45:9 and Exod 3:18.

1:6   הַמִבְּלִי

Three times   גׄ   Mp

1–4   Exod 14:11; 2 Kgs 1:3; **1:6**; **1:16**

| | Mm | הַמְבִלִי (ג) [ד] | הַמִבְלִי *four times* |

1–4 Exod 14:11   אין קברים
     2 Kgs 1:3   אין אלהים בישראל
     And its companion (2 Kgs 1:6)   וחבירו
     <2 Kgs 1:16>

Com.: The Mp heading of *three times* is inexact since there are *four* occurrences of this lemma. The note more precisely should have read *three times in the section* or *three times in the book*.

The Masorah notes the *four* occurrences of this lemma with the interrog. ה, to distinguish them from its more numerous occurrences (20x) written without this interrogative.

Neither M^C nor M^A has a note on this lemma here.

2 KINGS 1:7

וַיְדַבֵּר אֲלֵהֶם מֶה מִשְׁפַּט הָאִישׁ אֲשֶׁר עָלָה לִקְרַאתְכֶם וַיְדַבֵּר אֲלֵיכֶם אֶת־הַדְּבָרִים הָאֵלֶּה:

1:7   מֶה

Twenty-five times   כֹּה   Mp

Com.: See **1 Sam 4:6**.

2 KINGS 1:8

וַיֹּאמְרוּ אֵלָיו אִישׁ בַּעַל שֵׂעָר וְאֵזוֹר עוֹר אָזוּר בְּמָתְנָיו וַיֹּאמַר אֵלִיָּה הַתִּשְׁבִּי הוּא:

1:8   אֵזוֹר

Unique and plene   ל ומל׳   Mp

Com.: By noting that this lemma is *unique* and written plene ו, the Masorah is also implying (correctly) that this lemma does not occur elsewhere written defective.

1:8   אֵלִיָּה

Five times   ה֑   Mp

Com.: See directly above at **2 Kgs 1:3**.

> **2 KINGS 1:9**
>
> וַיִּשְׁלַח אֵלָיו שַׂר־חֲמִשִּׁים וַחֲמִשָּׁיו וַיַּעַל אֵלָיו וְהִנֵּה יֹשֵׁב עַל־רֹאשׁ הָהָר וַיְדַבֵּר אֵלָיו אִישׁ הָאֱלֹהִים הַמֶּלֶךְ דִּבֶּר רֵדָה:

1:9   וַחֲמִשָּׁיו

Three times   ג֫   Mp

2 Kgs 1:9; 1:11; 1:13

Com.: The Masorah notes the *three* occurrences of this lemma with a ו cj., to distinguish them from its *two* occurrences without a cj. at 2 Kgs 1:10 and 12.

1:9   וְהִנֵּה יֹשֵׁב עַל־רֹאשׁ הָהָר

Unique   ל֫   Mp

In M^L there are only *three* circelli on this *five-word* phrase; see **Josh 1:6** and *passim*.

> **2 KINGS 1:10**
>
> וַיַּעֲנֶה אֵלִיָּהוּ וַיְדַבֵּר אֶל־שַׂר הַחֲמִשִּׁים וְאִם־אִישׁ אֱלֹהִים אָנִי תֵּרֶד אֵשׁ מִן־הַשָּׁמַיִם וְתֹאכַל אֹתְךָ וְאֶת־חֲמִשֶּׁיךָ וַתֵּרֶד אֵשׁ מִן־הַשָּׁמַיִם וַתֹּאכַל אֹתוֹ וְאֶת־חֲמִשָּׁיו:

1:10   הַחֲמִשִּׁים

Eight times   ח֫   Mp

1–5   Lev 25:10; **25:11**; **Num 16:35**; **31:30**; 31:47
6–8   **2 Kgs 1:10; 1:13; 1:14**

Com.: The Masorah notes the *eight* occurrences of this lemma with the def. article, to distinguish them from its far more numerous occurrences (97x) without a def. article.

All the above highlighted Mp headings read *eight times* apart from that at Lev 25:11, which incorrectly reads *four times*, although its Mm heading reads *eight times* and correctly lists *eight* references.

1:10   וְאִם־אִישׁ

Three times   גׄ   Mp

Deut 24:12; 2 Kgs 1:10; **Job 11:2**

Com.: The Masorah notes the *three* occurrences of this lemma with a ו cj., to distinguish them from its more numerous occurrences (10x) written without a cj.

1:10   וְתֹאכַל

Six times   וׄ   Mp

Com.: See **Judg 9:20**.

---

2 KINGS 1:11

וַיָּשָׁב וַיִּשְׁלַח אֵלָיו שַׂר־חֲמִשִּׁים אַחֵר וַחֲמִשָּׁיו וַיַּעַן וַיְדַבֵּר אֵלָיו אִישׁ הָאֱלֹהִים כֹּה־אָמַר הַמֶּלֶךְ מְהֵרָה רֵדָה׃

1:11   וַחֲמִשָּׁיו

Three times   גׄ   Mp

Com.: See directly above at **2 Kgs 1:9**.

1:11   רֵדָה

Twice   בׄ   Mp

2 Kgs 1:9; **1:11**

The Masorah notes the *two* occurrences of this lemma pointed with a *ṣerê* (pausal), to distinguish them from its *two* occurrences pointed with a *šəwâ* (רְדָה) at Gen 45:9 and Ezek 32:19.

---

2 KINGS 1:12

וַיַּעַן אֵלִיָּה וַיְדַבֵּר אֲלֵיהֶם אִם־אִישׁ הָאֱלֹהִים אָנִי תֵּרֶד אֵשׁ מִן־הַשָּׁמַיִם וְתֹאכַל אֹתְךָ וְאֶת־חֲמִשֶּׁיךָ וַתֵּרֶד אֵשׁ־אֱלֹהִים מִן־הַשָּׁמַיִם וַתֹּאכַל אֹתוֹ וְאֶת־חֲמִשָּׁיו׃

1:12   וְתֹאכַל

Six times   וׄ   Mp

Com.: See **Judg 9:20**.

1:12 אֵשׁ־אֱלֹהִים

Twice   בׄ   Mp

2 Kgs 1:12; Job 1:16

Com.: The Masorah notes the *two* occurrences of אֵשׁ with אֱלֹהִים, to distinguish them from its *three* occasions with יְהוָה (אֵשׁ יְהוָה).

> **2 KINGS 1:13**
> וַיָּשָׁב וַיִּשְׁלַח שַׂר־חֲמִשִּׁים שְׁלִשִׁים וַחֲמִשָּׁיו וַיַּעַל וַיָּבֹא שַׂר־הַחֲמִשִּׁים הַשְּׁלִישִׁי וַיִּכְרַע עַל־בִּרְכָּיו ׀ לְנֶגֶד אֵלִיָּהוּ וַיִּתְחַנֵּן אֵלָיו וַיְדַבֵּר אֵלָיו אִישׁ הָאֱלֹהִים תִּיקַר־נָא נַפְשִׁי וְנֶפֶשׁ עֲבָדֶיךָ אֵלֶּה חֲמִשִּׁים בְּעֵינֶיךָ:

1:13 וַחֲמִשָּׁיו

Three times   גׄ   Mp

Com.: See directly above at **2 Kgs 1:9**.

1:13 הַחֲמִשִּׁים

Eight times   חׄ   Mp

Com.: See directly above at **2 Kgs 1:10**.

1:13 וַיִּכְרַע

Twice   בׄ   Mp

2 Kgs 1:13; 9:24

Com.: The Masorah notes the *two* occurrences of this lemma with a ו consec., to distinguish them from its *two* occurrences without it (יִכְרַע) at Judg 7:5; Esth 3:2.

1:13 לְנֶגֶד אֵלִיָּהוּ

Unique   לׄ   Mp

1:13 תִּיקַר

Twice   בׄ   Mp

2 Kgs 1:13; 1:14

2 Kings 1:14

הִנֵּה יָרְדָה אֵשׁ מִן־הַשָּׁמַיִם וַתֹּאכַל אֶת־שְׁנֵי שָׂרֵי הַחֲמִשִּׁים הָרִאשֹׁנִים וְאֶת־חֲמִשֵּׁיהֶם וְעַתָּה תִּיקַר נַפְשִׁי בְּעֵינֶיךָ׃ ס

1:14   הַחֲמִשִּׁים

Eight times   ח֮   Mp

Com.: See directly above at **2 Kgs 1:10**.

1:14   הָרִאשֹׁנִים

Thirty times   ל֮   Mp

1–5   Exod 34:1; Num 6:12; Deut 10:2; 10:10; **2 Kgs 1:14**
6–10   2 Kgs 17:34; Jer 11:10; 34:5; 36:28; Zech 1:4
11–15   Zech 7:7; 7:12; 8:11; Ps 89:50; Qoh 7:10
16–20   Dan 10:13; **Neh 5:15**; 1 Chr 9:2; **18:17**; 29:29
21–25   2 Chr 9:29; 12:15; **16:11** (הָרִאשׁוֹנִים); 17:3; **20:34**
26–30   **2 Chr 22:1**; 25:26; 26:22; **28:26**; 35:27

Com.: The Masorah notes the *thirty* occurrences of this lemma with the def. article, to distinguish them from its *five* occurrences without the article.

All the Mp headings highlighted above read *thirty times* except for *two* headings at 2 Chr 16:11 and 22:1.

At 2 Chr 16:11 the Mp reads *unique plene* noting the specific form of הָרִאשׁוֹנִים.

At 2 Chr 22:1 the Mp reads *sixteen times in the book*, but there are only *thirteen* occurrences of this lemma in the book of Chronicles. Dotan/Reich (*Masora Thesaurus, ad loc.*) suggest that the original reading may have been, not *in the book*, but *in the Writings*, and the writing י֮ *sixteen* be considered a graphic error for י֮ *seventeen*, which would be the correct total of occurrences of this lemma in the Writings.

1:14   תִּיקַר

Twice   ב֮   Mp

2 Kgs 1:13; **1:14**

> **2 KINGS 1:15**
>
> וַיְדַבֵּ֞ר מַלְאַ֤ךְ יְהוָה֙ אֶל־אֵ֣לִיָּ֔הוּ רֵ֥ד אוֹת֖וֹ אַל־תִּירָ֣א מִפָּנָ֑יו וַיָּ֥קָם וַיֵּ֛רֶד אוֹת֖וֹ אֶל־הַמֶּֽלֶךְ׃

1:15   וַיְדַבֵּ֞ר מַלְאַ֤ךְ יְהוָה֙

Unique   ל   Mp

Com.: The Masorah notes the *sole* occurrence of מַלְאַ֤ךְ יְהוָה֙ with וַיְדַבֵּ֞ר, to distinguish it from its *sole* occurrence with כִּדְבֵ֖ר (כִּדְבֵ֖ר מַלְאַ֤ךְ יְהוָה֙) at Judg 2:4.

1:15   אוֹתוֹ¹

Twenty-five times plene   כֹה מל   Mp

Com.: See **Josh 16:6**.

> **2 KINGS 1:16**
>
> וַיְדַבֵּ֨ר אֵלָ֜יו כֹּֽה־אָמַ֣ר יְהוָ֗ה יַ֚עַן אֲשֶׁר־שָׁלַ֣חְתָּ מַלְאָכִים֮ לִדְרֹשׁ֮ בְּבַ֣עַל זְבוּב֮ אֱלֹהֵ֣י עֶקְרוֹן֒ הַֽמִבְּלִ֤י אֵין־אֱלֹהִים֙ בְּיִשְׂרָאֵ֔ל לִדְרֹ֖שׁ בִּדְבָר֑וֹ לָ֠כֵן הַמִּטָּ֞ה אֲשֶׁר־עָלִ֥יתָ שָּׁ֛ם לֹֽא־תֵרֵ֥ד מִמֶּ֖נָּה כִּֽי־מ֥וֹת תָּמֽוּת׃

1:16   הַֽמִבְּלִ֤י

Three times   ג   Mp

Com.: See directly above at **2 Kgs 1:6**.

> **2 KINGS 1:17**
>
> וַיָּ֜מָת כִּדְבַ֥ר יְהוָ֣ה ׀ אֲשֶׁר־דִּבֶּ֣ר אֵלִיָּ֗הוּ וַיִּמְלֹ֤ךְ יְהוֹרָם֙ תַּחְתָּ֔יו פ בִּשְׁנַ֣ת שְׁתַּ֗יִם לִיהוֹרָ֥ם בֶּן־יְהוֹשָׁפָ֖ט מֶ֣לֶךְ יְהוּדָ֑ה כִּ֛י לֹֽא־הָ֥יָה ל֖וֹ בֵּֽן׃

1:17   לִיהוֹרָם

Twice   ב   Mp

2 Kgs 1:17; 2 Chr 21:3

Com.: The Masorah notes the *two* occurrences of this lemma written with a ה, to distinguish them from its *three* occurrences without a ה (לְיוֹרָם).

For the distinction in the writing of Jehoram's name as יְהוֹרָם or יוֹרָם, see the Mm at <u>2 Kgs 8:16</u> *sub* יְהוֹרָם.

> ## 2 KINGS 1:18
> וְיֶ֛תֶר דִּבְרֵ֥י אֲחַזְיָ֖הוּ אֲשֶׁ֣ר עָשָׂ֑ה הֲלוֹא־הֵ֣מָּה כְתוּבִ֗ים עַל־סֵ֛פֶר דִּבְרֵ֥י הַיָּמִ֖ים לְמַלְכֵ֥י יִשְׂרָאֵֽל׃ פ

1:18   הֲלוֹא

Seventeen times plene in the book   יז מל בסיפ   Mp

Com.: See **1 Kgs 2:42**.

> ## 2 KINGS 2:1
> וַיְהִ֗י בְּהַעֲל֤וֹת יְהוָה֙ אֶת־אֵ֣לִיָּ֔הוּ בַּֽסְעָרָ֖ה הַשָּׁמָ֑יִם וַיֵּ֧לֶךְ אֵלִיָּ֛הוּ וֶאֱלִישָׁ֖ע מִן־הַגִּלְגָּֽל׃

2:1   בְּהַעֲלוֹת

Three times   ג׃   Mp

2 Kgs 2:1; Ezek 26:19; 2 Chr 35:14

Com.: The Masorah notes the *three* occurrences of this lemma with the prep. ב to distinguish them from its *sole* occurrence with the prep. כ (כְּהַעֲלוֹת) at Ezek 26:3.

2:1   בַּסְעָרָה

Twice written with ס   ב כת ס   Mp

2 Kgs 2:1; 2:11

בְּסְעָרָה *twice* written with ס, and their references   בסערה ב כתב ס וסימנהון   Mm

ויהי בהעלות יהוה את אליהו   2 Kgs 2:1
ויהי המה הלכים הלוך   2 Kgs 2:11

Com.: The Masorah notes the *two* occurrences of this lemma written with a ס, to distinguish them from its *sole* occurrence written a שׂ (בִּשְׂעָרָה) at Job 9:17.

> **2 KINGS 2:3**
> וַיֵּצְא֨וּ בְנֵֽי־הַנְּבִיאִ֥ים אֲשֶׁר־בֵּֽית־אֵל֮ אֶל־אֱלִישָׁע֒ וַיֹּאמְר֣וּ אֵלָ֔יו הֲיָדַ֕עְתָּ כִּ֣י הַיּ֗וֹם יְהוָ֛ה לֹקֵ֥חַ אֶת־אֲדֹנֶ֖יךָ מֵעַ֣ל רֹאשֶׁ֑ךָ וַיֹּ֛אמֶר גַּם־אֲנִ֥י יָדַ֖עְתִּי הֶחֱשֽׁוּ׃

2:3   וַיֵּצְא֨וּ בְנֵֽי־הַנְּבִיאִ֥ים

Mm   קדמייה ויצאו בני הנביאים   *The first occurrence is* וַיֵּצְא֨וּ בְנֵֽי־הַנְּבִיאִ֥ים (2 Kgs 2:3)
תנינה ויגשו בני הנביאים   *The second occurrence is* וַיִּגְּשׁ֖וּ בְנֵֽי־הַנְּבִיאִ֥ים (2 Kgs 2:5)

וסימנהון ויבא דוד אל מאתים האנשים   And their *sîman* is 1 Sam 30:21

Com.: The Masorah compares the *two* parallel phrases of 2 Kgs 2:3 and 2 Kgs 2:5 and notes their difference by means of a *third verse sîman*.

In the *first* verse, the verb that occurs is וַיֵּצְא֨וּ, whereas in the *second* verse it is וַיִּגְּשׁ֖וּ.

The verse 1 Sam 30:21 is cited as the *third verse sîman* because it contains the elements of this difference, namely both verbs occurring in the same order (וַיֵּצְא֨וּ...וַיִּגַּשׁ) as in the two verses from Kings.

2:3   אֲשֶׁר־בֵּֽית־אֵל֮

Mp   בֿ   *Twice*

2 Kgs 2:3; 10:29

Com.: The Masorah notes the *two* occurrences of אֲשֶׁר with בֵּֽית־אֵל, to distinguish them from its *two* occurrences with אֲשֶׁר בְּבֵֽית־אֵל (בְּבֵֽית־אֵל) at 1 Kgs 13:32 and 2 Kgs 23:15.

Com.: In M^L the circellus has been placed only on the two words אֲשֶׁר־בֵּית but, since this phrase occurs *nine* times, it is most likely that, as in M^A, the note belongs with the three words אֲשֶׁר־בֵּֽית־אֵל that only occur *twice*. M^C has no note here.

2:3   הֲיָדַ֕עְתָּ

Mp   הֿ   *Five times*

1–5   **2 Kgs 2:3**; 2:5; Job 38:33; 39:1; Dan 10:20

Mm	הידעת ה׳	הֲיָדַעְתָּ *five times*

1–5	2 Kgs 2:3	לקח את אדניך
	2 Kgs 2:5	לקח את אדניך
	Job 38:33	חקות שמים
	Job 39:1	עת לדת (ועלי) [יעלי] סלע
	Dan 10:20	למה באתי אליך

Com.: The Masorah notes the *five* occurrences of this lemma with the interrog. ה, to distinguish them from its more numerous occurrences (47x) written without this interrogative.

2:3 לֹקֵחַ

Mp	ח׳	*Eight times*

1–5	**Gen 27:46**; Deut 27:25; **2 Kgs 2:3**; 2:5; Ezek 24:16
6–8	Ezek 37:19; 37:21; Prov 9:7

Mm	לקח ח׳ וחס׳ וסימנהון	לֹקֵחַ *eight times* and defective, and their references

1–5	Gen 27:46	קצתי בחיי
	2 Kgs 2:3	אשר (בבית) [בית] אל
	2 Kgs 2:5	אשר ביריחו
	Ezek 24:16	את מחמד עיניך
	Ezek 37:19	את עץ יוסף
6–8	Ezek 37:21	את בני ישראל
	Deut 27:25	ארור
	Prov 9:7	יסר לץ

And once (וְלֹקֵחַ):	Prov 11:30	ו׳ ולקח נפשות

Com.: The Masorah notes the *eight* occurrences of this lemma as a ptcp., to distinguish it from its more numerous occurrences (45x) as a perf. (לָקַח).

All the Mp headings highlighted above, apart from Prov 9:7, read *eight times*. The one at Prov 9:7 reads *nine times* to include the lemma with the ו cj. (וְלֹקֵחַ) at Prov 11:30.

By noting in the heading of the Mm that the *eight* occurrences of this lemma are all written defective ו, the Masorah is also implying (correctly) that this lemma does not occur elsewhere written plene.

2:3   רֹאשְׁךָ

Four times   ד֗   Mp

Gen 40:13; 2 Sam 1:16; **2 Kgs 2:3**; 2:5

רֹאשְׁךָ *four times*, and their references   ראשך ד וסימנהון   Mm

Gen 40:13   בעוד שלשת ימים
2 Sam 1:16   ויאמר אליו דוד
<u>2 Kgs 2:3</u>   ויצאו בני הנביאים
2 Kgs 2:5   ויגשו בני הנביאים

Com.: The Masorah notes the *four* occurrences of this lemma with a *sɘḡôl* under the שׁ (pausal), to distinguish them from its *five* occurrences written with a *šɘwâ* (רֹאשְׁךָ).

2:3   הֶחֱשׁוּ

Twice   ב֗   Mp

2 Kgs 2:3; 2:5

> ### 2 KINGS 2:4
> וַיֹּ֩אמֶר֩ ל֨וֹ אֵלִיָּ֜הוּ אֱלִישָׁ֗ע שֵֽׁב־נָ֣א פֹה֮ כִּ֣י יְהוָה֮ שְׁלָחַ֣נִי יְרִיחוֹ֒ וַיֹּ֙אמֶר֙ חַי־יְהוָ֣ה וְחֵֽי־נַפְשְׁךָ֖ אִם־אֶעֶזְבֶ֑ךָּ וַיָּבֹ֖אוּ יְרִיחֽוֹ׃

2:4   וַיֹּ֩אמֶר֩ ל֨וֹ אֵלִיָּ֜הוּ

Twice   ב֗   Mp

2 Kgs 2:4; 2:6

Com.: The Masorah notes the *two* occurrences of this lemma with לֹ֨ו, to distinguish them from its *sole* occurrence with אֵלִיָּ֖ה (וַיֹּ֥אמֶר אֵלִיָּ֛ה אֵלִיָּ֖הוּ) at 1 Kgs 17:13.

2 KINGS 2:5

וַיִּגְּשׁ֨וּ בְנֵֽי־הַנְּבִיאִ֥ים אֲשֶׁר־בִּירִיחוֹ֮ אֶל־אֱלִישָׁע֒ וַיֹּאמְר֣וּ אֵלָ֔יו הֲיָדַ֕עְתָּ כִּ֣י הַיּ֗וֹם יְהוָ֛ה לֹקֵ֥חַ אֶת־אֲדֹנֶ֖יךָ מֵעַ֣ל רֹאשֶׁ֑ךָ וַיֹּ֛אמֶר גַּם־אֲנִ֥י יָדַ֖עְתִּי הֶחֱשֽׁוּ׃

2:5   הֲיָדַ֕עְתָּ

Five times   ה֮   Mp

Com.: See directly above at **2 Kgs 2:3**.

2:5   לֹקֵ֥חַ

Eight times   ח֮   Mp

Com.: See directly above at **2 Kgs 2:3**.

2:5   רֹאשֶׁ֑ךָ

Four times   ד֮   Mp

Com.: See directly above at **2 Kgs 2:3**.

2:5   הֶחֱשֽׁוּ

Twice   ב֮   Mp

2 Kgs 2:3; 2:5

2 KINGS 2:6

וַיֹּאמֶר֩ ל֨וֹ אֵלִיָּ֜הוּ שֵֽׁב־נָ֣א פֹ֗ה כִּ֤י יְהוָה֙ שְׁלָחַ֣נִי הַיַּרְדֵּ֔נָה וַיֹּ֕אמֶר חַי־יְהוָ֥ה וְחֵֽי־נַפְשְׁךָ֖ אִם־אֶעֶזְבֶ֑ךָּ וַיֵּלְכ֖וּ שְׁנֵיהֶֽם׃

2:6   הַיַּרְדֵּ֔נָה

Four times   ד֮   Mp

Num 34:12; Judg 8:4; **2 Kgs 2:6**; 6:4

Mm	הירדנה ד וסימנהון	הַיַּרְדֵּנָה *four times*, and their references

Num 34:12   וירד הגבול הירדנה
Judg 8:4   ויבא גדעון
2 Kgs 2:6   שלחני
2 Kgs 6:4   ויגזרו

Com.: The Masorah notes the *four* occurrences of this lemma with the locative ה, to distinguish them from its more numerous occurrences (100+) written without this adverbial ending (הַיַּרְדֵּן).

---

2 KINGS 2:8

וַיִּקַּח אֵלִיָּהוּ אֶת־אַדַּרְתּוֹ וַיִּגְלֹם וַיַּכֶּה אֶת־הַמַּיִם וַיֵּחָצוּ הֵנָּה וָהֵנָּה וַיַּעַבְרוּ שְׁנֵיהֶם בֶּחָרָבָה׃

2:8   וַיִּגְלֹם

Unique   ל   Mp

Com.: The Masorah notes the *sole* occurrence of this lemma (from גָּלַם, *he wrapped*), possibly to distinguish it from its *two* occurrences pointed as וַיַּגְלֵם (from גָּלָה, *he exiled them*) at **2 Kgs 15:29** and 1 Chr 5:26.

2:8   וַיַּכֶּה

Ten times   ֹי   Mp

Com.: See **Josh 10:40**.

2:8   וַיֵּחָצוּ

Twice   ב   Mp

2 Kgs 2:8; 2:14

---

2 KINGS 2:9

וַיְהִי כְעָבְרָם וְאֵלִיָּהוּ אָמַר אֶל־אֱלִישָׁע שְׁאַל מָה אֶעֱשֶׂה־לָּךְ בְּטֶרֶם אֶלָּקַח מֵעִמָּךְ וַיֹּאמֶר אֱלִישָׁע וִיהִי־נָא פִּי־שְׁנַיִם בְּרוּחֲךָ אֵלָי׃

2:9   כְעָבְרָם

Unique   ל   Mp

Com.: This lemma is featured in a Masoretic list of words occurring only *once* with a ב at the beginning of the word; see Frensdorff, *Ochlah*, §19, and Díaz-Esteban, *Sefer Oklah we-Oklah*, §20.

2:9	אֶלָּקַח		
Unique		ל	Mp

2:9	וִיהִי		
Thirty-two times		לב	Mp

Com.: See **1 Sam 10:5**.

> **2 KINGS 2:10**
> וַיֹּאמֶר הִקְשִׁיתָ לִשְׁאוֹל אִם־תִּרְאֶה אֹתִי לֻקָּח מֵאִתָּךְ יְהִי־לְךָ כֵן וְאִם־אַיִן לֹא יִהְיֶה׃

2:10	הִקְשִׁיתָ		
Unique		ל	Mp

2:10	לֻקָּח		
Five times with a *qameṣ*		הָ	Mp

1–5 **Gen 3:23** (לָקַח); **Judg 17:2** (לָקַח); 2 Kgs 2:10; **Isa 52:5** (לֻקָּח); 53:8

Com.: The Mp heading here of *five times* with a *qameṣ* is incorrect since there are only *two* occurrences of this lemma with a *qameṣ*. The note should have read, like M^A here and the other Mp headings just *five times*, or like M^C here *twice* with a *qameṣ*.

This lemma is also featured in a Masoretic list of doublets occurring exceptionally with a *qameṣ*; see Frensdorff, *Ochlah*, §25, and Díaz-Esteban, *Sefer Oklah we-Oklah*, §26.

2:10	מֵאִתָּךְ		
Five times		ה	Mp

Com.: See **1 Kgs 2:16**.

2 KINGS 2:11

וַיְהִ֗י הֵ֣מָּה הֹלְכִ֤ים הָלוֹךְ֙ וְדַבֵּ֔ר וְהִנֵּ֤ה רֶֽכֶב־אֵשׁ֙ וְס֣וּסֵי אֵ֔שׁ וַיַּפְרִ֖דוּ בֵּ֣ין שְׁנֵיהֶ֑ם וַיַּ֙עַל֙ אֵ֣לִיָּ֔הוּ בַּֽסְעָרָ֖ה הַשָּׁמָֽיִם׃

2:11   וְס֣וּסֵי

Unique   ל   Mp

2:11   וַיַּפְרִ֖דוּ

Unique and defective   ל וחס   Mp

Com.: By noting that this lemmma is *unique* and written defective י, the Masorah is also implying (correctly) that this lemma does not occur elsewhere written plene.

2:11   אֵ֣לִיָּ֔הוּ

Twice with the accents (*mûnaḥ* and *zaqep̄*)   ב֣ בטע   Mp

Com.: See **1 Kgs 17:23**.

2 KINGS 2:12

וֶאֱלִישָׁ֣ע רֹאֶ֗ה וְה֤וּא מְצַעֵק֙ אָבִ֣י ׀ אָבִ֗י רֶ֤כֶב יִשְׂרָאֵל֙ וּפָ֣רָשָׁ֔יו וְלֹ֥א רָאָ֖הוּ ע֑וֹד וַֽיַּחֲזֵק֙ בִּבְגָדָ֔יו וַיִּקְרָעֵ֖ם לִשְׁנַ֥יִם קְרָעִֽים׃

2:12   וְה֤וּא מְצַעֵק֙

Unique   ל   Mp

2 KINGS 2:13

וַיָּ֙רֶם֙ אֶת־אַדֶּ֣רֶת אֵלִיָּ֔הוּ אֲשֶׁ֥ר נָפְלָ֖ה מֵעָלָ֑יו וַיָּ֥שׇׁב וַֽיַּעֲמֹ֖ד עַל־שְׂפַ֥ת הַיַּרְדֵּֽן׃

2:13   וַיָּ֙רֶם֙

Eight times   ח֗   Mp

Com.: See **1 Kgs 11:26**.

2 KINGS 2:14

וַיִּקַּח֙ אֶת־אַדֶּ֣רֶת אֵלִיָּ֔הוּ אֲשֶׁר־נָפְלָ֖ה מֵעָלָ֑יו וַיַּכֶּ֣ה אֶת־הַמַּ֗יִם וַיֹּאמַ֔ר אַיֵּ֕ה יְהוָ֖ה אֱלֹהֵ֣י אֵלִיָּ֑הוּ אַף־ה֣וּא ׀ וַיַּכֶּ֣ה אֶת־הַמַּ֗יִם וַיֵּחָצ֖וּ הֵ֣נָּה וָהֵ֑נָּה וַֽיַּעֲבֹ֖ר אֱלִישָֽׁע׃

2:14   וַיַּכֶּה¹

Ten times   יׄ   Mp

Com.: See **Josh 10:40**.

2:14   וַיַּכֶּה²

Ten times   יׄ   Mp

Com.: See **Josh 10:40**.

2:14   וַיֵּחָצוּ

Twice   בׄ   Mp

2 Kgs 2:8; 2:14

2 KINGS 2:15

וַיִּרְאֻ֨הוּ בְנֵי־הַנְּבִיאִ֤ים אֲשֶׁר־בִּֽירִיחוֹ֙ מִנֶּ֔גֶד וַיֹּ֣אמְר֔וּ נָ֛חָה ר֥וּחַ אֵלִיָּ֖הוּ עַל־אֱלִישָׁ֑ע וַיָּבֹ֙אוּ֙ לִקְרָאת֔וֹ וַיִּשְׁתַּחֲווּ־ל֖וֹ אָֽרְצָה׃

2:15   נָחָה

Three times accented (*mil'êl*)   גׄ בטע   Mp

2 Kgs 2:15; Isa 7:2; 14:7

Com.: The Masorah notes the *three* occurrences of this form accented *mil'êl*, to distinguish them from its *sole* occurrence accented *milra'* (וְנָחָה) at Isa 11:2.

The Mp headings at Isa 7:2 and 14:7 just read *three times*.

In M^L the heading at Isa 14:7 has mistakenly been placed in the right column alongside חָשַׁךְ instead of in the left column alongside נָחָה.

2 KINGS 2:16

וַיֹּאמְר֣וּ אֵלָ֡יו הִנֵּה־נָ֣א יֵֽשׁ־אֶת־עֲבָדֶיךָ֩ חֲמִשִּׁ֨ים אֲנָשִׁ֜ים בְּֽנֵי־חַ֗יִל יֵ֣לְכוּ נָא֮ וִיבַקְשׁ֣וּ אֶת־אֲדֹנֶיךָ֒ פֶּן־נְשָׂאוֹ֙ ר֣וּחַ יְהוָ֔ה וַיַּשְׁלִכֵ֙הוּ֙ בְּאַחַ֣ד הֶהָרִ֔ים א֖וֹ בְּאַחַ֣ת הַגֵּיאָי֑וֹת וַיֹּ֖אמֶר לֹ֥א תִשְׁלָֽחוּ׃

2:16   וִיבַקְשׁוּ

Three times   גׄ   Mp

2 Kgs 2:16; <u>Ps 83:17</u>; **2 Chr 7:14**

Com.: The Masorah notes the *three* occurrences of this lemma with a ו cj., to distinguish them from its more numerous occurrences (9x) written with a ו consec. (וַיְבַקְשׁוּ).

2:16   נְשָׂאוֹ

Three times   גׄ   Mp

Exod 35:21; 36:2; **2 Kgs 2:16**

Com.: The Masorah notes the *three* occurrences of this lemma with a masc. sg. sfx., to distinguish them from its more numerous occurrences (11x) pointed as a 3rd pers. pl. נָשְׂאוּ.

2:16   הַגֵּיאָיוֹת

Read   הַגֵּאָיוֹת   הגיאות ק   Mp

Com.: The *kəṯîḇ* (הגיאות), and the *qərê* (הַגֵּאָיוֹת) represent miscellaneous variations in nouns; see Gordis, *The Biblical Text*, 124.

2 KINGS 2:17

וַיִּפְצְרוּ־ב֥וֹ עַד־בֹּ֖שׁ וַיֹּ֣אמֶר שְׁלָ֑חוּ וַֽיִּשְׁלְחוּ֙ חֲמִשִּׁ֣ים אִ֔ישׁ וַיְבַקְשׁ֥וּ שְׁלֹשָֽׁה־יָמִ֖ים וְלֹ֥א מְצָאֻֽהוּ׃

2:17   מְצָאֻהוּ

Unique and defective   ל וחס   Mp

Com.: By noting that this lemma is *unique* and written defective י, the Masorah is also implying (correctly) that this lemma does not occur elsewhere written plene.

2 KINGS 2:18

וַיָּשֻׁבוּ אֵלָיו וְהוּא יֹשֵׁב בִּירִיחוֹ וַיֹּאמֶר אֲלֵהֶם הֲלוֹא־אָמַרְתִּי אֲלֵיכֶם אַל־תֵּלֵכוּ׃

2:18 אֲלֵהֶם

Thirteen times defective in the book   יֹגׄ חסׄ בסיפׄ   Mp

Com.: See **1 Kgs 12:16**.

2 KINGS 2:19

וַיֹּאמְרוּ אַנְשֵׁי הָעִיר אֶל־אֱלִישָׁע הִנֵּה־נָא מוֹשַׁב הָעִיר טוֹב כַּאֲשֶׁר אֲדֹנִי רֹאֶה וְהַמַּיִם רָעִים וְהָאָרֶץ מְשַׁכָּלֶת׃

2:19 מְשַׁכָּלֶת

Unique with *qameṣ*   לׄ   Mp

Com.: By noting that this lemma is *unique* and written with a *qameṣ* (לׄ), the Masorah is also implying (correctly) that this lemma does not occur elsewhere written with a *səḡôl*.

By contrast, the *sole* occurrence of this lemma with ו cj. is written both with a *səḡôl* (וּמְשַׁכֶּלֶת) at Ezek 36:13, and with a *qameṣ* (וּמְשַׁכָּלֶת) in v. 21.

2 KINGS 2:20

וַיֹּאמֶר קְחוּ־לִי צְלֹחִית חֲדָשָׁה וְשִׂימוּ שָׁם מֶלַח וַיִּקְחוּ אֵלָיו׃

2:20 צְלֹחִית

Unique   לׄ   Mp

2 KINGS 2:21

וַיֵּצֵא אֶל־מוֹצָא הַמַּיִם וַיַּשְׁלֶךְ־שָׁם מֶלַח וַיֹּאמֶר כֹּה־אָמַר יְהוָה רִפִּאתִי לַמַּיִם הָאֵלֶּה לֹא־יִהְיֶה מִשָּׁם עוֹד מָוֶת וּמְשַׁכָּלֶת׃

2:21 רִפִּאתִי

Twice written like this   בׄ כתׄ כן   Mp

Com.: The Mp heading here of *twice* is incorrect as this word only occurs this *once*.

Both M^C and M^A correctly read here *unique*.

This lemma is featured in a Masoretic list of words where an א is written but not read: see the Mm to Num 11:4 *sub* וְהָאסַפְסֻף, Frensdorff, *Ochlah*, §103, and Díaz-Esteban, *Sefer Oklah we-Oklah*, §86.

2:21   לַמַּיִם

Five times   ה̈   Mp

1–5   **Exod 17:3**; **2 Kgs 2:21**; **Isa 55:1**; Jer 14:3; **Amos 8:11**

Com.: The Masorah notes the *five* occurrences of this lemma, to distinguish them from its *two* occurrences pointed differently, as לְמָיִם at **Josh 7:5** and as לְמָיִם at Gen 1:6.

2:21   וּמְשַׁכָּלֶת

Unique   ל̇   Mp

Com.: The Masorah notes the *sole* occurrence of this lemma with a ו cj., to distinguish it from its occurrence without a cj. in v. 19.

---

2 KINGS 2:22

וַיֵּרָפוּ הַמַּיִם עַד הַיּוֹם הַזֶּה כִּדְבַר אֱלִישָׁע אֲשֶׁר דִּבֵּר׃ פ

2:22   וַיֵּרָפוּ

Unique   ל̇   Mp

Com.: This lemma is featured in a Masoretic list of words where an א, normally in a word, is omitted; see the Mm to 1 Chr 12:39 *sub* שְׂרִית, Frensdorff, *Ochlah*, §199, and Ognibeni, *'Oklah*, §153.

2 Kings 2:23

וַיַּעַל מִשָּׁם בֵּית־אֵל וְהוּא ׀ עֹלֶה בַדֶּרֶךְ וּנְעָרִים קְטַנִּים יָצְאוּ מִן־הָעִיר וַיִּתְקַלְּסוּ־בוֹ וַיֹּאמְרוּ לוֹ עֲלֵה קֵרֵחַ עֲלֵה קֵרֵחַ:

2:23   וְהוּא ׀ עֹלֶה

Unique   ל   Mp

Com.: This lemma is featured in a Masoretic list of words preceded only *once* by וְהוּא; see Frensdorff, *Ochlah*, §264.

2:23   וַיִּתְקַלְּסוּ

Unique   ל   Mp

Com.: The Masorah notes the *sole* occurrence of this lemma with a ו consec., to distinguish it from its occurrence without a ו (יִתְקַלָּסוּ) at Ezek 22:5.

2 Kings 2:24

וַיִּפֶן אַחֲרָיו וַיִּרְאֵם וַיְקַלְלֵם בְּשֵׁם יְהוָה וַתֵּצֶאנָה שְׁתַּיִם דֻּבִּים מִן־הַיַּעַר וַתְּבַקַּעְנָה מֵהֶם אַרְבָּעִים וּשְׁנֵי יְלָדִים:

2:24   וַיְקַלְלֵם

Unique   ל   Mp

Com.: The Masorah notes the *sole* occurrence of this lemma with a sfx., to distinguish it from its *four* occurrences without a sfx. (וַיְקַלֵּל).

2:24   וַתֵּצֶאנָה

Unique   ל   Mp

1–2   1 Sam 18:6; **2 Kgs 2:24**

Com.: The Mp heading of *unique* is inexact since there are *two* occurrences of this lemma. The note more precisely should have read *unique in the book*.

Neither M^C nor M^A has a note on this lemma here.

2:24   וַתְּבַקַּעְנָה

Unique   ל   Mp

2 KINGS 2:25

וַיֵּלֶךְ מִשָּׁם אֶל־הַר הַכַּרְמֶל וּמִשָּׁם שָׁב שֹׁמְרֽוֹן׃ פ

2:25   וּמִשָּׁם

Eight times   ח   Mp

Com.: See **Josh 19:13**.

2 KINGS 3:2

וַיַּעֲשֶׂה הָרַע בְּעֵינֵי יְהוָה רַק לֹא כְאָבִיו וּכְאִמּוֹ וַיָּסַר אֶת־מַצְּבַת הַבַּעַל אֲשֶׁר עָשָׂה אָבִֽיו׃

3:2   וַיַּעֲשֶׂה הָרַע

Three times   ג   Mp

1 Kgs 16:25 (וַיַּעֲשֶׂה עָמְרִי הָרַע); **2 Kgs 3:2**; **13:11**

Com.: The Masorah notes the *three* occurrences of this lemma with the unapocopated verbal form וַיַּעֲשֶׂה, to distinguish them from its more numerous occurrences (26x) with the apocopated form וַיַּעַשׂ.

The 1 Kgs 16:25 occurrence alone has the subject of the verb (Omri) between the verb and the object.

3:2   מַצְּבַת

Twice   ב   Mp

2 Kgs 3:2; 10:27

Com.: The Masorah notes the *two* occurrences of this lemma, possibly to distinguish them from its *four* occurrences pointed as מַצֶּבֶת.

This lemma is featured in a Masoretic list of doublets that have a *pataḥ*; see Frensdorff, *Ochlah*, §24, and Díaz-Esteban, *Sefer Oklah we-Oklah*, §25.

2 KINGS 3:3

רַ֣ק בְּחַטֹּ֞אות יָרׇבְעָ֧ם בֶּן־נְבָ֛ט אֲשֶׁר־הֶחֱטִ֥יא אֶת־יִשְׂרָאֵ֖ל דָּבֵ֑ק לֹא־סָ֖ר מִמֶּֽנָּה׃ ס

3:3   דָּבֵק

Twice   בׄ   Mp

2 Kgs 3:3; Prov 18:24

Com.: The Masorah notes the *two* occurrences of this lemma with a *ṣere* under the ב, to distinguish them from its *four* occurrences with a *pataḥ* (דָּבַק).

2 KINGS 3:4

וּמֵישַׁ֣ע מֶלֶךְ־מוֹאָ֔ב הָיָ֖ה נֹקֵ֑ד וְהֵשִׁ֤יב לְמֶֽלֶךְ־יִשְׂרָאֵל֙ מֵאָה־אֶ֣לֶף כָּרִ֔ים וּמֵ֥אָה אֶ֖לֶף אֵילִ֥ים צָֽמֶר׃

3:4   וּמֵישַׁע

Unique   לׄ   Mp

Com.: This lemma is featured in two Masoretic lists. One is in a list of words that occur *twice*, *once* with a ו cj. (here), and *once* without (1 Chr 2:42); see Frensdorff, *Ochlah*, §1, and Díaz-Esteban, *Sefer Oklah we-Oklah*, §1.

The second is in a list of words occurring *once* with a *qameṣ* (מֵישָׁע, 1 Chr 2:42), and *once* with a *pataḥ* (here); see Frensdorff, *Ochlah*, §23, and Díaz-Esteban, *Sefer Oklah we-Oklah*, §24.

3:4   נֹקֵד

Unique and defective   לׄ וחס   Mp

Com.: By noting that this lemmma is *unique* and written defective י, the Masorah is also implying (correctly) that this lemma does not occur elsewhere written plene.

3:4   אֵילִים צָמֶר

Unique and with a ר (*resh*)   לׄ וריש   Mp

Com.: By noting that this lemma is *unique* and written with a ר, the Masorah appears to be trying to prevent the second part of the lemma (צָמֶר, *wool*) being mistakenly written with a ד (as צָמֶד, *pair/team*).

Both M^C and M^A just read here *unique*.

> ## 2 KINGS 3:5
> וַיְהִי כְּמוֹת אַחְאָב וַיִּפְשַׁע מֶלֶךְ־מוֹאָב בְּמֶלֶךְ יִשְׂרָאֵל׃

3:5   כְּמוֹת

Three times   ג̇   Mp

Num 16:29; **2 Kgs 3:5**; Qoh 3:19

כְּמוֹת *three times* and plene, and their references   כמות ג̇ ומל̇ וסימנהון   Mm

Num 16:29   אם כמות כל האדם ימתון
Qoh 3:19   כמות זה כן מות זה
2 Kgs 3:5   ויהי כמות אחאב

Com.: The Masorah notes the *three* occurrences of this lemma, to distinguish them from its *three* occurrences written as כְּמָוֶת.

By noting in the Mm that the *three* occurrences of this lemma are all written plene ו, the Masorah is also implying (correctly) that this lemma does not occur elsewhere written defective.

> ## 2 KINGS 3:7
> וַיֵּלֶךְ וַיִּשְׁלַח אֶל־יְהוֹשָׁפָט מֶלֶךְ־יְהוּדָה לֵאמֹר מֶלֶךְ מוֹאָב פָּשַׁע בִּי הֲתֵלֵךְ אִתִּי אֶל־מוֹאָב לַמִּלְחָמָה וַיֹּאמֶר אֶעֱלֶה כָּמוֹנִי כָמוֹךָ כְּעַמִּי כְעַמֶּךָ כְּסוּסַי כְּסוּסֶיךָ׃

3:7   כְּסוּסַי

Twice   ב̇   Mp

1 Kgs 22:4; **2 Kgs 3:7**

> ## 2 KINGS 3:8
> וַיֹּאמֶר אֵי־זֶה הַדֶּרֶךְ נַעֲלֶה וַיֹּאמֶר דֶּרֶךְ מִדְבַּר אֱדוֹם׃

3:8   אֵי

Thirty-one times   לא̇   Mp

Com.: See **1 Sam 9:18**.

> **2 KINGS 3:9**
> וַיֵּ֣לֶךְ מֶ֣לֶךְ יִשְׂרָאֵ֡ל וּמֶֽלֶךְ־יְהוּדָ֣ה וּמֶלֶךְ֩ אֱד֨וֹם וַיָּסֹ֜בּוּ דֶּ֣רֶךְ שִׁבְעַ֣ת יָמִ֗ים וְלֹא־הָיָ֥ה מַ֛יִם לַֽמַּחֲנֶ֖ה וְלַבְּהֵמָ֥ה אֲשֶׁ֥ר בְּרַגְלֵיהֶֽם׃

3:9   דֶּ֣רֶךְ שִׁבְעַ֣ת יָמִים

Twice   בׄ   Mp

Gen 31:23; **2 Kgs 3:9**

דֶּ֣רֶךְ שִׁבְעַ֣ת יָמִים *twice, and their references*   דרך שבעת ימים בׄ וסימנהון   Mm

Gen 31:23   וידבק אתו בהר הגלעד
2 Kgs 3:9   וילך מלך ישראל ⟨ומלך יהודה⟩ ומלך אדום

Com.: The Masorah notes the *two* occurrences of דֶּ֣רֶךְ with שִׁבְעַ֣ת יָמִים, to distinguish them from its more numerous occurrences (7x) with a similar phrase שְׁלֹ֣שֶׁת יָמִים (דֶּ֣רֶךְ שְׁלֹ֣שֶׁת יָמִים).

3:9   וְלֹא־הָיָה

Twenty-seven times   כׄז   Mp

Com.: See **Josh 8:20**.

3:9   וְלַבְּהֵמָה

וְלַבְּהֵמָה *three times*   ולבהמה גׄ   Mm

Lev 7:26   וכל דם לא תאכלו
2 Kgs 3:9   ולא היה (מהם) [מים] למחנה
Isa 46:1   היו עצביהם לחיה

Com.: The Masorah notes the *three* occurrences of this lemma with a ו cj., to distinguish them from its *three* occurrences written without a cj.

This lemma occurs in the ms. in folio 203v, but the Mm note appears on the top right of the following folio 204r.

2 KINGS 3:10

וַיֹּ֙אמֶר֙ מֶ֣לֶךְ יִשְׂרָאֵ֔ל אֲהָ֕הּ כִּֽי־קָרָ֣א יְהוָ֗ה לִשְׁלֹ֙שֶׁת֙ הַמְּלָכִ֣ים הָאֵ֔לֶּה לָתֵ֥ת אוֹתָ֖ם בְּיַד־מוֹאָֽב׃

3:10 אוֹתָם

Nine times plene in the book   ט מל בסיפ   Mp

Com.: See **1 Kgs 20:25**.

2 KINGS 3:11

וַיֹּ֣אמֶר יְהוֹשָׁפָ֗ט הַאֵ֙ין פֹּ֤ה נָבִיא֙ לַֽיהוָ֔ה וְנִדְרְשָׁ֥ה אֶת־יְהוָ֖ה מֵאוֹת֑וֹ וַ֠יַּעַן אֶחָ֞ד מֵעַבְדֵ֤י מֶֽלֶךְ־יִשְׂרָאֵל֙ וַיֹּ֔אמֶר פֹּ֚ה אֱלִישָׁ֣ע בֶּן־שָׁפָ֔ט אֲשֶׁר־יָ֥צַק מַ֖יִם עַל־יְדֵ֥י אֵלִיָּֽהוּ׃

3:11 מֵאוֹתוֹ

Six times plene in the book   ו מל בסיפ   Mp

1–5   **2 Kgs 1:15**^a (אוֹתוֹ); 1:15^b (אוֹתוֹ); 3:11; 3:12 (אוֹתוֹ); 3:26 (אוֹתוֹ)
6   **2 Kgs 8:8**

Com.: The Masorah notes the *six* occurrences of אוֹתוֹ that occur in the book written plene first ו, to distinguish them from its more numerous occurrences (59x) in the book written defective first ו (אֹתוֹ/מֵאֹתוֹ).

M[L], contrary to M (מֵאֹתוֹ), has a *seventh* occurrence of this lemma since it reads the form at 1 Kgs 22:7 plene first ו (מֵאוֹתוֹ); see Breuer, *The Biblical Text*, 117. However, the Mp headings here and at 2 Kgs 8:8 of *six* support the enumeration inherent in the text of M.

The Mp headings at 2 Kgs 1:15^a, 3:12, and 3:26 read *twenty-five*, the total of occurrences in all the books; see **Josh 16:6**.

3:11 יָצַק

Unique accented (*mil‘êl*)   ל בטע   Mp

Com.: The Masorah notes the *sole* occurrence of the form יָצַק accented *mil‘êl*, to distinguish it from its *two* other occurrences accented *milra‘* (at Lev 8:15 and 9:9); see also Frensdorff, *Ochlah*, §372.

2 KINGS 3:12

וַיֹּ֙אמֶר֙ יְה֣וֹשָׁפָ֔ט יֵ֥שׁ אוֹת֖וֹ דְּבַר־יְהוָ֑ה וַיֵּרְד֣וּ אֵלָ֗יו מֶ֧לֶךְ יִשְׂרָאֵ֛ל וִיהוֹשָׁפָ֖ט וּמֶ֥לֶךְ אֱדֽוֹם׃

3:12　אוֹתוֹ

Twenty-five times plene　　כֹּה מל　　Mp

Com.: See **Josh 16:6**.

2 KINGS 3:13

וַיֹּ֙אמֶר אֱלִישָׁ֜ע אֶל־מֶ֣לֶךְ יִשְׂרָאֵ֗ל מַה־לִּ֣י וָלָ֔ךְ לֵ֚ךְ אֶל־נְבִיאֵ֣י אָבִ֔יךָ וְאֶל־נְבִיאֵ֖י אִמֶּ֑ךָ וַיֹּ֤אמֶר לוֹ֙ מֶ֣לֶךְ יִשְׂרָאֵ֔ל אַ֗ל כִּֽי־קָרָ֤א יְהוָה֙ לִשְׁלֹ֙שֶׁת֙ הַמְּלָכִ֣ים הָאֵ֔לֶּה לָתֵ֥ת אוֹתָ֖ם בְּיַד־מוֹאָֽב׃

3:13　אוֹתָם

Nine times plene in the book　　ט׳ מל בסיפ　　Mp

Com.: See **1 Kgs 20:25**.

2 KINGS 3:14

וַיֹּ֣אמֶר אֱלִישָׁ֗ע חַי־יְהוָ֤ה צְבָאוֹת֙ אֲשֶׁ֣ר עָמַ֣דְתִּי לְפָנָ֔יו כִּ֗י לוּלֵ֗י פְּנֵ֛י יְהוֹשָׁפָ֥ט מֶֽלֶךְ־יְהוּדָ֖ה אֲנִ֣י נֹשֵׂ֑א אִם־אַבִּ֥יט אֵלֶ֖יךָ וְאִם־אֶרְאֶֽךָּ׃

3:14　נֹשֵׂא

Thirty-eight times　　לֹח　　Mp

Com.: The enumeration given in the Mp heading here of *thirty-eight* is incorrect as there are *thirty-nine* occurrences of this lemma; see **1 Sam 16:21**.

2 KINGS 3:15

וְעַתָּ֖ה קְחוּ־לִ֣י מְנַגֵּ֑ן וְהָיָה֙ כְּנַגֵּ֣ן הַֽמְנַגֵּ֔ן וַתְּהִ֥י עָלָ֖יו יַד־יְהוָֽה׃

3:15　כְּנַגֵּן

Unique　　ל׳　　Mp

2 KINGS 3:16

וַיֹּ֕אמֶר כֹּ֖ה אָמַ֣ר יְהוָ֑ה עָשֹׂ֛ה הַנַּ֥חַל הַזֶּ֖ה גֵּבִ֥ים ׀ גֵּבִֽים׃

3:16   עָשֹׂה

Twenty-three times   כג   Mp

Com.: See **1 Sam 25:28**.

3:16   גֵּבִים ׀ גֵּבִים

Unique   ל   Mp

Com.: This lemma is featured in a Masoretic list of words occurring together only *once*; see Frensdorff, *Ochlah*, §72.

2 KINGS 3:17

כִּֽי־כֹ֣ה ׀ אָמַ֣ר יְהוָ֗ה לֹֽא־תִרְא֥וּ ר֙וּחַ֙ וְלֹֽא־תִרְא֣וּ גֶ֔שֶׁם וְהַנַּ֥חַל הַה֖וּא יִמָּ֣לֵא מָ֑יִם וּשְׁתִיתֶ֛ם אַתֶּ֥ם וּמִקְנֵיכֶ֖ם וּֽבְהֶמְתְּכֶֽם׃

3:17   כִּֽי־כֹה ׀ אָמַר יְהוָה

Thirty unusual (occurrences)   כֹּ מיח   Mp

1–5   **2 Kgs 3:17**; 4:43; Isa 8:11; 18:4; 21:16
6–10   Isa 31:4; 45:18; 49:25; 52:3; 56:4
11–15   Isa 66:12; Jer 4:3; 4:27; 10:18; 16:3
16–20   Jer 16:5; 20:4; 22:6; 22:11; 24:8
21–25   **Jer 29:10**; 29:16; 30:5; 30:12; 31:7
26–30   Jer 32:42; 33:17; 48:40; 49:12; Amos 5:4

כִּֽי־כֹה ׀ אָמַר יְהוָה   *thirty* unusual (occurrences)   כי כה אמר יהוה כֹּ מיחד   Mm

1–5   2 Kgs 3:17   לא תראו
      2 Kgs 4:43   [אכל] (אכול)
      Jer 4:3   נירו לכם
      Jer 4:27   שממה תהיה
      Jer 10:18   הנני (קלע) [קולע]

6–10	Jer 16:3	על הבנים
	Jer 16:5	(בת) [בית] מרזח ואל
	Jer 20:4	הנני נתנך
	Jer 22:6	גלעד אתה
	Jer 22:11	המלך (תחתו) [תחת]
11–15	Jer 24:8	(כתאנים) [וכתאנים]
	Jer 29:10	מלאת לבבל
	Jer 29:16	אל המלך היושב
	Jer 30:5	קול חרדה
	Jer 30:12	אנוש לשברך
16–20	Jer 31:7	רנו ליעקב
	Jer 32:42	כאשר הבאתי
	Jer 33:17	(כסא יכרת) [יכרת...כסא]
	Jer 48:40	הנה כנשר
	Jer 49:12	משפטם
21–25	Isa 8:11	(בחזקת) [כחזקת] היד
	Isa 18:4	אשקוטה ואביטה
	Isa 21:16	בעוד שנה
	Isa 31:4	כאשר יהגה
	Isa 45:18	בורא
26–30	Isa 49:25	גם שבי גבור
	Isa 52:3	נמכרתם
	Isa 56:4	לסריסים
	Isa 66:12	הנני (נוטה) [נטה]
	Amos 5:4	דרשוני

Com.: The Masorah notes the *thirty* occurrences of the phrase כִּי־כֹה ׀ אָמַר יְהוָה, which is considered to be unusual because it differs from similar phrases that occur where the Tetragrammaton is followed by צְבָאוֹת אֱלֹהֵי יִשְׂרָאֵל or אֱלֹהֵי יִשְׂרָאֵל, צְבָאוֹת, אֱלֹהִים.

The Mp heading at Jer 29:10 reads *six times with these accents in the book* and refers to the *six* occurrences of this phrase in Jeremiah with the accents *paštâ, mûnaḥ, zaqep̄* (כִּי־כֹה אָמַר יְהוָה) in 4:27, 10:18, 29:10, 30:5, 32:42, and 48:40.

It is noteworthy that in the Mm list, *all* the Jeremiah references precede those of Isaiah.

In M^L there are only *two* circelli on this *four-word* phrase: one on כִּי־כֹה and one on אָמַר יְהוָה. With *four-* or *five-word* phrases it is not unusual for only *two* circelli to be given; see **Josh 1:6** and *passim*.

3:17   וְלֹא־תִרְאוּ

Twice   בׄ   Mp

2 Kgs 3:17; Jer 42:18

וְלֹא־תִרְאוּ *twice*   ולא תראו בׄ   Mm

2 Kgs 3:17   כי כה אמר יהוה
Jer 42:18   את המקום

Com.: The Masorah notes the *two* occurrences of this lemma with a ו cj., to distinguish them from its *six* occurrences written without a cj.

This lemma occurs in the ms. in folio 204r, but the Mm note appears on the top left of the preceding folio 203v.

3:17   יִמָּלֵא

Eight times   חׄ   Mp

1–5   **2 Sam 23:7**; **2 Kgs 3:17**; Isa 6:4; Jer 13:12ᵃ; **13:12**ᵇ
6–8   **Pss 71:8**; **126:2**; Prov 20:17

יִמָּלֵא *eight times*   ימלא חׄ   Mm

1–5   2 Sam 23:7   ואיש יגע בהם
         2 Kgs 3:17   והנחל ההוא
         Isa 6:4   וינעו אמות הספים
         Jer 13:12ᵃ   כל נבל ימלא
         Twice in it (Jer 13:12ᵇ)   בׄ בו
6–8   Ps 71:8   ימלא פי תהלתך
         Ps 126:2   אז ימלא שחוק (פיד) [פינו]
         Prov 20:17   ערב לאיש

Com.: The Masorah notes the *eight* occurrences of this lemma in the *niphal*, to distinguish them from its *six* occurrences in the *piel* (יְמַלֵּא); see **1 Kgs 13:33**.

This lemma occurs in the ms. in folio 204r, but the Mm note appears on the bottom right of the preceding folio 203v.

2 KINGS 3:18

וְנָקַ֥ל זֹ֖את בְּעֵינֵ֣י יְהוָ֑ה וְנָתַ֥ן אֶת־מוֹאָ֖ב בְּיֶדְכֶֽם׃

3:18   וְנָקַל

Unique   לׄ   Mp

Com.: The Masorah notes the *sole* occurrence of this lemma with a ו cj., to distinguish it from its occurrence without a cj. at Prov 14:6.

2 KINGS 3:19

וְהִכִּיתֶ֞ם כָּל־עִ֣יר מִבְצָ֗ר וְכָל־עִיר֙ מִבְח֔וֹר וְכָל־עֵ֥ץ טוֹב֙ תַּפִּ֔ילוּ וְכָל־מַעְיְנֵי־מַ֖יִם תִּסְתֹּ֑מוּ וְכֹל֙ הַחֶלְקָ֣ה הַטּוֹבָ֔ה תַּכְאִ֖בוּ בָּאֲבָנִֽים׃

3:19   מִבְחוֹר

Twice   בׄ   Mp

2 Kgs 3:19; 19:23

מִבְחוֹר *twice* and plene   מבחור בׄ ומל   Mm

2 Kgs 3:19   וכל עיר
בְּרֹשָׁיו *of Kings* (2 Kgs 19:23)   דמלכים [ברשיו] (ברושיו)

Com.: The Masorah notes the *two* occurrences of this lemma written with a *holem*, to distinguish them from its more numerous occurrences (8x) written with a *patah* (מִבְחַר).

This distinction is implied in the addition in the Mm *of Kings* to the catchword בְּרֹשָׁיו of 2 Kgs 19:23, to distinguish that reference from its parallel in Isa 37:24, where the lemma appears as מִבְחַר.

This lemma is featured in two Masoretic lists. One is in a list of doublets that begin with the letter מ (see Frensdorff, *Ochlah*, §69, and Díaz-Esteban, *Sefer Oklah we-Oklah*, §70).

The other is in a list of words that appear in one form in a particular book of the Bible and in another form in another book. Here מִבְחוֹר is the form that occurs in Kings, whereas מִבְחָר is the form that occurs in Isaiah; see Frensdorff, *Ochlah*, §272 and Ognibeni, *'Oklah*, §113.

This lemma occurs in the ms. in folio 204r, but the Mm note appears on the bottom left of the preceding folio 203v.

3:19   וְכָל־עֵץ

Five times   הׄ   Mp

1–5 **2 Kgs 3:19**; **3:25**; Isa 44:23; **Ezek 20:28**; **21:3**

Com.: The Masorah notes the *five* occurrences of this lemma with a ו cj., to distinguish them from its more numerous occurrences (20x) written without a cj.

3:19   מַעְיְנֵי־מָיִם

Unique   ל   Mp

Com.: The Masorah notes the *sole* occurrence of מַעְיְנֵי with מָיִם, to distinguish it from its *sole* occurrence with הַמַּיִם (מַעְיְנֵי הַמַּיִם) at 1 Kgs 18:5.

3:19   תִּסְתֹּמוּ

Unique   ל   Mp

Com.: The Masorah notes the *sole* occurrence of this lemma in the 2nd pers. pl., to distinguish it from its *sole* occurrence in the 3rd pers. pl. (יִסְתֹּמוּ) in v. 25.

---

2 KINGS 3:20

וַיְהִי בַבֹּקֶר כַּעֲלוֹת הַמִּנְחָה וְהִנֵּה־מַיִם בָּאִים מִדֶּרֶךְ אֱדוֹם וַתִּמָּלֵא הָאָרֶץ אֶת־הַמָּיִם:

3:20   וְכָל־מוֹאָב

Unique   ל   Mp

2 Kings 3:21

וְכָל־מוֹאָב֙ שָׁמְע֔וּ כִּי־עָל֥וּ הַמְּלָכִ֖ים לְהִלָּ֣חֶם בָּ֑ם וַיִּצָּעֲק֗וּ מִכֹּ֨ל חֹגֵ֤ר חֲגֹרָה֙ וָמַ֔עְלָה וַיַּעַמְד֖וּ עַל־הַגְּבֽוּל׃

3:21   וַיִּצָּעֲק֗וּ

Three times   גׄ   Mp

Com.: See **Judg 10:17**.

3:21   חֹגֵ֤ר

Twice   בׄ   Mp

Com.: See **1 Kgs 20:11**.

2 Kings 3:22

וַיַּשְׁכִּ֣ימוּ בַבֹּ֔קֶר וְהַשֶּׁ֖מֶשׁ זָרְחָ֣ה עַל־הַמָּ֑יִם וַיִּרְא֨וּ מוֹאָ֧ב מִנֶּ֛גֶד אֶת־הַמַּ֖יִם אֲדֻמִּ֥ים כַּדָּֽם׃

3:22   וְהַשֶּׁ֖מֶשׁ

Twice   בׄ   Mp

Com.: See **2 Sam 2:24**.

3:22   זָרְחָ֣ה

Four times, and their references   זרחה דׄ וסימנהון   Mm

Exod 22:2   השמש
2 Kgs 3:22   והשמש
2 Chr 26:19   והצרעת
Nah 3:17   (השמש) [שמש]

Com.: This lemma is featured in a Masoretic list of words that occur *five times*, *four times* without a ו cj. (see above), and *once* with a cj. (Mal 3:20); see Frensdorff, *Ochlah*, §17, and Díaz-Esteban, *Sefer Oklah we-Oklah*, §18.

This lemma occurs in the ms. in folio 204r, but the Mm note appears on the top left of the preceding folio 203v.

3:22　עַל־הַמָּֽיִם

Mp　ד֗ וכל תלים דכות　*Four times*, and similarly *all* Psalms

Exod 7:17 (הַמַּ֣יִם); **15:27**; Lev 14:6 (הַמַּ֔יִם); <u>**2 Kgs 3:22**</u>

Mm　על המים ד֗ וסימנהון　עַל־הַמָּֽיִם *four times*, and their references

Exod 7:17　מכה
Exod 15:27　(אלימה) [אילמה]
Lev 14:6　הצפר
2 Kgs 3:22　זרחה

Com.: The Masorah notes the *four* occurrences, apart from Psalms, of this lemma with עַל, to distinguish them from its *five* occurrences with אֶל (אֶל־הַמַּ֫יִם/הַמָּֽיִם).

In M^L a ד has been superimposed over an original ל, with the upper part of the ל still visible. This lemma occurs in the ms. in folio 204r, but the Mm note appears on the bottom left of the preceding folio 203v.

3:22　אֲדֻמִּ֥ים כַּדָּֽם

Mp　ל֗　*Unique*

Com.: The second part of this lemma is featured in a Masoretic list of words that only occur *once* beginning with כ; see Frensdorff, *Ochlah*, §19.

2 KINGS 3:23

וַיֹּאמְרוּ֙ דָּ֣ם זֶ֔ה הָחֳרֵ֤ב נֶֽחֶרְבוּ֙ הַמְּלָכִ֔ים וַיַּכּ֖וּ אִ֣ישׁ אֶת־רֵעֵ֑הוּ וְעַתָּ֥ה לַשָּׁלָ֖ל מוֹאָֽב׃

3:23　לַשָּׁלָ֖ל

M_F　ל֗　*Unique*

Com.: This lemma is featured in a Masoretic list of words that only occur *once* beginning with a ל and vowel; see Frensdorff, *Ochlah*, §26, and Díaz-Esteban, *Sefer Oklah we-Oklah*, §27.

2 Kings 3:24

וַיָּבֹאוּ֙ אֶל־מַחֲנֵ֣ה יִשְׂרָאֵ֔ל וַיָּקֻ֤מוּ יִשְׂרָאֵל֙ וַיַּכּ֣וּ אֶת־מוֹאָ֔ב וַיָּנֻ֖סוּ מִפְּנֵיהֶ֑ם וַיַּבּוּ־בָ֔הּ וְהַכּ֖וֹת אֶת־מוֹאָֽב׃

3:24   וַיַּבּוּ

Read   וַיַּכּוּ ק   ויכו ק   Mp

Com.: The *kətîb* (ויבו), and the *qərê* (וַיַּכּוּ) are examples of cases where both the *kətîb* and the *qərê* are unsatisfactory; see Gordis, *The Biblical Text*, 155.

The *kətîb* ויבו is unintelligible unless it stands for וַיָּבֹ֫אוּ, *they came*, as occurs early in the verse. The more likely reading is the *qərê*, which reads וַיַּכּוּ, *they smote*, a form that also occurs earlier in the verse.

This lemma is featured in a Masoretic list of words that have a ב read as a כ; see Frensdorff, *Ochlah*, §149, and Díaz-Esteban, *Sefer Oklah we-Oklah*, §137.

2 Kings 3:25

וְהֶעָרִ֣ים יַהֲרֹ֡סוּ וְכָל־חֶלְקָ֣ה ט֠וֹבָה יַשְׁלִ֨יכוּ אִישׁ־אַבְנ֜וֹ וּמִלְא֗וּהָ וְכָל־מַעְיַן־מַ֤יִם יִסְתֹּ֙מוּ֙ וְכָל־עֵץ־ט֣וֹב יַפִּ֔ילוּ עַד־הִשְׁאִ֧יר אֲבָנֶ֛יהָ בַּקִּ֖יר חֲרָ֑שֶׂת וַיָּסֹ֥בּוּ הַקַּלָּעִ֖ים וַיַּכּֽוּהָ׃

3:25   חֶלְקָה טוֹבָה

Unique   ל   Mp

Com.: The Masorah notes the *sole* occurrence of this lemma (*fertile plot*), to distinguish it from its *sole* occurrence as a def. הַחֶלְקָה הַטּוֹבָה (*the fertile plot*) in v. 19.

3:25   מַעְיַן

Four times   ד   Mp

Com.: See **Josh 15:9**.

3:25   יִסְתֹּמוּ

Unique   ל   Mp

Com.: The Masorah notes the *sole* occurrence of this lemma in the 3rd pers. plur., to distinguish it from its *sole* occurrence in the 2nd pers. plur. (תִּסְתֹּמוּ) in v. 19.

3:25 וְכָל־עֵץ

Five times ה̇ Mp

Com.: See directly above at **2 Kgs 3:19**.

3:25 חֲרֹשֶׂת

Unique with *qameṣ* ל̇ Mp

Com.: The Masorah notes the *sole* occurrence of this lemma with a *qameṣ*, to distinguish it from its *sole* occurrence with a *səḡôl* (חֲרֶשֶׂת) at Isa 16:7.

3:25 הַקַּלָּעִים

Unique ל̇ Mp

> ## 2 KINGS 3:26
> וַיַּרְא מֶלֶךְ מוֹאָב כִּי־חָזַק מִמֶּנּוּ הַמִּלְחָמָה וַיִּקַּח אוֹתוֹ שְׁבַע־מֵאוֹת אִישׁ שֹׁלֵף חֶרֶב לְהַבְקִיעַ אֶל־מֶלֶךְ אֱדוֹם וְלֹא יָכֹלוּ:

3:26 חָזַק

Five times ה̇ Mp

Com.: See **Judg 1:28**.

3:26 אוֹתוֹ

Twenty-five times plene כֹּה מל Mp

Com.: See **Josh 16:6**.

3:26 וְלֹא יָכֹלוּ

Three times ג̇ Mp

Exod 8:14; **2 Kgs 3:26**; **Jonah 1:13**

2 KINGS

Mm	ולא יכלו ג׳ וסימנהון	לֹא יָכְלוּ *three times*, and their references

Exod 8:14   ויעשו כן החרטמים
2 Kgs 3:26   להבקיע
Jonah 1:13   ויחתרו האנשים

Com.: The Masorah notes the *three* occurrences of this lemma with a *ḥolem* on the כ, to distinguish them from its more numerous occurrences (20x) written with a *šəwâ* (יָכְלוּ).

This lemma occurs in the ms. in folio 204r, but the Mm note appears on the bottom right of the preceding folio 203v.

2 KINGS 3:27

וַיִּקַּח אֶת־בְּנוֹ הַבְּכוֹר אֲשֶׁר־יִמְלֹךְ תַּחְתָּיו וַיַּעֲלֵהוּ עֹלָה עַל־הַחֹמָה וַיְהִי קֶצֶף־גָּדוֹל עַל־יִשְׂרָאֵל וַיִּסְעוּ מֵעָלָיו וַיָּשֻׁבוּ לָאָרֶץ: פ

3:27   הַחֹמָה

Six times defective   ו חס׳   Mp

1–5   **2 Kgs 3:27**; **6:26**; 6:30; 18:26; 18:27
6   2 Kgs 25:4 (הַחֹמֹתַיִם)

Com.: The Masorah notes the *six* occurrences of this lemma in various forms written in the book defective ו, to distinguish them from its *two* occurrences in the book written plene ו (חוֹמָה in **1 Kgs 4:13**, and הַחוֹמָה in **1 Kgs 20:30**).

2 KINGS 4:1

וְאִשָּׁה אַחַת מִנְּשֵׁי בְנֵי־הַנְּבִיאִים צָעֲקָה אֶל־אֱלִישָׁע לֵאמֹר עַבְדְּךָ אִישִׁי מֵת וְאַתָּה יָדַעְתָּ כִּי עַבְדְּךָ הָיָה יָרֵא אֶת־יְהוָה וְהַנֹּשֶׁה בָּא לָקַחַת אֶת־שְׁנֵי יְלָדַי לוֹ לַעֲבָדִים:

4:1   וְאִשָּׁה

Twenty-two times   כב   Mp

Com.: See **1 Sam 27:11**.

4:1   אִישִׁי

Eight times   ח   Mp

1–5   Gen 29:32; 29:34; **30:15**; 30:20; 2 Sam 14:5
6–8   **2 Kgs 4:1**; **Hos 2:9**; 2:18

Com.: The Masorah notes the *eight* occurrences of this lemma without a prep., to distinguish them from its *two* occurrences with a prep. (לְאִישִׁי) at Gen 30:18 and 2 Sam 14:7.

This distinction is implied in the additional notation to the Mm at 2 Sam 14:5 of *and twice* לְאִישִׁי.

4:1   וְהַנָּשָׁה

Unique   ל   Mp

---

2 KINGS 4:2

וַיֹּאמֶר אֵלֶיהָ אֱלִישָׁע מָה אֶעֱשֶׂה־לָּךְ הַגִּידִי לִי מַה־יֶּשׁ־לָכִי בַּבָּיִת וַתֹּאמֶר אֵין לְשִׁפְחָתְךָ כֹל בַּבַּיִת כִּי אִם־אָסוּךְ שָׁמֶן׃

4:2   לָכִי

Read לָךְ   לך ק   Mp

Com.: The *kətîb* (לכי) represents the older 2nd pers. fem. sg. sfx. לָכִי, whereas the *qərê* (לָךְ) represents the regular form; see Gordis, *The Biblical Text*, 103.

This lemma is featured in a Masoretic list of words that have a י at the end of a word that is not read; see Frensdorff, *Ochlah*, §127, and Díaz-Esteban, *Sefer Oklah we-Oklah*, §111.

In M^L this lemma has no circellus.

4:2   אָסוּךְ

Unique and plene   ל ומל   Mp

Com.: By noting that this lemmma is *unique* and written plene ו, the Masorah is also implying (correctly) that this lemma does not occur elsewhere written defective.

---

2 KINGS 4:3

וַיֹּאמֶר לְכִי שַׁאֲלִי־לָךְ כֵּלִים מִן־הַחוּץ מֵאֵת כָּל־שְׁכֵנָכִי כֵּלִים רֵקִים אַל־תַּמְעִיטִי׃

4:3   שְׁכֵנָכִי

Read שְׁכֵנָיִךְ   שכניך קר   Mp

Com.: The *kətîb* (שכנבי) represents the older 2nd pers. fem. sg. sfx. שְׁכֵנַיְכִי, whereas the *qərê* (שְׁכֵנַיִךְ) represents the regular form; see Gordis, *The Biblical Text*, 103.

This lemma is featured in a Masoretic list of words that have a י at the end of a word that is not read; see Frensdorff, *Ochlah*, §127, and Díaz-Esteban, *Sefer Oklah we-Oklah*, §111.

---

2 KINGS 4:4
וּבָאת וְסָגַרְתְּ הַדֶּלֶת בַּעֲדֵךְ וּבְעַד־בָּנַיִךְ וְיָצַקְתְּ עַל כָּל־הַכֵּלִים הָאֵלֶּה וְהַמָּלֵא תַּסִּיעִי׃

4:4   וּבָאת

וּבָאת *five times*	וּבָאת ה	Mm

1–5	2 Sam 14:3	אל המלך
	1 Kgs 14:3	עשרה לחם
	<u>2 Kgs 4:4</u>	וסגרת
	Mic 4:10	עד בבל
	Ruth 3:4	וגלית

And *once* (וּבָת): Dan 6:19   וא ובת טות

Com.: The Masorah notes the *five* occurrences of this lemma written without a vowel under the ת (2nd pers. fem.), to distinguish them from its more numerous occurrences (19x) written with a *qameṣ* (וּבָאתָ, 2nd pers masc.).

The Masorah also notes the occurrence of this lemma without a medial א at Dan 6:19. This form, however, is derived from an Aramaic verb בּוּת *to spend the night*, whereas the other forms in the list are derived from the Hebrew verb בּוֹא *to come*.

4:4   בָּנַיִךְ

Eighteen times	יח	Mp

1–5	**2 Kgs 4:4**; **4:7** (וּבָנַיִךְ, *qərê*); Isa 49:17; 49:22; 49:25
6–10	Isa 51:20; 54:13ᵃ; 54:13ᵇ; 60:4; **60:9**
11–15	Isa 62:5; Jer 5:7; Ezek 16:20; 16:36; 23:25
16–18	Zech 9:13ᵃ; 9:13ᵇ; **Ps 147:13**

Com.: The Masorah notes the *eighteen* occurrences of this lemma with a fem. sfx., to distinguish them from its more numerous occurrences (46x) with a masc. sfx. (בָּנֶיךָ/וּבָנֶיךָ).

4:4   וְיָצְקְתְּ

Unique   ל   Mp

Com.: The Masorah notes the *sole* occurrence of this lemma in the fem., to distinguish it from its *five* occurrences in the masc. (וְיָצְקְתָּ).

4:4   וְהַמָּלֵא

Unique   ל   Mp

Com.: This lemma is featured in a Masoretic list of words that occur *twice*, *once* with a prefixed וְ, and *once* with a prefixed וְהַ; see Frensdorff, *Ochlah*, §9, and Díaz-Esteban, *Sefer Oklah we-Oklah*, §9.

4:4   תַּסִּיעִי

Unique   ל   Mp

Com.: The Masorah notes the *sole* occurrence of this lemma in the fem., to distinguish it from its *sole* occurrence in the masc. (תַּסִּיע) at Ps 80:9.

---

2 KINGS 4:5
וַתֵּלֶךְ מֵאִתּוֹ וַתִּסְגֹּר הַדֶּלֶת בַּעֲדָהּ וּבְעַד בָּנֶיהָ הֵם מַגִּשִׁים אֵלֶיהָ וְהִיא מֵיצָקֶת׃

4:5   מַגִּשִׁים

Three times   ג   Mp

1 Kgs 5:1; **2 Kgs 4:5** (מַגִּישִׁים)*; **Mal 1:7** (מַגִּישִׁים)

מגשים *three times, twice* defective and *once* plene   (מגישים) [מגשים] ג֣ ב׳ חסירין וא׳ מל   Mm

1 Kgs 5:1   מנחה
2 Kgs 4:5   הם (מגישים) [מגשים] אליה
Mal 1:7   על מזבחי

Com.: The Masorah notes the *three* occurrences of this lemma, *twice* written plene first י (here and Mal 1:7), and *once* written defective first י (1 Kgs 5:1). This is expressly stated in the Mm heading of Mal 1:7, and in the Mm of M^C at 1 Kgs 5:1, which read *twice plene, and once defective*.

*M^L, contrary to M (מַגִּשִׁים), reads the form here defective first י (מַגִּשִׁם); see Breuer, *The Biblical Text*, 120.

The heading of the Mm here is contrary to that of the heading of the Mm of Mal 1:7, and to that of the Mm of M^C at 1 Kgs 5:1. The Mm here reads *twice defective and once plene*, whereas the others read *twice plene, and once defective*.

M^A reads here מַגִּישִׁים, whereas M^C, as M^L, reads מַגִּשִׁים. Both have Mp notes that read *three times*.

4:5   מיצֶקֶת

Mp   מוצקת קרי   מוּצֶקֶת Read

Com.: The *kətîb* (מיצקת) and *qərê* (מוּצֶקֶת) represent examples of interchanges between original initial ו and initial י verbs; see Gordis, *The Biblical Text*, 130.

This lemma is featured in a Masoretic list of words that have a י in the middle of word that is read as a ו; see the Mm at Num 1:16 *sub* קריא, Frensdorff, *Ochlah*, §80, and Díaz-Esteban, *Sefer Oklah we-Oklah*, §71.

2 KINGS 4:6

וַיְהִי ׀ כִּמְלֹאת הַכֵּלִים וַתֹּאמֶר אֶל־בְּנָהּ הַגִּישָׁה אֵלַי עוֹד כֶּלִי וַיֹּאמֶר אֵלֶיהָ אֵין עוֹד כֶּלִי וַיַּעֲמֹד הַשָּׁמֶן:

4:6   כִּמְלֹאת

Mp   גׄ   Three times

2 Kgs 4:6; **Jer 25:12** (כִּמְלֹאות); **Ezek 5:2**

Mm   כמלאת גׄ בׄ חסירין וחד מל וסימנהון   כִּמְלֹאת *three times, twice* defective and *once* plene, and their references

2 Kgs 4:6   הכלים
Jer 25:12   שבעים שנה
Ezek 5:2   ימי המצור

Com.: The Masorah notes the *three* occurrences of this lemma, *twice* written defective ו (2 Kgs 4:6 and Ezek 5:2), and *once* written plene ו (Jer 25:12).

This lemma occurs in the ms. in folio 204v, but the Mm note appears on the top left of the preceding folio 204r.

> **2 KINGS 4:7**
> וַתָּבֹא וַתַּגֵּד לְאִישׁ הָאֱלֹהִים וַיֹּאמֶר לְכִי מִכְרִי אֶת־הַשֶּׁמֶן וְשַׁלְּמִי אֶת־נִשְׁיֵכִי וְאַתְּ ◦בָּנַיְכִי תִחְיִי בַּנּוֹתָר: פ

4:7   מִכְרִי

Mp   בֿ   *Twice*

2 Kgs 4:7; 1 Chr 9:8

Com.: The Masorah notes the *two* occurrences of this lemma but does not distinguish between its different meanings. Here the form is a fem. imper. sg. *sell!*, whereas in 1 Chr 9:8 it is a person's name *Michri*.

4:7   נִשְׁיֵכִי

Mp   נשיך קֿ   נִשְׁיֵךְ Read

Com.: The *kǝtîb* (נשיכי) represents the older second pers. fem. sg. sfx. נִשְׁיֵכִי, whereas the *qǝrê* (נִשְׁיֵךְ) represents the regular form; see Gordis, *The Biblical Text*, 103.

This lemma is featured in a Masoretic list of words in which a י is written at the end but is not read; see Frensdorff, *Ochlah*, §127, and Díaz-Esteban, *Sefer Oklah we-Oklah*, §111.

4:7   ◦בָּנַיְכִי

Mp   ובניך קֿ   וּבָנַיִךְ Read

Com.: The *kǝtîb* (בניכי) represents the older 2nd pers. fem. sg. sfx. בָּנַיְכִי, whereas the *qǝrê* (וּבָנַיִךְ) represents the regular form; see Gordis, *The Biblical Text*, 103. The *kǝtîb* (בניכי) and *qǝrê* (וּבָנַיִךְ) also represent examples where a ו at the beginning of a word is not written yet it is read; see ibid, 144.

This lemma is featured in two Masoretic lists. One is in a list of words in which a י is written at the end but is not read; see Frensdorff, *Ochlah*, §127.

The other is in a list of words where a ו cj. is missing in the writing at the beginning of a word but is read; see the Mm at <u>Dan 2:43</u> *sub* דִּי, Frensdorff, *Ochlah*, §117, and Díaz-Esteban, *Sefer Oklah we-Oklah*, §103.

2 KINGS 4:8

וַיְהִי הַיּוֹם וַיַּעֲבֹר אֱלִישָׁע אֶל־שׁוּנֵם וְשָׁם אִשָּׁה גְדוֹלָה וַתַּחֲזֶק־בּוֹ לֶאֱכָל־לָחֶם וַיְהִי מִדֵּי עָבְרוֹ יָסֻר שָׁמָּה לֶאֱכָל־לָחֶם:

4:8   מִדֵּי עָבְרוֹ

Twice   בֿ   Mp

2 Kgs 4:8; **Isa 28:19**

מִדֵּי עָבְרוֹ *twice, and their references*   מדי עברו בֿ וסימנהון   Mm

2 Kgs 4:8   (והיה) [ויהי] מדי עברו
Isa 28:19   מדי עברו יקח

4:8   יָסֻר

Three times defective   גֿ חס   Mp

2 Kgs 4:8; **Prov 9:4**; **9:16**

יָסֻר *three times defective, and their references*   יסר גֿ חסירין וסימנהון   Mm

2 Kgs 4:8   (והיה) [ויהי] מדי עברו
Prov 9:4   מי (פתו) [פתי] יסר הנה
<Prov 9:16>

Com.: The Masorah notes the *three* occurrences of this lemma written defective ו, to distinguish them from its more numerous occurrences (13x) written plene ו (יָסוּר).

2 KINGS 4:9

וַתֹּאמֶר אֶל־אִישָׁהּ הִנֵּה־נָא יָדַעְתִּי כִּי אִישׁ אֱלֹהִים קָדוֹשׁ הוּא עֹבֵר עָלֵינוּ תָּמִיד:

4:9   אִישָׁהּ

Twenty-one times   כֿא   Mp

Com.: See **Judg 19:3**.

> **2 KINGS 4:10**
> נַעֲשֶׂה־נָּא עֲלִיַּת־קִיר קְטַנָּה וְנָשִׂים לוֹ שָׁם מִטָּה וְשֻׁלְחָן וְכִסֵּא וּמְנוֹרָה וְהָיָה בְּבֹאוֹ אֵלֵינוּ יָסוּר שָׁמָּה:

4:10   שָׁם

Five verses containing the sequence שָׁם...שָׁמָּה   ה̇ פסוק שם שמה   Mp

1–5   Deut 12:5; 12:11; **2 Kgs 4:10**; Jer 22:27; **Ezek 1:20**
6   Ezek 47:9

Six verses containing the sequence שָׁם...שָׁמָּה, and their references   ו̇ פסוקין אית בהון שם שמה וסימנהון   Mm

1–5   Deut 12:5   כי אם אל המקום אשר
      Deut 12:11   (יהיה) [והיה] המקום אשר יבחר
      <u>2 Kgs 4:10</u>   נעשה נא עלית קיר
      Jer 22:27   ועל הארץ אשר הם מנשאים
      <u>Ezek 1:20</u>   על אשר
6   <Ezek 47:9>

Com.: The Mp heading here incorrectly reads *five*, similarly the Mp heading at Ezek 1:20 incorrectly reads *seven*. The correct number *six* for the sequence שָׁם...שָׁמָּה is given in the heading to the Mm here, at <u>Ezek. 1:20</u>, and Frensdorff, *Ochlah*, §336. However, both the Mm at Ezek 1:20 and *Ochlah* list 2 Kgs 4:8, which has a slightly different sequence of וְשָׁם...שָׁמָּה, as the sixth reference.

In M^L the circellus for this note has been attached to the first word in the verse נַעֲשֶׂה.

4:10   שָׁמָּה

Eighteen times at the end of a verse   י̇ח̇ סוף פסוק   Mp

1–5   Gen 23:13; **24:6**; 24:8; **39:1**; 43:30
6–10   Num 15:18; 17:19; 35:26; Josh 2:1; 1 Sam 22:1
11–15   **2 Kgs 4:10**; 4:11; Isa 65:9; **Ezek 29:13**; **36:21**
16–18   Ezek 40:1; **48:35**; Qoh 9:10

Com.: The Masorah notes the *eighteen* occurrences at the end of a verse of שָׁמָּה, to distinguish them from the more numerous occurrences (80x) at the end of a verse of its parallel form שָׁם.

This enumeration does not include the *nine* occurrences of this lemma in the books of Exodus and Deuteronomy; see Breuer, *Masora Magna*, 309.

The Mp heading at Ezek 29:13 mistakenly reads *fifteen*, whereas its Mm only lists the *four* occurrences of this lemma in the book of Ezekiel.

---

2 KINGS 4:13

וַיֹּ֣אמֶר ל֗וֹ אֱמָר־נָ֣א אֵלֶיהָ֮ הִנֵּ֣ה חָרַ֣דְתְּ ׀ אֵלֵינוּ֮ אֶת־כָּל־הַחֲרָדָ֣ה הַזֹּאת֒ מֶ֤ה לַעֲשׂ֣וֹת לָ֔ךְ הֲיֵ֤שׁ לְדַבֶּר־לָךְ֙ אֶל־הַמֶּ֔לֶךְ א֖וֹ אֶל־שַׂ֣ר הַצָּבָ֑א וַתֹּ֕אמֶר בְּת֥וֹךְ עַמִּ֖י אָנֹכִ֥י יֹשָֽׁבֶת׃

4:13	חָרַ֣דְתְּ		
Unique	ל	Mp	

4:13	הֲיֵ֤שׁ לְדַבֶּר		
Unique	ל	Mp	

4:13   יֹשָֽׁבֶת

יֹשָׁבֶת *twice, once* defective *and once* plene	ישבת בׄ חד חסׄ וחׄ מלׄ	Mm

Josh 2:15   (יוֹשֶׁבֶת)   היא [ובחומה] (ובחוסה)
2 Kgs 4:13   (יֹשָׁבֶת)   בתוך עמי

Com.: The Masorah notes the *two* occurrences of this lemma, *one* written plene ו (Josh 2:15), and *one* written defective ו (here).

The Mp heading at **Josh 2:15**, reads *twice with qameṣ* (בָ) to distinguish these forms from the more numerous occurrences (23x) of the non-pausal form of this lemma written with a *səḡôl* under the שׁ (יוֹשֶׁבֶת).

---

2 KINGS 4:15

וַיֹּ֖אמֶר קְרָא־לָ֑הּ וַיִּקְרָא־לָ֔הּ וַֽתַּעֲמֹ֖ד בַּפָּֽתַח׃

4:15	בַּפָּֽתַח		
Unique with *qameṣ*	ל קמׄ	Mp	

Com.: The Masorah notes the *sole* occurrence of this lemma with *qameṣ*, to distinguish it from its *sole* occurrence with *səḡôl* (בַּפֶּתַח) at 1 Kgs 14:6.

> ### 2 KINGS 4:16
> וַיֹּאמֶר לַמּוֹעֵד הַזֶּה כָּעֵת חַיָּה אַתִּי חֹבֶקֶת בֵּן וַתֹּאמֶר אַל־אֲדֹנִי אִישׁ הָאֱלֹהִים אַל־תְּכַזֵּב בְּשִׁפְחָתֶךָ׃

4:16   אַתִּי

Read   אַתְּ ק   את כ   Mp

Com.: The *kǝtîb* (אתי) represents the older 2nd pers. fem. sg. form of the pron. אַתְּ, whereas the *qǝrê* (אַתְּ) represents the regular form; see Gordis, *The Biblical Text*, 102.

This lemma is featured in a Masoretic list of words in which a י is written at the end but is not read; see Frensdorff, *Ochlah*, §127, and Díaz-Esteban, *Sefer Oklah we-Oklah*, §111.

This lemma is one of *seven* occurrences where אתי, with and without ו cj., is written but אַתְּ is read; see the Mm to 2 Kgs 8:1 *sub* אַתִּי.

4:16   אַל־תְּכַזֵּב

Unique   ל   Mp

> ### 2 KINGS 4:18
> וַיִּגְדַּל הַיָּלֶד וַיְהִי הַיּוֹם וַיֵּצֵא אֶל־אָבִיו אֶל־הַקֹּצְרִים׃

4:18   וַיֵּצֵא אֶל־אָבִיו

Unique   ל   Mp

> ### 2 KINGS 4:19
> וַיֹּאמֶר אֶל־אָבִיו רֹאשִׁי ׀ רֹאשִׁי וַיֹּאמֶר אֶל־הַנַּעַר שָׂאֵהוּ אֶל־אִמּוֹ׃

4:19   שָׂאֵהוּ

Twice   ב֗   Mp

Num 11:12; 2 Kgs 4:19

2 Kings 4:20

וַיִּשָּׂאֵהוּ וַיְבִיאֵהוּ אֶל־אִמּוֹ וַיֵּשֶׁב עַל־בִּרְכֶּיהָ עַד־הַצָּהֳרַיִם וַיָּמֹת:

4:20   וַיְבִיאֵהוּ

Mp   ח̇ מל̇ וכל כתיב דכות̇ ב̇ מ̇ א̇   *Eight times* plene, and similarly in *all* the Writings apart from *one*

Com.: The Mp heading here of *eight times* plene etc. is incorrect since there are only *five* occurrences of this lemma. Most probably this is the result of a graphic error of ח *eight* for ה *five*; see **Judg 19:21**.

M^A correctly reads here *five times plene*, whereas M^C has no note.

2 Kings 4:22

וַתִּקְרָא אֶל־אִישָׁהּ וַתֹּאמֶר שִׁלְחָה נָא לִי אֶחָד מִן־הַנְּעָרִים וְאַחַת הָאֲתֹנוֹת וְאָרוּצָה עַד־אִישׁ הָאֱלֹהִים וְאָשׁוּבָה:

4:22   אִישָׁהּ

Mp   כא̇   *Twenty-one times*

Com.: See **Judg 19:3**.

4:22   שִׁלְחָה

Mp   ו̇   *Six times*

Com.: See **1 Sam 16:11**.

4:22   מִן־הַנְּעָרִים

Mp   ל̇   *Unique*

Com.: This lemma is featured in a Masoretic list of words that are preceded only *once* by the separable prep. מִן, otherwise the prep. is directly attached to the word; see Frensdorff, *Ochlah*, §196, and Ognibeni, *'Oklah*, §151.

4:22   וְאַחַת הָאֲתֹנוֹת

Mp   ל̇   *Unique*

> **2 KINGS 4:23**
>
> וַיֹּ֗אמֶר מַ֠דּוּעַ אַ֣תְּ הֹלֶ֤כֶתי אֵלָיו֙ הַיּ֔וֹם לֹֽא־חֹ֖דֶשׁ וְלֹ֣א שַׁבָּ֑ת וַתֹּ֖אמֶר שָׁלֽוֹם׃

4:23   אַתְּי

Read אַתְּ   אתּ ק̇   Mp

Com.: See directly above at **2 Kgs 4:16**. In M^L this lemma has no circellus.

4:23   הֹלֶ֤כֶתי

Read הֹלֶ֤כֶת   הלכת ק̇   Mp

Com.: The *kətîb* (הלכתי) with its paragogic י, represents a remnant of the old Semitic case endings, whereas the *qərê* (הֹלֶ֤כֶת) represents the regular form; see Gordis, *The Biblical Text*, 104.

This lemma is featured in a Masoretic list of words in which a י is written at the end but is not read; see Frensdorff, *Ochlah*, §127. In M^L this lemma has no circellus.

> **2 KINGS 4:24**
>
> וַתַּחֲבֹשׁ֙ הָֽאָת֔וֹן וַתֹּ֥אמֶר אֶֽל־נַעֲרָ֖הּ נְהַ֣ג וָלֵ֑ךְ אַל־תַּעֲצָר־לִ֣י לִרְכֹּ֔ב כִּ֖י אִם־אָמַ֥רְתִּי לָֽךְ׃

4:24   אֶֽל־נַעֲרָ֖הּ

Unique   ל̇   Mp

Com.: The Masorah notes the *sole* occurrence of this lemma with the fem. sfx., to distinguish it from its *sole* occurrence with the masc. sfx. (אֶֽל־נַעֲרוֹ) at 1 Kgs 18:43.

4:24   לִרְכֹּ֔ב

Twice   ב̇   Mp

2 Sam 16:2; **2 Kgs 4:24**

2 Kings 4:25

וַתֵּ֨לֶךְ וַתָּב֜וֹא אֶל־אִ֤ישׁ הָאֱלֹהִים֙ אֶל־הַ֣ר הַכַּרְמֶ֔ל וַ֠יְהִי כִּרְא֨וֹת אִישׁ־הָאֱלֹהִ֤ים אֹתָהּ֙ מִנֶּ֔גֶד וַיֹּ֨אמֶר֙ אֶל־גֵּיחֲזִ֣י נַעֲר֔וֹ הִנֵּ֖ה הַשּׁוּנַמִּ֥ית הַלָּֽז׃

4:25	הַשּׁוּנַמִּית הַלָּז		
Unique		ל	Mp

Com.: In M^L the circellus has been placed over the two words הַלָּ֖ז׃ עַתָּ֔ה. Most likely, as suggested by *BHS*, it belongs on the phrase הַשּׁוּנַמִּית הַלָּז, which also occurs only this *once*. Neither M^C nor M^A has a note on this lemma here.

2 Kings 4:27

וַתָּבֹ֞א אֶל־אִ֤ישׁ הָאֱלֹהִים֙ אֶל־הָהָ֔ר וַֽתַּחֲזֵ֖ק בְּרַגְלָ֑יו וַיִּגַּ֨שׁ גֵּֽיחֲזִ֜י לְהָדְפָ֗הּ וַיֹּאמֶר֩ אִ֨ישׁ הָאֱלֹהִ֤ים הַרְפֵּֽה־לָהּ֙ כִּֽי־נַפְשָׁ֣הּ מָֽרָה־לָ֔הּ וַֽיהוָה֙ הֶעְלִ֣ים מִמֶּ֔נִּי וְלֹ֥א הִגִּ֖יד לִֽי׃

4:27	לְהָדְפָהּ		
Unique		ל	Mp

4:27	הַרְפֵּה		
Twice		ב	Mp

Com.: See **Judg 11:37**.

2 Kings 4:28

וַתֹּ֕אמֶר הֲשָׁאַ֥לְתִּי בֵ֖ן מֵאֵ֣ת אֲדֹנִ֑י הֲלֹ֣א אָמַ֔רְתִּי לֹ֥א תַשְׁלֶ֖ה אֹתִֽי׃

4:28	הֲשָׁאַלְתִּי		
Unique		ל	Mp

Com.: The Masorah notes the *sole* occurrence of this lemma with the interrog. ה, to distinguish it from its *three* occurrences without this interrogative.

4:28	תַשְׁלֶה		
Unique		ל	Mp

> **2 KINGS 4:29**
>
> וַיֹּ֨אמֶר לְגֵיחֲזִ֜י חֲגֹ֣ר מָתְנֶ֗יךָ וְקַ֨ח מִשְׁעַנְתִּ֣י בְיָדְךָ֮ וָלֵךְ֒ כִּֽי־תִמְצָ֥א אִישׁ֙ לֹ֣א תְבָרְכֶ֔נּוּ וְכִֽי־יְבָרֶכְךָ֥ אִ֖ישׁ לֹ֣א תַעֲנֶ֑נּוּ וְשַׂמְתָּ֥ מִשְׁעַנְתִּ֖י עַל־פְּנֵ֥י הַנָּֽעַר׃

4:29   וַיֹּ֨אמֶר לְגֵיחֲזִ֜י

Unique   ל̇   Mp

Com.: The Masorah notes the *sole* occurrence of this lemma with the prep. ל, to distinguish it from its *two* occurrences with the prep. אֶל (וַיֹּאמֶר אֶל גֵּיחֲזִי) in vv. 12 and 25.

4:29   וְקַ֨ח

Thirteen times   י̇ג̇   Mp

Com.: See **1 Sam 2:16**.

4:29   וָלֵךְ֒

Five times   ה̇   Mp

1–5   **Gen 12:19**; <u>24:51</u>; 2 Kgs 4:24; **4:29**; Jer 36:14

Com.: The Masorah notes the *five* occurrences of this lemma with a ו cj. pointed with a *qameṣ*, to distinguish them from its *ten* occurrences with a ו cj pointed with a *šəwâ* (וְלֵךְ).

In M^L at Gen 24:51, a Mp note reading *fourteen times rapê* has mistakenly been placed on וָלֵ֔ךְ, but it belongs on the following word וּתְהִי. The heading of the Mm there has the correct enumeration, and the Mm lists the above *five* occurrences.

4:29   כִּי

Thirty-one verses with the sequence כִּי...וְכִי   לא פסו כי וכי   Mp

1–5   Gen 3:6; 29:12; 33:11; Exod 3:11; 4:31
6–10   Num 5:20; Josh 7:15; 8:21; Josh 10:1; 10:2
11–15 Judg 6:30; 1 Sam 19:4; 31:7; 2 Sam 5:12; 1 Kgs 11:21
16–20 **2 Kgs 4:29**; Isa 30:21; 65:16; <u>Jer 38:15</u>; 40:7
21–25 Jer 40:11; 51:53; Ezek 11:16; Mic 5:4; 5:5
26–30 Mal 3:14; Job 7:17; 15:14; 31:14; 31:25
31–33 Job 38:20; Ruth 2:13; 1 Chr 10:7

	Mm	לא פסוק כי וכי	כִּי...וְכִי	Thirty-one verses with the sequence
1–5		Gen 3:6	תאוה הוא	
		Gen 29:12	ויגד יעקב לרחל	
		Gen 33:11	את ברכתי	
		Exod 3:11	וכי אוציא	
		Exod 4:31	ויאמן העם	
6–10		Num 5:20	ואת כי שטית	
		Josh 7:15	והיה הנלכד	
		Josh 8:21	ויהושע וכל	
		Josh 10:1	אדני צדק	
		Josh 10:2	כי עיר גדולה	
11–15		Judg 6:30	הוצא את בנך	
		1 Sam 31:7	בעבר העמק	
		2 Sam 5:12	כי הכינו יהוה	
		1 Kgs 11:21	והדד שמע במצרים	
		2 Kgs 4:29	ויאמר לגיחזי	
16–20		Isa 30:21	ואזניך תשמענה	
		Isa 65:16	המתברך	
		Jer 38:15	אל צדקיהו	
		Jer 40:7	שרי החילים	
		Jer 51:53	כי תעלה	
21–25		Ezek 11:16	[הרחקתים] (הרחקים)	
		Mic 5:4	והיה זה	
		Mic 5:5	ורעו את	
		Mal 3:14	שוא עבד	
		1 Chr 10:7	ויראו כל איש	
26–30		Job 7:17	מה אנוש כי תגדלנו	
		Job 15:14	מה אנוש כי יזכה	
		Job 31:14	ומה אעשה	
		Job 31:25	אם אשמח כי רב	
		Job 38:20	כי תקחנו אל גבולו [תקחנו] (תקוה)	
31		כי (נחמתי) [נחמתני] דרות	כִּי נִחַמְתָּנִי of Ruth (Ruth 2:13)	

Com.: Both the Mp and Mm have a heading of *thirty-one*, and the Mm lists *thirty-one* catchwords of verses with the sequence כִּי...וְכִי. However, there are *thirty-three* occurrences of this lemma, the other *two* being at 1 Sam 19:4 and Jer 40:11; see Jobin, *Concordance*, 106–07.

The addition *of Ruth* to the catchwords כִּי נִחַמְתָּנִי of Ruth 2:13 is simply a reference marker for Ruth since the phrase does not occur anywhere else. Curiously, the original reading in the Mm note of כִּי נִחַמְתִּי has a parallel in Gen 6:7, and there the sequence is not כִּי...וְכִי but כִּי...כִּי.

The Mm at Jer 38:15 lists only the references in Jeremiah and, just as the Mm here, it lists only *three* of them and omits Jer 40:11.

It should be noted that additions to the sequence כִּי...וְכִי are not counted, so that the *two* cases of כִּי...וְכִי...כִּי (1 Sam 22:17; Jer 14:12), or the *one* case of כִּי...וְכִי...וְכִי (Josh 2:9) are not included in this list.

Neither M^C nor M^A has a note on this lemma here.

In M^L this lemma has no circellus.

---

2 KINGS 4:31

וְגֵחֲזִ֞י עָבַ֣ר לִפְנֵיהֶ֗ם וַיָּ֤שֶׂם אֶת־הַמִּשְׁעֶ֙נֶת֙ עַל־פְּנֵ֣י הַנַּ֔עַר וְאֵ֥ין ק֖וֹל וְאֵ֣ין קָ֑שֶׁב וַיָּ֥שָׁב לִקְרָאת֖וֹ וַיַּגֶּד־ל֣וֹ לֵאמֹ֔ר לֹ֥א הֵקִ֖יץ הַנָּֽעַר׃

4:31   וְגֵחֲזִי

Four times defective   ד חס   Mp

2 Kgs 4:31; 5:25 (גֵחֲזִי); **8:4** (גֵחֲזִי); **8:5** (גֵחֲזִי)

Com.: The Masorah notes the *four* occurrences of this lemma written defective first י, to distinguish them from its more numerous occurrences (8x) written plene first י (גֵּיחֲזִי/לְגֵיחֲזִי), *six* of which are in this chapter.

M^L, contrary to M (גֵּיחֲזִי), has a *fifth* occurrence of this lemma at 2 Kgs 4:12 (גֵחֲזִי); see Breuer, *The Biblical Text*, 120. However, all the Mp headings and the Mm at **2 Kgs 8:4** support the enumeration inherent in the text of M.

4:31   וְאֵין

Sixteen verses with the sequence וְאֵין...וְאֵין   יו פסוק ואין ואין   Mp

Com.: See **1 Kgs 18:26**.

In M^L this lemma has no circellus.

---

2 KINGS 4:32

וַיָּבֹ֥א אֱלִישָׁ֖ע הַבָּ֑יְתָה וְהִנֵּ֤ה הַנַּ֙עַר֙ מֵ֔ת מֻשְׁכָּ֖ב עַל־מִטָּתֽוֹ׃

4:32   הַבָּיְתָה

Nineteen times   יט   Mp

Com.: See **Josh 2:18**.

4:32   מִשְׁכָּב

Unique   לׄ   Mp

Com.: The Masorah notes the *sole* occurrence of this lemma pointed with a *qibbûṣ* under the מ (*hophal* ptcp., *laid out*), to distinguish it from its *three* occurrences pointed with a *ḥîreq* (מִשְׁכָּב, *bed*).

---

2 KINGS 4:34

וַיַּ֜עַל וַיִּשְׁכַּ֣ב עַל־הַיֶּ֗לֶד וַיָּשֶׂם֩ פִּ֨יו עַל־פִּ֜יו וְעֵינָ֤יו עַל־עֵינָיו֙ וְכַפָּ֣יו עַל־כַּפָּ֔ו וַיִּגְהַ֖ר עָלָ֑יו וַיָּ֖חָם בְּשַׂ֥ר הַיָּֽלֶד׃

4:34   כַּפָּ֖ו

Read   כַּפָּ֖יו   כפיו ק   Mp

Com.: The *kətîb* (כפו) without a י represents the archaic form of the 3rd masc. sg. sfx. to a pl. noun, whereas the *qərê* (כַּפָּ֖יו) with a י represents the later form; see Cohen, *The Kethib and Qeri System*, 33.

This lemma is featured in a Masoretic list of *hapax legomena* in which a י is read though it is not written; see Frensdorff, *Ochlah*, §128, and Díaz-Esteban, *Sefer Oklah we-Oklah*, §112.

M^C, as M^L, has a *kətîb*/*qərê* here, but M^A reads here *unique defective*.

In M^L this lemma has no circellus.

4:34   וַיָּחָם

Twice   בׄ   Mp

2 Kgs 4:34; Isa 44:15

וַיָּחָם *twice*   ויחם בׄ   Mm

2 Kgs 4:34   ויחם בשר הילד
Isa 44:15   אף ישיק

Com.: This lemma is featured in a Masoretic list of doublets that start with a וי; see Frensdorff, *Ochlah*, §68, and Díaz-Esteban, *Sefer Oklah we-Oklah*, §69.

2 KINGS 4:35

וַיָּ֜שָׁב וַיֵּ֣לֶךְ בַּבַּ֗יִת אַחַ֥ת הֵ֙נָּה֙ וְאַחַ֣ת הֵ֔נָּה וַיַּ֖עַל וַיִּגְהַ֣ר עָלָ֑יו וַיְזוֹרֵ֤ר הַנַּ֙עַר֙ עַד־שֶׁ֣בַע פְּעָמִ֔ים וַיִּפְקַ֥ח הַנַּ֖עַר אֶת־עֵינָֽיו:

4:35   אַחַ֥ת הֵ֙נָּה֙

Unique   ל   Mp

Com.: The Masorah notes the *sole* occurrence of this lemma without a ו cj., to distinguish it from its *sole* occurrence with a cj. (וְאַחַ֣ת הֵ֔נָּה) in the same verse.

4:35   וַיִּגְהַ֣ר

Three times   ג֗   Mp

1 Kgs 18:42; 2 Kgs 4:34; **4:35**

4:35   וַיְזוֹרֵ֤ר

Unique   ל   Mp

2 KINGS 4:36

וַיִּקְרָ֣א אֶל־גֵּיחֲזִ֗י וַיֹּ֙אמֶר֙ קְרָא֙ אֶל־הַשֻּׁנַמִּ֣ית הַזֹּ֔את וַיִּקְרָאֶ֖הָ וַתָּב֣וֹא אֵלָ֑יו וַיֹּ֖אמֶר שְׂאִ֥י בְנֵֽךְ:

4:36   הַשֻּׁנַמִּ֣ית

Three times defective   ג֗ חס   Mp

1 Kgs 2:21; 2:22; **2 Kgs 4:36**

הַשֻּׁנַמִּ֣ית *three times* defective   השנמית ג חס   Mm

<u>1 Kgs 2:21</u>   יתן את אבישג
1 Kgs 2:22   ויען המלך
<u>2 Kgs 4:36</u>   ויקרא אל גיחזי

Com.: The Masorah notes the *three* occurrences of this lemma written defective ו, to distinguish them from its *four* occurrences of this form written plene ו (הַשּׁוּנַמִּ֣ית).

4:36 שְׂאִֽי

Eight times ח̇ Mp

1–5 Gen 21:18; **2 Kgs 4:36**; Isa 49:18; 60:4; Jer 3:2
6–8 Ezek 16:52; 23:35; **Lam 2:19**

Com.: The Masorah notes the *eight* occurrences of this lemma without a ו cj., to distinguish them from the *two* occurrences with a ו cj. (וּשְׂאִי) at Jer 7:29 and Ezek 16:52.

> **2 KINGS 4:38**
> וֶאֱלִישָׁ֞ע שָׁ֤ב הַגִּלְגָּ֙לָה֙ וְהָרָעָ֣ב בָּאָ֔רֶץ וּבְנֵי֙ הַנְּבִיאִ֔ים יֹשְׁבִ֖ים לְפָנָ֑יו וַיֹּ֣אמֶר לְנַעֲר֗וֹ שְׁפֹת֙ הַסִּ֣יר הַגְּדוֹלָ֔ה וּבַשֵּׁ֥ל נָזִ֖יד לִבְנֵ֥י הַנְּבִיאִֽים׃

4:38 הַגִּלְגָּֽלָה

Six times ו̇ Mp

Com.: See **Josh 10:6**.

4:38 וּבְנֵי הַנְּבִיאִים

Unique ל̇ Mp

Com.: This lemma is featured in a Masoretic list of words that occur *once* with a preceding וּבְנֵי; see Frensdorff, *Ochlah*, §366.

4:38 שְׁפֹת

Three times ג̇ Mp

2 Kgs 4:38; **Ezek 24:3**ᵃ; 24:3ᵇ

Com.: The Masorah here notes the *three* occurrences of this lemma without a ו cj., to distinguish it from its *sole* occurrence with a ו cj. at 2 Sam 17:29 (וּשְׁפֹת).

The Mm at 2 Sam 17:29 *sub* שְׁפֹת וּשְׁפֹת lists all *four* forms.

2 Kings 4:39

וַיֵּצֵ֨א אֶחָ֜ד אֶל־הַשָּׂדֶה֮ לְלַקֵּ֣ט אֹרֹת֒ וַיִּמְצָ֣א גֶֽפֶן־שָׂדֶ֗ה וַיְלַקֵּ֤ט מִמֶּ֙נּוּ֙ פַּקֻּעֹ֣ת שָׂדֶ֔ה מְלֹ֖א בִגְד֑וֹ וַיָּבֹ֗א וַיְפַלַּ֛ח אֶל־סִ֥יר הַנָּזִ֖יד כִּי־לֹ֥א יָדָֽעוּ׃

4:39   אֹרֹת

Mp   בׄ בתרׄ לשנׄ   *Twice* in two meanings

2 Kgs 4:39 (אֹרֹת); **Isa 26:19** (אוֹרֹת)

Mm   ארת בׄ בתרי לשנין חד חס וחד מלֹ   אֹרֹת *twice* in *two* meanings, *once* defective and *once* plene

2 Kgs 4:39   ויצא אחד אל השדה
Isa 26:19   כי טל (ארת) [אורת] טלך

The *latter* is written this way (אוֹרֹת)   בתרׄ כת כן

Com.: The Masorah notes the occurrence of the homonym אֹרֹת written both defective (here) and plene (Isa 26:19) first ו. Here the meaning of the lemma is *sprouts*, whereas in Isa 26:19 it is *lights*, or perhaps *celestial dew*.

This lemma is featured in a Masoretic list of homonyms; see Frensdorff, *Ochlah*, §59, and Díaz-Esteban, *Sefer Oklah we-Oklah*, §60.

4:39   פַּקֻּעֹת

Mp   לׄ וחסׄ   *Unique* and defective

Com.: By noting that this lemmma is *unique* and written (doubly) defective ו, the Masorah is also implying (correctly) that this lemma does not occur elsewhere written plene.

4:39   וַיְפַלַּח

Mp   לׄ   *Unique*

Com.: The Masorah notes the *sole* occurrence of this lemma with a ו consec., to distinguish it from its *two* occurrences without this ו (יְפַלַּח) at Prov 7:23 and Job 16:13.

4:39	אֶל־סִיר		
Unique		ל	Mp

Com.: This lemma is featured in a Masoretic list of words occurring only *once* with a preceding אֶל, and only *once* with a preceding עַל; see Frensdorff, *Ochlah*, §2, and Díaz-Esteban, *Sefer Oklah we-Oklah*, §2.

> **2 KINGS 4:40**
>
> וַיִּצְקוּ לַאֲנָשִׁים לֶאֱכוֹל וַיְהִי כְּאָכְלָם מֵהַנָּזִיד וְהֵמָּה צָעָקוּ וַיֹּאמְרוּ מָוֶת בַּסִּיר אִישׁ הָאֱלֹהִים וְלֹא יָכְלוּ לֶאֱכֹל:

4:40	לַאֲנָשִׁים		
Eight times		ח	Mp

Com.: See **1 Sam 4:9**.

4:40	כְּאָכְלָם		
Unique		ל	Mp

Com.: This lemma is featured in a Masoretic list of words occurring only *once* with a prefix כ; see Frensdorff, *Ochlah*, §19, and Díaz-Esteban, *Sefer Oklah we-Oklah*, §20.

4:40	מֵהַנָּזִיד		
Unique		ל	Mp

Com.: This lemma is featured in a Masoretic list of words occurring only *once* with the inseparable prep. מ, whereas normally it is with the separable prep. מִן; see Frensdorff, *Ochlah*, §195.

> **2 KINGS 4:41**
>
> וַיֹּאמֶר וּקְחוּ־קֶמַח וַיַּשְׁלֵךְ אֶל־הַסִּיר וַיֹּאמֶר צַק לָעָם וְיֹאכֵלוּ וְלֹא הָיָה דָּבָר רָע בַּסִּיר: ס

4:41	וּקְחוּ־קֶמַח		
Unique		ל	Mp

4:41   צָק

Unique   לׄ   Mp

Com.: This lemma is featured in a Masoretic list of words containing *two* letters that occur only *once*; see Frensdorff, *Ochlah*, §40.

4:41   וְיֹאכֵלוּ

Three times   גׄ   Mp

2 Kgs 4:41; 4:42; 4:43

וְיֹאכֵלוּ *three times*   ויאכלו גׄ   Mm

2 Kgs 4:41   צק לעם ויאכלו
2 Kgs 4:42   ויאמר
2 Kgs 4:43   משרתו

Com.: The Masorah notes the *three* occurrences of this lemma with a ו cj., to distinguish them from its *six* occurrences of this form with a ו consec. (וַיֹּאכְלוּ).

In M^L the circellus has incorrectly been placed on the preceding word לָעָם, but that word occurs over *fifty* times.

4:41   וְלֹא הָיָה

Twenty-seven times   כׄזׄ   Mp

Com.: See **Josh 8:20**.

---

2 KINGS 4:42

וְאִישׁ בָּא מִבַּעַל שָׁלִשָׁה וַיָּבֵא לְאִישׁ הָאֱלֹהִים לֶחֶם בִּכּוּרִים עֶשְׂרִים־לֶחֶם שְׂעֹרִים וְכַרְמֶל בְּצִקְלֹנוֹ וַיֹּאמֶר תֵּן לָעָם וְיֹאכֵלוּ׃

4:42   שְׁלִשָׁה

Twice defective   בׄ חס   Mp

1 Sam 9:4; **2 Kgs 4:42**

| שְׁלֹשָׁה *twice* defective | שלשה בׄ חסׄ | Mm |

1 Sam 9:4   ויעבר בארץ
<u>2 Kgs 4:42</u>   ואיש בא מבעל

Com.: The Masorah notes the *two* occurrences of this lemma written defective יׄ, but there are no occurrences written plene יׄ so the note more precisely should have read *twice and defective*, as M^C writes at 1 Sam 9:4.

M^A also reads *twice* defective, but M^C has no note here.

4:42	עֶשְׂרִים־לֶחֶם		
	Unique	לׄ	Mp

This lemma is featured in a Masoretic list of word pairs occurring only once where a preceding וׄ cj. would be expected; see Frensdorff, *Ochlah*, §30, and Díaz-Esteban, *Sefer Oklah we-Oklah*, §31.

4:42	וַיֹּאכְלוּ		
	Three times	גׄ	Mp

Com.: See directly above at **2 Kgs 4:41**.

---

2 KINGS 4:44

וַיִּתֵּן לִפְנֵיהֶם וַיֹּאכְלוּ וַיּוֹתִרוּ כִּדְבַר יְהוָה: פ

4:44	וַיּוֹתִרוּ		
	Twice written like this	בׄ כתׄ כן	Mp

Exod 16:20; <u>2 Kgs 4:44</u>

| וַיּוֹתִרוּ *twice* written like this | (ויתרו) [ויותרו] בׄ כתׄ כן | Mm |

Exod 16:20   (ויתרו) [ויותרו] אנשים ממנו עד
<u>2 Kgs 4:44</u>   ויאכלו (ויתרו) [ויותרו] כדבר יהוה

Com.: The Masorah notes the *two* occurrences of this lemma written defective second יׄ. Normally a יׄ would be expected in the *hiphil* impf. of this verb, as it is in the *three* forms of תּוֹתִירוּ, or in the form יוֹתִיר at Deut 28:54.

2 KINGS 5:1

וְנַעֲמָ֞ן שַׂר־צְבָ֣א מֶֽלֶךְ־אֲרָ֗ם הָיָ֨ה אִישׁ֩ גָּד֨וֹל לִפְנֵ֤י אֲדֹנָיו֙ וּנְשֻׂ֣א פָנִ֔ים כִּי־ב֛וֹ נָֽתַן־יְהוָ֥ה תְּשׁוּעָ֖ה לַאֲרָ֑ם וְהָאִ֗ישׁ הָיָ֛ה גִּבּ֥וֹר חַ֖יִל מְצֹרָֽע׃

5:1 וּנְשֻׂא פָנִים

Four times   דֿ   Mp

2 Kgs 5:1; **Isa 3:3** (וּנְשׂוּא); **9:14** (וּנְשׂוּא); **Job 22:8** (וּנְשׂוּא)

Com.: The Masorah notes the *four* occurrences of this lemma, *three times* written plene and *once* written defective ו (here).

M^C reads here *four times, once defective*. However, M^A places the circellus only on the first word וּנְשֻׂא and reads *twice defective*, noting the form here with the cj., and the form without the cj. (נְשֻׂא) at Isa 33:24.

In the Isa 3:3 and 9:14 references, the circelli have been placed only on the first word וּנְשׂוּא.

2 KINGS 5:2

וַאֲרָם֙ יָצְא֣וּ גְדוּדִ֔ים וַיִּשְׁבּ֛וּ מֵאֶ֥רֶץ יִשְׂרָאֵ֖ל נַעֲרָ֣ה קְטַנָּ֑ה וַתְּהִ֕י לִפְנֵ֖י אֵ֥שֶׁת נַעֲמָֽן׃

5:2 וַיִּשְׁבּוּ

Nine times   טֿ   Mp

Com.: See **1 Sam 30:2**.

2 KINGS 5:3

וַתֹּ֙אמֶר֙ אֶל־גְּבִרְתָּ֔הּ אַחֲלֵ֣י אֲדֹנִ֔י לִפְנֵ֥י הַנָּבִ֖יא אֲשֶׁ֣ר בְּשֹׁמְר֑וֹן אָ֛ז יֶאֱסֹ֥ף אֹת֖וֹ מִצָּרַעְתּֽוֹ׃

5:3 גְּבִרְתָּהּ

Four times   דֿ   Mp

Gen 16:4; **2 Kgs 5:3**; **Ps 123:2**; **Prov 30:23**

	Mm	גברתה ד	*four times* גְּבִרְתָּהּ
Gen 16:4	ותקל גברתה בעיניה		
<u>2 Kgs 5:3</u>	ותאמר אל גברתה		
Ps 123:2	כעיני שפחה אל יד		
Prov 30:23	ושפחה כי תירש גברתה		

And *once* (כִּגְבִרְתָּהּ): Isa 24:2   וחד כשפחה כגברתה

Com.: The Masorah notes the *four* occurrences of this lemma, and the Mm additionally notes its *sole* occurrence with a prep. (כִּגְבִרְתָּהּ) at Isa 24:2.

5:3   אַחֲלֵי

Unique   לׄ   Mp

Com.: This lemma is featured in a Masoretic list of words with an initial א occurring only *once*; see Frensdorff, *Ochlah*, §35, and Díaz-Esteban, *Sefer Oklah we-Oklah*, §36.

5:3   מִצָּרַעְתּוֹ

Three times   גׄ   Mp

2 Kgs 5:3; 5:6; 5:7

Com.: The Masorah notes the *three* occurrences of this lemma, possibly to distinguish them from its *three* occurrences of a similar written lemma מְצֹרַעַת.

---

2 KINGS 5:5

וַיֹּאמֶר מֶלֶךְ־אֲרָם לֶךְ־בֹּא וְאֶשְׁלְחָה סֵפֶר אֶל־מֶלֶךְ יִשְׂרָאֵל וַיֵּלֶךְ וַיִּקַּח בְּיָדוֹ עֶשֶׂר כִּכְּרֵי־כֶסֶף וְשֵׁשֶׁת אֲלָפִים זָהָב וְעֶשֶׂר חֲלִיפוֹת בְּגָדִים׃

5:5   וְאֶשְׁלְחָה

Twice   בׄ   Mp

2 Sam 14:32; **2 Kgs 5:5**

Com.: The Masorah notes the *two* occurrences of this lemma with a ו cj., to distinguish them from its *four* occurrences with a ו consec. (וָאֶשְׁלְחָה).

5:5	וָאֶשְׁלְחָה סֵפֶר		
Unique		ל	Mp

5:5	כִּכְּרֵי־כֶסֶף		
Unique		ל	Mp

Com.: The Masorah notes the *sole* occurrence of כֶסֶף with the cstr. pl. כִּכְּרֵי, to distinguish it from its *sole* occurrence with the dual form כִּכְּרַיִם (כִּכְּרַיִם כֶסֶף) in v. 23, and from its more numerous occurrences (11x) with the sg. כִּכַּר (כִּכַּר כֶסֶף), *one* of which is in v. 22.

2 KINGS 5:6
וַיָּבֵא הַסֵּפֶר אֶל־מֶלֶךְ יִשְׂרָאֵל לֵאמֹר וְעַתָּה כְּבוֹא הַסֵּפֶר הַזֶּה אֵלֶיךָ הִנֵּה שָׁלַחְתִּי אֵלֶיךָ אֶת־נַעֲמָן עַבְדִּי וַאֲסַפְתּוֹ מִצָּרַעְתּוֹ:

5:6	וַיָּבֵא הַסֵּפֶר		
Unique		ל	Mp

5:6	וַאֲסַפְתּוֹ		
Twice		ב̇	Mp

Deut 22:2; **2 Kgs 5:6**

אֲסַפְתּוֹ	*twice*	ואספתו ב̇		Mm
Deut 22:2		אל תוך ביתך		
2 Kgs 5:6		מצרעתו		

Com.: The heading of the Mp for this doublet at Deut 22:2 contains the catchword מצרעתו (מִצָּרַעְתּוֹ), which refers the reader back to this verse.

5:6	מִצָּרַעְתּוֹ		
Three times		ג̇	Mp

Com.: See directly above at **2 Kgs 5:3**.

2 KINGS 5:7

וַיְהִ֡י כִּקְרֹא֩ מֶֽלֶךְ־יִשְׂרָאֵ֨ל אֶת־הַסֵּ֜פֶר וַיִּקְרַ֣ע בְּגָדָ֗יו וַיֹּ֙אמֶר֙ הַאֱלֹהִ֥ים אָ֙נִי֙ לְהָמִ֣ית וּֽלְהַחֲי֔וֹת כִּֽי־זֶה֙ שֹׁלֵ֣חַ אֵלַ֔י לֶאֱסֹ֥ף אִ֖ישׁ מִצָּֽרַעְתּ֑וֹ כִּ֤י אַךְ־דְּעֽוּ־נָא֙ וּרְא֔וּ כִּֽי־מִתְאַנֶּ֥ה ה֖וּא לִֽי׃

5:7   כִּקְרֹא

Twice   בׄ   Mp

2 Kgs 5:7; **Jer 36:23** (כִּקְרוֹא)

כִּקְרֹא *twice, once defective and once plene*   כקרא בׄ חד חסׄ וחד מלׄ   Mm

2 Kgs 5:7   (ויקרא) [ויהי כקרא] מלך ישראל
Jer 36:23   ויהי (כקרא) [כקרוא] יהודי

Com.: The Masorah notes the *two* occurrences with the prep. כְּ, to distinguish them from its *sole* occurrence with the prep. ב (בִּקְרֹא) at Jer 36:13.

5:7   וַיִּקְרַע בְּגָדָיו

Twice   בׄ   Mp

Com.: See **1 Kgs 21:27**.

5:7   וּלְהַחֲיוֹת

Three times   גׄ   Mp

Gen 45:7; **2 Kgs 5:7**; **Isa 57:15**

וּלְהַחֲיוֹת *three times*   ולהחיות גׄ   Mm

Gen 45:7   וישלחני אלהים לפניכם
2 Kgs 5:7   האלהים אני להמית ולהחיות
Isa 57:15   רוח שפלים

Com.: The Masorah notes the *three* occurrences of this lemma with a ו cj., to distinguish them from its *four* occurrences without a cj.

5:7 מִצָּרַעְתּוֹ

Three times   ג׳   Mp

Com.: See directly above at **2 Kgs 5:3**.

5:7 מִתְאַנֶּה

Unique   ל׳   Mp

> **2 KINGS 5:8**
>
> וַיְהִי כִּשְׁמֹעַ ׀ אֱלִישָׁע אִישׁ־הָאֱלֹהִים כִּי־קָרַע מֶלֶךְ־יִשְׂרָאֵל אֶת־בְּגָדָיו וַיִּשְׁלַח אֶל־הַמֶּלֶךְ לֵאמֹר לָמָּה קָרַעְתָּ בְּגָדֶיךָ יָבֹא־נָא אֵלַי וְיֵדַע כִּי יֵשׁ נָבִיא בְּיִשְׂרָאֵל׃

5:8 וַיְהִי

Nine times with the accent (geršayim) in the book   ט׳ בטע בסיפ   Mp

Com.: See **1 Kgs 3:18**.

5:8 קָרַעְתָּ בְּגָדֶיךָ

Unique   ל׳   Mp

5:8 וְיֵדַע

Three times   ג׳   Mp

2 Kgs 5:8; **Job 21:19** (וְיֵדַע); **31:6**

Com.: The Masorah notes the *three* occurrences of this lemma with a ו cj., to distinguish them from its more numerous occurrences (18x) written with a ו consec. (וַיֵּדַע).

The Mp heading at Job 21:19 reads *unique with qameṣ* (ל׳) noting the *sole* occurrence of the pausal form וְיֵדָע.

5:8 יֵשׁ נָבִיא

Unique   ל׳   Mp

2 KINGS 5:9

וַיָּבֹא נַעֲמָן בְּסוּסָו וּבְרִכְבּוֹ וַיַּעֲמֹד פֶּתַח־הַבַּיִת לֶאֱלִישָׁע׃

5:9   בְּסוּסָו

Read   בְּסוּסָיו   בסוסיו ק   Mp

Com.: The *kәtîb* (בסוסו) without the י represents the archaic form of the 3rd masc. sg. sfx. to a pl. noun, whereas the *qәrê* (בְּסוּסָיו) with the second י represents the later form; see Cohen, *The Kethib and Qeri System*, 33.

This lemma is featured in a Masoretic list of *hapax legomena* in which a י is read though it is not written; see Frensdorff, *Ochlah*, §128, and Díaz-Esteban, *Sefer Oklah we-Oklah*, §112.

5:9   פֶּתַח־הַבַּיִת לֶאֱלִישָׁע

Unique   ל   Mp

2 KINGS 5:10

וַיִּשְׁלַח אֵלָיו אֱלִישָׁע מַלְאָךְ לֵאמֹר הָלוֹךְ וְרָחַצְתָּ שֶׁבַע־פְּעָמִים בַּיַּרְדֵּן וְיָשֹׁב בְּשָׂרְךָ לְךָ וּטְהָר׃

5:10   וְיָשֹׁב

Fifteen times   הֹי   Mp

Com.: See **1 Sam 5:11**.

5:10   וּטְהָר

Three times   ג   Mp

2 Kgs 5:10; 5:13; Job 17:9 (וּטְהָר)

Com.: This lemma is featured in a Masoretic list of words that occur *four* times, *three times* with a ו cj. (as listed above), and *once* (Prov 22:11) without a cj.; see Frensdorff, *Ochlah*, §16, and Díaz-Esteban, *Sefer Oklah we-Oklah*, §17.

> ## 2 Kings 5:11
>
> וַיִּקְצֹ֥ף נַעֲמָ֖ן וַיֵּלַ֑ךְ וַיֹּ֗אמֶר הִנֵּ֤ה אָמַ֙רְתִּי֙ אֵלַ֔י | יֵצֵ֣א יָצ֗וֹא וְעָמַד֙ וְקָרָא֙ בְּשֵׁם־יְהוָ֣ה אֱלֹהָ֔יו וְהֵנִ֥יף יָד֛וֹ אֶל־הַמָּק֖וֹם וְאָסַ֥ף הַמְּצֹרָֽע׃

5:11   וַיֵּלַ֑ךְ

Seven times   ז̇   Mp

Com.: See **1 Sam 21:1**.

5:11   יֵצֵ֣א יָצ֗וֹא

Unique   ל̇   Mp

5:11   וְאָסַ֥ף

Three times   ג̇   Mp

Num 19:9; **2 Kgs 5:11**; Isa 11:12

Com.: The Masorah notes the *three* occurrences of this verbal form with a ו cj., to distinguish them from its *three* occurrences without this cj.

> ## 2 Kings 5:12
>
> הֲלֹ֣א טוֹב֩ אֲבָנָ֨ה וּפַרְפַּ֜ר נַהֲר֣וֹת דַּמֶּ֗שֶׂק מִכֹּל֙ מֵימֵ֣י יִשְׂרָאֵ֔ל הֲלֹֽא־אֶרְחַ֥ץ בָּהֶ֖ם וְטָהָ֑רְתִּי וַיִּ֥פֶן וַיֵּ֖לֶךְ בְּחֵמָֽה׃

5:12   אֲבָנָ֨ה

Read אֲמָנָה   אמנה ק   Mp

Com.: The *kətîb* (אבנה) and *qərê* (אֲמָנָה) give alternate names of the name of the Damascus river: the *kətîb*, supported by the Septuagint and Vulgate, reads *Abana*, the *qərê*, supported by the the Syriac and Targum, reads *Amana*. Both forms are correct, and reflect a ב and מ interchange; see Gordis, *The Biblical Text*, 157, 203.

This lemma is found in two Masoretic lists. One is in a list of words where ב is written but read מ (see Frensdorff, *Ochlah*, §154, and Díaz-Esteban, *Sefer Oklah we-Oklah*, §141).

The other is in a list of forms that occur *four times*, *three times* without a ו cj. (2 Kgs 5:12, Cant 4:8, and Neh 10:1), and *once* with a ו cj. (Neh 11:23); see Frensdorff, *Ochlah*, §15, Díaz-Esteban, *Sefer Oklah we-Oklah*, §16, and Ognibeni, *'Oklah*, §298.

5:12 נַהֲרוֹת

Three times   גׄ   Mp

2 Kgs 5:12; **Ps 74:15**; **137:1**

Com.: The Masorah notes the *three* occurrences of this lemma, to distinguish them from its more numerous occurrences (15x) written as נְהָרוֹת.

5:12 וְטָהָרְתִּי

Unique   לׄ   Mp

Com.: This lemma is featured in a Masoretic list of words that occur *twice*, *once* with a ו cj. (here), and *once* without (Prov 20:9); see Frensdorff, *Ochlah*, §1, and Díaz-Esteban, *Sefer Oklah we-Oklah*, §1.

---

2 KINGS 5:13

וַיִּגְּשׁוּ עֲבָדָיו וַיְדַבְּרוּ אֵלָיו וַיֹּאמְרוּ אָבִי דָּבָר גָּדוֹל הַנָּבִיא דִּבֶּר אֵלֶיךָ הֲלוֹא תַעֲשֶׂה וְאַף כִּי־אָמַר אֵלֶיךָ רְחַץ וּטְהָר:

5:13 הֲלוֹא

Seventeen times plene in the book   יׄז מל בסיפׄ   Mp

Com.: See **1 Kgs 2:42**.

---

2 KINGS 5:14

וַיֵּרֶד וַיִּטְבֹּל בַּיַּרְדֵּן שֶׁבַע פְּעָמִים כִּדְבַר אִישׁ הָאֱלֹהִים וַיָּשָׁב בְּשָׂרוֹ כִּבְשַׂר נַעַר קָטֹן וַיִּטְהָר:

5:14 כִּבְשַׂר

Twice   בׄ   Mp

2 Kgs 5:14; **Neh 5:5**

Com.: The Masorah notes the *two* occurrences of this lemma with the prep. כ, to distinguish them from its *sole* occurrence with the prep. ב (בִּבְשַׂר) at Lev 15:7.

> **2 KINGS 5:15**
>
> וַיָּ֩שָׁב֩ אֶל־אִ֨ישׁ הָאֱלֹהִ֜ים ה֣וּא וְכָֽל־מַחֲנֵ֗הוּ וַיָּבֹא֮ וַיַּעֲמֹ֣ד לְפָנָיו֒ וַיֹּ֗אמֶר הִנֵּה־נָ֤א יָדַ֨עְתִּי֙ כִּ֣י אֵ֤ין אֱלֹהִים֙ בְּכָל־הָאָ֔רֶץ כִּ֖י אִם־בְּיִשְׂרָאֵ֑ל וְעַתָּ֛ה קַח־נָ֥א בְרָכָ֖ה מֵאֵ֥ת עַבְדֶּֽךָ׃

5:15   כִּי אֵין אֱלֹהִים

Unique   ל   Mp

Com.: The Masorah notes the *sole* occurrence of אֵין אֱלֹהִים with כִּי, to distinguish it from its more numerous occurrences (8x) without כִּי.

5:15   וְעַתָּה

Nine times with the accent (*ṭəbîr*)   ט בטע   Mp

1–5   Gen 47:4; Num 11:6; 22:34; **2 Sam 19:10**; 1 Kgs 1:18b
6–10   **2 Kgs 5:15**; Isa 5:3; Hos 2:12; Mic 4:11; Mal 1:9
11–12   **Ezra 9:10**; 10:2

Com.: The Mp heading here of *nine* times is inexact since there are *twelve* occurrences of this lemma with the *ṭəbîr* accent. The note more precisely should have read *nine times with this accent in the Prophets and Writings*; see Dotan/Reich, *Masora Thesaurus*, ad loc.

The Mp notes at 2 Sam 19:10 and Ezra 9:10 read *twenty-seven*, a number which must include the *three* other forms עַתָּה, אַתָּה, and וְאַתָּה with some exceptions; see **1 Sam 27:1**.

The Mp note at Ezra 10:2 reads *four times with this accent in the Writings* and, as is indicated in the Mm to Ezra 9:10, deals with the *four* occurrences of both וְאַתָּה, (2 Chr 2:15 and 21:15) and וְעַתָּה (Ezra 9:10 and 10:2) with *ṭəbîr* in the Writings.

M[C] reads here incorrectly *seventeen times* (see Castro, *El codice*, 3:197), whereas M[A] has no note.

> **2 KINGS 5:16**
>
> וַיֹּ֕אמֶר חַי־יְהוָ֛ה אֲשֶׁר־עָמַ֥דְתִּי לְפָנָ֖יו אִם־אֶקָּ֑ח וַיִּפְצַר־בּ֥וֹ לָקַ֖חַת וַיְמָאֵֽן׃

5:16   אִם־אֶקָּח

Unique   ל   Mp

Com.: The Masorah notes the *sole* occurrence of this lemma without a ו cj., to distinguish it from its *sole* occurrence with a cj. (וְאִם־אֶקָּח) at Gen 14:23.

2 Kings

5:16 וַיִּפְצַר

Four times   ד֗   Mp

Com.: See **Judg 19:7**.

> **2 KINGS 5:17**
>
> וַיֹּאמֶר֮ נַעֲמָן֒ וָלֹ֕א יֻתַּן־נָ֣א לְעַבְדְּךָ֔ מַשָּׂ֥א צֶֽמֶד־פְּרָדִ֖ים אֲדָמָ֑ה כִּ֡י לֽוֹא־יַעֲשֶׂה֩ ע֨וֹד עַבְדְּךָ֜ עֹלָ֤ה וָזֶ֙בַח֙ לֵאלֹהִ֣ים אֲחֵרִ֔ים כִּ֖י אִם־לַיהוָֽה׃

5:17   וָלֹ֕א

Twice   ב֗   Mp

2 Sam 13:26; **2 Kgs 5:16**

Com.: The Masorah notes the *two* occurrences of this lemma with a *qameṣ* under the ו, to distinguish them from its over *fifteen-hundred* occurrences written with a *šəwâ* (וְלֹא).

5:17   יֻתַּן

Seven times   ז֗   Mp

Com.: See **1 Kgs 2:21**.

5:17   אֲדָמָה

Eleven times   יא֗   Mp

1–5   Gen 4:2; **Exod 20:24**; 2 Kgs 5:17; **Isa 15:9**; 45:9
6–10   **Joel 1:10**; 2:21; Amos 7:17; Zech 13:5; Ps 104:30
11   **2 Chr 26:10**

Com.: The Masorah notes the *eleven* occurrences of this lemma without the def. article, to distinguish them from its more numerous occurrences (100+) with the article (הָאֲדָמָה).

5:17   וָזֶבַח

Twice   ב֗   Mp

2 Kgs 5:17; **Jer 7:22** (וְזֶבַח)

Com.: The Masorah notes the *two* occurrences of this lemma pointed with *qameṣ* under the ו, to distinguish them from its *two* occurrences with a *šəwâ* (וְזֶבַח) at Judg 8:10 and Jer 17:26.

> **2 KINGS 5:18**
> לַדָּבָ֣ר הַזֶּ֗ה יִסְלַ֣ח יְהוָה֮ לְעַבְדֶּךָ֒ בְּב֣וֹא אֲדֹנִ֣י בֵית־רִמּוֹן֩ לְהִשְׁתַּחֲוֺ֨ת שָׁ֜מָּה וְה֣וּא ׀ נִשְׁעָ֣ן עַל־יָדִ֗י וְהִֽשְׁתַּחֲוֵ֙יתִי֙ בֵּ֣ית רִמֹּ֔ן בְּהִשְׁתַּחֲוָיָ֙תִי֙ בֵּ֣ית רִמֹּ֔ן יִסְלַח־נָ֥א יְהוָ֛ה לְעַבְדְּךָ֖ בַּדָּבָ֥ר הַזֶּֽה׃

5:18   בְּבוֹא

Nine times plene   ט׳ מל   Mp

1–5   **Gen 42:15**; **Deut 31:11**; <u>**2 Kgs 5:18**</u>; **12:10**; <u>**Ezek 46:8**</u> (וּבְבוֹא)
6–9   **Ezek 46:9** (וּבְבוֹא); **Ps 51:2**; **52:2**; **Prov 18:3**

בְּבוֹא *nine times* plene   בבוא ט׳ מל   Mm

1–5   Gen 42:15   כי אם בבוא אחיהם
       Deut 31:11   בבוא כל ישראל
       <u>2 Kgs 5:18</u>   לדבר הזה יסלח יהוה
       2 Kgs 12:10   ויקב חר
       Ezek 46:8   ובבוא (השמש) [הנשיא]
6–9   Ezek 46:9   עם הארץ
       Ps 52:2   דואג האדמי
       Ps 51:2   נתן הנביא
       Prov 18:3   בבוא רשע

Com.: The Masorah notes the *nine* occurrences of this lemma written plene ו, to distinguish them from its more numerous occurrences (11x) written defective ו (בְּבֹא/וּבְבֹא).

M^L, contrary to M (בְּבֹא), has a *tenth* occurrence of this lemma at Ps 54:2 (בְּבוֹא); see Breuer, *The Biblical Text*, 255. However, *four* of the Mp headings highlighted above (2 Kgs 12:10, Ps 51:2, Ps 52:2, and Prov 18:3), and the headings of both the Mp and Mm here, support the enumeration of *nine* inherent in the text of M.

Notes on the other Mp headings.

Gen 42:15   *Eight times plene.* This number appears to be incorrect. However, Dotan/Reich (*Masora Thesaurus, ad loc.*) suggest that this note deals only with occurrences without a ו cj., of which there are *seven* in the above list, and include as the *eighth* form Ps 54:2 (see above).

Deut 31:11   *Four times plene.* More precisely it should have read *four times plene in the Torah and Prophets* (Gen 42:15, Deut 31:11; 2 Kgs 5:18 and 12:10).

| Ezek 46:8 | *Four times* (וּבְבוֹא). Includes all *four* forms of this lemma with a ו cj.; *two* 46:9 that are plene ו (Ezek 46:8 and 9), and *two* that are defective ו (Exod 34:34 and Num 7:89); see the Mm notes at Exod 34:34, Num 7:89, and Ezek 46:8. |

5:18	לְהִשְׁתַּחֲוֹת שָׁמָּה		
Unique		ל	Mp

5:18	רִמֹּן²		
Nine times defective		ט֗ חס֗	Mp

1–5 **Exod 28:33** (רִמֹּנֵי); **39:26**ᵃ (וְרִמֹּן); 39:26ᵇ (וְרִמֹּן); **Num 33:19** (בְּרִמֹּן); 33:20 (מֵרִמֹּן);
6–9 **1 Kgs 15:18** (טַבְרִמֹּן); **2 Kgs 5:18**ᵇ; 5:18ᶜ; Cant 8:2 (רִמֹּנִי)

Com.: The Masorah notes the *nine* occurrences of this lemma in various forms written defective ו, to distinguish them from its more numerous occurrences in various forms written plene ו (e.g., רִמּוֹן).

Three of the above highlighted Mp headings (Exod 39:26ᵃ, Num 33:19, and 2 Kgs 5:18ᵇ) read *nine times defective*.

The Mp heading at Exod 28:33 on רִמֹּנֵי reads *twice, once plene* (for רִמּוֹנֵי at Exod 39:24) *and once defective* (רִמֹּנֵי), and the Mp heading at 1 Kgs 15:18 on טַבְרִמֹּן reads *unique and defective* for the *sole* occurrence of its particular form.

In Mᴸ the circellus has mistakenly been placed on the first רִמֹּן in this verse which, however, is written plene.

5:18	נא		
Written but not read		כת֗ ולא קרי	Mp

Com.: This lemma is featured in a Masoretic list of *eight* words that are written but not read; see the Mm at Jer 51:3 *sub* דְּרָךְ, and at Ruth 3:12 *sub* אִם, Frensdorff, *Ochlah*, §98, and Díaz-Esteban, *Sefer Oklah we-Oklah*, §81.

> ## 2 KINGS 5:19
>
> וַיֹּ֧אמֶר ל֛וֹ לֵ֥ךְ לְשָׁל֖וֹם וַיֵּ֣לֶךְ מֵאִתּ֑וֹ כִּבְרַת־אָֽרֶץ׃ ס

5:19	כִּבְרַת־אָֽרֶץ		
Unique		לֹ	Mp

Com.: The Masorah notes the *sole* occurrence of this lemma with a *qameṣ* under the א (pausal), to distinguish it from its *sole* occurrence with a *səḡôl* (כִּבְרַת־אֶרֶץ) at Gen 48:7.

> ## 2 KINGS 5:20
>
> וַיֹּ֣אמֶר גֵּיחֲזִ֗י נַעַר֮ אֱלִישָׁ֣ע אִישׁ־הָאֱלֹהִים֒ הִנֵּ֣ה ׀ חָשַׂ֣ךְ אֲדֹנִ֗י אֶֽת־נַעֲמָ֤ן הָֽאֲרַמִּי֙ הַזֶּ֔ה מִקַּ֥חַת מִיָּד֖וֹ אֵ֣ת אֲשֶׁר־הֵבִ֑יא חַי־יְהוָה֙ כִּֽי־אִם־רַ֣צְתִּי אַחֲרָ֔יו וְלָקַחְתִּ֥י מֵאִתּ֖וֹ מְאֽוּמָה׃

5:20	חָשַׂ֣ךְ		
Seven times		ז	Mp

Com.: See **1 Sam 25:39**.

> ## 2 KINGS 5:21
>
> וַיִּרְדֹּ֥ף גֵּיחֲזִ֖י אַחֲרֵ֣י נַעֲמָ֑ן וַיִּרְאֶ֤ה נַֽעֲמָן֙ רָ֣ץ אַחֲרָ֔יו וַיִּפֹּ֛ל מֵעַ֥ל הַמֶּרְכָּבָ֖ה לִקְרָאת֑וֹ וַיֹּ֖אמֶר הֲשָׁלֽוֹם׃

5:21	וַיִּרְאֶ֤ה		
Five times		ה	Mp

1–5 **1 Sam 17:42; 2 Kgs 5:21;** Ezek 18:14; 18:28; Job 42:16 (*qərê*)

וַיִּרְאֶה *five times*		ויראה ה	Mm

1–5	2 Kgs 5:21	ויראה נעמן רץ אחריו
	Ezek 18:14	ויראה ולא יעשה
	Ezek 18:28	וישוב מכל פשעיו
	1 Sam 17:42	את דוד ויבזהו
	וירא *of Job* (Job 42:16)	(ירא) [וירא] את בניו {ואת בניו}
	is defective	ואת בני בניו דאיוב חס׳

Com.: The Masorah notes the *five* occurrences of this lemma in its unapocopated form, to distinguish them from its vastly more numerous occurrences (100+) in its apocopated form (וַיַּרְא), *one* of which is in the *kǝtîb* form at Job 42:16.

In the catchwords for the Job 42:16 reference, the phrase וְאֶת בָּנָיו has mistakenly been added. At this reference, the *kǝtîb* form is וירא and the *qǝrê* form is וַיִּרְאֶה, and the note indicates that the *kǝtîb* form is written defective (ה), even though the *qǝrê* is the one required for the list.

---

2 KINGS 5:22

וַיֹּאמֶר ׀ שָׁלוֹם אֲדֹנִי שְׁלָחַנִי לֵאמֹר הִנֵּה עַתָּה זֶה בָּאוּ אֵלַי שְׁנֵי־נְעָרִים מֵהַר אֶפְרַיִם מִבְּנֵי הַנְּבִיאִים תְּנָה־נָּא לָהֶם כִּכַּר־כֶּסֶף וּשְׁתֵּי חֲלִפוֹת בְּגָדִים׃

5:22   חֲלִפוֹת

Mp	ג̇ חס̇ י̇	*Three times* defective י

Gen 45:22ᵃ; 2 Kgs 5:22; 5:23

Mm	חלפות ג̇ כת̇ כן	חֲלִפוֹת *three times* written like this

Gen 45:22ᵃ, *first* (occurrence) in the verse — לכלם נתן קדמיה דפסוק
2 Kgs 5:22 — תנה נא להם ככר
2 Kgs 5:23 — ויפרץ בו

And *twice* doubly defective (חֲלִפֹת) — ותרי חס̇ דחס̇
Gen 45:22ᵇ — (ולבנימין) [ולבנימן] נתן
Judg 14:12 — ויאמר להם שמשון

Com.: The Masorah notes the *three* occurrences of this lemma written defective י, to distinguish them from its *five* occurrences written plene י (חֲלִיפוֹת).

The Masorah also notes the *two* occurrences of this lemma written doubly defective (of the י and the ו) at Gen 45:22ᵇ and Judg 14:12.

The additional note to the Gen 45:22 reference of the "*first* (occurrence) in the verse" illustrates both forms. The first one is written defective י (חֲלִפוֹת), whereas the second one is written doubly defective (חֲלִפֹת).

> ## 2 KINGS 5:23
> וַיֹּאמֶר נַעֲמָן הוֹאֵל קַח כִּכָּרָיִם וַיִּפְרָץ־בּוֹ וַיָּצַר כִּכְּרַיִם כֶּסֶף בִּשְׁנֵי חֲרִטִים וּשְׁתֵּי חֲלִפוֹת בְּגָדִים וַיִּתֵּן אֶל־שְׁנֵי נְעָרָיו וַיִּשְׂאוּ לְפָנָיו׃

5:23   חֲלִפוֹת

Three times defective   ג̇ חס̇   Mp

Com.: See directly above at **2 Kgs 5:22**.

5:23   אֶל־שְׁנֵי

אֶל־שְׁנֵי *three times*   אל שני ג̇   Mm

Exod 28:7   (שני) [שתי] (כתפת) חברת יהיה
1 Sam 2:34   וזה לך האות אשר יבא אל שני
<u>2 Kgs 5:23</u>   הואל קח ככרים

Com.: The Masorah notes the *three* occurrences of שְׁנֵי with אֶל, to distinguish them from its more numerous occurrences (16x) with עַל (עַל שְׁנֵי).

> ## 2 KINGS 5:24
> וַיָּבֹא אֶל־הָעֹפֶל וַיִּקַּח מִיָּדָם וַיִּפְקֹד בַּבָּיִת וַיְשַׁלַּח אֶת־הָאֲנָשִׁים וַיֵּלֵכוּ׃

5:24   הָעֹפֶל

Unique   ל   Mp

1–3   **2 Kgs 5:24**; Neh 3:27; 2 Chr 27:3

Com.: The Mp heading here of *unique* is inexact since there are *three* occurrences of this lemma. The note more precisely should have read *unique in the book*.

M^A has no note here, but M^C reads *unique and defective*, but there are no plene forms of this lemma.

5:24   וַיְשַׁלַּח

Twenty-two times   כב̇   Mp

Com.: See **Judg 2:6**.

2 Kings 5:25

וְהוּא־בָא וַיַּעֲמֹד אֶל־אֲדֹנָיו וַיֹּאמֶר אֵלָיו אֱלִישָׁע מֵאָן גֵּחֲזִי וַיֹּאמֶר לֹא־הָלַךְ עַבְדְּךָ אָנֶה וָאָנָה׃

5:25   וְהוּא

Mp   לֹ֗ג ראש פסו   *Thirty-three times* at the beginning of a verse

Com.: See **2 Sam 17:10**.

5:25   מֵאָן

Mp   מאין ק   מֵאַיִן   Read

Com.: The *kǝtîb* (מאן) and the *qǝrê* (מֵאַיִן), represent miscellaneous variations in forms with the same meaning; see Gordis, *The Biblical Text*, 124.

5:25   אָנֶה וָאָנָה

Mp   ג֗   *Three times*

Com.: See **1 Kgs 2:36**.

2 Kings 5:26

וַיֹּאמֶר אֵלָיו לֹא־לִבִּי הָלַךְ כַּאֲשֶׁר הָפַךְ־אִישׁ מֵעַל מֶרְכַּבְתּוֹ לִקְרָאתֶךָ הַעֵת לָקַחַת אֶת־הַכֶּסֶף וְלָקַחַת בְּגָדִים וְזֵיתִים וּכְרָמִים וְצֹאן וּבָקָר וַעֲבָדִים וּשְׁפָחוֹת׃

5:26   לִקְרָאתֶךָ

Mp   ד֗   *Four times*

Exod 4:14; **Num 20:18**; <u>2 Kgs 5:26</u>; Prov 7:15

לִקְרָאתֶךָ *four times*   לקראתך ד֗   Mm

Exod 4:14   וגם הנה הוא יצא לקראתך
Num 20:18   פן בחרב אצא
2 Kgs 5:26   מעל מרכבתו לקראתך
Prov 7:15   על כן יצאתי לקראתך

Com.: The Masorah notes the *four* occurrences of this lemma with *sᵉgôl* under the ת, to distinguish them from its *sole* occurrence with a *šᵉwâ* (לִקְרָאתְךָ) at Gen 32:7. The first two letters of the lemma heading appear to have been written over two original ב letters.

5:26   הַעֵת

הַעֵת *twice* with *pataḥ*	העת ב̇ פת̇	Mm

<u>2 Kgs 5:26</u>   לקחת (אתה כסף) [את הכסף]
Hag 1:4   העת לכם אתם

Com.: The Masorah notes the *two* occurrences of this lemma with a *pataḥ* under the ה (the interrog. ה), to distinguish them from its *five* occurrences of this form written with a *qameṣ* (הָעֵת, the def. article).

This lemma is featured in a Masoretic list of doublets with an initial הַ; see Frensdorff, *Ochlah*, §64, and Díaz-Esteban, *Sefer Oklah we-Oklah*, §65.

5:26   וְלָקַחַת

Four times	ד̇	Mp

<u>Gen 30:15</u>; 43:18; <u>2 Kgs 5:26</u>; Mal 2:13

וְלָקַחַת *four times*, and their references	ולקחת ד̇ וסימנהון	Mm

<u>Gen 30:15</u>   (דּוּדָאֵי =)   יברוחוי
Gen 43:18   (יוֹסֵף =)   דיוסף
<u>2 Kgs 5:26</u>   (בְּגָדִים =)   לבושין
Mal 2:13   (רָצוֹן =)   דרעווה

Com.: The Masorah notes the *four* occurrences of this lemma without a *dageš* in the ת (infin.), to distinguish them from its *sole* occurrence written with a *dageš* (וְלָקַחְתָּ, perf. consec.) at 1 Kgs 14:3.

The heading to the Mm at <u>Gen 30:15</u> reads *four times rapê*, that is, without *dageš* (in the ת).

The catchwords in the Mm are in the form of an Aramaic mnemonic, which reads as follows: "the mandrakes of Joseph are clothed of (= with) pleasure"; see Marcus, *Scribal Wit*, 81–82. The Hebrew catchwords are given in the Mm to <u>Gen 30:15</u>.

This lemma occurs in the ms. in folio 205v, but the Mm note appears on the top right of the following folio 206r.

5:26   וְזֵיתִים וּכְרָמִים

Unique   ל   Mp

Com.: The Masorah notes the *sole* occurrence of this lemma in this order, to distinguish it from its *two* occurrences in the reverse order (כְּרָמִים וְזֵיתִים) at Deut 6:11 and Josh 24:13.

5:26   וְצֹאן וּבָקָר

Twice   בֿ   Mp

Exod 12:38; **2 Kgs 5:26**

Mm	וצאן ובקר בֿ	*twice* וְצֹאן וּבָקָר
Exod 12:38	וגם ערב רב עלה אתם וצאן ובקר	
2 Kgs 5:26	ויאמר אליו לא לבי הלך כאשר	

Com.: The Masorah notes the *two* occurrences of וּבָקָר with וְצֹאן, to distinguish them from its more numerous occurrences (16x) with צֹאן (צֹאן וּבָקָר).

2 KINGS 5:27

וְצָרַעַת נַעֲמָן תִּדְבַּק־בְּךָ וּבְזַרְעֲךָ לְעוֹלָם וַיֵּצֵא מִלְּפָנָיו מְצֹרָע כַּשָּׁלֶג׃ ס

5:27   וְצָרַעַת

Unique   ל   Mp

Com.: This lemma is featured in a Masoretic list of words that occur *once* with ו, and *once* with וה (וְהַצָּרַעַת, 2 Chr 26:19); see Frensdorff, *Ochlah*, §9, and Díaz-Esteban, *Sefer Oklah we-Oklah*, §9.

5:27   וּבְזַרְעֲךָ לְעוֹלָם

Unique   ל   Mp

Com.: This lemma is featured in a Masoretic list that shows the *three* different ways this lemma occurs, *once* as וּלְזַרְעֲךָ עַד־עוֹלָם (Gen 13:15), *once* as וּבְזַרְעֲךָ עַד־עוֹלָם (Deut 28:46), and *once* as בְזַרְעֲךָ לְעוֹלָם (here); see Frensdorff, *Ochlah*, §268.

> **2 KINGS 6:2**
> גֵלְכָה־נָּא עַד־הַיַּרְדֵּן וְנִקְחָה מִשָּׁם אִישׁ קוֹרָה אֶחָת וְנַעֲשֶׂה־לָּנוּ שָׁם מָקוֹם לָשֶׁבֶת שָׁם וַיֹּאמֶר לֵכוּ׃

6:2   וְנִקְחָה

Five times   הֿ   Mp

Com.: See **1 Sam 4:3**.

6:2   לֵכוּ

Three times   גֿ   Mp

Josh 2:16; **2 Kgs 6:2**; Ezek 20:19

Com.: The Masorah notes these *three* occurrences of the pausal form לֵכוּ, to distinguish them from its much more numerous occurrences (65x) of the regular imper. pl. לְכוּ.

In M^L the circellus has mistakenly been placed on the two words וַיֹּאמֶר לֵכוּ, but this phrase only occurs this once.

> **2 KINGS 6:4**
> וַיֵּלֶךְ אִתָּם וַיָּבֹאוּ הַיַּרְדֵּנָה וַיִּגְזְרוּ הָעֵצִים׃

6:4   הַיַּרְדֵּנָה

Four times   דֿ   Mp

Com.: See **2 Kgs 2:6**.

> **2 KINGS 6:5**
> וַיְהִי הָאֶחָד מַפִּיל הַקּוֹרָה וְאֶת־הַבַּרְזֶל נָפַל אֶל־הַמָּיִם וַיִּצְעַק וַיֹּאמֶר אֲהָהּ אֲדֹנִי וְהוּא שָׁאוּל׃

6:5   מַפִּיל

Twice   בֿ   Mp

2 Kgs 6:5; Jer 38:26

Com.: The Masorah notes the *two* occurrences of this lemma written without a ו cj. to distinguish them from its *sole* occurrence with a ו cj. at Dan 9:20.

2 Kings

6:5 שָׁאוּל

| *Twice* in this meaning | ב׳ בליש׳ | Mp |

1 Sam 1:28; **2 Kgs 6:5**

| שָׁאוּל *twice*, and their references | שאול ב׳ וסימנהון | Mm |

1 Sam 1:28   (שאול ליהוה כל הימים) [כל הימים...שאול ליהוה]
2 Kgs 6:5   מפיל הקורה ואת הברזל

| And *every* name of a person similarly (has the same form) | וכל שם ברנש דכותהון | |

Com.: The Masorah notes the *two* occurrences of this lemma in the meaning of *borrowed*, and the Mm additionally notes that the same form elsewhere is used to designate the name *Saul*.

2 KINGS 6:6

וַיֹּאמֶר אִישׁ־הָאֱלֹהִים אָנָה נָפָל וַיַּרְאֵהוּ אֶת־הַמָּקוֹם וַיִּקְצָב־עֵץ וַיַּשְׁלֶךְ־שָׁמָּה וַיָּצֶף הַבַּרְזֶל׃

6:6 וַיַּרְאֵהוּ

| Twice | ב׳ | Mp |

Deut 34:1; 2 Kgs 6:6

Com.: The Masorah notes the *two* occurrences of this lemma in the *hiphil*, to distinguish it from its *sole* occurrence in the *qal* (וַיִּרְאֵהוּ) at Judg 19:3.

2 KINGS 6:8

וּמֶלֶךְ אֲרָם הָיָה נִלְחָם בְּיִשְׂרָאֵל וַיִּוָּעַץ אֶל־עֲבָדָיו לֵאמֹר אֶל־מְקוֹם פְּלֹנִי אַלְמֹנִי תַּחֲנֹתִי׃

6:8 פְּלֹנִי אַלְמֹנִי

| *Three times* | ג׳ | Mp |

Com.: See **1 Sam 21:3**.

6:8 תַּחֲנֹתִי

| *Unique* | ל׳ | Mp |

> ### 2 KINGS 6:10
> וַיִּשְׁלַ֞ח מֶ֣לֶךְ יִשְׂרָאֵ֗ל אֶֽל־הַמָּק֞וֹם אֲשֶׁ֨ר אָֽמַר־ל֧וֹ אִישׁ־הָאֱלֹהִ֛ים וְהִזְהִירֹ֖ה וְנִשְׁמַ֣ר שָׁ֑ם לֹ֥א אַחַ֖ת וְלֹ֥א שְׁתָֽיִם׃

6:10   וְהִזְהִירֹ֖ה

Read וְהִזְהִירוֹ ק   והזהירו   Mp

Com.: The *kǝtîb* (והזהירה) contains the older masc. sg ending *ḥolem* ה whereas the *qǝrê* (וְהִזְהִירוֹ) contains the later masc sg. sfx. in ו; see Gordis, *The Biblical Text*, 93.

This lemma is featured in a Masoretic list of words ending in a ה but read as a ו; see the Mm at Lev 21:5 *sub* יִקְרְחָה, and the Mm at Lam 4:17 *sub* עוֹדֵינָה.

M^C, as M^L, has a *kǝtîb/qǝrê* here, but M^A reads *unique and written (with)* ה.

6:10   וְנִשְׁמַ֣ר

Unique   ל   Mp

Com.: The Masorah notes the *sole* occurrence of this lemma with a ו cj., to distinguish it from its occurrence without a cj. at 2 Sam 20:10.

Com.: In M^L this lemma has no circellus.

> ### 2 KINGS 6:11
> וַיִּסָּעֵר֙ לֵ֣ב מֶֽלֶךְ־אֲרָ֔ם עַל־הַדָּבָ֖ר הַזֶּ֑ה וַיִּקְרָ֤א אֶל־עֲבָדָיו֙ וַיֹּ֣אמֶר אֲלֵיהֶ֔ם הֲלוֹא֙ תַּגִּ֣ידוּ לִ֔י מִ֥י מִשֶּׁלָּ֖נוּ אֶל־מֶ֥לֶךְ יִשְׂרָאֵֽל׃

6:11   וַיִּסָּעֵר֙

Unique   ל   Mp

6:11   עַל

Fourteen verses having the sequence עַל...אֶל...אֶל   יד פסוק על אל אל   Mp

1–5   Exod 19:20; **25:20**; **37:9**; Lev 17:5; Josh 17:7
6–10   Josh 18:9; Judg 19:22; **2 Kgs 6:11**; Isa 18:2; **Ezek 43:20** (עַל...וְאֶל...וְאֶל)
11–14   Ezek 46:19; 1 Chr 11:15; **19:2**; Neh 2:5

Com.: The Masorah notes the *fourteen* verses containing the sequence אֶל...אֶל...עַל or עַל...וְאֶל...וְאֶל; see Frensdorff, *Ochlah*, §350, and Díaz-Esteban, *Sefer Oklah we-Oklah*, §158B.

In M^L this lemma has no circellus.

6:11   הֲלוֹא

Seventeen times plene in the book   יֹז מל בסיפֹ   Mp

Com.: See **1 Kgs 2:42**.

---

2 KINGS 6:12

וַיֹּאמֶר אַחַד מֵעֲבָדָיו לוֹא אֲדֹנִי הַמֶּלֶךְ כִּי־אֱלִישָׁע הַנָּבִיא אֲשֶׁר בְּיִשְׂרָאֵל יַגִּיד לְמֶלֶךְ יִשְׂרָאֵל אֶת־הַדְּבָרִים אֲשֶׁר תְּדַבֵּר בַּחֲדַר מִשְׁכָּבֶךָ׃

6:12   לוֹא

Thirty-five times plene   לֹה מל   Mp

Com.: See **1 Sam 19:4**.

---

2 KINGS 6:13

וַיֹּאמֶר לְכוּ וּרְאוּ אֵיכֹה הוּא וְאֶשְׁלַח וְאֶקָּחֵהוּ וַיֻּגַּד־לוֹ לֵאמֹר הִנֵּה בְדֹתָן׃

6:13   אֵיכֹה

Unique   לֹ   Mp

Com.: The Masorah notes the *sole* occurrence of this lemma with a *ḥolem* (אֵיכֹה, where?) to distinguish it from its more numerous occurrences (18x) with a *qameṣ* (אֵיכָה, how?).

6:13   וְאֶשְׁלַח

Unique   לֹ   Mp

Com.: The Masorah notes the *sole* occurrence of this lemma with a ו cj., to distinguish it from its more numerous occurrences (8x) with a ו consec. (וָאֶשְׁלַח).

6:13   וְאֶקָּחֵהוּ

Unique   לֹ   Mp

6:13	בְּדֹתָ֖ן		
Twice	בּ֫	Mp	

Gen 37:17; 2 Kgs 6:13

---

2 KINGS 6:14

וַיִּשְׁלַח־שָׁ֧מָּה סוּסִ֛ים וְרֶ֥כֶב וְחַ֖יִל כָּבֵ֑ד וַיָּבֹ֣אוּ לַ֔יְלָה וַיַּקִּ֖פוּ עַל־הָעִֽיר׃

6:14	שָׁ֖מָּה		

Ten times when שָׁ֖מָּה is the second word in a verse	י ראש פסוק ומלא אחר שמה	Mp

1–5   **Gen 29:3**; Exod 29:43; Deut 4:42; **12:6**; Josh 20:3
6–10 Judg 18:15; **2 Kgs 6:14**; **9:2**; **Ezek 11:18**; Ps 122:5

Com.: The Masorah notes the *ten* occurrences when the adverb שָׁ֖מָּה follows the first word in a verse; see also Frensdorff, *Ochlah*, §338.

The phrase ומלא אחר stands for ומילה אחריתא *and the last* (= *second*) *word*. At Gen 29:3, 2 Kgs 9:2, and Ezek 11:18 the circellus has been placed between the first word and שָׁ֖מָּה.

6:14	וַיַּקִּ֖פוּ		

Unique defective	ל חס֗	Mp

Com.: The Mp heading of *unique defective* (י) is inexact since there is no occurrence of this lemma written plene י. The note more precisely should have read *unique and defective*. However, the form without the ו consec. is written plene י (יַקִּיפוּ) at Ps 17:9.

Neither M^C nor M^A has a note on this lemma here.

6:14	עַל־הָעִֽיר		

עַל־הָעִ֖יר	*seventeen times*	על העיר יז	Mm

1–5	Gen 34:25	כאבים
	Deut 20:20	מצור
	Judg 9:33	כזרח
	2 Sam 12:28	וחנה
	1 Kgs 20:12	בסכות

6–10	2 Kgs 6:14	ויקפו
	2 Kgs 10:5	והאמנים
	2 Kgs 24:11	נבוכדנאצר
	2 Kgs 25:4	ותבקע
	And its companion (Jer 52:7)	וחבירו
11–15	Jer 22:8	ועברו
	Jer 37:8	ונלחמו
	Jer 32:29	הנלחמים
	Jer 26:20	וגם איש
	Ezek 10:2	וזרק
16–17	Neh 11:9	ויואל
	Neh 13:18	כה עשו

And likewise every instance of וְגַנּוֹתִי apart from *one* (אֶל־הָעִיר): of Kings (2 Kgs 19:34)	וכל וגנותי דכות ב̇ מ̇ א̇ דמלכים

Com.: The Masorah notes the *seventeen* occurrences of the phrase עַל־הָעִיר, to distinguish them from its slightly more numerous occurrences (21x) with the prep. אֶל (אֶל־הָעִיר).

This distinction is implied in the additional notation that the verbal form וְגַנּוֹתִי also occurs with the phrase עַל־הָעִיר with *one* exception, that of **2 Kgs 19:34**, where it occurs with אֶל (וְגַנּוֹתִי אֶל הָעִיר).

---

2 KINGS 6:17

וַיִּתְפַּלֵּל אֱלִישָׁע וַיֹּאמַר יְהוָה פְּקַח־נָא אֶת־עֵינָיו וְיִרְאֶה וַיִּפְקַח יְהוָה אֶת־עֵינֵי הַנַּעַר וַיַּרְא וְהִנֵּה הָהָר מָלֵא סוּסִים וְרֶכֶב אֵשׁ סְבִיבֹת אֱלִישָׁע׃

6:17	וְיִרְאֶה		
Unique		ל	Mp

Com.: The Masorah notes the *sole* occurrence of this lemma with a ו cj., to distinguish it from its more numerous occurrences (47x) without a cj.

This lemma is featured in a Masoretic list of words that occur *once* with ר, and *once* with ד; see Frensdorff, *Ochlah*, §7, and Díaz-Esteban, *Sefer Oklah we-Oklah*, §7.

6:17   סְבִיבֹת

| Mp | ל חס בנביא | *Unique* defective in the Prophets |

Com.: The Masorah notes the *sole* occurrence of this lemma in the Prophets written defective ו, to distinguish it from its more numerous occurrences (7x) in the Prophets that are written plene ו (סְבִיבוֹת).

---

2 KINGS 6:18

וַיֵּרְדוּ֘ אֵלָיו֒ וַיִּתְפַּלֵּ֣ל אֱלִישָׁ֣ע אֶל־יְהוָה֮ וַיֹּאמַר֒ הַךְ־נָ֥א אֶת־הַגּוֹי־הַזֶּ֖ה בַּסַּנְוֵרִ֑ים וַיַּכֵּ֥ם בַּסַּנְוֵרִ֖ים כִּדְבַ֥ר אֱלִישָֽׁע׃

6:18   הַךְ־נָא

| Mp | ל | *Unique* |

In M^L the circellus has been placed only on הַךְ but since that form occurs *four times*, it is most likely that the note refers to the phrase הַךְ־נָא which only occurs this once; see also Dotan/Reich, *Masora Thesaurus*, ad loc. Neither M^C nor M^A has a note on this lemma here.

6:18   בַּסַּנְוֵרִים²

| Mp | ג̇ | *Three times* |

Gen 19:11; 2 Kgs 6:18ᵃ; **6:18**ᵇ

---

2 KINGS 6:19

וַיֹּ֨אמֶר אֲלֵהֶ֜ם אֱלִישָׁ֗ע לֹ֣א זֶ֣ה הַדֶּרֶךְ֮ וְלֹ֣א זֶ֣ה הָעִיר֒ לְכ֣וּ אַחֲרַ֔י וְאוֹלִ֣יכָה אֶתְכֶ֔ם אֶל־הָאִ֖ישׁ אֲשֶׁ֣ר תְּבַקֵּשׁ֑וּן וַיֹּ֥לֶךְ אוֹתָ֖ם שֹׁמְרֽוֹנָה׃

6:19   אֲלֵהֶם

| Mp | יג̇ חס בסיפ | *Thirteen times* defective in the book |

Com.: See **1 Kgs 12:16**.

6:19   זֶה

| Mp | י̇ | *Ten times* |

1–5   **2 Kgs 6:19**; <u>Ezek 40:45</u>; **Hos 7:16** (זֹ̇ה); **Ps 132:12** (זֹ̇ה); **Qoh 2:2**
6–10 **Qoh 2:24; 5:15; 5:18;** <u>7:23</u>**; 9:13**

Com.: The Masorah notes the *ten* occurrences of this lemma written with ה and ו, to distinguish them from its more numerous occurrences (200+) written as זֹאת.

The Mp headings at Hos 7:16 and Ps 132:12, both of which have forms of זוֹ, correctly read *twice written with* ו.

In M^L the circellus has been placed between this word and the preceding word וְלֹא but it belongs on this one.

6:19   תְּבַקֵּשׁוּן

Unique   ל̇   Mp

Com.: This lemma is featured in a Masoretic list of words occurring only *once* with a paragogic נ; see Frensdorff, *Ochlah*, §75.

6:19   וַיֹּלֶךְ

		Mm
וַיֹּלֶךְ *four times, three* defective *and one* plene	וילך ד̇ ג̇ חסירין וחד מל	

Exod 14:21 (וַיּוֹלֶךְ)	את הים
2 Kgs 6:19	שמרונה
2 Kgs 25:20	נבוזראדן
And its companion (Jer 52:26)	וחבירו

Com.: The Masorah notes the *four* occurrences of this lemma with a *sǝḡōl, three times* written defective ו (2 Kgs 6:19, 25:20, and Jer 52:26), and *once* written plene וֹ (Exod 14:21).

In the Mm at Exod 14:21, there is an additional note that this form occurs *once* with a *pataḥ* (וַיֹּלַךְ) at Lam 3:2.

6:19   שֹׁמְרוֹנָה

Three times   ג̇   Mp

Com.: See **1 Kgs 20:43**.

> ### 2 KINGS 6:20
> וַיְהִ֣י כְּבֹאָ֣ם שֹׁמְר֗וֹן וַיֹּ֤אמֶר אֱלִישָׁע֙ יְהוָ֔ה פְּקַ֥ח אֶת־עֵינֵֽי־אֵ֖לֶּה וְיִרְא֑וּ וַיִּפְקַ֤ח יְהוָה֙ אֶת־עֵ֣ינֵיהֶ֔ם וַיִּרְא֕וּ וְהִנֵּ֖ה בְּת֥וֹךְ שֹׁמְרֽוֹן׃

6:20   כְּבֹאָ֣ם

Twice, *once* defective, and *once* plene   ב֘ חד חס̇ וחד מל̇   Mp

2 Kgs 6:20; Jer 41:7 (כְּבוֹאָם)

Com.: The Masorah notes the *two* occurrences of this lemma with the prep. כ, to distinguish them from its more numerous occurrences (11x) written with a ב (בְּבוֹאָם/בְּבֹאָם).

6:20   וְיִרְא֑וּ

Three times   ג֘   Mp

2 Kgs 6:20; Ps 52:8; **86:17**

Com.: The Masorah notes the *three* occurrences of this lemma with a ו cj., to distinguish them from its more numerous occurrences (48x) with a ו consec (וַיִּרְאוּ).

Since there are *two* other occurrences of this lemma at Isa 59:19 (written plene second י in M^L [וְיִירְאוּ] but written defective in M [וְיִרְאוּ]; see Breuer, *The Biblical Text*, 160), and at Mic 7:17, it seems that the Masorah is here making an unusual semantic distinction between identical forms. The forms in this note are derived from the verb רָאָה *to see*, whereas the forms at Isa 59:19 and Mic 7:17 are derived from the verb יָרֵא *to fear*.

> ### 2 KINGS 6:21
> וַיֹּ֤אמֶר מֶֽלֶךְ־יִשְׂרָאֵל֙ אֶל־אֱלִישָׁ֔ע כִּרְאֹת֖וֹ אוֹתָ֑ם הַאַכֶּ֥ה אַכֶּ֖ה אָבִֽי׃

6:21   כִּרְאֹת֖וֹ

Twice defective   ב֘ חס̇   Mp

2 Kgs 6:21; **23:29**

Com.: The Masorah notes the *two* occurrences of this lemma written defective ו, to distinguish them from its *two* occurrences written plene ו (כִּרְאֹתוֹ) at Gen 44:31 and Judg 11:35.

The Mp heading at 2 Kgs 23:29 of *twice, once defective* (ו) is incorrect since both forms are written defective ו as correctly indicated in the heading of the Mp here, and in the Mm heading at 2 Kgs 23:29.

6:21   אוֹתָם

Nine times plene in the book   ט׳ מל בסיפ   Mp

Com.: See **1 Kgs 20:25**.

> **2 KINGS 6:22**
>
> וַיֹּאמֶר לֹא תַכֶּה הַאֲשֶׁר שָׁבִיתָ בְּחַרְבְּךָ וּבְקַשְׁתְּךָ אַתָּה מַכֶּה שִׂים לֶחֶם וָמַיִם לִפְנֵיהֶם וְיֹאכְלוּ וְיִשְׁתּוּ וְיֵלְכוּ אֶל־אֲדֹנֵיהֶם׃

6:22   בְּחַרְבְּךָ

Twice   ב׳   Mp

Josh 24:12; **2 Kgs 6:22**

Com.: The Masorah notes the *two* occurrences of this lemma with the prep. בְּ, to distinguish them from its more numerous occurrences (8x) without this preposition

---

6:22   מַכֶּה

Five times   ה׳   Mp

1–5   Exod 2:11; 7:17; 2 Kgs 6:22; Isa 14:6; Ezek 7:9

Com.: The Masorah notes the *five* occurrences of this lemma with a *səḡōl*, to distinguish them from its more numerous occurrences with a *qameṣ* (מַכָּה, 17x), or with a *ṣērê* (מַכֵּה, 12x).

This distinction is implied in the Mp heading at Exod 2:11, which reads *five times with səḡōl* (הֶ), thereby assuming a contrast with a form with a different vowel under the כ, which could be either a *qameṣ* or a *ṣērê*.

6:22 שִׂים

Twenty-two times   כֿב   Mp

1–5   Gen 24:2; 31:37; 47:29; 48:18; Josh 7:19
6–10   Josh 8:2; Judg 18:19; 1 Sam 9:23; 9:24; **2 Sam 14:7** (*qərê*)
11–15 **2 Kgs 6:22**; Jer 38:12; 39:12; Ezek 6:2; 13:17
16–20 Ezek 21:2; 21:7; 21:24; 25:2; 28:21
21–25 Ezek 29:2; 35:2; 38:2; 44:5; Obad 4
26–30 **Job 20:4**; 40:32; Dan 3:29; 4:3; 6:27
31–35 Ezra 4:19; 5:17; 6:8; 6:11; 7:13
36   Ezra 7:21

Com.: The Mp's heading here of *twenty-two* is incorrect since there are *thirty-six* occurrences of this lemma.

Dotan/Reich (*Masora Thesaurus*, ad loc.) suggest that the *twenty-two* consist of occurrences only in the Prophets and Writings with all (= 11) occurrences in Ezekiel taken as one reference.

The Mp at Job 20:4 reads *twice*, correctly counting the *two* occurrences in that book.

Neither M^C nor M^A has a note on this lemma here.

6:22 וַיְשִׁתוּ

Unique   ל   Mp

Com.: The Masorah notes the *sole* occurrence of this lemma with a ו cj., to distinguish it from its more numerous occurrences (12x) with a ו consec. (וַיָּשִׁתוּ), *one* of which occurs in v. 23.

6:22 וְיֵלְכוּ

Twice   בֿ   Mp

2 Kgs 6:22; 17:27

Com.: The Masorah notes the *two* occurrences of this lemma, a jussive with a ו cj, written with a *šəwâ* under the ל, to disinguish them from the *two* occurrences of this form in pause written with a *ṣerê* under the ל at 1 Sam 30:22 and Job 38:35. This lemma is featured in a Masoretic list of doublets that start with a וי; see Frensdorff, *Ochlah*, §68.

2 Kings 6:23

וַיִּכְרֶה לָהֶם כֵּרָה גְדוֹלָה וַיֹּאכְלוּ וַיִּשְׁתּוּ וַיְשַׁלְּחֵם וַיֵּלְכוּ אֶל־אֲדֹנֵיהֶם וְלֹא־יָסְפוּ עוֹד גְּדוּדֵי אֲרָם לָבוֹא בְּאֶרֶץ יִשְׂרָאֵל: פ

6:23   וְלֹא־יָסְפוּ

Four times   ד   Mp

Com.: See **Judg 8:28**.

2 Kings 6:24

וַיְהִי אַחֲרֵי־כֵן וַיִּקְבֹּץ בֶּן־הֲדַד מֶלֶךְ־אֲרָם אֶת־כָּל־מַחֲנֵהוּ וַיַּעַל וַיָּצַר עַל־שֹׁמְרוֹן:

6:24   כָּל־מַחֲנֵהוּ

Unique   ל   Mp

Com.: The Masorah notes the *sole* occurrence of this lemma without a ו cj., to distinguish it from its *sole* occurrence with a cj. (וְכָל־מַחֲנֵהוּ) at 2 Kgs 5:15.

2 Kings 6:25

וַיְהִי רָעָב גָּדוֹל בְּשֹׁמְרוֹן וְהִנֵּה צָרִים עָלֶיהָ עַד הֱיוֹת רֹאשׁ־חֲמוֹר בִּשְׁמֹנִים כֶּסֶף וְרֹבַע הַקַּב חִרְיוֹנִים בַּחֲמִשָּׁה־כָסֶף:

6:25   חִרְיוֹנִים

Read דִּבְיוֹנִים   דביונים ק   Mp

Com.: The *kətîb* (חרייונים), and the *qərê* (דִּבְיוֹנִים) are examples of *kətîb*/*qərê* variations where the reader is enjoined to substitute the *kətîb* because it was thought to be too coarse; see Gordis, *The Biblical Text*, 86.

The *kətîb* contains the phrase חֲרֵי יוֹנִים, *doves' dung* (a plant = carob), whereas the *qərê* reads דִּבְיוֹנִים, another word for the carob plant known as *doves' dung*; see Held, "Studies," 395–98.

> **2 KINGS 6:26**
> וַיְהִי מֶלֶךְ יִשְׂרָאֵל עֹבֵר עַל־הַחֹמָה וְאִשָּׁה צָעֲקָה אֵלָיו לֵאמֹר הוֹשִׁיעָה אֲדֹנִי הַמֶּלֶךְ׃

6:26   הַחֹמָה

Six times defective   ו חס̇   Mp

Com.: See **2 Kgs 3:27**.

6:26   וְאִשָּׁה

Twenty-two times   כ̇ב̇   Mp

Com.: See **1 Sam 27:11**.

> **2 KINGS 6:27**
> וַיֹּאמֶר אַל־יוֹשִׁעֵךְ יְהוָה מֵאַיִן אוֹשִׁיעֵךְ הֲמִן־הַגֹּרֶן אוֹ מִן־הַיָּקֶב׃

6:27   יוֹשִׁעֵךְ

Unique and defective   ל̇ וחס̇   Mp

Com.: By noting that this lemma is *unique* and written defective י, the Masorah is also implying (correctly) that this lemma does not occur elsewhere written plene י.

In M^L this lemma was originally written plene י as there is a space between the שׁ and the ע, and some traces of an original י can still be seen.

6:27   הֲמִן

Three times   ג̇   Mp

Gen 3:11; **Num 20:10**; 2 Kgs 6:27

Com.: The Masorah notes the *three* occurrences of this lemma with the interrog. ה, to distinguish them from its more numerous occurrences (600+) without this interrogative.

2 KINGS 6:28

וַיֹּאמֶר־לָהּ הַמֶּלֶךְ מַה־לָּךְ וַתֹּאמֶר הָאִשָּׁה הַזֹּאת אָמְרָה אֵלַי תְּנִי אֶת־בְּנֵךְ וְנֹאכְלֶנּוּ הַיּוֹם וְאֶת־בְּנִי נֹאכַל מָחָר:

6:28   וְנֹאכְלֶנּוּ

Twice   בֿ   Mp

2 Kgs 6:28; 6:29

6:28   וְאֶת־בְּנִי

Twice   בֿ   Mp

2 Sam 14:16; **2 Kgs 6:28**

וְאֶת־בְּנִי *twice, and their references*   ואת בני בֿ וסימנהון   Mm

2 Sam 14:16   להשמיד (את יואב) [אתי] ואת בני יחד
2 Kgs 6:28   ונאכלנו היום

Com.: The Masorah notes the *two* occurrences of this lemma with a ו cj., to distinguish them from its more numerous occurrences (8x) without a cj.

2 KINGS 6:29

וַנְּבַשֵּׁל אֶת־בְּנִי וַנֹּאכְלֵהוּ וָאֹמַר אֵלֶיהָ בַּיּוֹם הָאַחֵר תְּנִי אֶת־בְּנֵךְ וְנֹאכְלֶנּוּ וַתַּחְבִּא אֶת־בְּנָהּ:

6:29   בַּיּוֹם הָאַחֵר

Unique   ל   Mp

Com.: The Masorah notes the *sole* occurrence of this lemma, a def. *on the next day*, to distinguish it from its *sole* occurrence as an indef. בְּיוֹם אַחֵר, *on another day*, at 2 Sam 18:20.

6:29   הָאַחֵר

Three times   גֿ   Mp

2 Kgs 6:29; **2 Chr 3:11**; 3:12

	Mm	הָאַחֵר גׄ	*three times* הָאַחֵר

2 Kgs 6:29   ואמר אליה ביום האחר
2 Chr 3:11   מגיע לכנף הכרוב
2 Chr 3:12   דבקה לכנף הכרוב (האחד) [האחר]

Com.: The Masorah notes the *three* occurrrences of this lemma with a ר, to distinguish them from its more numerous occurrences (100x) written with a ד (הָאֶחָד).

The Mp headings at 2 Chr 3:11 and 3:12 supports this distinction by noting that the *three* occurrences of this lemma are written with a ר (גׄ בריש).

6:29   וַתִּחָבֵא

	Mp	ל וחסׄ	*Unique* and defective

Com.: By noting that this lemmma is *unique* and written defective י, the Masorah is also implying (correctly) that this lemma does not occur elsewhere written plene.

---

2 KINGS 6:31

וַיֹּאמֶר כֹּה־יַעֲשֶׂה־לִּי אֱלֹהִים וְכֹה יוֹסִף אִם־יַעֲמֹד רֹאשׁ אֱלִישָׁע בֶּן־שָׁפָט עָלָיו הַיּוֹם׃

6:31   לִּי אֱלֹהִים

	Mp	יאׄ	*Eleven times*

Com.: See **Judg 1:7**.

---

2 KINGS 6:32

וֶאֱלִישָׁע יֹשֵׁב בְּבֵיתוֹ וְהַזְּקֵנִים יֹשְׁבִים אִתּוֹ וַיִּשְׁלַח אִישׁ מִלְּפָנָיו בְּטֶרֶם יָבֹא הַמַּלְאָךְ אֵלָיו וְהוּא ׀ אָמַר אֶל־הַזְּקֵנִים הַרְאִיתֶם כִּי־שָׁלַח בֶּן־הַמְרַצֵּחַ הַזֶּה לְהָסִיר אֶת־רֹאשִׁי רְאוּ ׀ כְּבֹא הַמַּלְאָךְ סִגְרוּ הַדֶּלֶת וּלְחַצְתֶּם אֹתוֹ בַּדֶּלֶת הֲלוֹא קוֹל רַגְלֵי אֲדֹנָיו אַחֲרָיו׃

6:32   וֶאֱלִישָׁע

	Mp	כוׄ פסוק אית בהון אלף בית	*Twenty-six* verses in which there are all the letters of the alphabet

1–5	**Exod 16:16**; **Deut 4:34**; Josh 23:13; 2 Kgs 4:39; **6:32**
6–10	2 Kgs 7:8; **Isa 5:25**; 66:17; Jer 22:3; 32:29
11–15	Ezek 17:9; 38:12; Hos 10:8; 13:2; Amos 9:13
16–20	Zeph 3:8; **Zech 6:11**; Qoh 4:8; **Esth 3:13**; Dan 2:45
21–25	Dan 3:22; 4:20; 7:19; Ezra 7:28; Neh 3:7
26	2 Chr 26:11

Com.: The Masorah notes the *twenty-six* verses in which all letters of the alphabet appear; see Ginsburg, 2, פ, §227. In M^L this lemma has no circellus.

6:32 מִלְּפָנָיו

Eight times   ח׳   Mp

1–5	2 Kgs 5:27; **6:32**; **Qoh 3:14**; 8:12; Esth 1:19
6–8	Esth 4:8; **Dan 11:22**; <u>1 Chr 16:30</u>

Com.: The Masorah notes the *eight* occurrences of this lemma, to distinguish them from the more numerous occurrences (23x) of its parallel form מִפָּנָיו.

This distinction is implied in the Mm of <u>1 Chr 16:30</u> where there is an addition *of Psalms* to the catchword of the 1 Chr 16:30 reference, to distinguish this reference from its parallel passage in Ps 96:9, where the lemma appears as מִפָּנָיו.

6:32 הַרְאִיתֶם

הַרְאִיתֶם *three times*, and their references   הראיתם ג׳ וסימנהון   Mm

1 Sam 10:24	אשר בחר בו יהוה
1 Sam 17:25	הראיתם האיש (העולה) [העלה]
<u>2 Kgs 6:32</u>	הראיתם כי שלח בן המרצח הזה להסיר את ראשי

Com.: The Masorah notes the *three* unusual occurrences of the interrog. ה followed by a *dageš* in the letter ר; see *GKC*, §100l.

6:32 כְּבֹא

Six times and defective   ו׳ וחס   Mp

Com.: The Mp heading here of *six times and defective* (implying that there are no other occurrences of the lemma written plene) is inaccurate. More precisely it should have read, just *six times defective*; see **1 Kgs 22:36**.

Both M^C and M^A correctly read here *six times defective*.

6:32　הֲלוֹא

Seventeen times plene in the book　יז מל בסיפ　Mp

Com.: See **1 Kgs 2:42**.

---

2 KINGS 6:33

עוֹדֶ֙נּוּ֙ מְדַבֵּ֣ר עִמָּ֔ם וְהִנֵּ֥ה הַמַּלְאָ֖ךְ יֹרֵ֣ד אֵלָ֑יו וַיֹּ֗אמֶר הִנֵּה־זֹ֤את הָֽרָעָה֙ מֵאֵ֣ת יְהוָ֔ה מָֽה־אוֹחִ֥יל לַיהוָ֖ה עֽוֹד׃ ס

6:33　אוֹחִיל

Three times　ג֗　Mp

2 Kgs 6:32; **Lam 3:21**; **3:24**

Com.: The Masorah notes the *three* occurrences of this lemma without the cohortative ה, to distinguish them from its *three* occurrences with the cohortative (אוֹחִילָה/אֹחִילָה).

---

2 KINGS 7:2

וַיַּ֣עַן הַשָּׁלִ֡ישׁ אֲשֶׁר־לַמֶּלֶךְ֩ נִשְׁעָ֨ן עַל־יָד֜וֹ אֶת־אִ֣ישׁ הָאֱלֹהִים֮ וַיֹּאמַר֒ הִנֵּ֣ה יְהוָ֗ה עֹשֶׂ֤ה אֲרֻבּוֹת֙ בַּשָּׁמַ֔יִם הֲיִהְיֶ֖ה הַדָּבָ֣ר הַזֶּ֑ה וַיֹּ֗אמֶר הִנְּכָ֤ה רֹאֶה֙ בְּעֵינֶ֔יךָ וּמִשָּׁ֖ם לֹ֥א תֹאכֵֽל׃ ס

7:2　הִנְּכָה

Unique plene　ל מל　Mp

Com.: This lemma is featured in a Masoretic list of words in which the final ך is written as כה; see **1 Kgs 18:10**, the Mm at <u>Num 22:33</u> *sub* אִתָּךְ, Frensdorff, *Ochlah*, §92, and Díaz-Esteban, *Sefer Oklah we-Oklah*, §74.

7:2　וּמִשָּׁם

Eight times　ח֗　Mp

1–5　**Gen 2:10**; **11:9**; **Num 21:16**; **Deut 30:4**; <u>**Josh 19:13**</u>
6–8　**2 Kgs 2:25**; <u>**7:2**</u>; **7:19**

| וּמִשָּׁם *eight times* | וּמשם ח׳ | Mm |

1–5 Gen 2:10   יפרד והיה לארבעה
      Gen 11:9   הפיצם יהוה
      Num 21:16   בארה (היא) [הוא] הבאר
      Deut 30:4   יקחך
      <u>Josh 19:13</u>   עבר
6–8 2 Kgs 2:25   שב שמרון
      <u>2 Kgs 7:2</u>   ומשם לא תאכל
      And its companion (2 Kgs 7:19)   וחבירו

Com.: The Masorah notes the *eight* occurrences of this lemma with a ו cj., to distinguish them from its more numerous occurrences (100+) without a cj.

7:2 תֹּאכֵל

| *Seventeen times* | י״ז | Mp |

1–5   Gen 2:16; Lev 22:12; **<u>22:13</u>**; **Deut 12:27**; **<u>15:23</u>**
6–10   **Deut 20:19; 2 Sam 22:9; <u>2 Kgs 7:2</u>; 7:19; Isa 9:17**
11–15 **Ezek 12:18; 24:17; <u>Ps 18:9</u>; 50:3; 128:2**
16–17 **Prov 31:27; Job 31:12**

| תֹּאכֵל *seventeen times,* and their references | תאכל י״ז וסימנהון | Mm |

1–5   Gen 2:16   ויצו
       Lev 22:12   ובת
       <u>Lev 22:13</u>   ובת
       Deut 12:27   ועשית
       <u>Deut 15:23</u>   את דמו
6–10   Deut 20:19   כי תצור
       2 Sam 22:9   עלה
       <u>2 Kgs 7:2</u>   השליש
       2 Kgs 7:19   השליש
       Isa 9:17   בערה
11–15 Ezek 12:18   לחמך
       Ezek 24:17   האנק דם
       Job 31:12   אש
       Prov 31:27   צופיה
       <<u>Ps 18:9</u>>
16–17 Ps 50:3   (ובא) [יבא]
       Ps 128:2   יגיע

Com.: The Masorah notes the *seventeen* occurrences of this lemma pointed with a *ṣerê*, to distinguish them from its more numerous occurrences (35x) pointed with a *pataḥ* (תֹּאכַל).

Although the Mm here has the correct heading of *seventeen times* only *sixteen* catchwords have been listed, with Ps 18:9 being omitted.

---

2 KINGS 7:3

וְאַרְבָּעָה אֲנָשִׁים הָיוּ מְצֹרָעִים פֶּתַח הַשָּׁעַר וַיֹּאמְרוּ אִישׁ אֶל־רֵעֵהוּ מָה אֲנַחְנוּ יֹשְׁבִים פֹּה עַד־מָתְנוּ:

7:3　　וְאַרְבָּעָה אֲנָשִׁים

Unique　　ל　　Mp

---

2 KINGS 7:4

אִם־אָמַרְנוּ נָבוֹא הָעִיר וְהָרָעָב בָּעִיר וָמַתְנוּ שָׁם וְאִם־יָשַׁבְנוּ פֹה וָמָתְנוּ וְעַתָּה לְכוּ וְנִפְּלָה אֶל־מַחֲנֵה אֲרָם אִם־יְחַיֻּנוּ נִחְיֶה וְאִם־יְמִיתֻנוּ וָמָתְנוּ:

7:4　　וָמַתְנוּ¹

Five times　　ה　　Mp

Com.: See **1 Kgs 17:12**.

7:4　　וָמָתְנוּ²

Five times　　ה　　Mp

Com.: See **1 Kgs 17:12**.

7:4　　יְחַיֻּנוּ

Unique and defective　　ל וחס　　Mp

Com.: By noting that this lemma is *unique* and written defective ו, the Masorah is also implying (correctly) that this lemma does not occur elsewhere written *plene*.

This lemma is featured in a Masoretic list of doublets with different hierarchial vowels, in a list termed *milʿêl* and *milraʿ*; see Yeivin, *Introduction*, §132, p. 103. In this connection, the higher vowel, the *milʿêl*, is the vowel *qibbûṣ*, and the lower vowel, the *milraʿ*, is the vowel *ṣerê*. Thus יְחַיֻּנוּ (here) having the *qibbûṣ* is *milʿêl*, whereas יְחַיֵּנוּ (Hos 6:2) having the *ṣerê* is *milraʿ*; see Frensdorff, *Ochlah*, §5, and Díaz-Esteban, *Sefer Oklah we-Oklah*, §5.

7:4   יְמִיתֻנוּ

Unique and defective   ל וחסׄ   Mp

Com.: By noting that this lemma is *unique* and written defective ו, the Masorah is also implying (correctly) that this lemma does not occur elsewhere written plene וּ.

In M^L this Mp note has been placed in the left column adjacent to the note on וַיָּקוּמוּ instead of in the right one adjacent to the note on וָמָתְנוּ³.

7:4   וָמָֽתְנוּ³

Five times   הׄ   Mp

Com.: See **1 Kgs 17:12**.

2 KINGS 7:5

וַיָּקוּמוּ בַנֶּשֶׁף לָבוֹא אֶל־מַחֲנֵה אֲרָם וַיָּבֹאוּ עַד־קְצֵה מַחֲנֵה אֲרָם וְהִנֵּה אֵין־שָׁם אִישׁ׃

7:5   וַיָּקוּמוּ

Nine times plene*   ט מל   Mp

Com.: See **Judg 20:19**.

*M^L, contrary to M (וַיָּקֻמוּ) writes the lemma here plene first ו (וַיָּקוּמוּ); see Breuer, *The Biblical Text*, 123.

Both M^C and M^A read וַיָּקֻמוּ, but neither of them has a note here.

2 KINGS 7:6

וַאדֹנָי הִשְׁמִיעַ ׀ אֶת־מַחֲנֵה אֲרָם קוֹל רֶכֶב קוֹל סוּס קוֹל חַיִל גָּדוֹל וַיֹּאמְרוּ אִישׁ אֶל־אָחִיו הִנֵּה שָׂכַר־עָלֵינוּ מֶלֶךְ יִשְׂרָאֵל אֶת־מַלְכֵי הַחִתִּים וְאֶת־מַלְכֵי מִצְרַיִם לָבוֹא עָלֵינוּ׃

7:6   וַאדֹנָי

Three times written with א   ג כתׄ אׄ   Mp

2 Kgs 7:6; Isa 49:14; Ps 35:23

Com.: The Masorah notes the *three* occurrences where יְהוָה with a וֹ cj. is written with the letters אדני.

This enumeration excludes the *three* occurrences of וַאדֹנָי when it is followed by יְהוָה (= אֱלֹהִים) at Isa 50:7, Amos 9:5, and Zech 9:14.

This lemma is also featured in a Masoretic list of the 134 occurrences of אֲדֹנָי when it is not followed by יְהוָה; see 1 **Kgs 3:10**, and Ognibeni, *'Oklah*, §151.

7:6   שָׂכַר

Twice   בֿ   Mp

Deut 23:5; **2 Kgs 7:6**

Com.: This lemma is featured in two Masoretic lists. One is in a list of doublets that have a *pataḥ*; see Frensdorff, *Ochlah*, §24, and Díaz-Esteban, *Sefer Oklah we-Oklah*, §25.

The other is in a list of doublets that are accented *once milʿêl* (שָׂכַר, here), and *once milraʿ* (שָׂכָר, Deut 23:5); see Frensdorff, *Ochlah*, §51, and Díaz-Esteban, *Sefer Oklah we-Oklah*, §52.

7:6   הַחִתִּים

Five times   הֿ   Mp

Com.: See **Judg 1:26**.

---

2 KINGS 7:7

וַיָּק֣וּמוּ וַיָּנ֣וּסוּ בַנֶּ֗שֶׁף וַיַּעַזְב֤וּ אֶת־אָהֳלֵיהֶם֙ וְאֶת־סוּסֵיהֶ֣ם וְאֶת־חֲמֹרֵיהֶ֔ם הַֽמַּחֲנֶ֖ה כַּאֲשֶׁר־הִ֑יא וַיָּנֻ֖סוּ אֶל־נַפְשָֽׁם׃

7:7   וַיָּקוּמוּ

Nine times plene   ט מלֿ   Mp

Com.: See **Judg 20:19**.

7:7   וַיָּנוּסוּ

Four times plene   דֿ מלֿ   Mp

2 Kgs 7:7[a]; **1 Chr 19:14**; 19:15; 2 Chr 13:16

| Mm | וינוסו ד׳ מל׳ וסימנהון | וְיָנֻסוּ *four times* plene, and their references |

2 Kgs 7:7[a]   ויקומו וינוסו בנשף (ויּ֫) [ויעזבו]
1 Chr 19:14   ויגש יואב והעם
(And) the *one* after it (1 Chr 19:15)   דבתריה
2 Chr 13:16   וינוסו בני ישראל

Com.: The Masorah notes the *four* occurrences of this lemma written plene וּ, to distinguish them from its more numerous occurrences (25x) written defective וּ as וַיָּנֻסוּ, *one* of which occurs in the same verse.

M[L], contrary to M (וַיָּנֻסוּ), has a *fifth* occurrence of this lemma since it writes the form at Judg 8:12 plene וּ (וַיָּנוּסוּ); see Breuer, *The Biblical Text*, 60. However, the Mp headings here and at 1 Chr 19:14, and the Mm here lists only *four* occurrences, thus supporting the enumeration inherent in the text of M.

Not included in this list is the *qərê* form (וַיָּנֻסוּ) at Judg 7:21, which has a *kətîb* וינסו.

7:7   וְאֶת־חֲמֹרֵיהֶם

Unique   ל   Mp

Gen 34:28; **2 Kgs 7:7**

Com.: The Mp heading of *unique* is inexact since there are *two* occurrences of this lemma. The note more precisely should have read *unique in the book*.

M[C], as M[L], mistakenly reads *unique* (see Castro, *El codice*, 3:209). M[A] has no note here.

7:7   כַּאֲשֶׁר־הִיא

Unique   ל   Mp

Com.: The Masorah notes the *sole* occurrence of this lemma with the prep. כַּ, to distinguish it from its *five* occurrences without this preposition (אֲשֶׁר־הִיא).

7:7   אֶל־נַפְשָׁם

Unique   ל   Mp

Com.: The Masorah notes the *sole* occurrence of נַפְשָׁם with אֶל, to distinguish it from its *three* occurrences with עַל (עַל־נַפְשָׁם).

This lemma is featured in a Masoretic list of words that usually occur with עַל but occur *once* אֶל; see Frensdorff, *Ochlah*, §77, and Díaz-Esteban, *Sefer Oklah we-Oklah*, §156A.

2 Kings 7:8

וַיָּבֹאוּ הַמְצֹרָעִים הָאֵלֶּה עַד־קְצֵה הַמַּחֲנֶה וַיָּבֹאוּ אֶל־אֹהֶל אֶחָד וַיֹּאכְלוּ וַיִּשְׁתּוּ וַיִּשְׂאוּ מִשָּׁם כֶּסֶף וְזָהָב וּבְגָדִים וַיֵּלְכוּ וַיַּטְמִנוּ וַיָּשֻׁבוּ וַיָּבֹאוּ אֶל־אֹהֶל אַחֵר וַיִּשְׂאוּ מִשָּׁם וַיֵּלְכוּ וַיַּטְמִנוּ׃

7:8   וַיַּטְמִנוּ

Twice and defective   ב׳ וחס׳   Mp

2 Kgs 7:8ᵃ; 7:8ᵇ

Com.: By noting that this lemma occurs *twice* and written defective י, the Masorah is also implying (correctly) that this lemma does not occur elsewhere written plene.

This lemma is featured in a Masoretic list of doublets that occur in the same verse; see Frensdorff, *Ochlah*, §58, and Díaz-Esteban, *Sefer Oklah we-Oklah*, §59.

2 Kings 7:9

וַיֹּאמְרוּ אִישׁ אֶל־רֵעֵהוּ לֹא־כֵן ׀ אֲנַחְנוּ עֹשִׂים הַיּוֹם הַזֶּה יוֹם־בְּשֹׂרָה הוּא וַאֲנַחְנוּ מַחְשִׁים וְחִכִּינוּ עַד־אוֹר הַבֹּקֶר וּמְצָאָנוּ עָווֹן וְעַתָּה לְכוּ וְנָבֹאָה וְנַגִּידָה בֵּית הַמֶּלֶךְ׃

7:9   לֹא־כֵן

Nineteen times   יט׳   Mp

Com.: See **2 Sam 20:21**.

7:9   בְּשֹׂרָה

Three times defective   ג׳ חס׳   Mp

Com.: See **2 Sam 4:10**.

7:9   אוֹר הַבֹּקֶר

Six times   ו׳   Mp

Com.: See **Judg 16:2**.

7:9   עָווֹן

Four times plene   ד׳ מל׳   Mp

2 Kgs 7:9; **Ps 51:7** (בְּעָווֹן); **Prov 5:22** (עֲווֹנוֹתָיו); **1 Chr 21:8** (עֲווֹן)

Com.: The Masorah notes the *four* occurrences of various forms of this lemma written plene second ו, to distinguish them from its more numerous occurrences (82x) of various forms written defective second ו (e.g., עָוֹן, עֲוֹן).

This lemma is featured in a Masoretic list of words with a double ו in the middle of a word; see the Mm at Exod 39:4 *sub* קְצוֹוֹתָיו, and Frensdorff, *Ochlah*, §184.

7:9   וְנָבֹאָה

Three times   ג̇   Mp

2 Kgs 7:9; **Jer 4:5** (וְנָבוֹאָה); **Ps 132:7** (נָבוֹאָה)

Mm¹   ונבאה ג̇ חד חסיר וב̇ מל   וְנָבֹאָה *three times*, *once* defective, and *twice* plene

2 Kgs 7:9   לכו ונבאה ונגידה
Jer 4:5   האספו ונבואה אל ערי המבצר
Ps 132:7   נבואה למשכנותיו

Mm²   ונבאה ג̇ חד חס̇ וב̇ מל   וְנָבֹאָה *three times*, *once* defective and *twice* plene

2 Kgs 7:9   לכו ונבאה ונגידה
Jer 4:5   האספו (ונבאה) [ונבואה] אל ערי המבצר
Ps 132:7   נבואה למשכנותיו

Com.: The Masorah notes the *three* occurrences of this lemma, *twice* written *plene* ו (Jer 4:5 and Ps 132:7), and *once* written defective ו (here).

The Mp heading at Ps 132:7 of *unique and plene* for נָבוֹאָה refers just to that specific reference.

This lemma is featured in a Masoretic list of words that occur *three times*, *twice* with ו cj. and *once* without; see Frensdorff, *Ochlah*, §14, and Díaz-Esteban, *Sefer Oklah we-Oklah*, §15.

The Mm has been written *twice* at this reference, *once* on the top right of fol. 207r, and *once* on the bottom right of the same folio.

2 KINGS 7:10

וַיָּבֹאוּ וַיִּקְרְאוּ אֶל־שֹׁעֵר הָעִיר וַיַּגִּידוּ לָהֶם לֵאמֹר בָּאנוּ אֶל־מַחֲנֵה אֲרָם וְהִנֵּה אֵין־שָׁם אִישׁ וְקוֹל אָדָם כִּי אִם־הַסּוּס אָסוּר וְהַחֲמוֹר אָסוּר וְאֹהָלִים כַּאֲשֶׁר־הֵמָּה׃

7:10   וְקוֹל אָדָם

Unique   ל   Mp

Com.: The Masorah notes the *sole* occurrence of this lemma with a ו cj., to distinguish it from its *sole* occurrence without a cj. at Dan 8:16.

2 KINGS 7:11

וַיִּקְרָא הַשֹּׁעֲרִים וַיַּגִּידוּ בֵּית הַמֶּלֶךְ פְּנִימָה׃

7:11   וַיִּקְרָא הַשֹּׁעֲרִים

Unique   ל   Mp

Com.: A circellus has been placed on each of these words but, since both occur many times, the note must refer to the combination of both words which occur only this once.

2 KINGS 7:12

וַיָּקָם הַמֶּלֶךְ לַיְלָה וַיֹּאמֶר אֶל־עֲבָדָיו אַגִּידָה־נָּא לָכֶם אֵת אֲשֶׁר־עָשׂוּ לָנוּ אֲרָם יָדְעוּ כִּי־רְעֵבִים אֲנַחְנוּ וַיֵּצְאוּ מִן־הַמַּחֲנֶה לְהֵחָבֵה בהשדה לֵאמֹר כִּי־יֵצְאוּ מִן־הָעִיר וְנִתְפְּשֵׂם חַיִּים וְאֶל־הָעִיר נָבֹא׃

7:12   לְהֵחָבֵה

Twice written with ה   בׄ כתׄ הׄ   Mp

Com.: See **1 Kgs 22:25**.

7:12   בהשׂדה

Read   בַּשָּׂדֶה   בשדה ק   Mp

Com.: The *kәtîb* (בהשדה) and *qәrê* (בַּשָּׂדֶה) represent examples where the letter ה is assimilated; see Gordis, *The Biblical Text*, 116.

This lemma is featured in a Masoretic list of words where a ה is written in the middle of a word but it is not read; see Frensdorff, *Ochlah*, §110, and Díaz-Esteban, *Sefer Oklah we-Oklah*, §92.

In M^L this lemma has no circellus.

7:12   נְבֹא

Three times defective   ג֗ חס֗   Mp

Deut 1:22; 1:19 (וַנָּבֹא); <u>**2 Kgs 7:12**</u>

נְבֹא *three times* defective   נבא ג֗ חס֗   Mm

Deut 1:22   ואת הערים אשר
Deut 1:19   ונבא עד קדש
<u>2 Kgs 7:12</u>   ואל העיר נבא

Com.: The Masorah notes the *three* occurrences of this lemma written defective ו, to distinguish them from its more numerous occurrences (9x) written plene ו (נְבוֹא/וַנָּבוֹא), *one of* which is in v. 4.

---

2 KINGS 7:13

וַיַּ֨עַן אֶחָ֜ד מֵעֲבָדָ֗יו וַיֹּ֘אמֶר֮ וְיִקְחוּ־נָ֣א חֲמִשָּׁה֮ מִן־הַסּוּסִים֮ הַנִּשְׁאָרִים֒ אֲשֶׁ֣ר נִשְׁאֲרוּ־בָ֔הּ הִנָּ֕ם כְּכָל־הֲמ֣וֹן יִשְׂרָאֵ֔ל אֲשֶׁ֥ר נִשְׁאֲרוּ־בָ֖הּ הִנָּ֛ם כְּכָל־הֲמ֥וֹן יִשְׂרָאֵ֖ל אֲשֶׁר־תָּ֑מּוּ וְנִשְׁלְחָ֖ה וְנִרְאֶֽה׃

7:13   וְיִקְחוּ

Six times   ו   Mp

1–5   Exod 12:3; 25:2; <u>27:20</u>; Lev 24:2; <u>Num 19:2</u>
6   <u>**2 Kgs 31:7**</u>

	Mm	ויקחו וֹ	*six times* וְיִקְחוּ
1–5	**Exod 12:3**	איש שה לבית (אבות) [אבת]	
	Exod 25:2	ויקחו לי תרומה	
	Num 19:2	פרה אדמה תמימה אשר	
	Exod 27:20	שמן זית זך כתית	
	Lev 24:2	שמן זית	
6	2 Kgs 7:13	מן הסוסים	

Com.: The Masorah notes the *six* occurrences of this lemma with a ו cj., to distinguish them from its more numerous occurrences (54x) with a ו consec. (וַיִּקְחוּ).

This distinction is implied in the headings of the Mm notes at Exod 27:20 and Num 19:2, which read *six times rapê*, that is, *six times* without *dageš*, e.g., as a ו cj. (as opposed to being with *dageš*, e.g., as a ו consec.).

7:13   הַהֲמוֹן

Mp	המון קׄ	הֲמוֹן Read

Com.: The *kətîb* (ההמון), and the *qərê* (הֲמוֹן) represent examples of the omission of a definite article; see Gordis, *The Biblical Text*, 147.

This lemma is featured in a Masoretic list of words where a ה is written at the beginning of a word but it is not read; see Frensdorff, *Ochlah*, §166, and Díaz-Esteban, *Sefer Oklah we-Oklah*, §91.

7:13   וְנִרְאֶה

Mp	דׄ	*Four times*

Gen 37:20; **2 Kgs 7:13**; **Isa 41:23** (*qərê*); 66:5

Com.: The Masorah notes the *four* occurrences of this lemma in the *qal*, to distinguish them from its *five* occurrences in the *niphal* (וְנִרְאָה).

2 Kings 7:15

וַיֵּלְכ֣וּ אַחֲרֵיהֶם֮ עַד־הַיַּרְדֵּן֒ וְהִנֵּ֣ה כָל־הַדֶּ֗רֶךְ מְלֵאָ֤ה בְגָדִים֙ וְכֵלִ֔ים אֲשֶׁר־הִשְׁלִ֥יכוּ אֲרָ֖ם בְּהֵחָפְזָ֑ם וַיָּשֻׁ֙בוּ֙ הַמַּלְאָכִ֔ים וַיַּגִּ֖דוּ לַמֶּֽלֶךְ׃

7:15   וְהִנֵּה כָל

Five times   הֿ   Mp

1–5   2 Sam 19:42; **2 Kgs 7:15**; Jer 38:22; Ezek 8:10; **Zech 1:11**

Com.: The Masorah notes the *five* occurrences of this lemma with a ו cj., to distinguish them from its *two* occurrences without a cj. at Ezek 16:44 and Job 1:12.

7:15   בְּהֵחָפְזָם

Read   בְּחָפְזָם ק   בהחפזם   Mp

Com.: The *kətîb* (בההחפזם, *niphal*), and the *qərê* (בְּחָפְזָם, *qal*) are examples of *kətîb/qərê* forms occurring in different conjugations with identical meanings; see Gordis, *The Biblical Text*, 133–34.

This lemma is featured in a Masoretic list of words where a ה is written in the middle of a word but it is not read; see Frensdorff, *Ochlah*, §110, and Díaz-Esteban, *Sefer Oklah we-Oklah*, §92.

2 Kings 7:17

וְהַמֶּ֣לֶךְ הִפְקִ֡יד אֶת־הַשָּׁלִישׁ֩ אֲשֶׁר־נִשְׁעָ֨ן עַל־יָד֜וֹ עַל־הַשַּׁ֗עַר וַיִּרְמְסֻ֧הוּ הָעָ֛ם בַּשַּׁ֖עַר וַיָּמֹ֑ת כַּאֲשֶׁ֣ר דִּבֶּ֗ר אִ֤ישׁ הָאֱלֹהִים֙ אֲשֶׁ֣ר דִּבֶּ֔ר בְּרֶ֥דֶת הַמֶּ֖לֶךְ אֵלָֽיו׃

7:17   עַל־הַשַּׁעַר

Four times in various forms   ד בליש   Mp

2 Kgs 7:17; Ezek 21:27 (עַל שְׁעָרִים); **Prov 14:19** (עַל שַׁעֲרֵי); **Cant 7:5** (עַל שַׁעַר)

Com.: The Masorah notes the *four* occurrences of שַׁעַר in various forms with עַל, to distinguish them from its more numerous occurrences (14x) in various forms with אֶל (e.g., שַׁעַר).

This enumeration does not include occurrences of this lemma in Chronicles and in parts of the book of Nehemiah (from 9:4 to the end); see Ginsburg 2, שׁ, §855, and Dotan/Reich, *Masora Thesaurus, ad loc.*

The Mp heading at Prov 14:19 reads *twice* for the *two* forms of עַל שַׁעֲרֵי, *one* of which is in 2 Chr 23:19, and thus is not included in this list.

The Mp heading at Cant 7:5 reads *twice* for the two forms of עַל שַׁעַר, *one* of which is in 2 Chr 26:9, and thus is also not included in this list.

2 KINGS 7:18

וַיְהִ֡י כְּדַבֵּר֩ אִ֨ישׁ הָאֱלֹהִ֜ים אֶל־הַמֶּ֣לֶךְ לֵאמֹ֗ר סָאתַ֨יִם שְׂעֹרִ֤ים בְּשֶׁ֙קֶל֙ וּסְאָה־סֹ֣לֶת בְּשֶׁ֔קֶל יִהְיֶ֛ה כָּעֵ֥ת מָחָ֖ר בְּשַׁ֥עַר שֹׁמְרֽוֹן׃

7:18   וּסְאָה

Unique   ל   Mp

Com.: The Masorah notes the *sole* occurrence of this lemma with a ו cj., to distinguish it from its *two* occurrences without a cj. in vv. 1 and 16.

2 KINGS 7:19

וַיַּ֨עַן הַשָּׁלִ֜ישׁ אֶת־אִ֣ישׁ הָאֱלֹהִים֮ וַיֹּאמַר֒ וְהִנֵּ֣ה יְהוָ֗ה עֹשֶׂ֤ה אֲרֻבּוֹת֙ בַּשָּׁמַ֔יִם הֲיִהְיֶ֖ה כַּדָּבָ֣ר הַזֶּ֑ה וַיֹּ֗אמֶר הִנְּךָ֤ רֹאֶה֙ בְּעֵינֶ֔יךָ וּמִשָּׁ֖ם לֹ֥א תֹאכֵֽל׃

7:19   וְהִנֵּה יְהוָה

Four times   ד   Mp

Com.: See **1 Kgs 19:11**.

7:19   עֹשֶׂה

Twenty-two times   כב   Mp

1–5   Deut 5:10 (וְעֹשֶׂה); 10:18; **31:21**; 2 Kgs 7:2; **7:19**
6–10   Amos 9:12; Nah 1:9; Zeph 3:19; Zech 10:1; Mal 3:17
11–15   Mal 3:21; **Ps 18:51** (וְעֹשֶׂה); **37:7**; **104:4**; **106:21**
16–20   Ps 146:6; **146:7**; Qoh 8:12; **Neh 2:16**; **4:11**
21–22   **Neh 6:3**; **1 Chr 18:14**

Com.: The Masorah notes the *twenty-two* occurrences of this form with a *sẹḡōl* in the books of Deuteronomy, Kings, The Twelve, Psalms, Qoheleth, Ezra-Nehemiah and Chronicles, to distinguish them from its more numerous occurrences (37x) in these books with a *serê* (עֹשֵׂה/וְעֹשֵׂה).

The Mm at Exod 15:11 *sub* עָשָׂה gives the note in reverse form: עָשָׂה occurs *eight times* and similarly in the books of Deuteronomy, Kings, The Twelve, Chronicles, Psalms, Qoheleth, and Ezra-Nehemiah apart from *twenty-two times* (when it occurs as עֹשֵׂה). Then the *twenty-two* occurrences of עֹשֵׂה are listed.

Notes on the headings highlighted above.

Deut 31:21	*Three times in the book* (Deut 5:10, 10:18 and 31:21).
2 Kgs 7:19	*Twenty-two times.* All the above references.
Ps 18:51 (וְעֹשֶׂה)	*Five times in the book with səḡôl* (ֶה). Incorrect, since there are *six* occurrences of this lemma in the book of Psalms, and this *one* is the only *one* with a ו cj. The note should read *five times with səḡôl*, and would include the *five* occurrences of this lemma with a ו cj. (Exod 20:6, Deut 5:10, 2 Sam 22:51, Jer 33:18, and Ps 18:51); see Dotan/Reich, *Masora Thesaurus, ad loc.*
Ps 37:7; 106:21; 146:7	*Five times in the book with səḡôl* (ֶה). Notes the *five* occurrences in Psalms that occur without a ו cj. (Ps 37:7, 104:4, 106:21, 146:6, and 146:7).
Ps 104:4	*Five times* (in the book without a ו cj, see directly above).
Qoh 8:12; Neh 2:16 Neh 6:3; 1 Chr 18:14	*Twenty-two times with səḡôl* (כֶב). All the above references.
Neh 4:11	*Twenty-five times with səḡôl* (כֶה). *Three of them are in the book* (of Ezra/Nehemiah, Neh 2:16, 4:11, and 6:3). According to Dotan/Reich (*Masora Thesaurus, ad loc.*) the extra *three* references are those in Judges (11:27; 15:3; 18:3).

7:19   וּמִשָּׁם

Eight times   ח̇   Mp

Com.: See above at **2 Kgs 7:2**.

> **2 KINGS 8:1**
> וֶאֱלִישָׁ֞ע דִּבֶּ֣ר אֶל־הָאִשָּׁ֣ה אֲשֶׁר־הֶחֱיָ֣ה אֶת־בְּנָ֡הּ לֵאמֹר֩ ק֨וּמִי וּלְכִ֜י אַ֣תְּי וּבֵיתֵ֗ךְ וְג֙וּרִי֙ בַּאֲשֶׁ֣ר תָּג֔וּרִי כִּֽי־קָרָ֤א יְהוָה֙ לָֽרָעָ֔ב וְגַם־בָּ֥א אֶל־הָאָ֖רֶץ שֶׁ֥בַע שָׁנִֽים׃

8:1   אַ֣תְּי

Mp   את ק   Read אַתְּ

Mm   אתי ז כת כן   אַ֣תְּי *seven times* written like this

1–5   Judg 17:2   ואת אלית וגם
       2 Kgs 4:16   את חבקת בן
       1 Kgs 14:2   אשת ירבעם
       2 Kgs 4:23   הלכת אליו
       <u>2 Kgs 8:1</u>   קומי ולכי
6–7   Jer 4:30   ואת שדוד
       Ezek 36:13   אכלת אדם אתי

Com.: The *kǝtîb* (אתי) represents the older 2nd pers. fem. sg. form of the pron. אַ֣תְּי, whereas the *qǝrê* (אַתְּ) represents the regular form; see Gordis, *The Biblical Text*, 102.

The Mm notes the *seven* occurrences where אתי is written but אַתְּ is read. However, in most of the catchwords in this list the *qǝrê* form (אַתְּ) is written.

This lemma is featured in a Masoretic list of words in which a י is written at the end but is not read; see Frensdorff, *Ochlah*, §127, and Díaz-Esteban, *Sefer Oklah we-Oklah*, §111.

In M^L this lemma has no circellus.

8:1   בַּאֲשֶׁ֣ר

Mp   ט֗ו   *Fifteen times*

Com.: See **Judg 5:27**.

8:1   אֶל־הָאָ֖רֶץ

Mp   ל בסיפ   *Unique* in the book

Com.: This lemma is featured in a Masoretic list of the prepositions עַל and אֶל that precede הָאָ֖רֶץ in the book of Kings. There are *five* occurrences of עַל הָאָ֖רֶץ, but only this *one* of אֶל הָאָ֖רֶץ; see Díaz-Esteban, *Sefer Oklah we-Oklah*, §160E.

2 KINGS 8:3

וַיְהִ֗י מִקְצֵה֙ שֶׁ֣בַע שָׁנִ֔ים וַתָּ֥שָׁב הָאִשָּׁ֖ה מֵאֶ֣רֶץ פְּלִשְׁתִּ֑ים וַתֵּצֵא֙ לִצְעֹ֣ק אֶל־הַמֶּ֔לֶךְ אֶל־בֵּיתָ֖הּ וְאֶל־שָׂדָֽהּ׃

8:3   וַיְהִ֗י מִקְצֵה֙

Five times   הׄ   Mp

Com.: See **Josh 3:2**.

2 KINGS 8:4

וְהַמֶּ֗לֶךְ מְדַבֵּר֙ אֶל־גֵּ֣חֲזִ֔י נַ֥עַר אִישׁ־הָאֱלֹהִ֖ים לֵאמֹ֑ר סַפְּרָה־נָּ֣א לִ֔י אֵ֥ת כׇּל־הַגְּדֹל֖וֹת אֲשֶׁר־עָשָׂ֥ה אֱלִישָֽׁע׃

8:4   גֵּ֣חֲזִ֔י

Four times   דׄ   Mp

2 Kgs 4:31 (וְגֵחֲזִ֔י); 5:25; **8:4**; 8:5

גֵּ֣חֲזִ֔י *four times* defective in this and a similar form   גחזי דׄ חסׄ בליש   Mm

2 Kgs 4:31	וגחזי עבר לפניהם
2 Kgs 5:25	ויאמר אליו אלישע מאן
<u>2 Kgs 8:4</u>	והמלך מדבר
2 Kgs 8:5	ויהי הוא מספר

Com.: The Masorah notes the *four* occurrences of this lemma written defective first י, to distinguish them from its more numerous occurrences (8x) written plene first י (גֵּחֲזִי/לְגֵיחֲזִי).

M^L, contrary to M (גֵּיחֲזִי), has a *fifth* occurrence of this lemma at 2 Kgs 4:12 (גֵּחֲזִי); see Breuer, *The Biblical Text*, 120. However, all the Mp headings and the Mm here support the enumeration inherent in the text of M.

> **2 KINGS 8:5**
>
> וַיְהִ֣י ה֣וּא מְסַפֵּ֣ר לַמֶּ֗לֶךְ אֵ֣ת אֲשֶׁר־הֶחֱיָה֮ אֶת־הַמֵּת֒ וְהִנֵּ֨ה הָאִשָּׁ֜ה אֲשֶׁר־הֶחֱיָ֤ה אֶת־בְּנָהּ֙ צֹעֶ֣קֶת אֶל־הַמֶּ֔לֶךְ עַל־בֵּיתָ֖הּ וְעַל־שָׂדָ֑הּ וַיֹּ֤אמֶר גֵּֽחֲזִי֙ אֲדֹנִ֣י הַמֶּ֔לֶךְ זֹ֚את הָאִשָּׁ֔ה וְזֶה־בְּנָ֖הּ אֲשֶׁר־הֶחֱיָ֥ה אֱלִישָֽׁע׃

8:5   ה֣וּא

Twice with the accent (*mêrəkâ*)   ב בטע   Mp

2 Kgs 8:5; 2 Chr 6:32 (לֹא)

Twice with the accent (*mêrəkâ*)   ב בטע   Mm

2 Kgs 8:5   הוא מספר למלך
2 Chr 6:32   לא מעמד יש־אל

Com.: The Masorah notes the *two* instances where the *second* servus before *zarqâ* (ה֣וּא מְסַפֵּ֣ר לַמֶּ֗לֶךְ (here) and לֹ֣א מֵעַמְּךָ֮ יִשְׂרָאֵל֒ (2 Chr 6:32) is marked with *mêrəkâ*, and not with an expected *mûnaḥ*; see Yeivin, *Introduction*, §261 (p. 206). Note that the accent *mêrəkâ* has been written in the Mm note.

In M^L the circellus has been placed between this word and the preceding word וַיְהִי but, as is clear from the intent of the note and the Mm references, the circellus belongs on this lemma.

8:5   צֹעֶ֣קֶת

Unique   ל   Mp

Com.: The Masorah notes the *sole* occurrence of this lemma pointed this way (fem. ptcp., *crying*), to distinguish it from its more numerous occurrences (6x) pointed as צַעֲקַת (noun, *cry of*).

8:5   וְעַל־שָׂדָ֑הּ

Unique   ל   Mp

Com.: This lemma is featured in a Masoretic list of phrases that occur *once* with וְעַל, and *once* with וְאֶל; see Frensdorff, *Ochlah*, §86, and Díaz-Esteban, *Sefer Oklah we-Oklah*, §156C.

8:5 גֵּחֲזִי

Four times defective   ד֗ חס   Mp

Com.: See directly above at **2 Kgs 8:4**.

---

2 KINGS 8:6

וַיִּשְׁאַ֨ל הַמֶּ֤לֶךְ לָֽאִשָּׁה֙ וַתְּסַפֶּר־ל֔וֹ וַיִּתֶּן־לָ֣הּ הַמֶּ֣לֶךְ סָרִ֣יס אֶחָ֗ד לֵאמֹר֙ הָשֵׁ֣יב אֶת־כָּל־אֲשֶׁר־לָ֔הּ וְאֵת֙ כָּל־תְּבוּאֹ֣ת הַשָּׂדֶ֔ה מִיּ֛וֹם עָזְבָ֥ה אֶת־הָאָ֖רֶץ וְעַד־עָֽתָּה׃ פ

8:6 לָאִשָּׁה

Five times   ה֗   Mp

Com.: See **Judg 14:7**.

8:6 הָשֵׁיב

Unique plene   ל מל֗   Mp

Com.: The Masorah notes the *sole* occurrence of this lemma written plene י, to distinguish it from its more numerous occurrences (14x) written defective י (הָשֵׁב).

8:6 תְּבוּאֹת

Seven times   ז֗   Mp

1–5   **Gen 47:24** (בִּתְבוּאֹת); Lev 25:15; **25:16**; **Deut 33:14**; **2 Kgs 8:6**
6–7   **Prov 14:4** (תְּבוּאוֹת); **16:8** (תְּבוּאֹות)

תְּבוּאֹת *seven times*   ז֗ [תבואת] (תבואות)   Mm

1–5	Gen 47:24	והיה
	Lev 25:16	מספר (תבואות) [תבואת]
	Lev 25:15	במספר
	Deut 33:14	וממגד
	2 Kgs 8:6	וישאל
6–7	Prov 14:4	ורב
	Prov 16:8	מרב

Com.: The Masorah notes the *seven* occurrences of this lemma in various forms in the pl., to distinguish them from its *twelve* occurrences in various forms in the sg. (e.g., תְּבוּאַת); see Ognibeni, *'Oklah*, §1L.

The Mp headings at Prov 14:4 and 16:8 (תְּבוּאוֹת) read *twice plene*, noting the *two* occurrences of this form written plene second ו.

8:6   עֲזֻבָה

Mp   ב׳   *Twice*

2 Kgs 8:6; Jer 49:11

Mm   עזבה ב׳   *twice* עֲזֻבָה

2 Kgs 8:6   השדה מיום עזבה
Jer 49:11   יתמיד

Com.: The Masorah notes the *two* occurrences of this lemma (3rd fem. sg.), to distinguish them from its *sole* occurrence in pause (עֲזָבָה) in Ezek 23:8.

2 KINGS 8:7
וַיָּבֹא אֱלִישָׁע דַּמֶּשֶׂק וּבֶן־הֲדַד מֶלֶךְ־אֲרָם חֹלֶה וַיֻּגַּד־לוֹ לֵאמֹר בָּא אִישׁ הָאֱלֹהִים עַד־הֵנָּה׃

8:7   חֹלֶה

Mp   ח׳   *Eight times*

Com.: See **1 Sam 22:8**.

8:7   וַיֻּגַּד

Mp   כד׳   *Twenty-four times*

Com.: See **Josh 10:17**.

2 KINGS 8:8

וַיֹּ֤אמֶר הַמֶּ֙לֶךְ֙ אֶל־חֲזָהאֵ֔ל קַ֥ח בְּיָדְךָ֖ מִנְחָ֑ה וְלֵ֗ךְ לִקְרַאת֙ אִ֣ישׁ הָאֱלֹהִ֔ים וְדָרַשְׁתָּ֧ אֶת־יְהוָ֛ה מֵאוֹת֖וֹ לֵאמֹ֑ר הַאֶחְיֶ֖ה מֵחֳלִ֥י זֶֽה׃

8:8   חֲזָהאֵל

Five times written with a ה   ה̇ כת̇ ה̇   Mp

1–5   **2 Kgs 8:8; 8:13; 8:15; 8:29; <u>2 Chr 22:6</u>**

חֲזָהאֵל *five times* written with a ה   חזהאל ה̇ כת̇ ה̇   Mm

1–5   <u>2 Kgs 8:8</u>   ויאמר המלך אל חזהאל
       2 Kgs 8:13   כי מה עבדך
       2 Kgs 8:15   ויהי ממחרת ויקח המכבר
       וַיָּ֤שָׁב יוֹרָ֣ם הַמֶּ֙לֶךְ֙ *the first occurrence*   וישב (יואב) [יורם] המלך
      in Kings (2 Kgs 8:29)   קדמייה דמלכים
       בְּהִלָּחֲמ֖וֹ *of Chronicles* (<u>2 Chr 22:6</u>)   בהלחמו דדבר ימ׳

Com.: The Masorah notes the *five* occurrences of this lemma written with a medial ה, to distinguish them from its more numerous occurrences (16x) written without this ה (חֲזָאֵל).

This distinction is implied in the *two* additional notations in the Mm here.

The additional notation of *the first occurrence in Kings* to the catchwords of the 2 Kgs 8:29 reference is to distinguish that verse from a later verse in which these catchwords occur (2 Kgs 9:15), and in which the lemma is written differently as חֲזָאֵל.

The additional notation *of Chronicles* to the 2 Chr 22:6 reference is to distinguish that verse from its parallel in 2 Kgs 9:15 where, as noted above, the lemma is written as חֲזָאֵל.

M^L, contrary to M (חֲזָאֵל), has a *sixth* occurrence of this lemma at 2 Kgs 8:28 (חֲזָהאֵל); see Breuer, *The Biblical Text*, 124. Nevertheless, all the Mp headings in Kings highlighted above, read *five times*, and the Mm listings here only give *five* references, thus supporting the enumeration inherent in the text of M.

The Mp heading at 2 Chr 22:6 of *unique plene in the book* notes this *one* occurrence in Chronicles.

8:8   מֵאוֹתוֹ

Six times plene in the book   ו מל בסיפ   Mp

Com.: See **2 Kgs 3:11**.

---

2 KINGS 8:9

וַיֵּ֣לֶךְ חֲזָאֵל֮ לִקְרָאתוֹ֒ וַיִּקַּ֨ח מִנְחָ֤ה בְיָדוֹ֙ וְכׇל־ט֣וּב דַּמֶּ֔שֶׂק מַשָּׂ֖א אַרְבָּעִ֣ים גָּמָ֑ל וַיָּבֹא֙ וַיַּעֲמֹ֣ד לְפָנָ֔יו וַיֹּ֗אמֶר בִּנְךָ֨ בֶן־הֲדַ֧ד מֶֽלֶךְ־אֲרָ֛ם שְׁלָחַ֥נִי אֵלֶ֖יךָ לֵאמֹ֑ר הַאֶחְיֶ֖ה מֵחֳלִ֥י זֶֽה׃

8:9   וְכׇל־טוּב

Twice   בׄ   Mp

Gen 24:10; 2 Kgs 8:9

וְכׇל־טוּב *twice*   וכל טוב בׄ   Mm

2 Kgs 8:9   דמשק משא ארבעים
Gen 24:10   ויקח העבד

Com.: The Masorah notes the *two* occurrences of this lemma written with a ו cj., to distinguish them from its *three* occurrences without a cj. (כׇּל־טוּב).

---

2 KINGS 8:10

וַיֹּ֤אמֶר אֵלָיו֙ אֱלִישָׁ֔ע לֵ֥ךְ אֱמׇר־לֹ֖א חָיֹ֣ה תִחְיֶ֑ה וְהִרְאַ֥נִי יְהֹוָ֖ה כִּי־מ֥וֹת יָמֽוּת׃

8:10   לֹא

Read לוֹ   לו ק   Mp

Com.: The *kəṯîḇ* (לֹא, *not*), and the *qərê* (לוֹ, *to him*) represent variants of equal value; see Gordis, *The Biblical Text*, 151.

This lemma is featured in a Masoretic list of occurrences when לא is written, but read as לו; see the Mm at **2 Sam 16:18**, Frensdorff, *Ochlah*, §105, and Díaz-Esteban, *Sefer Oklah we-Oklah*, §88.

8:10   מוֹת יָמוּת

Three times   גׁ   Mp

1 Sam 14:39; 2 Sam 12:14; <u>2 Kgs 8:10</u>

מוֹת יָמוּת *three times*   מות ימות גׁ   Mm

1 Sam 14:39   כי חי יהוה המושיע
<u>2 Kgs 8:10</u>   אמר (לי) [לו]
2 Sam 12:14   כי נאץ

Com.: The Masorah notes the *three* occurrences of this lemma, to distinguish them from the more numerous occurrences (24x) of its parallel expression מוֹת יוּמָת; see Ognibeni, *'Oklah*, §191.

---

2 KINGS 8:11

וַיַּעֲמֵד אֶת־פָּנָיו וַיָּשֶׂם עַד־בֹּשׁ וַיֵּבְךְּ אִישׁ הָאֱלֹהִים׃

8:11   וַיַּעֲמֵד

Four times   דׁ   Mp

<u>Num 11:24</u>; <u>2 Kgs 8:11</u>; Job 34:24; Ps 107:25

וַיַּעֲמֵד *four times*   ויעמד דׁ   Mm

Num 11:24   (סביבות) [סביבת]
<u>2 Kgs 8:11</u>   פניו
Job 34:24   אחרים
Ps 107:25   סערה
And similarly *all* of Chronicles apart from *seven* (וַיַּעֲמֹד)   וכל דברי ימׁ דכותהון בר מן זׁ

Com.: The Masorah notes the *four* occurrences of this lemma in the *hiphil*, to distinguish them from its more numerous occurrences (57x) in the *qal* (וַיַּעֲמֹד); see Ognibeni, *'Oklah*, §166.

The Mm additionally notes that this lemma also occurs (11x) in Chronicles in the *hiphil*, apart from *seven* times when it is in the *qal*.

The Mp headings at Num 11:24 and Ps 107:25 read *four times, and similarly all Chronicles apart from seven*.

8:11   בֹּשׁ

Three times defective   ג̇ חס   Mp

2 Kgs 2:17; **8:11**; **Jer 48:13** (וּבֹשׁ)

Com.: The Masorah notes the *three* occurrences of this lemma, written defective ו, to distinguish them from its *four* occurrences written plene ו as בוֹשׁ.

2 KINGS 8:12

וַיֹּאמֶר חֲזָאֵל מַדּוּעַ אֲדֹנִי בֹּכֶה וַיֹּאמֶר כִּי־יָדַעְתִּי אֵת אֲשֶׁר־תַּעֲשֶׂה לִבְנֵי יִשְׂרָאֵל רָעָה מִבְצְרֵיהֶם תְּשַׁלַּח בָּאֵשׁ וּבַחֻרֵיהֶם בַּחֶרֶב תַּהֲרֹג וְעֹלְלֵיהֶם תְּרַטֵּשׁ וְהָרֹתֵיהֶם תְּבַקֵּעַ׃

8:12   תְּשַׁלַּח

Five times   ה̇   Mp

1–5   **Exod 15:7**; **Deut 22:7**; 2 Kgs 8:12; **Pss 80:12**; **104:30**

Com.: The Masorah notes the *five* occurrences of this lemma in the *piel* to distinguish them from its *six* occurrences in the *qal* (תִּשְׁלַח).

8:12   וּבַחֻרֵיהֶם

Three times   ג̇   Mp

2 Kgs 8:12; **Jer 18:21** (בַּחוּרֵיהֶם); 2 Chr 36:17 (בַּחוּרֵיהֶם)

Com.: The Masorah notes the *three* occurrences of this lemma, *twice* written plene ו without a ו cj. (Jer 18:21 and 2 Chr 36:17), and *once* written defective ו with a ו cj. (here).

8:12   וְעֹלְלֵיהֶם

Three times   ג̇   Mp

2 Kgs 8:12; Isa 13:16; Hos 14:1 (עֹלְלֵיהֶם)

Com.: The Masorah notes the *three* occurrences of this lemma written defective ו, to distinguish them from its *sole* occurrence written plene ו (לְעוֹלְלֵיהֶם) at Ps 17:14.

8:12   תְּרַטֵּשׁ

Unique   ל̇   Mp

2 KINGS 8:13

וַיֹּאמֶר חֲזָהאֵל כִּי מָה עַבְדְּךָ הַכֶּלֶב כִּי יַעֲשֶׂה הַדָּבָר הַגָּדוֹל הַזֶּה וַיֹּאמֶר אֱלִישָׁע הִרְאַנִי יְהוָה אֹתְךָ מֶלֶךְ עַל־אֲרָם׃

8:13   חֲזָהאֵל

Five times written with a ה   ה̇ כת̇ ה̇   Mp

Com.: See directly above at **2 Kgs 8:8**.

8:13   מָה

Five times with *qameṣ* adjacent to an ע or a ח   הָ דסמיך לעין ולחית   Mp

1–5   Gen 31:32; **2 Kgs 8:13**; Mal 2:14; **Dan 4:32**; **Ezra 6:9** (וּמָה)

מָה *five times* with *qameṣ* adjacent to an ע or a ח   מה ה̇ קמץ דסמיכין לעין ולחית   Mm

1–5   Gen 31:32   עם אשר תמצא
       2 Kgs 8:13   ויאמר חזהאל
       Mal 2:14   ואמרתם על מה
       Ezra 6:9   ומה חשחן
       Dan 4:32   וכל דארי ארעא

Com.: The Masorah notes the *five* occurrences of the interrog. pron. מָה, pointed with a *qameṣ* before words beginning with the letters ע and ח. Normally the interrog. is pointed with a *sᵊgôl* before an ע or ח; see **1 Sam 4:6**.

8:13   הַדָּבָר הַגָּדוֹל הַזֶּה

Three times   גׄ   Mp

Deut 4:32 (כַּדָּבָר); 1 Sam 12:16; **2 Kgs 8:13**

Com.: The Masorah notes the *three* occurrences of this phrase with הַגָּדוֹל, to distinguish them from its many occurrences (100+) without it; see Ginsburg, 4, ד, §84.

In M^L the circellus has been placed only on הַדָּבָר הַגָּדוֹל, but the note belongs, as the Mm of M^A indicates here, with the three words הַדָּבָר הַגָּדוֹל הַזֶּה.

2 KINGS 8:15

וַיְהִי מִמָּחֳרָת וַיִּקַּח הַמַּכְבֵּר וַיִּטְבֹּל בַּמַּיִם וַיִּפְרֹשׂ עַל־פָּנָיו וַיָּמֹת וַיִּמְלֹךְ חֲזָהאֵל תַּחְתָּיו: פ

8:15   הַמַּכְבֵּר

Unique   לׄ   Mp

8:15   חֲזָהאֵל

Five times written with a ה   הׄ כת הי   Mp

Com.: See above at **2 Kgs 8:8**.

2 KINGS 8:16

וּבִשְׁנַת חָמֵשׁ לְיוֹרָם בֶּן־אַחְאָב מֶלֶךְ יִשְׂרָאֵל וִיהוֹשָׁפָט מֶלֶךְ יְהוּדָה מָלַךְ יְהוֹרָם בֶּן־יְהוֹשָׁפָט מֶלֶךְ יְהוּדָה:

8:16   וּבִשְׁנַת

Ten times   יׄ   Mp

Com.: See **1 Kgs 15:1**.

2 KINGS

8:16   יְהוֹרָ֥ם

	יְהוֹרָם *sixteen times* in the Prophets	יהורם יֹ֨ בנביא֙	Mm
1–5	1 Kgs 22:51	וישכב	
	2 Kgs 1:17a	וימת	
	Twice in the verse (2 Kgs 1:17b; לִיהוֹרָ֖ם)	שנים בפסוקה	
	2 Kgs 3:1 (וִיהוֹרָ֣ם)	ויהורם בן אחאב	
	2 Kgs 3:6	ויצא המלך יהורם	
	{the *second* (occurrence) in the verse}	{בתריה דפסוק}	
6	<2 Kgs 8:16>		
7	2 Kgs 8:25	מלך אחזיהו בן יהורם	
	the *second* (occurrence) in the verse	בתרי דפסוק	
8	the *first* (occurrence) of לְהִתְרַפֵּ֣א (2 Kgs 8:29) in the *second* part of the verse	להתרפא קדמיה תנינא דפסוק	
9	the *second* (occurrence) of לְהִתְרַפֵּ֣א (2 Kgs 9:15)	להתרפא בתרייה	
10–15	*Six* cases from 2 Kgs 9:17–9:25 [2 Kgs 9:17; 9:21a; 9:21b; 9:22; 9:23; 9:24]	ומן קח רכב עד בדקר וֹ	
16	2 Kgs 12:19 (וִיהוֹרָ֖ם)	ויקח יהואש	
	And *all* of the Writings apart from *four*	וכל כתיבייה בֹּ מֹ דֹ	
1–4	1 Chr 3:11	יורם בנו	
	1 Chr 26:25 (ויורם) [וירם] בנו		
	2 Chr 22:5	ויכו	
	2 Chr 22:7 (מהאלהים) [ומאלהים] היתה		

Com.: The Masorah notes the *sixteen* occurrences of יְהוֹרָם (Joram) in various forms in the Prophets which are spelled with a ה, to distinguish them from its *sixteen* occurrences in various forms in the Prophets written without the ה (e.g., יוֹרָם).

The Masorah also notes that this lemma also occurs (15 x) in the Writings (in various forms, such as יְהוֹרָם), apart from *four* cases that are listed in the note, when it is יוֹרָם.

In this Mm there are several additional notations.

The addition of *the second (occurrence) in the verse* to the 2 Kgs 3:6 reference [no. 5] is misplaced since there is only *one* occurrence of Joram's name in that verse.

However, the same addition at the 2 Kgs 8:25 reference [no. 7] is to distinguish the *second* occurrence of Joram's name in the verse, which is written as יְהוֹרָם, from the first occurrence, which is written as לְיוֹרָם.

The additional notations concerning the phrase לְהִתְרַפֵּא [nos. 8 and 9] can be explained as follows. The phrase לְהִתְרַפֵּא occurs *twice* in this section concerning Joram (2 Kgs 8:16–9:37). The *first* time it occurs in 2 Kgs 8:29 Joram's name is written יְהוֹרָם in the *second* part of the verse, but as יוֹרָם in the *first* and *third* part of the verse.

The *second* time לְהִתְרַפֵּא occurs is in 2 Kgs 9:15, and there Joram only occurs *once*, and his name in that verse is spelled יְהוֹרָם.

2 KINGS 8:17

בֶּן־שְׁלֹשִׁים וּשְׁתַּיִם שָׁנָה הָיָה בְמָלְכוֹ וּשְׁמֹנֶה שָׁנָה מָלַךְ בִּירוּשָׁלָֽם׃

8:17   הָיָה בְמָלְכוֹ

Seven times   ז̇   Mp

1–5   **2 Kgs 8:17; 14:2;** 15:2; **15:33; 18:2**
6–7   **2 Chr 21:20; 27:8**

Com.: The Masorah notes the *seven* occurrences of the form בְּמָלְכוֹ preceded by הָיָה, possibly to distinguish them from its more numerous occurrences (30x) without הָיָה preceding it.

In M^L the circellus has been placed only on הָיָה but it belongs on the two words.

8:17   שָׁנָה

Read שָׁנִים   שנים ק̇   Mp

Com.: The *kətîb* (שנה) and *qərê* (שָׁנִים) represent examples where the *kətîb* and the *qərê* fluctuate between the sg. and the pl.; see Gordis, *The Biblical Text*, 143.

This lemma is featured in a Masoretic list of words where a מ is not written at the end of a word nevertheless it is read; see the Mm at 1 Sam 20:38 *sub* הַחֵצִי, Frensdorff, *Ochlah*, §157, and Díaz-Esteban, *Sefer Oklah we-Oklah*, §143.

2 Kings 8:19

וְלֹא־אָבָה יְהוָה לְהַשְׁחִית אֶת־יְהוּדָה לְמַעַן דָּוִד עַבְדּוֹ כַּאֲשֶׁר אָמַר־לוֹ לָתֵת לוֹ נִיר לְבָנָיו כָּל־הַיָּמִים׃

8:19   נִיר

Eight times   ח֗   Mp

Com.: See **1 Kgs 15:4**.

2 Kings 8:20

בְּיָמָיו פָּשַׁע אֱדוֹם מִתַּחַת יַד־יְהוּדָה וַיַּמְלִכוּ עֲלֵיהֶם מֶלֶךְ׃

8:20   וַיַּמְלִכוּ

Five times defective   ה֗ חס   Mp

Com.: See **1 Sam 11:15**.

2 Kings 8:21

וַיַּעֲבֹר יוֹרָם צָעִירָה וְכָל־הָרֶכֶב עִמּוֹ וַיְהִי־הוּא קָם לַיְלָה וַיַּכֶּה אֶת־אֱדוֹם הַסֹּבֵיב אֵלָיו וְאֵת שָׂרֵי הָרֶכֶב וַיָּנָס הָעָם לְאֹהָלָיו׃

8:21   וַיַּכֶּה

Ten times   י֗   Mp

Com.: See **Josh 10:40**.

8:21   הַסֹּבֵיב

Three times defective   ג֗ חס   Mp

Gen 2:11 (הַסֹּבֵב); **2 Kgs 8:21**; **Qoh 1:6**ᶜ (סֹבֵב)

Com.: The Masorah notes the *three* occurrences of this lemma written defective ו, to distinguish them from its *five* occurrences in various forms written plene ו (e.g., סוֹבֵב).

The Mp heading at Qoh 1:6ᶜ reads *twice*, and the Mm there lists only the Gen 2:11 and Qoh 1:6ᵇ references omitting this 2 Kgs 8:21 reference.

8:21   וְאֵת שָׂרֵי

Three times   ג׳   Mp

2 Kgs 8:21; <u>Jer 24:1</u>; **2 Chr 21:9**

Com.: The Masorah notes the *three* occurrences of this phrase written with a ו cj., to distinguish them from its more numerous occurrences (17x) written without a cj.

---

2 KINGS 8:25

בִּשְׁנַת שְׁתֵּים־עֶשְׂרֵה שָׁנָה לְיוֹרָם בֶּן־אַחְאָב מֶלֶךְ יִשְׂרָאֵל מָלַךְ אֲחַזְיָהוּ בֶן־יְהוֹרָם מֶלֶךְ יְהוּדָה׃

8:25   יְהוֹרָם

Three times plene   ג׳ מל   Mp

<u>2 Kgs 8:16</u>; **8:25**; 8:29

Com.: The Masorah notes the *three* occurrences of this lemma in this section; see directly above at <u>2 Kgs 8:16</u>.

---

2 KINGS 8:27

וַיֵּלֶךְ בְּדֶרֶךְ בֵּית אַחְאָב וַיַּעַשׂ הָרַע בְּעֵינֵי יְהוָה כְּבֵית אַחְאָב כִּי חֲתַן בֵּית־אַחְאָב הוּא׃

8:27   חֲתַן

Four times   ד׳   Mp

Com.: See **Judg 15:6**.

---

2 KINGS 8:29

וַיָּשָׁב יוֹרָם הַמֶּלֶךְ לְהִתְרַפֵּא בְיִזְרְעֶאל מִן־הַמַּכִּים אֲשֶׁר יַכֻּהוּ אֲרַמִּים בָּרָמָה בְּהִלָּחֲמוֹ אֶת־חֲזָהאֵל מֶלֶךְ אֲרָם וַאֲחַזְיָהוּ בֶן־יְהוֹרָם מֶלֶךְ יְהוּדָה יָרַד לִרְאוֹת אֶת־יוֹרָם בֶּן־אַחְאָב בְּיִזְרְעֶאל כִּי־חֹלֶה הוּא׃ פ

8:29   חֲזָהאֵל

Five times written with a ה   ה׳ כת ה   Mp

Com.: See above at **2 Kgs 8:8**.

8:29   חֹלֵה

Eight times   ח֗   Mp

Com.: See **1 Sam 22:8**.

---

2 KINGS 9:1

וֶאֱלִישָׁע הַנָּבִיא קָרָא לְאַחַד מִבְּנֵי הַנְּבִיאִים וַיֹּאמֶר לוֹ חֲגֹר מָתְנֶיךָ וְקַח פַּךְ הַשֶּׁמֶן הַזֶּה בְּיָדֶךָ וְלֵךְ רָמֹת גִּלְעָד׃

9:1   לְאַחַד

Seven times   ז֗   Mp

Com.: See **2 Sam 1:15**.

9:1   חֲגֹר

Four times   ד֗   Mp

2 Sam 20:8 (חָגוֹר); 2 Kgs 4:29; **9:1**; <u>**Ps 45:4**</u> (חֲגוֹר)

Com.: The Masorah notes the *four* occurrences of this lemma, *twice* written plene ו (2 Sam 20:8 and Ps 45:4), and *twice* written defective ו (2 Kgs 4:29 and here).

The heading of the Mp at Ps 45:4 reads *five times* to include the form at Prov 31:24 with a ו cj.

This lemma is featured in a Masoretic list of words that occur *five* times, *four* times without a ו cj. and *once* with a cj.; see Frensdorff, *Ochlah*, §17, and Díaz-Esteban, *Sefer Oklah we-Oklah*, §18.

9:1   וְלֵךְ

Eleven times   יא֗   Mp

1–5   Gen 22:2 (וְלֶךְ); **27:13**; <u>**Judg 18:19**</u>; <u>**1 Sam 16:1**</u>; <u>**29:7**</u>
6–10   **2 Sam 14:21**; 2 Kgs 6:3; 8:8; <u>**9:1**</u>; **Ezek 3:1**
11   Ezek 3:11

		Mm	וֹלֵךְ יא	וְלֵךְ *eleven times*
1–5	Gen 22:2	המריה		
	<Gen 27:13>			
	Judg 18:19	שים ידך על (פני) [פיך]		
	1 Sam 16:1	מתאבל		
	1 Sam 29:7	ועתה שוב		
6–10	2 Sam 14:21	השב את (הנע) [הנער]		
	2 Kgs 9:1	רמת גלעד		
	2 Kgs 8:8	אל (חזאל) [חזהאל]		
	2 Kgs 6:3	הואל נא		
	Ezek 3:11	בא אל		
11	Ezek 3:1	המגלה		

One (of them) is וְלֶךְ (Gen 22:2)   חד ולך

Com.: The Masorah notes the *eleven* occurrences of this lemma with the ו cj. pointed with a *šəwâ*, to distinguish them from its *five* occurrences with the ו cj. pointed with a *qameṣ* (וָלֵךְ).

The last reference in the Mm, that of וְלֵךְ of Gen 22:2, is a repetition of the same reference given at the beginning of the list, but here the lemma is pointed in the note with a *səḡôl*.

2 KINGS 9:2

וּבָאתָ שָׁמָּה וּרְאֵה־שָׁם יֵהוּא בֶן־יְהוֹשָׁפָט בֶּן־נִמְשִׁי וּבָאתָ וַהֲקֵמֹתוֹ מִתּוֹךְ אֶחָיו וְהֵבֵיאתָ אֹתוֹ חֶדֶר בְּחָדֶר׃

9:2   וּבָאתָ שָׁמָּה

Mp   י ראש פסוק   *Ten times* at the beginning of a verse

Com.: See **2 Kgs 6:14**.

9:2   וַהֲקֵמֹתוֹ

Mp   ל   *Unique*

9:2   וְהֵבֵיאתָ

Mp   ב מל   *Twice* plene

2 Kgs 9:2; Isa 43:23 (הֵבֵיאתָ)

Com.: The Masorah notes the *two* occurrences of this lemma written plene י, to distinguish them from its more numerous occurrences (15x) written defective י (הֵבֵאתָ/וְהֵבֵאתָ).

2 KINGS 9:3

וְלָקַחְתָּ פַךְ־הַשֶּׁמֶן וְיָצַקְתָּ עַל־רֹאשׁוֹ וְאָמַרְתָּ כֹּה־אָמַר יְהֹוָה מְשַׁחְתִּיךָ לְמֶלֶךְ אֶל־יִשְׂרָאֵל וּפָתַחְתָּ הַדֶּלֶת וְנַסְתָּה וְלֹא תְחַכֶּה׃

9:3   וְנַסְתָּה

Unique plene   ל מל   Mp

Com.: By noting that this lemma is *unique* written plene ה the Masorah is implying that this lemma occurs elsewhere written defective ה. But there is no other occurrence of this lemma written defective ה, so the note should properly have read *unique and plene* (ל ומל).

M^C reads here the same as M^L, but M^A correctly reads *unique*.

2 KINGS 9:4

וַיֵּלֶךְ הַנַּעַר הַנַּעַר הַנָּבִיא רָמֹת גִּלְעָד׃

9:4   הַנַּעַר הַנַּעַר

Unique   ל   Mp

Com.: This lemma is featured in a Masoretic list of words occurring together only *once*; see Frensdorff, *Ochlah*, §72.

2 KINGS 9:5

וַיָּבֹא וְהִנֵּה שָׂרֵי הַחַיִל יֹשְׁבִים וַיֹּאמֶר דָּבָר לִי אֵלֶיךָ הַשָּׂר וַיֹּאמֶר יֵהוּא אֶל־מִי מִכֻּלָּנוּ וַיֹּאמֶר אֵלֶיךָ הַשָּׂר׃

9:5   אֶל־מִי

Three times   ג   Mp

2 Kgs 9:5; Ezek 31:2; 31:18

Com.: The Masorah notes the *three* occurrences of this lemma with the separable prep. אֶל, to distinguish them from its more numerous occurrences (17x) with the inseparable prep. לְ (לְמִי), and from its *four* occurrences with a ו cj. (וְאֶל־מִי); see **1 Sam 6:20**.

9:5   מִכֻּלָּנוּ

Unique   ל   Mp

> **2 KINGS 9:6**
>
> וַיָּקָם וַיָּבֹא הַבַּיְתָה וַיִּצֹק הַשֶּׁמֶן אֶל־רֹאשׁוֹ וַיֹּאמֶר לוֹ כֹּה־אָמַר יְהוָה אֱלֹהֵי יִשְׂרָאֵל מְשַׁחְתִּיךָ לְמֶלֶךְ אֶל־עַם יְהוָה אֶל־יִשְׂרָאֵל׃

9:6   הַבַּיְתָה

Nineteen times   יֹט   Mp

Com.: See **Josh 2:18**.

9:6   רֹאשׁוֹ

Thirty-two times   לֹב   Mp

Com.: See **Judg 16:19**.

9:6   כֹּה־אָמַר יְהוָה אֱלֹהֵי יִשְׂרָאֵל

Twenty-four times   כֹד   Mp

Com.: See **1 Sam 10:18**.

In some of the Mp references there is only *one* circellus between *two* of the words in the phrase, e.g., at 1 Kgs 14:7 and 2 Kgs 22:18 just on כֹּה־אָמַר; and here and Isa 37:21 just on אֱלֹהֵי יִשְׂרָאֵל.

> **2 KINGS 9:7**
>
> וְהִכִּיתָה אֶת־בֵּית אַחְאָב אֲדֹנֶיךָ וְנִקַּמְתִּי דְּמֵי ׀ עֲבָדַי הַנְּבִיאִים וּדְמֵי כָּל־עַבְדֵי יְהוָה מִיַּד אִיזָבֶל׃

9:7   וְהִכִּיתָה

Three times plene   גֹ מל   Mp

Com.: See **1 Sam 15:3**.

9:7   וְנִקַּמְתִּי

Three times   גֹ   Mp

1 Sam 14:24; **2 Kgs 9:7**; Jer 51:36

| וְנִקַמְתִּי | *three times* | וְנִקַמְתִּי ג׳ | Mm |

1 Sam 14:24 — ארור האיש אשר יאכל
2 Kgs 9:7 — עבדי הנביאים
Jer 51:36 — את נקמתך

Com.: The Masorah notes the *three* occurrences of this lemma with a ו cj., to distinguish them from its *sole* occurrence without a cj. at Judg 15:7.

---

2 KINGS 9:8

וְאָבַד כָּל־בֵּית אַחְאָב וְהִכְרַתִּי לְאַחְאָב מַשְׁתִּין בְּקִיר וְעָצוּר וְעָזוּב בְּיִשְׂרָאֵל׃

9:8 וְעָצוּר וְעָזוּב

| *Twice* | ב׳ | Mp |

Com.: See **1 Kgs 21:21**.

---

2 KINGS 9:10

וְאֶת־אִיזֶבֶל יֹאכְלוּ הַכְּלָבִים בְּחֵלֶק יִזְרְעֶאל וְאֵין קֹבֵר וַיִּפְתַּח הַדֶּלֶת וַיָּנֹס׃

9:10 וְאֶת־אִיזֶבֶל

| *Unique* | ל׳ | Mp |

Com.: The Masorah notes the *sole* occurrence of this lemma with a ו cj., to distinguish it from its *two* occurrences without a cj. at 1 Kgs 16:31 and 21:23.

9:10 קֹבֵר

| *Twice, once* defective *and once* plene | ב׳ חד חס׳ וחד מל׳ | Mp |

2 Kgs 9:10; **Ps 79:3** (קוֹבֵר)

Com.: The Masorah notes the *two* occurrences of this lemma, *one* written plene ו (Ps 79:3), and *one* written defective ו (here).

> **2 KINGS 9:11**
> וְיֵה֗וּא יָצָא֙ אֶל־עַבְדֵ֣י אֲדֹנָ֔יו וַיֹּ֤אמֶר לוֹ֙ הֲשָׁל֔וֹם מַדּ֛וּעַ בָּֽא־הַמְשֻׁגָּ֥ע הַזֶּ֖ה אֵלֶ֑יךָ וַיֹּ֣אמֶר אֲלֵיהֶ֔ם אַתֶּ֛ם יְדַעְתֶּ֥ם אֶת־הָאִ֖ישׁ וְאֶת־שִׂיחֽוֹ׃

9:11   הַמְשֻׁגָּע

Unique   לׄ   Mp

Com.: The Masorah notes the *sole* occurrence of this lemma with the def. article, to distinguish it from its *three* occurrences without this def. article (מְשֻׁגָּע).

9:11   אַתֶּם יְדַעְתֶּם

אַתֶּם יְדַעְתֶּם *twice*   אתם ידעתם בׄ   Mm

Gen 44:27   כי שנים ילדה לי
2 Kgs 9:11   את האיש ואת

Com.: The Masorah notes the *two* occurrences of this lemma, to distinguish them from its *sole* occurrence with a ו cj. (וְאַתֶּם יְדַעְתֶּם) in Exod 23:9.

The problem with this note is that there is another occurrence of this lemma at Deut 29:15.

A possible origin of this confusion is suggested by Dotan/Reich (*Masora Thesaurus, ad loc.*). They point out that in M^S5 at Deut 29:15 there is a Mp note, that reads *twice*, and that the *twice* there may have stood for *twice* (in the Torah, e.g., Gen 44:27 and Deut 29:15) or *twice* (with these accents, that is, *mûnaḥ zaqep̄*, since only the Genesis and Deuteronomy occurrences have *mûnaḥ zaqep̄* accents, whereas the occurrence here at 1 Kgs 9:11 has *ṭəḇîr* and *mêrəḵā*).

Thus, as posited by Dotan/Reich, the original note before getting confused, might have meant to indicate: *twice* (1) the *two* Torah references; (2) 2 Kgs 9:11.

Neither M^C nor M^A has a note on this lemma here.

9:11   שִׂיחוֹ

Twice   בׄ   Mp

2 Kgs 9:11; Ps 102:1

Com.: At Ps 102:1 the Mp contains the catchwords אתם ידעתם (אַתֶּם יְדַעְתֶּם) referring the reader back to this verse.

2 KINGS 9:14

וַיִּתְקַשֵּׁ֣ר יֵה֔וּא בֶּן־יְהוֹשָׁפָ֖ט בֶּן־נִמְשִׁ֑י אֶל־יוֹרָ֑ם וְיוֹרָם֩ הָיָ֨ה שֹׁמֵ֜ר בְּרָמֹ֣ת גִּלְעָ֗ד ה֚וּא וְכָל־יִשְׂרָאֵ֔ל מִפְּנֵ֖י חֲזָאֵ֥ל מֶֽלֶךְ־אֲרָֽם׃

9:14 יוֹרָם

Ten times   י̇   Mp

Com.: See **2 Sam 8:10**.

2 KINGS 9:15

וַיָּשָׁב֩ יְהוֹרָ֨ם הַמֶּ֜לֶךְ לְהִתְרַפֵּ֣א בְיִזְרְעֶ֗אל מִן־הַמַּכִּים֙ אֲשֶׁ֣ר יַכֻּ֣הוּ אֲרַמִּ֔ים בְּהִלָּ֣חֲמ֔וֹ אֶת־חֲזָאֵ֖ל מֶ֣לֶךְ אֲרָ֑ם וַיֹּ֣אמֶר יֵה֗וּא אִם־יֵ֣שׁ נַפְשְׁכֶ֔ם אַל־יֵצֵ֤א פָלִיט֙ מִן־הָעִ֔יר לָלֶ֖כֶת לְגִ֥יד בְּיִזְרְעֶֽאל׃

9:15 יְהוֹרָם

Sixteen times in the Prophets   יו̇ בנביא   Mp

1–5 1 Kgs 22:51; 2 Kgs 1:17ᵃ; **1:17ᵇ** (לִיהוֹרָם); 3:1 (וִיהוֹרָם); 3:6
6–10 2 Kgs 8:16; **8:25**; 8:29; **9:15**; 9:17
11–15 2 Kgs 9:21ᵃ; **9:21ᵇ**; 9:22; 9:23; 9:24
16 2 Kgs 12:19 (וִיהוֹרָם)

Com.: The Masorah notes the *sixteen* occurrences of יְהוֹרָם (Joram) in various forms in the Prophets which are spelled with a ה, to distinguish them from its *sixteen* occurrences in various forms in the Prophets written without the ה (e.g., יוֹרָם).

This distinction is implied in the various additional notations in the Mm at 2 Kgs 8:25 where the occurrences of יְהוֹרָם are distinguished in the parallel passages from יוֹרָם.

The Mp heading at 2 Kgs 1:17ᵇ (לִיהוֹרָם) reads *twice* to enumerate the *two* occurrences of לִיהוֹרָם, there and at 2 Chr 21:3.

The Mp heading at 2 Kgs 8:25 reads *three times* enumerating the *three* occurrences of this lemma in that section (2 Kgs 8:16, 25, and 29).

9:15 אַל־יֵצֵא

Three times   ג̇   Mp

Exod 16:29; **2 Kgs 9:15**; 10:25

Mm	אל (יוצא) [יצא] ג׳ וסימנהון	אַל־יֵצֵא *three times*, and their references

אל יצא איש ממקמו ביום	Exod 16:29
אל יצא פליט	2 Kgs 9:15
איש אל יצא	2 Kgs 10:25

Com.: The Masorah notes the *three* occurrences of this lemma with אַל, to distinguish them from its *five* occurrences with לֹא.

9:15   לַגִּיד

Mp   לְהַגִּיד קׄ   Read לְהַגִּיד

Mm	ג׳ חסירין ה׳ (בסוף) [במצע׳] תיבותה	*Three times* lacking a ה in the middle of a word

ויאהבהו	1 Sam 18:1
להגיד	2 Kgs 9:15
והכרמל	Isa 32:15

וסימנהון	And their references
רחמת	1 Sam 18:1 (= וַיֶּאֱהָבֵהוּ)
למתנייה	2 Kgs 9:15 (= לְהַגִּיד)
בכרמלה	Isa 32:15 (= וְהַכַּרְמֶל)

Com.: The *kətîb* (לגיד) and *qərê* (לְהַגִּיד) represent examples where the letter ה is assimilated; see Gordis, *The Biblical Text*, 116.

The Masorah notes the *three* occurrences of where a ה is lacking in the middle of a word; see also Frensdorff, *Ochlah*, §109, and Díaz-Esteban, *Sefer Oklah we-Oklah*, §92.

The catchwords in the Mm are given both in Hebrew and Aramaic. The Aramaic catchwords are in the form of a mnemonic "she loved to tell it on the Carmel"; see Marcus, *Scribal Wit*, 83.

2 KINGS 9:16

וַיִּרְכַּב יֵהוּא וַיֵּלֶךְ יִזְרְעֶאלָה כִּי יוֹרָם שֹׁכֵב שָׁמָּה וַאֲחַזְיָה מֶלֶךְ יְהוּדָה יָרַד לִרְאוֹת אֶת־יוֹרָם:

9:16   יִזְרְעֶאלָה

Seven times   זֹ   Mp

Com.: See **Josh 19:18**.

9:16   יוֹרָם¹

Ten times   יֹ   Mp

Com.: See **2 Sam 8:10**.

9:16   שֹׁכֵב שָׁמָּה

Three times   גֹ   Mp

Com.: See **Josh 2:1**.

9:16   וַאֲחַזְיָה

Three times   גֹ   Mp

1–5   **2 Kgs 1:2**; **9:16**; 9:23ᵇ; 9:27; 9:29
6–7   **2 Kgs 11:2ᵇ**; **2 Chr 20:35**

וַאֲחַזְיָה *seven times*   ואחזיה ז   Mm

1–5	2 Kgs 1:2	בעד השבכה
	2 Kgs 9:27	וינס דרך בית הגן
	2 Chr 20:35	ואחריכן אתחבר
	2 Kgs 9:16	וירכב יהוא וילך
	2 Kgs 9:29	ובשנת אחת עשרה
6–7	2 Kgs 11:2ᵇ	ותקח (יהושעת) [יהושבע]
	the *second* (form of אֲחַזְיָה) *in the verse*	תינינה דפסוק
	2 Kgs 9:23ᵇ	ויהפך תינינה דפסוק
	the *second* (form of אֲחַזְיָה) *in the verse*	

Com.: The heading of the Mp here of *three* is incorrect as there are *seven* occurrences of this lemma with, and without a ו cj. All the other highlighted Mp headings have *seven* as does M[C] and M[A] here.

It is possible that the enumeration of *three* orginally was to indicate the parallel form with a ו cj. וַאֲחַזְיָהוּ, which does occur *three times* (2 Kgs 8:29, 9:21, and 12:19).

The Masorah notes the *seven* occurrences of this lemma in various forms ending in ה, to distinguish them from its more numerous occurrences (30x) in various forms ending in הו (e.g., אֲחַזְיָהוּ).

This distinction is implied in the additions in the Mm of the notation *second* (form of אֲחַזְיָה) *in the verse* to the 2 Kgs 11:2[b] and 9:23[b] references because the *first form* of Ahaziah's name in both verses is written אֲחַזְיָהוּ.

9:16   יוֹרָם֨²

Ten times   ׳   Mp

Com.: See **2 Sam 8:10**.

---

2 KINGS 9:17

וְהַצֹּפֶה֩ עֹמֵ֨ד עַל־הַמִּגְדָּ֜ל בְּיִזְרְעֶ֗אל וַיַּ֞רְא אֶת־שִׁפְעַ֤ת יֵהוּא֙ בְּבֹא֔וֹ וַיֹּ֕אמֶר שִׁפְעַ֥ת אֲנִ֖י רֹאֶ֑ה וַיֹּ֣אמֶר יְהוֹרָ֗ם קַ֥ח רַכָּ֛ב וּשְׁלַ֥ח לִקְרָאתָ֖ם וְיֹאמַ֥ר הֲשָׁלֽוֹם׃

9:17   וְיֹאמַר

Six times   ו   Mp

1–5   **2 Kgs 9:17;** Isa 44:16; 44:17; Isa 58:9; **Hab 2:6**
6   **Ps 58:12**

Com.: The Masorah notes the *six* occurrences of this lemma with a ו cj., to distinguish them from its more numerous occurrences (100+) with a ו consec. (וַיֹּאמֶר); see Ognibeni, *'Oklah*, §9E.

2 KINGS 9:18

וַיֵּ֣לֶךְ רֹכֵ֣ב הַסּוּס֮ לִקְרָאתוֹ֒ וַיֹּ֗אמֶר כֹּֽה־אָמַ֤ר הַמֶּ֙לֶךְ֙ הֲשָׁל֔וֹם וַיֹּ֧אמֶר יֵה֛וּא מַה־לְּךָ֥ וּלְשָׁל֖וֹם סֹ֣ב אֶל־אַחֲרָ֑י וַיַּגֵּ֨ד הַצֹּפֶ֜ה לֵאמֹ֗ר בָּֽא־הַמַּלְאָ֥ךְ עַד־הֵ֖ם וְלֹא־שָֽׁב׃

9:18   וּלְשָׁל֖וֹם

Three times   ג̇   Mp

2 Kgs 9:18; 9:19; Isa 9:6

וּלְשָׁלוֹם *three times* ולשלום ג   Mm

2 Kgs 9:18	מה לך ולשלום סב אל אחרי
And its companion (2 Kgs 9:19)	(וחבי) [וחבירו]
Isa 9:6	למרבה המשרה

Com.: The Masorah notes the *three* occurrences of this lemma in the absol., to distinguish them from its *two* occurrences in the cstr. (וּלְשָׁלוֹם) at 2 Sam 11:7; see Ognibeni, *'Oklah*, §21D.

9:18   סֹ֣ב

Six times   ו̇   Mp

1–5   **Deut 2:3**; 1 Sam 22:18; 2 Sam 18:30; **2 Kgs 9:18**; 9:19
6   Cant 2:17

סֹב *six times* defective   סב ו חס   Mm

1–5	Deut 2:3	ההר הזה
	1 Sam 22:18	לדויג
	2 Sam 18:30	התיצב
	2 Kgs 9:18	אל אחרי
	And its companion (2 Kgs 9:19)	וחבירו
6	Cant 2:17	דמה

Com.: The Mp notes the *six* occurrences of this lemma but the Mm, which reads *six times defective* (ו), is inexact since there are no occurrences of this lemma written plene ו. This heading more precisely should have read, as the Mp heading at 2 Sam 18:30 and the Mm heading at <u>Deut 2:3</u> read, *six times and defective* (ו).

M^A reads here, with the Mp of M^L, *six times*, and M^C has no note.

9:18   וְלֹא־שָׁב

Five times   הֹ   Mp

1–5   **1 Kgs 13:10**; <u>**2 Kgs 9:18**</u>; <u>**9:20**</u>; <u>**Ezek 3:19**</u>; <u>**33:9**</u>

וְלֹא־שָׁב *five times*, and their references   ולא שב הֹ וסימנהון   Mm

1–5   <u>2 Kgs 9:18</u>   בא המלאך
       2 Kgs 9:20   בא עד אליהם
       <u>Ezek 3:19</u>   מרשעו
       1 Kgs 13:10   בדרך
       <u>Ezek 33:9</u>   ואתה כי הזהרת

Com.: The Masorah notes the *five* occurrences of this lemma with a ו cj., to distinguish them from its more numerous occurrences (9x) without a cj.

---

2 KINGS 9:19

וַיִּשְׁלַח רֹכֵב סוּס שֵׁנִי וַיָּבֹא אֲלֵהֶם וַיֹּאמֶר כֹּה־אָמַר הַמֶּלֶךְ שָׁלוֹם וַיֹּאמֶר יֵהוּא מַה־לְּךָ וּלְשָׁלוֹם סֹב אֶל־אַחֲרָי׃

9:19   אֲלֵהֶם

Thirteen times defective in the book   יגׄ חסׄ בסיפׄ   Mp

Com.: See <u>**1 Kgs 12:16**</u>.

2 KINGS 9:20

וַיַּגֵּ֤ד הַצֹּפֶה֙ לֵאמֹ֔ר בָּ֥א עַד־אֲלֵיהֶ֖ם וְלֹֽא־שָׁ֑ב וְהַמִּנְהָ֗ג כְּמִנְהַג֙ יֵה֣וּא בֶן־נִמְשִׁ֔י כִּ֥י בְשִׁגָּע֖וֹן יִנְהָֽג׃

9:20   וְלֹֽא־שָׁ֑ב

Five times   הׄ   Mp

Com.: See directly above at **2 Kgs 9:18**.

9:20   בְשִׁגָּע֖וֹן

Twice   בׄ   Mp

Deut 28:28; 2 Kgs 9:20

Com.: At Deut 28:28 the Mp heading contains a catchword ינהג (יִנְהָג) referring the reader back to this verse.

2 KINGS 9:21

וַיֹּ֤אמֶר יְהוֹרָם֙ אֱסֹ֔ר וַיֶּאְסֹ֖ר רִכְבּ֑וֹ וַיֵּצֵ֣א יְהוֹרָ֣ם מֶֽלֶךְ־יִ֠שְׂרָאֵל וַאֲחַזְיָ֨הוּ מֶֽלֶךְ־יְהוּדָ֜ה אִ֣ישׁ בְּרִכְבּ֗וֹ וַיֵּֽצְאוּ֙ לִקְרַ֣את יֵה֔וּא וַיִּמְצָאֻ֔הוּ בְּחֶלְקַ֖ת נָב֥וֹת הַיִּזְרְעֵאלִֽי׃

9:21   יְהוֹרָם֙[2]

Sixteen times in the Prophets   יו֛ בנב   Mp

Com.: See directly above at **2 Kgs 9:15**.

9:21   וַיִּמְצָאֻ֔הוּ

Three times   גׄ   Mp

Com.: See **1 Sam 31:3**.

2 KINGS 9:22

וַיְהִ֗י כִּרְא֤וֹת יְהוֹרָם֙ אֶת־יֵה֔וּא וַיֹּ֖אמֶר הֲשָׁל֣וֹם יֵה֑וּא וַיֹּ֙אמֶר֙ מָ֣ה הַשָּׁל֔וֹם עַד־זְנוּנֵ֞י אִיזֶ֧בֶל אִמְּךָ֛ וּכְשָׁפֶ֖יהָ הָרַבִּֽים׃

9:22   יְהוֹרָם

Mp   יוֹ בנב   *Sixteen times* in the Prophets

Com.: See above at **2 Kgs 9:15**.

9:22   הֲשָׁלוֹם

Mp   ד   *Four times*

2 Kgs 9:22; **Jer 25:37**; **33:9**; **Zech 8:12**

Mm   השלום ד   *four times* הַשָּׁלוֹם

2 Kgs 9:22   ויאמר מה השלום
Zech 8:12   כי זרע השלום הגפן
Jer 25:37   ונדמו נאות השלום
Jer 33:9   ופחדו ורגזו (אל) [על]

Com.: The Masorah notes the *four* occurrences of this lemma with the def. article ה, to distinguish them from its more numerous occurrences (14x) with the interrog. הֲ (הֲשָׁלוֹם), *one* of which is in this verse; see Ognibeni, *'Oklah*, §21C.

In M^L the circellus has mistakenly been placed on the interrog. הֲשָׁלוֹם that occurs early in the verse and directly above the correct lemma in the ms. but, as indicated in the Mm, it belongs on this lemma.

2 KINGS 9:23

וַיַּהֲפֹ֧ךְ יְהוֹרָ֛ם יָדָ֖יו וַיָּנֹ֑ס וַיֹּ֥אמֶר אֶל־אֲחַזְיָ֖הוּ מִרְמָ֥ה אֲחַזְיָֽה׃

9:23   אֲחַזְיָה

Mp   ז   *Seven times*

Com.: See directly above at **2 Kgs 9:16**.

2 Kings 9:25

וַיֹּאמֶר אֶל־בִּדְקַר שָׁלִשֹׁה שָׂא הַשְׁלִכֵהוּ בְּחֶלְקַת שְׂדֵה נָבוֹת הַיִּזְרְעֵאלִי כִּי־זְכֹר אֲנִי וָאַתָּה אֵת רֹכְבִים צְמָדִים אַחֲרֵי אַחְאָב אָבִיו וַיהוָה נָשָׂא עָלָיו אֶת־הַמַּשָּׂא הַזֶּה:

9:25   בִּדְקַר

Unique   לׄ   Mp

9:25   שָׁלִשֹׁה

Read (שָׁלִשׁוֹ)   שׁו ק   Mp¹

Twice   בׄ   Mp²

2 Kgs 9:25; **15:25** (שָׁלִישׁוֹ)

Com.: The *kəṯîḇ* (שלשה) contains the older masc. sg. ending *ḥolem* ה whereas the *qərê* (שָׁלִשׁוֹ) contains the later masc. sg. sfx. in ו; see Gordis, *The Biblical Text*, 93.

In the second Mp the Masorah notes the *two* occurrences of this lemma, *one* written plene י (2 Kgs 15:25), and *one* written defective י (here).

M^C, as M^L, has a *kəṯîḇ/qərê* here, but M^A reads *twice, one written* שה *and once written* שו.

In M^L there are two Mp notes but only one circellus.

9:25   וָאַתָּה

Three times   גׄ   Mp

Gen 31:44 (וְאַתָּה); **1 Sam 20:23** (וָאַתָּה); **2 Kgs 9:25**

וָאַתָּה *three times*   ואתה ג   Mm

Gen 31:44   לכה נכרתה ברית
1 Sam 20:23   והדבר אשר דברנו
2 Kgs 9:25   כי זכר אני ואתה

Com.: The Masorah notes the *three* occurrences of this lemma, which has a ו cj. pointed with a *qames* before a tone syllable. *Two* of these occurrences are with a *qames* under the א (Gen 31:44 and 1 Sam 20:23), and *one* is with a *pataḥ* (here).

The heading to the Mm at Gen 31:44 reads *three times, twice with qames and once with pataḥ*.

---

2 KINGS 9:26

אִם־לֹא אֶת־דְּמֵי נָבוֹת וְאֶת־דְּמֵי בָנָיו רָאִיתִי אֶמֶשׁ נְאֻם־יְהוָה וְשִׁלַּמְתִּי לְךָ בַּחֶלְקָה הַזֹּאת נְאֻם־יְהוָה וְעַתָּה שָׂא הַשְׁלִכֵהוּ בַּחֶלְקָה כִּדְבַר יְהוָה:

9:26   אִם־לֹא

Eight times at the beginning of a verse   ח׳ ראש פסוק   Mp

1–5   Gen 24:38; Exod 22:7; **Deut 28:58; 2 Kgs 9:26; Mal 2:2**
6–8   Pss 7:13; **131:2;** Cant 1:8

Com.: The Masorah notes the *eight* occurrences of this lemma at the beginning of a verse without a ו cj., to distinguish it from its more numerous occurrences (27x) at the beginning of a verse with a cj. (וְאִם־לֹא); see Ognibeni, *'Oklah*, §90B.

This enumeration does not include the *six* occurrences of this lemma in the book of Job.

The Mp heading at Mal 2:2 reads *eight times at the beginning of a verse and similarly all Job apart from two* (וְאִם־לֹא). A similar formulation occurs in the Mm at Mal 2:2 and Ps 131:2.

9:26   וְאֶת־דְּמֵי

וְאֶת־דְּמֵי *twice*   ואת דמי ב׳   Mm

2 Kgs 9:26   אם לא את דמי נבות
Isa 4:4   ירושלם ידיח

Com.: The Masorah notes the *two* occurrences of this lemma with a ו cj., to distinguish them from its *three* occurrences without a cj., *one* of which is in the same verse.

2 KINGS 9:27

וַאֲחַזְיָה מֶלֶךְ־יְהוּדָה רָאָה וַיָּנָס דֶּרֶךְ בֵּית הַגָּן וַיִּרְדֹּף אַחֲרָיו יֵהוּא וַיֹּאמֶר גַּם־אֹתוֹ הַכֻּהוּ אֶל־הַמֶּרְכָּבָה בְּמַעֲלֵה־גוּר אֲשֶׁר אֶת־יִבְלְעָם וַיָּנָס מְגִדּוֹ וַיָּמָת שָׁם:

9:27   וַאֲחַזְיָה

Seven times   ז̇   Mp

Com.: See directly above at **2 Kgs 9:16**.

9:27   הַכֻּהוּ

Five times defective   ה̇ חס̇   Mp

1–5   **2 Kgs 9:27**; 12:22 (הַכֻּהוּ); 19:37 (הַכֻּהוּ); **Isa 37:38** (הַכֻּהוּ); 2 Chr 22:6 (הַכֻּהוּ)

הַכֻּהוּ *five times* defective, *and their references*   הכהו ה̇ חס̇ וסימנהון   Mm

1–5   2 Kgs 9:27   וְאַחְזִיָּה] (אחזיהו)
        2 Kgs 12:22   וַיּוֹזָבָד] (ויזכד)
        2 Kgs 19:37   בית נסרך
        And its companion (Isa 37:38)   וחבירו
        2 Chr 22:6   להתרפא ביזרעאל

Com.: The headings of both the Mp and Mm of *five times defective* (first ו) are inexact since there are no occurrences of this lemma written plene first ו. The headings more precisely should have read *five times and defective*.

Four of these forms (הַכֻּהוּ) are 3rd masc. pl. perfects with a sfx., and *one* (הַכֻּהוּ, here) is a pl. imper. with a sfx.

Neither M^C nor M^A has a note on this lemma here.

2 KINGS 9:28

וַיִּרְכִּ֧בוּ אֹת֣וֹ עֲבָדָ֗יו יְרוּשָׁלְָ֔מָה וַיִּקְבְּר֨וּ אֹת֧וֹ בִקְבֻרָת֛וֹ עִם־אֲבֹתָ֖יו בְּעִ֥יר דָּוִֽד: פ

9:28   יְרוּשָׁלְָמָה

Five times with qameṣ   ָה   Mp

1–5   1 Kgs 10:2; **2 Kgs 9:28**; Isa 36:2; Ezek 8:3; 2 Chr 32:9

יְרוּשָׁלְָמָה *five times*   ירושלמה ה̇   Mm

1–5   1 Kgs 10:2   (ותבוא) [ותבא]
      2 Kgs 9:28   וירכבו
      רַב שָׁקֵה *of Isaiah* (Isa 36:2)   רב שקה דישעיה
      Ezek 8:3   (בציית) [בציצת]
      2 Chr 32:9   (אחרי) [אחר] זה

Com.: The Masorah notes the *five* occurrences of this lemma with the locative ה, to distinguish them from its vastly more numerous occurrences (over 300) without this adverbial ה.

This distinction is implied in the Mm list in the additional note to the Isa 36:2 reference, where the addition *of Isaiah* to this reference distinguishes it from its parallel verse at 2 Kgs 18:17, where the lemma occurs as יְרוּשָׁלַ֔ם.

The heading of the Mm at Isa 36:2 reads *five times, four defective, and one plene* referring to the fact that only the form יְרוּשָׁלַ֫יְמָה at 2 Chr 32:9 is written with a medial י, whereas in the other forms only the vowel for this י is written between the ל and the מ.

The distinctiveness of the 2 Chr 32:9 form is also indicated in the Mp heading there which reads *unique plene*.

2 KINGS 9:29

וּבִשְׁנַת֙ אַחַ֣ת עֶשְׂרֵ֣ה שָׁנָ֔ה לְיוֹרָ֖ם בֶּן־אַחְאָ֑ב מָלַ֥ךְ אֲחַזְיָ֖ה עַל־יְהוּדָֽה:

9:29   וּבִשְׁנַת

Ten times   י̇   Mp

Com.: See **1 Kgs 15:1**.

2 KINGS

9:29   אֲחַזְיָה

Seven times   ז̇   Mp

Com.: See **2 Kgs 1:2**.

2 KINGS 9:30

וַיָּבוֹא יֵהוּא יִזְרְעֶאלָה וְאִיזֶבֶל שָׁמְעָה וַתָּשֶׂם בַּפּוּךְ עֵינֶיהָ וַתֵּיטֶב אֶת־רֹאשָׁהּ וַתַּשְׁקֵף בְּעַד הַחַלּוֹן׃

9:30   וַיָּבוֹא

Sixteen times plene   יו̇ מל   Mp

Com.: See **1 Sam 4:13**.

9:30   וַתֵּיטֶב

Unique   ל̇   Mp

Com.: The Masorah notes the *sole* occurrence of this lemma in the *hiphil*, to distinguish it from its *sole* occurrence in the *qal* (וַתִּיטַב) at Esth 2:9.

2 KINGS 9:32

וַיִּשָּׂא פָנָיו אֶל־הַחַלּוֹן וַיֹּאמֶר מִי אִתִּי מִי וַיַּשְׁקִיפוּ אֵלָיו שְׁנַיִם שְׁלֹשָׁה סָרִיסִים׃

9:32   מִי אִתִּי

Unique   ל̇   Mp

2 KINGS 9:33

וַיֹּאמֶר שִׁמְטֻהָ וַיִּשְׁמְטוּהָ וַיִּז מִדָּמָהּ אֶל־הַקִּיר וְאֶל־הַסּוּסִים וַיִּרְמְסֶנָּה׃

9:33   שִׁמְטֻהָ

Read   שִׁמְטוּהָ ק   שמטהו   Mp

Com.: The *kəṯîḇ* (שמטהו, *throw him down*), and the *qərê* (שִׁמְטוּהָ, *throw her down*) represent variant forms where the *qərê* is preferable to the *kəṯîḇ*; see Gordis, *The Biblical Text*, 152.

This form is featured in a Masoretic list of words where a ו written at the end of a word is not read; see Frensdorff, *Ochlah*, §120, and Díaz-Esteban, *Sefer Oklah we-Oklah*, §106.

9:33   וַיִּשְׁמְטוּהָ וַיִּז

Unique   לׄ   Mp

In M^L the circellus has been placed between these two words, but in M^C and M^A the circellus is only on וַיִּז. Placing the circellus solely on וַיִּז allows a contrast to be made between the *qal* (וַיִּז) and the *hiphil* (וַיַּז), which occurs *twice* at Lev 8:11 and 8:30; see the Mm at Lev 8:11 *sub* וַיַּז.

9:33   וַיִּז מִדָּמָהּ אֶל

Four times   דׄ   Mp

Lev 14:51 (וְהִזָּה אֶל); Num 19:4 (וְהִזָּה אֶל); **2 Kgs 9:33**ᵃ; 33ᵇ (וְאֶל)

Com.: The Masorah notes the *four* occurrences of various forms of *sprinkling towards* (הַזָּאָה אֶל), utilizing both the *qal* (וַיִּז) and the *hiphil* (וְהִזָּה).

The form וַיִּז in this verse serves double duty. It is counted *first* with אֶל הַקִּיר and *then* with the following וְאֶל הַסּוּסִים; see Ginsburg, 2, נ, §155, and Dotan/Reich, *Masora Thesaurus*, *ad loc*.

In M^L a circellus has been placed only between מִדָּמָהּ and אֶל, but the note applies to all three words.

9:33   מִדָּמָהּ

Seven times   זׄ   Mp

1–5   **Lev 4:30**; 6:20; **6:23**; **Num 19:4**ᵃ; **19:4**ᵇ
6   **2 Kgs 9:33**

Com.: The Mp heading here of *seven times* is incorrect since there are only *six* occurrences of this lemma. The error is no doubt a graphic one, a confusion of ז *seven* with ו *six*; see also Dotan/Reich, *Masora Thesaurus*, *ad loc*.

The Masorah notes the *six* occurrences of this lemma with the prep. מ, to distinguish them from its *seven* occurrences without this preposition.

The Mp headings at Lev 6:23, Num 19:4ᵃ, and Num 19:4ᵇ read correctly *five times in the Torah*.

The Mp heading at Lev 4:30 of *twice in the Torah* is incorrect, but the heading of its Mm is correct and it lists the *five* Torah references.

Neither M^C nor M^A has a note on this lemma here.

2 KINGS 9:35

וַיֵּלְכוּ לְקָבְרָהּ וְלֹא־מָצְאוּ בָהּ כִּי אִם־הַגֻּלְגֹּלֶת וְהָרַגְלַיִם וְכַפּוֹת הַיָּדָיִם׃

9:35   וְהָרַגְלַיִם

Unique   ל   Mp

Com.: This lemma is featured in a Masoretic list of words that occur *once* with prefix ו and *once* with prefix זה; see Frensdorff, *Ochlah*, §9, and Díaz-Esteban, *Sefer Oklah we-Oklah*, §9.

9:35   וְכַפּוֹת

Three times   ג̇   Mp

2 Kgs 9:35; Dan 10:10; **2 Chr 24:14**

Com.: The Masorah notes the *three* occurrences of this lemma with a ו cj., to distinguish them from its more numerous occurrences (10x) without a cj.

2 KINGS 9:37

וְהָיְתָ֞ נִבְלַת אִיזֶבֶל כְּדֹמֶן עַל־פְּנֵי הַשָּׂדֶה בְּחֵלֶק יִזְרְעֶאל אֲשֶׁר לֹא־יֹאמְרוּ זֹאת אִיזָבֶל׃ פ

9:37   וְהָיְתָ֞

Read   וְהָיְתָה   והיתה ק   Mp¹

Three times with the accent (*geršayim*)   ג̇ בטע   Mp²

1 Sam 13:21; **2 Kgs 9:37**; Zeph 2:6

Com.: In the first Mp, the *kǝtîb* (והית) reads the fem. archaic form וְהָיְת and the *qǝrê* (וְהָיְתָה) reads the more usual fem. form; see Gordis, *The Biblical Text*, 105.

This lemma is featured in a Masoretic list of words in which a ה at the end of a word that is not written is read; see Frensdorff, *Ochlah*, §111, and Díaz-Esteban, *Sefer Oklah we-Oklah*, §93.

For the second Mp note of *three times with the accent* (*geršayim*), see **1 Sam 13:21**.

In M^L there are two Mp notes but only one circellus.

2 KINGS 10:1

וּלְאַחְאָ֡ב שִׁבְעִ֣ים בָּנִים֮ בְּשֹׁמְר֒וֹן֒ וַיִּכְתֹּב֩ יֵה֨וּא סְפָרִ֜ים וַיִּשְׁלַ֣ח שֹׁמְר֗וֹן אֶל־שָׂרֵ֤י יִזְרְעֶאל֙ הַזְּקֵנִ֔ים וְאֶל־הָאֹמְנִ֖ים אַחְאָ֥ב לֵאמֹֽר׃

10:1 וּלְאַחְאָב

Unique   ל   Mp

Com.: The Masorah notes the *sole* occurrence of this lemma with a ו cj., to distinguish it from its more numerous occurrences (8x) without a cj., *one* of which occurs in v. 17.

10:1 הָאֹמְנִים

Unique   ל   Mp

Com.: The Masorah notes the *sole* occurrence of this lemma pointed as an active ptcpl. (*the guardians*), possibly to distinguish it from its *sole* occurrence pointed as a passive ptcpl. (הָאֱמֻנִים, *the supported ones*) at Lam 4:5.

2 KINGS 10:2

וְעַתָּ֗ה כְּבֹ֨א הַסֵּ֤פֶר הַזֶּה֙ אֲלֵיכֶ֔ם וְאִתְּכֶ֖ם בְּנֵ֣י אֲדֹנֵיכֶ֑ם וְאִתְּכֶם֙ הָרֶ֣כֶב וְהַסּוּסִ֔ים וְעִ֥יר מִבְצָ֖ר וְהַנָּֽשֶׁק׃

10:2 כְּבֹא

Six times defective   ו חס   Mp

Com.: See **1 Kgs 22:36**.

10:2 וְאִתְּכֶם¹

Three times   ג   Mp

Num 1:4; 2 Kgs 10:2ᵃ;10:2ᵇ

Com.: The Masorah notes the *three* occurrences of this lemma with a ו cj., to distinguish them from its more numerous occurrences (48x) without a cj.

10:2 וְאִתְּכֶם²

Three times   ג   Mp

Com.: See directly above.

10:2	וְהַנֶּ֫שֶׁק
Unique	ל Mp

Com.: The Masorah notes the *sole* occurrence of this lemma with a ו cj., to distinguish it from its *sole* occurrence without a cj. at Neh 3:19.

2 KINGS 10:3

וּרְאִיתֶ֞ם הַטּ֣וֹב וְהַיָּשָׁר֮ מִבְּנֵ֣י אֲדֹנֵיכֶם֒ וְשַׂמְתֶּ֗ם עַל־כִּסֵּ֣א אָבִ֔יו וְהִלָּחֲמ֖וּ עַל־בֵּ֥ית אֲדֹנֵיכֶֽם׃

10:3	וְהִלָּחֲמ֖וּ
Twice:	ב֗ Mp

2 Kgs 10:3; Neh 4:8

Com.: The Mp heading at Neh 4:8 contains the catchwords על בית אדניכם (עַל־בֵּ֥ית אֲדֹנֵיכֶֽם) referring the reader back to this verse.

2 KINGS 10:4

וַיִּֽרְא֖וּ מְאֹ֣ד מְאֹ֑ד וַיֹּ֣אמְר֔וּ הִנֵּה֙ שְׁנֵ֣י הַמְּלָכִ֔ים לֹ֥א עָמְד֖וּ לְפָנָ֑יו וְאֵ֖יךְ נַעֲמֹ֥ד אֲנָֽחְנוּ׃

10:4	וַיִּֽרְא֖וּ
Four times defective	ד֗ חס Mp

Com.: See **Josh 4:14**.

10: 4	מְאֹ֣ד מְאֹ֑ד
Six times:	ו֗ Mp

Com.: See **1 Kgs 7:47**.

> **2 KINGS 10:5**
>
> וַיִּשְׁלַ֣ח אֲשֶׁר־עַל־הַבַּ֡יִת וַאֲשֶׁ֣ר עַל־הָעִיר֩ וְהַזְּקֵנִ֨ים וְהָאֹמְנִ֜ים אֶל־יֵה֗וּא לֵאמֹר֙ עֲבָדֶ֣יךָ אֲנַ֔חְנוּ וְכֹ֥ל אֲשֶׁר־תֹּאמַ֛ר אֵלֵ֖ינוּ נַעֲשֶׂ֑ה לֹֽא־נַמְלִ֣יךְ אִ֔ישׁ הַטּ֥וֹב בְּעֵינֶ֖יךָ עֲשֵֽׂה׃

10:5   וַאֲשֶׁ֣ר עַל־הָעִיר֩

Mp   ז֗ בטע   *Sixteen times* with the accents (*galgal* and *pazer gadôl*)

Com.: See **Josh 19:51**.

In M[L] there is only one circellus on this phrase between וַאֲשֶׁר and עַל.

10:5   נַמְלִ֣יךְ

Mp   ל וחס   *Unique* and *defective**

Com.: By noting that this lemma is *unique* and written defective י, the Masorah is also implying (correctly) that this lemma does not occur elsewhere written *plene*.

*M[L], contrary to M (נַמְלִךְ), writes this lemma *plene* י (נַמְלִיךְ); see Breuer, *The Biblical Text*, 125. However, the Masoretic note *unique and defective* supports the text of M.

Both M[C] and M[A], in conformity with M, read here נַמְלִךְ. The Mp of M[A] reads *unique and defective*, and the Mp of M[C] reads the same but adds *and once* וַנַמְלִיךְ מֶלֶךְ, Isa 7:6).

This lemma is featured in a Masoretic list of words that occur *twice*, *once* with a ו cj. (Isa 7:6), and *once* without (here); see Frensdorff, *Ochlah*, §1, and Díaz-Esteban, *Sefer Oklah we-Oklah*, §1. In Frensdorff this form is written defective י, but in Díaz-Esteban it is written *plene* י.

> **2 KINGS 10:6**
>
> וַיִּכְתֹּ֨ב אֲלֵיהֶ֥ם סֵ֙פֶר֙ שֵׁנִ֣ית לֵאמֹ֔ר אִם־לִ֨י אַתֶּ֜ם וּלְקֹלִ֣י ׀ אַתֶּ֣ם שֹׁמְעִ֗ים קְחוּ֙ אֶת־רָאשֵׁי֙ אַנְשֵׁ֣י בְנֵֽי־אֲדֹנֵיכֶ֔ם וּבֹ֧אוּ אֵלַ֛י כָּעֵ֥ת מָחָ֖ר יִזְרְעֶ֑אלָה וּבְנֵ֨י הַמֶּ֜לֶךְ שִׁבְעִ֣ים אִ֗ישׁ אֶת־גְּדֹלֵ֥י הָעִ֖יר מְגַדְּלִ֥ים אוֹתָֽם׃

10:6   וּלְקֹלִ֣י

Mp   ל   *Unique*

Com.: The Masorah notes the *sole* occurrence of this lemma with a ו cj., to distinguish it from its *two* occurrences without a cj. (לְקוֹלִי) at Judg 2:20 and Ps 81:12.

10:6	אַנְשֵׁי בְנֵי־אֲדֹנֵיכֶם

Unique	ל	Mp

Com.: The Masorah notes the *sole* occurrence of בְנֵי־אֲדֹנֵיכֶם with אַנְשֵׁי, to distinguish it from its *sole* occurrence without אַנְשֵׁי in v. 2.

2 KINGS 10:7

וַיְהִי כְּבֹא הַסֵּפֶר אֲלֵיהֶם וַיִּקְחוּ אֶת־בְּנֵי הַמֶּלֶךְ וַיִּשְׁחֲטוּ שִׁבְעִים אִישׁ וַיָּשִׂימוּ אֶת־רָאשֵׁיהֶם בַּדּוּדִים וַיִּשְׁלְחוּ אֵלָיו יִזְרְעֶאלָה׃

10:7	כְּבֹא

Six times defective	ו חס	Mp

Com.: See **1 Kgs 22:36**.

In M^L the circellus has mistakenly been placed on גְּדֹלֵי of the preceding line in the ms. but it belongs on כְּבֹא since גְּדֹלֵי occurs only *once*.

10:7	יִזְרְעֶאלָה

Seven times:	ז	Mp

Com.: See **Josh 19:18**.

2 KINGS 10:8

וַיָּבֹא הַמַּלְאָךְ וַיַּגֶּד־לוֹ לֵאמֹר הֵבִיאוּ רָאשֵׁי בְנֵי־הַמֶּלֶךְ וַיֹּאמֶר שִׂימוּ אֹתָם שְׁנֵי צִבֻּרִים פֶּתַח הַשַּׁעַר עַד־הַבֹּקֶר׃

10:8	צִבֻּרִים

Unique	ל	Mp

> **2 KINGS 10:9**
> וַיְהִ֤י בַבֹּ֙קֶר֙ וַיֵּצֵ֣א וַֽיַּעֲמֹ֔ד וַיֹּ֙אמֶר֙ אֶל־כָּל־הָעָ֔ם צַדִּקִ֖ים אַתֶּ֑ם הִנֵּ֨ה אֲנִ֜י קָשַׁ֤רְתִּי עַל־אֲדֹנִי֙ וָאֶהְרְגֵ֔הוּ וּמִ֥י הִכָּ֖ה אֶת־כָּל־אֵֽלֶּה׃

10:9   צַדִּקִים

Seven times defective in the Prophets   ז חֹס בנביא   Mp

1–3   **1 Kgs 2:32; <u>2 Kgs 10:9</u>; <u>Hos 14:10</u>** (וְצַדִּקִים)

צַדִּקִים *three times* defective in the Prophets, and their references   צדקים ג חֹס בנביא וסימנהון   Mm

1–3   1 Kgs 2:32   והשיב יהוה את דמו
       <u>2 Kgs 10:9</u>   ויהי בבקר
       <u>Hos 14:10</u>   מי חכם ויבן אלה

Com.: The heading of the Mp here of *seven* is incorrect since there are only *three* occurrences of this lemma as correctly noted in the Mm and in all the headings highlighted above.

The Masorah notes the *three* occurrences of this lemma in the Prophets that are written defective first י, to distinguish them from its *two* occurrences in the Prophets that are written plene first י (צַדִּיקִים) at Isa 5:23 and 60:21.

M^A correctly reads here *three times* defective. M^C has a circellus but no note here; see Castro, *El codice*, 3:228.

10:9   וָאֶהְרְגֵהוּ

Twice: ב   Mp

2 Sam 4:10; 2 Kgs 10:9

2 Kings 10:10

דְּעוּ אֵפוֹא כִּי לֹא יִפֹּל מִדְּבַר יְהוָה אַרְצָה אֲשֶׁר־דִּבֶּר יְהוָה עַל־בֵּית אַחְאָב וַיהוָה עָשָׂה אֵת אֲשֶׁר דִּבֶּר בְּיַד עַבְדּוֹ אֵלִיָּהוּ:

10:10   מִדְּבַר

Three times   גׄ   Mp

Com.: See **2 Sam 19:44**.

2 Kings 10:11

וַיַּךְ יֵהוּא אֵת כָּל־הַנִּשְׁאָרִים לְבֵית־אַחְאָב בְּיִזְרְעֶאל וְכָל־גְּדֹלָיו וּמְיֻדָּעָיו וְכֹהֲנָיו עַד־בִּלְתִּי הִשְׁאִיר־לוֹ שָׂרִיד:

10:11   וַיַּךְ

The *first* (phrase)   קדמייה   Mm
2 Kgs 10:11   ויך יהוא את כל הנשארים לבית אחאב

The *second* (phrase)   תנינה
2 Kgs 10:17   ויבא שמרון ויך את כל הנשארים

Com.: The Masorah indicates the difference between parallel phrases in a similar context.

The *first* time that the phrase occurs in v. 11 it is וַיַּךְ יֵהוּא אֵת כָּל־הַנִּשְׁאָרִים לְבֵית־אַחְאָב, but the *second* time it occurs in v. 17 Jehu is not mentioned nor is *the house* (of Ahab) וַיַּךְ אֶת־כָּל־הַנִּשְׁאָרִים לְאַחְאָב.

10:11   גְּדֹלָיו

Twice   בׄ   Mp

2 Kgs 10:11; Jonah 3:7 (וּגְדֹלָיו)

Com.: The Masorah notes the *two* occurrences of this lemma, *one* with a ו cj. (Jonah 3:7), and *one* without a cj. (here).

10:11 וְכֹהֲנָיו

Unique   ל   Mp

1–2   **2 Kgs 10:11; 2 Chr 13:12**

וְכֹהֲנָיו   \<twice\>   \<בׄ\>   וכהניו   Mm

1–2   2 Kgs 10:11 ומידעיו וכהניו
         2 Chr 13:12 והנה עמנו בראש

Com.: The Mp heading here *of unique* is inexact since there are *two* occurrences of this lemma. The note more precisely should have read *unique in the book*.

The Masorah notes the *two* occurrences of this lemma with a ו cj., to distinguish them from its *four* occurrences written without a cj. (כֹּהֲנָיו), *one* of which is found in this same chapter in v. 19.

Both M^C and M^A correctly read here *twice*.

2 KINGS 10:12

וַיָּקָם וַיָּבֹא וַיֵּלֶךְ שֹׁמְרוֹן הוּא בֵּית־עֵקֶד הָרֹעִים בַּדָּרֶךְ׃

10:12   וַיָּבֹא וַיֵּלֶךְ

Unique   ל   Mp

Com.: The Masorah notes the *sole* occurrence of this lemma in this order, to distinguish it from its occurrence in the reverse order (וַיֵּלֶךְ וַיָּבֹא) at Judg 19:10.

10:12   עֵקֶד

Twice: בׄ   Mp

2 Kgs 10:12; 10:14

2 Kings 10:13

וְיֵה֗וּא מָצָא֙ אֶת־אֲחֵי֙ אֲחַזְיָ֣הוּ מֶֽלֶךְ־יְהוּדָ֔ה וַיֹּ֖אמֶר מִ֣י אַתֶּ֑ם וַיֹּאמְר֗וּ אֲחֵ֤י אֲחַזְיָ֙הוּ֙ אֲנַ֔חְנוּ וַנֵּ֛רֶד לִשְׁל֥וֹם בְּנֵֽי־הַמֶּ֖לֶךְ וּבְנֵ֥י הַגְּבִירָֽה׃

10:13   לִשְׁלוֹם

Four times: ד   Mp

2 Sam 11:7ᵃ; 11:7ᵇ (וְלִשְׁלוֹם); **2 Sam 11:7ᶜ** (וְלִשְׁלוֹם); **2 Kgs 10:13**

לִשְׁלוֹם *four times*, and their references   לשלום ד וסימנהון   Mm

2 Sam 11:7ᵃ   ויבא אוריה ‹אליו› וישאל דוד
Three times in the verse (11:7ᵇ; 11:7ᶜ)   שלשה בפסוקה
2 Kgs 10:13   ונרד לשלום

Com.: The Masorah notes the *four* occurrences of this lemma in the cstr., to distinguish them from its more numerous occurrences (29x) in the absol. (לִשְׁלוֹם/וְלִשְׁלוֹם).

The Mp headings at 2 Sam 11:7ᵇ and 11:7ᶜ both read *twice* indicating the *two* occurrences of this lemma with a ו cj. (וְלִשְׁלוֹם).

2 Kings 10:14

וַיֹּ֛אמֶר תִּפְשׂ֥וּם חַיִּ֖ים וַֽיִּתְפְּשׂ֣וּם חַיִּ֑ים וַיִּשְׁחָט֞וּם אֶל־בּ֣וֹר בֵּֽית־עֵ֗קֶד אַרְבָּעִ֤ים וּשְׁנַ֙יִם֙ אִ֔ישׁ וְלֹֽא־הִשְׁאִ֥יר אִ֖ישׁ מֵהֶֽם׃ ס

10:14   תִּפְשׂוּם

Three times: ג   Mp

Com.: See **1 Kgs 20:18ᵇ**.

10:14   וַיִּשְׁחָטוּם

Twice: ב   Mp

2 Kgs 10:14; 2 Chr 29:24

Com.: The Masorah notes the *two* occurrences of this lemma with the masc. pl. sfx., to distinguish them from its more numerous occurrences (11x) without a sfx. (וַיִּשְׁחָטוּ).

10:14   וַיִּשְׁחָטוּם אֶל

Mm   שחיטא אל ה׳   שְׁחִיטָא אֶל *five times*

1–5	2 Kgs 10:14	(וַיִּשְׁחָטוּם)	[עקר] אל בור בית (עקד)
	Judg 12:6	(וַיִּשְׁחָטוּהוּ)	אל מעברות הירדן
	Jer 41:7	(וַיִּשְׁחָטֵם)	וישחטם ישמעאל בן נתניה
	Ezek 40:39	(לִשְׁחוֹט)	לשחוט אליהם
	Ezek 40:41	(יִשְׁחֲטוּ)	שמונה שלחנות אליהם

Com.: The Masorah notes the *five* occurrences of forms of the verb שָׁחַט together with the prep. אֶל, to distinguish them from occurrences of forms of this verb with the prep. עַל, such as תִּשְׁחַט עַל (Exod 34:25) and וְשָׁחַט אֹתוֹ עַל (Lev 1:11).

10:14   וְלֹא־הִשְׁאִיר

Unique   ל   Mp

Com.: The Masorah notes the *sole* occurrence of this lemma with a ו cj., to distinguish it from its more numerous occurrences (8x) without a cj.

2 KINGS 10:15

וַיֵּלֶךְ מִשָּׁם וַיִּמְצָא אֶת־יְהוֹנָדָב בֶּן־רֵכָב לִקְרָאתוֹ וַיְבָרְכֵהוּ וַיֹּאמֶר אֵלָיו הֲיֵשׁ אֶת־לְבָבְךָ יָשָׁר כַּאֲשֶׁר לְבָבִי עִם־לְבָבֶךָ וַיֹּאמֶר יְהוֹנָדָב יֵשׁ וָיֵשׁ תְּנָה אֶת־יָדֶךָ וַיִּתֵּן יָדוֹ וַיַּעֲלֵהוּ אֵלָיו אֶל־הַמֶּרְכָּבָה׃

10:15   יֵשׁ וָיֵשׁ

Unique   ל   Mp

Com.: The second part of this lemma וָיֵשׁ is featured in a Masoretic list of words only occurring *once* that start with a ו; see Frensdorff, *Ochlah*, §.71.

10:15   אֶל־הַמֶּרְכָּבָה

Four times   ד   Mp

1–2   2 Kgs 9:27; **10:15**

Com.: The Mp heading of *four times* is incorrect since there are only *two* occurrences of this lemma.

The Masorah notes the *two* occurrences of הַמֶּרְכָּבָה with אֶל, to distinguish them from its *sole* occurrence with עַל in 1 Kgs 20:33.

In some printed editions this phrase here is found with the prep. עַל; it is even featured in *Ochla* in a list of phrases occurring only *once* with the prep. עַל; see Frensdorff, *Ochlah*, §76, and Díaz-Esteban, *Sefer Oklah we-Oklah*, §155.

Neither M^C nor M^A has a note on this lemma here.

---

2 KINGS 10:17

וַיָּבֹא שֹׁמְרוֹן וַיַּךְ אֶת־כָּל־הַנִּשְׁאָרִים לְאַחְאָב בְּשֹׁמְרוֹן עַד־הִשְׁמִדוֹ כִּדְבַר יְהוָה אֲשֶׁר דִּבֶּר אֶל־אֵלִיָּהוּ׃ פ

10:17   כִּדְבַר יְהוָה

Four times with the accents (*mûnaḥ* and *zaqep*)   ד בט׳   Mp

Com.: The Mp heading here of *four times with these accents* (*mûnaḥ* and *zaqep* in the book) seems to be incorrect since there are *five* occurrences of this lemma. M^C similarly reads here *four times with these accents in the book*. For a possible explanation of this difference, see **1 Kgs 15:29**.

M^A has no note here.

---

2 KINGS 10:18

וַיִּקְבֹּץ יֵהוּא אֶת־כָּל־הָעָם וַיֹּאמֶר אֲלֵהֶם אַחְאָב עָבַד אֶת־הַבַּעַל מְעָט יֵהוּא יַעַבְדֶנּוּ הַרְבֵּה׃

10:18   אֲלֵהֶם

Thirteen times defective in the book   יג׳ חס׳ בסיפ׳   Mp

Com.: See **1 Kgs 12:16**.

---

2 KINGS 10:19

וְעַתָּה כָל־נְבִיאֵי הַבַּעַל כָּל־עֹבְדָיו וְכָל־כֹּהֲנָיו קִרְאוּ אֵלַי אִישׁ אַל־יִפָּקֵד כִּי זֶבַח גָּדוֹל לִי לַבַּעַל כֹּל אֲשֶׁר־יִפָּקֵד לֹא יִחְיֶה וְיֵהוּא עָשָׂה בְעָקְבָּה לְמַעַן הַאֲבִיד אֶת־עֹבְדֵי הַבָּעַל׃

10:19   כֹּל

Four unusual verses   ד פסו׳ מיוח׳   Mp

Gen 8:19; **2 Kgs 10:19**; **Ezek 44:30**; **Dan 3:7**

| Mm | ד פסוקין דמיחד אית בהון כל כל וכל כל | *Four* unusual verses containing the sequence כָּל...כָּל...וְכָל...כָּל |

Gen 8:19   כל החיה כל הרמש
<u>2 Kgs 10:19</u>   ועתה כל נביאי הבעל
Ezek 44:30   וראשית כל בכורי
Dan 3:7   כל קבל דנה בה זמנא

Com.: This Masoretic note of *four* verses that contain the sequence כָּל...כָּל...וְכָל...כָּל is also found in the *Ochlah* lists; see Frensdorff, *Ochlah*, §311, and Jobin, *Concordance*, 121.

It is not clear why this particular sequence of *four* forms of כָּל, with and without a ו cj., is considered to be unusual. There does not seem to be anything that sets this sequence apart from other sequences containing *four* forms such as these, as listed in Frensdorff, *Ochlah*, §305 and §306, and Jobin, *Concordance*, 121.

M[A] reads *four verses containing the sequence* כָּל...כָּל...וְכָל...כָּל. (without the term *unusual*). M[C] has no note here.

In M[L] the circellus has been placed on וְעַתָּה because it is the first word in the verse.

10:19   יִחְיֶה

Eighteen times   יח   Mp

1–5   **Gen 17:18**; 31:32; **Exod 19:13**; Num 24:23; **Deut 8:3**[a]
6–10   Deut 8:3[b]; 2 Sam 1:10; **2 Kgs 10:19**; **Ezek 18:13**; 18:22
11–15   Ezek 33:19; **47:9; Hab 2:4**; Ps 89:49; **Prov 15:27**
16–18   Qoh 6:3; **11:8; Neh 2:3**

Com.: The Masorah notes the *eighteen* occurrences of this lemma written with a ח, to distinguish them from the more frequent occurrences (400+) of this form written with a ה; see Ognibeni, *'Oklah*, §18C.

This enumeration does not include the *nine* occurrences of this lemma when it is part of the phrase חָיֹה/חָיוֹ יִחְיֶה.

Most of the Mp headings, and all the Mm lists highlighted above, include the additional note after the numeral *eighteen* of *and similarly all* (occurrences of) חָיוֹ יִחְיֶה.

10:19   בְּעָקְבָּה

Unique   ל   Mp

2 KINGS 10:20

וַיֹּאמֶר יֵהוּא קַדְּשׁוּ עֲצָרָה לַבַּעַל וַיִּקְרָאוּ׃

10:20   וַיִּקְרָאוּ

Unique   ל̇   Mp

Com.: The Masorah notes the *sole* occurrence of this lemma with a *qameṣ* under the ר (pausal), to distinguish it from its more numerous occurrences (31x) with a *šəwâ* (וַיִּקְרְאוּ).

In M^L this lemma has no circellus.

2 KINGS 10:21

וַיִּשְׁלַח יֵהוּא בְּכָל־יִשְׂרָאֵל וַיָּבֹאוּ כָּל־עֹבְדֵי הַבַּעַל וְלֹא־נִשְׁאַר אִישׁ אֲשֶׁר לֹא־בָא וַיָּבֹאוּ בֵּית הַבַּעַל וַיִּמָּלֵא בֵית־הַבַּעַל פֶּה לָפֶה׃

10:21   וְלֹא־נִשְׁאַר

Four times   ד̇   Mp

Josh 8:17; **2 Kgs 10:21**; Dan 10:8; **2 Chr 21:17**

וְלֹא־נִשְׁאַר *four times*, and their references   ולא נשאר ד̇ וסימנהון   Mm

Josh 8:17   איש בעי ובית אל
2 Kgs 10:21   וישלח יהוא בכל
2 Chr 21:17   ויעלו ביהודה
Dan 10:8   ואני נשארתי לבדי

Com.: The Masorah notes the *four* occurrences of this lemma with a ו cj., to distinguish them from its *seven* occurrences without a cj.

10:21   וַיִּמָּלֵא

Six times   ו̇   Mp

Com.: See **1 Kgs 7:14**.

10:21	פֶּה לָפֶה
Twice	בׄ Mp

2 Kgs 10:21; 21:16

Com.: The Masorah notes the *two* occurrences of this phrase with the inseparable prep. ל, to distinguish it from its *sole* occurrence with the separable prep. אֶל (פֶּה אֶל פֶּה) at Num 12:8.

---

2 KINGS 10:22

וַיֹּאמֶר לַאֲשֶׁר עַל־הַמֶּלְתָּחָה הוֹצֵא לְבוּשׁ לְכֹל עֹבְדֵי הַבָּעַל וַיֹּצֵא לָהֶם הַמַּלְבּוּשׁ׃

10:22	הַמֶּלְתָּחָה
Unique	לׄ Mp

10:22	הוֹצֵא
Five times	הׄ Mp

Com.: See **Judg 6:30**.

10:22	וַיֹּצֵא
Thirteen times defective	יׄגׄ חס Mp

1–5	**Num 17:23**; 17:24; Judg 19:25; **2 Sam 10:16**; 13:18
6–10	2 Sam 22:20; **2 Kgs 10:22**; 15:20; 23:6; Jer 20:3
11–13	Jer 52:31; Job 12:22; 2 Chr 16:2

| וַיֹּצֵא *thirteen times* defective, and their references | ויצא יׄגׄ חסירין וסימנהון | Mm |

1–5	Num 17:23	פרח
	Num 17:24	(המטות) [המטת]
	Judg 19:25	בפילגשו
	2 Sam 10:16	הדדעזר
	2 Sam 13:18	משרתו

6–10	לְמֶרְחָב *of Samuel* (2 Sam 22:20)	למרחב דשמואל
	2 Kgs 15:20	מנחם
	2 Kgs 23:6	את האשרה
	2 Kgs 10:22	המלתחה
	Jer 20:3	פשחור
11–13	2 Chr 16:2	(מאצרת) [מאצרות]
	Job 12:22	מגלה
	Jer 52:31	נשא

Com.: The Masorah notes the *thirteen* occurrences of this lemma written defective ו, to distinguish them from its *twelve* occurrences written plene וֹ (וַיּוֹצֵא); see **Judg 6:19**.

In the Mm, the addition *of Samuel* to the catchword לְמֶרְחָב of 2 Sam 22:20 is to distinguish that reference from its parallel in Ps 18:20, where the lemma appears as וַיּוֹצִיאֵנִי.

M^L, contrary to M (וַיּוֹצֵא), has a *fourteenth* occurrence of this lemma since it writes the form at Jer 51:16 defective ו (וַיֹּצֵא); see Breuer, *The Biblical Text*, 196. However, virtually all the Mp headings and Mm notes highlighted above read *thirteen times*, thus supporting the enumeration inherent in the text of M.

The Mp heading at Job 12:22 reads *twenty-five* which includes the *thirteen* defective and *twelve* plene occurrences of this lemma.

2 KINGS 10:23

וַיָּבֹא יֵהוּא וִיהוֹנָדָב בֶּן־רֵכָב בֵּית הַבָּעַל וַיֹּאמֶר לְעֹבְדֵי הַבַּעַל חַפְּשׂוּ וּרְאוּ פֶּן־יֶשׁ־פֹּה עִמָּכֶם מֵעַבְדֵי יְהוָה כִּי אִם־עֹבְדֵי הַבַּעַל לְבַדָּם׃

| 10:23 | פֶּן־יֶשׁ־פֹּה | | |
| Unique | ל | Mp | |

Com.: The Masorah notes the *sole* occurrence of פֶּן־יֶשׁ with פֹּה, to distinguish it from its *two* occurrences without פֹּה at Deut 29:17ᵃ and 29:17ᵇ.

2 KINGS 10:24

וַיָּבֹאוּ לַעֲשׂוֹת זְבָחִים וְעֹלוֹת וְיֵהוּא שָׂם־לוֹ בַחוּץ שְׁמֹנִים אִישׁ וַיֹּאמֶר הָאִישׁ אֲשֶׁר־יִמָּלֵט מִן־הָאֲנָשִׁים אֲשֶׁר אֲנִי מֵבִיא עַל־יְדֵיכֶם נַפְשׁוֹ תַּחַת נַפְשׁוֹ׃

| 10:24 | זְבָחִים וְעֹלוֹת | | |
| Twice | ב֗ | Mp | |

Exod 10:25; 2 Kgs 10:24

Com.: The Mp heading at Exod 10:25 contains the catchwords וַיָּבֹאוּ וִיבאו לעשות (לַעֲשׂוֹת) referring the reader back to this verse.

10:24　וְיֵהוּא שָׁם

Unique　ל　Mp

10:24　יִמָּלֵט

Thirteen times　יג　Mp

Com.: See **1 Kgs 18:40**.

---

2 KINGS 10:25

וַיְהִי כְּכַלֹּתוֹ ׀ לַעֲשׂוֹת הָעֹלָה וַיֹּאמֶר יֵהוּא לָרָצִים וְלַשָּׁלִשִׁים בֹּאוּ הַכּוּם אִישׁ אַל־יֵצֵא וַיַּכּוּם לְפִי־חָרֶב וַיַּשְׁלִכוּ הָרָצִים וְהַשָּׁלִשִׁים וַיֵּלְכוּ עַד־עִיר בֵּית־הַבָּעַל׃

10:25　וַיְהִי

Nine times with the accent (*geršayim*) in the book　ט בטע בסיפׄר　Mp

Com.: See **1 Kgs 3:18**.

10:25　וַיַּכּוּם

Eleven times　יא　Mp

Com.: See **Josh 7:5**.

---

2 KINGS 10:26

וַיֹּצִאוּ אֶת־מַצְּבוֹת בֵּית־הַבַּעַל וַיִּשְׂרְפוּהָ׃

10:26　וַיֹּצִאוּ

Twelve times　יב　Mp

Com.: See **Josh 6:23**.

2 Kings 10:27

וַיִּתְּצ֕וּ אֵ֖ת מַצְּבַ֣ת הַבָּ֑עַל וַֽיִּתְּצוּ֙ אֶת־בֵּ֣ית הַבַּ֔עַל וַיְשִׂמֻ֥הוּ לְמֽוֹצָא֖וֹת עַד־הַיּֽוֹם׃

10:27   מַצְּבַת

Twice   בֿ   Mp

Com.: See **2 Kgs 3:2**.

10:27   לְמֽחֳרָאוֹת

Read למוצאות ק   למוצאות   Mp

Com.: The *katîb* (לְמחראות), and the *qərê* (לְמוצאות) both meaning *latrines*, are examples of *katîb/qərê* variations where the reader is enjoined to substitute the *katîb* because it was thought to be too coarse; see Gordis, *The Biblical Text*, 86.

2 Kings 10:29

רַ֚ק חֲטָאֵ֣י יָרָבְעָ֣ם בֶּן־נְבָ֗ט אֲשֶׁ֤ר הֶחֱטִיא֙ אֶת־יִשְׂרָאֵ֔ל לֹא־סָ֥ר יֵה֖וּא מֵאַֽחֲרֵיהֶ֑ם עֶגְלֵי֙ הַזָּהָ֔ב אֲשֶׁ֥ר בֵּֽית־אֵ֖ל וַאֲשֶׁ֥ר בְּדָֽן׃ ס

10:29   חֲטָאֵי יָרָבְעָם

Unique   ל   Mp

Com.: The Masorah notes the *sole* occurrence of יָרָבְעָם with חֲטָאֵי, to distinguish it from its more numerous occurrences (9x) with חַטֹּאות/חַטַּאת (e.g., חַטֹּאות יָרָבְעָם).

10:29   אֲשֶׁר בֵּית־אֵל

Unique   ל   Mp

1–2   **2 Kgs 2:3**; **10:29**

Com.: The Mp heading here of *unique* is incorrect since there are *two* occurrences of this lemma; see **2 Kgs 2:3**.

M^A correctly reads here *twice*, whereas M^C has no note.

In M^L and M^A the circellus has been placed only on the two words אֲשֶׁר בֵּית but, since this phrase occurs *nine* times, it is most likely that the note belongs with the three words אֲשֶׁר בֵּית־אֵל that only occur *twice*.

10:29 בְּדָן

Four times   דׄ   Mp

Com.: See **1 Sam 12:11**.

---

2 KINGS 10:30

וַיֹּאמֶר יְהוָה אֶל־יֵהוּא יַעַן אֲשֶׁר־הֱטִיבֹתָ לַעֲשׂוֹת הַיָּשָׁר בְּעֵינַי כְּכֹל אֲשֶׁר בִּלְבָבִי עָשִׂיתָ לְבֵית אַחְאָב בְּנֵי רְבִעִים יֵשְׁבוּ לְךָ עַל־כִּסֵּא יִשְׂרָאֵל:

10:30   הֱטִיבֹתָ

Three times   גׄ   Mp

1 Kgs 8:18; **2 Kgs 10:30**; **2 Chr 6:8** (הֱטִיבוֹתָ)

הֱטִיבֹתָ *three times, twice* defective and *once* plene   הטיבת גׄ בׄ חסׄ וא׳ מלׄ   Mm

1 Kgs 8:18   כי היה
And its companion (2 Chr 6:8)   וחבירו
2 Kgs 10:30   יהוא

Com.: The Masorah notes the *three* occurrences of this lemma written *twice* defective ו (1 Kgs 8:18 and here) and *once* plene ו (2 Chr 6:8).

The lengthy Mp heading at 2 Chr 6:8 reads *three times, in Chronicles* הטיבות *is written, in Kings* הטיבת *is written*.

10:30   בִּלְבָבִי

Three times   גׄ   Mp

1 Sam 2:35; **2 Kgs 10:30**; **Ps 13:3**

Com.: The Masorah notes the *three* occurrences of this lemma with the prep. ב, to distinguish them from its more numerous occurrences (21x) without this preposition.

In M^L the circellus has been placed on the phrase אֲשֶׁר בִּלְבָבִי which only occurs *once*.

10:30   רְבִעִים

Twice   בֿ   Mp

2 Kgs 10:30; **15:12** (רְבִיעִים)

Com.: The Masorah notes the *two* occurrences of this lemma, *one* written plene first י (2 Kgs 15:12), and *one* written defective first י (here).

The Mp and Mm headings at 2 Kgs 15:12 read *twice, once plene and once defective*.

---

2 KINGS 10:31

וְיֵהוּא לֹא שָׁמַר לָלֶכֶת בְּתוֹרַת־יְהוָה אֱלֹהֵי־יִשְׂרָאֵל בְּכָל־לְבָבוֹ לֹא סָר מֵעַל חַטֹּאות יָרָבְעָם אֲשֶׁר הֶחֱטִיא אֶת־יִשְׂרָאֵל׃

10:31   מֵעַל חַטֹּאות

Twice   בֿ   Mp

2 Kgs 10:31; 15:18

Com.: This lemma features in a Masoretic list showing how the phrase *from the sins* (of Jeroboam son of Nebat) is used in connection with various kings; see Frensdorff, *Ochlah*, §294, and Ognibeni, *'Oklah*, §128.

With Jehu (here) and Menahem (**2 Kgs 15:18**), it is מֵעַל חַטֹּאות.

With Joash (2 Kgs 13:11) and Jeroboam son of Joash (**2 Kgs 14:24**), it is מִכָּל חַטֹּאות.

With Jehoahaz (2 Kgs 13:6), Zechariah (2 Kgs 15:9), and Pekahiah (2 Kgs 15:24), it is מֵחַטֹּאות.

---

2 KINGS 10:32

בַּיָּמִים הָהֵם הֵחֵל יְהוָה לְקַצּוֹת בְּיִשְׂרָאֵל וַיַּכֵּם חֲזָאֵל בְּכָל־גְּבוּל יִשְׂרָאֵל׃

10:32   לְקַצּוֹת

Unique   ל   Mp

Com.: The Masorah notes the *sole* occurrence of this lemma pointed this way (*piel, to break off*), possibly to distinguish it from its occurrence pointed differently as לִקְצוֹת (*to the ends of*) at Job 28:24.

2 Kings 10:33

מִן־הַיַּרְדֵּן֙ מִזְרַ֣ח הַשֶּׁ֔מֶשׁ אֵ֚ת כָּל־אֶ֣רֶץ הַגִּלְעָ֔ד הַגָּדִ֥י וְהָרֻאוּבֵנִ֖י וְהַֽמְנַשִּׁ֑י מֵעֲרֹעֵר֙ אֲשֶׁ֣ר עַל־נַ֣חַל אַרְנֹ֔ן וְהַגִּלְעָ֖ד וְהַבָּשָֽׁן׃

10:33   אֵת כָּל־אֶרֶץ הַגִּלְעָד

Unique   ל   Mp

Com.: The Masorah notes the *sole* occurrence of this lemma with כָּל, to distinguish it from its *sole* occurrence without כָּל (אֶת־אֶרֶץ הַגִּלְעָד) at Num 32:29.

In M^L there are only *two* circelli on this *four-word* phrase: *one* on אֵת כָּל and *one* on אֶרֶץ הַגִּלְעָד. With *four-* or *five-word* phrases it is not unusual for only *two* circelli to be given; see **Josh 1:6** and *passim*.

10:33   וְהַמְנַשִּׁי

Four times   ד   Mp

Deut 4:43 (לַמְנַשִּׁי); **29:7** (הַמְנַשִּׁי); **2 Kgs 10:33**; **1 Chr 26:32** (הַמְנַשִּׁי)

Com.: The Masorah notes the *four* occurrences of this lemma in various forms with the gentilic י, to distinguish them from its vastly more numerous occurrences (100+) in various forms without this gentilic, such as מְנַשֶּׁה, וּמְנַשֶּׁה, etc.

10:33   מֵעֲרֹעֵר

Five times defective   ה חס   Mp

Com.: See **1 Sam 30:28**.

10:33   אֲשֶׁר עַל־נַחַל אַרְנֹן

Twice: ב   Mp

Deut 3:12; 2 Kgs 10:33

Mm	אשר על נחל ארנן ב׳ וסימנהון	*twice*, and their references	אֲשֶׁר עַל־נַחַל אַרְנֹן

Deut 3:12   ואת הארץ הזאת ירשנו

<u>2 Kgs 10:33</u>   מן הירדן מזרח השמש

Com.: The Masorah notes the *two* occurrences of this lemma, to distinguish them from the *five* occurrences of this phrase that includes שְׂפַת (אֲשֶׁר עַל־שְׂפַת נַחַל אַרְנֹן).

In M^L there are only *two* circelli on this *four-word* phrase: *one* on אֲשֶׁר עַל, and *one* on נַחַל אַרְנֹן. With *four-* or *five-word* phrases it is not unusual for only *two* circelli to be given; see **Josh 1:6** and *passim*.

10:33   וְהַגִּלְעָד וְהַבָּשָׁן

Mp	ל	*Unique*

Com.: The Masorah notes the *sole* occurrence of וְהַבָּשָׁן with וְהַגִּלְעָד, to distinguish it from its *two* occurrences with הַגִּלְעָד (הַגִּלְעָד וְהַבָּשָׁן) at Josh 17:1 and 17:5.

---

2 KINGS 10:34

וְיֶתֶר דִּבְרֵי יֵהוּא וְכָל־אֲשֶׁר עָשָׂה וְכָל־גְּבוּרָתוֹ הֲלוֹא־הֵם כְּתוּבִים עַל־סֵפֶר דִּבְרֵי הַיָּמִים לְמַלְכֵי יִשְׂרָאֵל׃

10:34   וְיֶתֶר דִּבְרֵי יֵהוּא

Mp	ב׳ בט בסי׳	*Twice* with the accents (*ʾazlâ*, *mêrəkâ*, and *təbîr*) in the book

1 Kgs 16:5 (Baasha); **2 Kgs 10:34**

Com.: The Masorah notes the *two* occurrences of the phrase וְיֶתֶר דִּבְרֵי with the accents *ʾazlâ* and *mêrəkâ* followed by a king's name with *təbîr*.

The Mp heading at 1 Kgs 16:5 reads *five times* with these accents in the book noting the fact that in addition to these *two* occurrences in the book of this lemma with (*ʾazlâ*, *mêrəkâ*, and *təbîr*), there are *three* others with the combination *ʾazlâ*, *dargâ* and *təbîr*; (1 Kgs 11:41 with Solomon, 1 Kgs 22:46 with Jehoshaphat, and 2 Kgs 13:8 with Jehoahaz).

10:34   הֲלוֹא

Mp	יז מל בסיפ׳	*Seventeen times* plene in the book

Com.: See **1 Kgs 2:42**.

2 KINGS 11:1
וַעֲתַלְיָה אֵם אֲחַזְיָהוּ וְרָאֲתָה כִּי מֵת בְּנָהּ וַתָּקָם וַתְּאַבֵּד אֵת כָּל־זֶרַע הַמַּמְלָכָה:

11:1   וַעֲתַלְיָה

Seven times   ז   Mp

1–5   **2 Kgs 11:1; 11:3**; 11:13 (עֲתַלְיָה); **11:14** (עֲתַלְיָה); Ezra 8:7 (עֲתַלְיָה)
6–7   **1 Chr 8:26; 2 Chr 22:12**

Com.: The Masorah notes the *seven* occurrences of this name ending in a ה, to distinguish them from its *ten* occurrences ending in יהו (עֲתַלְיָהוּ/וַעֲתַלְיָהוּ), *two* of which are in vv. 2 and 20 of this chapter.

In M^L this lemma has a circellus but no note, but there is a note of *seven times* at vv. 3 and 14.

11:1   וְרָאֲתָה

Read   רָאֲתָה   ק   ראתה   Mp

Com.: This lemma is featured in a Masoretic list of words where a ו is written at the beginning of a word but is not read; see Frensdorff, *Ochlah*, §118, and Díaz-Esteban, *Sefer Oklah we-Oklah*, §104.

2 KINGS 11:2
וַתִּקַּח יְהוֹשֶׁבַע בַּת־הַמֶּלֶךְ־יוֹרָם אֲחוֹת אֲחַזְיָהוּ אֶת־יוֹאָשׁ בֶּן־אֲחַזְיָה וַתִּגְנֹב אֹתוֹ מִתּוֹךְ בְּנֵי־הַמֶּלֶךְ הַמּוּמָתִים אֹתוֹ וְאֶת־מֵינִקְתּוֹ בַּחֲדַר הַמִּטּוֹת וַיַּסְתִּרוּ אֹתוֹ מִפְּנֵי עֲתַלְיָהוּ וְלֹא הוּמָת:

11:2   יְהוֹשֶׁבַע

Unique   ל   Mp

Com.: The Masorah notes the *sole* occurrence of this lemma, to distinguish it from the form יְהוֹשַׁבְעַת that occurs in the parallel text of 2 Chr 22:11.

11:2   אֲחַזְיָה

Seven times   ז   Mp

Com.: See **2 Kgs 1:2**.

11:2   הַמְמוֹתָתִים

Mp   הממתים קרי   הַמּוּמָתִים   Read

Com.: The *kǝtîb* (הממותתים, *polal*), and the *qǝrê* (הַמּוּמָתִים, *hophal*) are examples of *kǝtîb/qǝrê* forms occurring in different conjugations with identical meanings; see Gordis, *The Biblical Text*, 133–34.

Com.: This lemma is featured in a number of Masoretic lists.

1   In a list of doublets beginning with הַ; see Frensdorff, *Ochlah*, §64, and Díaz-Esteban, *Sefer Oklah we-Oklah*, §65.

2   In a list of words in which there is a metathesis of letters; see Frensdorff, *Ochlah*, §91, and Díaz-Esteban, *Sefer Oklah we-Oklah*, §73.

3   In a list of words in which a ת is written but is not read or read as a different letter; see the Mm at Ezek 7:2 *sub* אַרְבַּעַת, the Mm at Mic 1:10 *sub* הִתְפַּלָּשְׁתִּי, Frensdorff, *Ochlah*, §163, and Díaz-Esteban, *Sefer Oklah we-Oklah*, §149.

In M^L this lemma has no circellus.

11:2   הַמִּטּוֹת

Mp   בֹּ   *Twice*

2 Kgs 11:2; 2 Chr 22:11

Com.: The Masorah notes the *two* occurrences of this lemma in these parallel passages written with a *ḥîreq* under the מ, to distinguish them from its more numerous occurrences (10x) with a *pataḥ* (הַמַּטּוֹת); see Ognibeni, *'Oklah*, §280, no.27.

11:2   וַיַּסְתִּרוּ

Mm   ויסתרו (ו) [i] חסירין לישׂ וסימנהון   *six times* defective in this and וַיַּסְתִּרוּ other forms, and their references

1–5	וַיַּסְתִּרוּ *of Athaliah* (2 Kgs 11:2) אֹתוֹ מִפְּנֵי	ויסתרו אתו מפני דעתליה
	Isa 29:15 (לַסְתִּר)	הוי המעמיקים מיהוה
	Jer 36:26 (וַיַּסְתִּרֵם)	את ירחמאל בן המלך
	Ezek 39:23 (וָאַסְתִּר)	וידעו הגוים כי (בעתם) [בעונם] גלו
	Ezek 39:24 (וָאַסְתִּר)	כטמאתם וכפשעיהם
6	Ps 27:5 (יַסְתִּרֵנִי)	כי יצפנני בסכה ביום

Com.: The Masorah notes the *six* occurrences of various forms of the *hiphil* of סָתַר written defective י, to distinguish them from the more numerous occurrences of forms of the *hiphil* written plene י such as הִסְתִּיר or אַסְתִּיר.

This distinction is implied in the addition *of Athaliah* to the catchwords וַיִּסְתְּרוּ אֹתוֹ מִפְּנֵי of the 2 Kgs 11:2, to distinguish that reference from its parallel in 2 Chr 22:11, where the lemma appears as וַתַּסְתִּירֵהוּ.

---

2 KINGS 11:3

וַיְהִי אִתָּהּ בֵּית יְהוָה מִתְחַבֵּא שֵׁשׁ שָׁנִים וַעֲתַלְיָה מֹלֶכֶת עַל־הָאָרֶץ׃ פ

11:3   וַעֲתַלְיָה

Seven times   ז̇   Mp

Com.: See directly above at **2 Kgs 11:1**.

---

2 KINGS 11:4

וּבַשָּׁנָה הַשְּׁבִיעִית שָׁלַח יְהוֹיָדָע וַיִּקַּח ׀ אֶת־שָׂרֵי הַמֵּאוֹת לַכָּרִי וְלָרָצִים וַיָּבֵא אֹתָם אֵלָיו בֵּית יְהוָה וַיִּכְרֹת לָהֶם בְּרִית וַיַּשְׁבַּע אֹתָם בְּבֵית יְהוָה וַיַּרְא אֹתָם אֶת־בֶּן־הַמֶּלֶךְ׃

11:4   וּבַשָּׁנָה הַשְּׁבִיעִית

Three pairs   ג̇ זוג   Mp

1   **2 Kgs 11:4** and 2 Chr 23:1
2   Ps 42:10 and Ps 43:2
3   **Ps 59:10** and **Ps 59:18**

Com.: The Masorah notes *three* pairs of phrases in similar contexts where one word of the pair has a שׁ, but the equivalent of that word in the second of the pairs has a ז; see Frensdorff, *Ochlah*, §204, and Ognibeni, *'Oklah*, §133B.

The first pair. In 2 Kgs 11:4 the phrase occurs as וּבַשָּׁנָה הַשְּׁבִיעִית שָׁלַח יְהוֹיָדָע whereas in 2 Chr 23:1 it occurs as וּבַשָּׁנָה הַשְּׁבִעִית הִתְחַזַּק יְהוֹיָדָע, the difference being that in the Kings passage the verb is שָׁלַח whereas in the Chronicles passage it is הִתְחַזַּק, the former having a שׁ, and the latter a ז.

The second pair. In Ps 42:10 the word containing the שׁ is שְׁכַחְתָּנִי, whereas in the parallel phrase in Ps 43:2 the word with the ז is זְנַחְתָּנִי.

The third pair. In Ps 59:10 the word containing the שׁ is אֶשְׁמֹרָה, whereas in the parallel phrase in Ps 59:18 the word with the ז is אֲזַמֵּרָה.

The Mp heading at Ps 59:10 also *reads three pairs*, but that at Ps 59:18 reads *three pairs (involving) two words in the same section.*

The Mm for this lemma may be found at Exod 20:8, where examples of the reverse (ז first word, שׁ second word) are also listed, and 2 Chr 23:1, which only lists this one pair (2 Kgs 11:4 and 2 Chr 23:1).

11:4   הַמֵּאיוֹת

Read הַמֵּאוֹת   המאות ק   Mp

Com.: This *kǝtîb* (המאיות) and *qǝrê* (הַמֵּאוֹת) is an example of a י under certain conditions morphing into an א; see Gordis, *The Biblical Text*, 110–11.

11:4   בְּבֵית יְהוָה

Thirty-nine times   לט   Mp

Com.: See **1 Sam 1:7**.

---

2 KINGS 11:5

וַיְצַוֵּם לֵאמֹר זֶה הַדָּבָר אֲשֶׁר תַּעֲשׂוּן הַשְּׁלִשִׁית מִכֶּם בָּאֵי הַשַּׁבָּת וְשֹׁמְרֵי מִשְׁמֶרֶת בֵּית הַמֶּלֶךְ:

11:5   וַיְצַוֵּם

Four times   ד   Mp

Exod 6:13; **34:32**; **2 Kgs 11:5**; 17:35

וַיְצַוֵּם *four times*, and their references   ויצום ד וסימנהון   Mm

Exod 6:13	ויצום אל בני ישראל
Exod 34:32	ואחריכן
2 Kgs 11:5	ויצום לאמר
2 Kgs 17:35	ויכרת יהוה

Com.: The Masorah notes the *four* occurrences of this lemma with a 3rd masc. pl. sfx., possibly to distinguish them from occurrences with other sfxs. such as וַיְצַוֻּהוּ or וַיְצַוֵּנוּ.

11:5   תַּעֲשׂוּן

Fourteen times   יֹד   Mp

Com.: See **Judg 7:17**.

---

2 KINGS 11:6

וְהַשְּׁלִשִׁית֙ בְּשַׁ֣עַר ס֔וּר וְהַשְּׁלִשִׁ֥ית בַּשַּׁ֖עַר אַחַ֣ר הָרָצִ֑ים וּשְׁמַרְתֶּ֛ם אֶת־מִשְׁמֶ֥רֶת הַבַּ֖יִת מַסָּֽח׃

11:6   בְּשַׁעַר סוּר

Unique   ל   Mp

Com.: The Masorah notes the *sole* occurrence of this lemma, to distinguish it from the phrase בְּשַׁעַר הַיְסוֹד that occurs in the parallel text of 2 Chr 23:5.

11:6   מַסָּח

Unique   ל   Mp

---

2 KINGS 11:8

וְהִקַּפְתֶּ֨ם עַל־הַמֶּ֜לֶךְ סָבִ֗יב אִ֚ישׁ וְכֵלָ֣יו בְּיָד֔וֹ וְהַבָּ֥א אֶל־הַשְּׂדֵר֖וֹת יוּמָ֑ת וִהְי֥וּ אֶת־הַמֶּ֖לֶךְ בְּצֵאת֥וֹ וּבְבֹאֽוֹ׃

11:8   עַל־הַמֶּלֶךְ

Eight times   ח   Mp

1–5   **2 Kgs 11:8**; 11:11; <u>21:24</u>; 25:11; 2 Chr 23:10
6–8   **2 Chr 23:13**; 33:25; Esth 1:16

עַל־הַמֶּלֶךְ *eight times*, and their references   על המלך ח וסימנהון   Mm

1–5   <u>2 Kgs 21:24</u>   ויד עם הארץ
       2 Chr 33:25   ויכו עם הארץ
       2 Kgs 11:11   ויעמדו הרצים
       2 Chr 23:10   ויעמד את כל העם
       2 Kgs 25:11   ואת יתר העם

6–8	2 Kgs 11:8	והקפתם
	וַתֵּרֶא וְהִנֵּה *of Chronicles* (2 Chr 23:13)	ותרא והנה דדברי הימים
	Esth 1:16	ויאמר ממוכן

And similarly all cases of עַל־הַמֶּלֶךְ טוֹב [ג.] (ב) בֹּ מֹ ב דכות טוב המלך על וכל apart from *three* (אֶל הַמֶּלֶךְ):

1 Kgs 22:13	(והמלך) [והמלאך]
And its companion (2 Chr 18:12)	וחבירו
1 Kgs 2:18	בת שבע

Com.: The Masorah notes the *eight* occurrences of הַמֶּלֶךְ with עַל, to distinguish them from its more numerous occurrences (100+) with אֶל (אֶל הַמֶּלֶךְ).

This distinction is implied in the addition *of Chronicles* to the catchword of the 2 Chr 23:13 reference, to distinguish this verse from its parallel in 2 Kgs 11:14 where the lemma appears as אֶל־הַמֶּלֶךְ.

The Mm additionally notes that this lemma also occurs with טוֹב in the phrase עַל־הַמֶּלֶךְ טוֹב, apart from *three* cases listed when it is with אֶל (e.g., טוֹב אֶל הַמֶּלֶךְ). In the Mp note only traces of a letter are visible.

11:8   וְהָיוּ

Seven times   i̇   Mp

Com.: See **1 Sam 4:9**.

---

2 KINGS 11:9

וַיַּעֲשׂוּ שָׂרֵי הַמֵּאיוֹת כְּכֹל אֲשֶׁר־צִוָּה יְהוֹיָדָע הַכֹּהֵן וַיִּקְחוּ אִישׁ אֶת־אֲנָשָׁיו בָּאֵי הַשַּׁבָּת עִם יֹצְאֵי הַשַּׁבָּת וַיָּבֹאוּ אֶל־יְהוֹיָדָע הַכֹּהֵן׃

11:9   הַמֵּאיוֹת

Read הַמֵּאוֹת   המאות ק   Mp

Com.: See directly above at **2 Kgs 11:4**.

2 KINGS 11:10

וַיִּתֵּן הַכֹּהֵן לְשָׂרֵי הַמֵּאיׄות אֶת־הַחֲנִית וְאֶת־הַשְּׁלָטִים אֲשֶׁר לַמֶּלֶךְ דָּוִד אֲשֶׁר בְּבֵית יְהוָה׃

11:10   וַיִּתֵּן הַכֹּהֵן

Unique   ל   Mp

Com.: The Masorah notes the *sole* occurrence of this lemma without יְהוֹיָדָע, to distinguish it from its *sole* occurrence with יְהוֹיָדָע (וַיִּתֵּן יְהוֹיָדָע הַכֹּהֵן) in the parallel text of 2 Chr 23:9.

11:10   הַמֵּאיׄות

Read הַמֵּאוֹת   המאות ק̇   Mp

Com.: See directly above at **2 Kgs 11:4**.

11:10   בְּבֵית יְהוָה

Thirty-nine times   לט̇   Mp

Com.: See **1 Sam 1:7**.

2 KINGS 11:12

וַיּוֹצִא אֶת־בֶּן־הַמֶּלֶךְ וַיִּתֵּן עָלָיו אֶת־הַנֵּזֶר וְאֶת־הָעֵדוּת וַיַּמְלִכוּ אֹתוֹ וַיִּמְשָׁחֻהוּ וַיַּכּוּ־כָף וַיֹּאמְרוּ יְחִי הַמֶּלֶךְ׃
ס

11:12   וַיּוֹצִא

Four times   ד̇   Mp

Deut 4:20; 2 Kgs 11:12; Ps 78:16; 105:43

Com.: The Masorah notes the *four* occurrences of this lemma pointed with a *ḥîreq*, to distinguish them from its more numerous occurrences (12x) pointed with a *ṣerê* (וַיּוֹצֵא); see Ognibeni, *'Oklah*, §2L.

11:12	וְאֶת־הָעֵדוּת
Twice	בֿ	Mp

2 Kgs 11:12; 2 Chr 23:11

Com.: The Masorah notes the *two* occurrences of this lemma in the parallel passages of 2 Kings and 2 Chronicles.

11:12	וַיִּמְשָׁחֵהוּ
Twice	בֿ	Mp

2 Kgs 11:12; 2 Chr 23:11

| וַיִּמְשָׁחֵהוּ *twice* and defective, and their references | וימשחהו בֿ וחסירין וסימנהון | Mm |

| 2 Chr 23:11 | ויוציאו את בן |
| 2 Kgs 11:12 | ויוצא את בן המלך |

Com.: By noting that the *two* occurrences of this lemma in these parallel passages are both written defective ו, the Masorah is also implying (correctly) that this lemma does not occur elsewhere written plene.

11:12	כָּף
Unique zaqep qameṣ	ל זק קמֿ	Mp

Com.: The Masorah notes the *sole* occurrence of this lemma with a *qameṣ* and *zaqep* accent, to distinguish it from its *six* occurrences with a *qameṣ* and an *ʾatnaḥ* or *sôp pasûq*.

This lemma is featured in two Masoretic lists. One is in a list of words occurring only *once* with a *qameṣ* and *zaqep*; see Frensdorff, *Ochlah*, §21, and Díaz-Esteban, *Sefer Oklah we-Oklah*, §22).

The other is in a list of two-letter words occurring only *once*; see Frensdorff, *Ochlah*, §40, and Díaz-Esteban, *Sefer Oklah we-Oklah*, §41).

In M[L] the circellus has been placed between וַיַּכּוּ and כָּף, but the note belongs only with כָּף.

> **2 KINGS 11:14**
> וַתֵּ֡רֶא וְהִנֵּ֣ה הַמֶּ֩לֶךְ֩ עֹמֵ֨ד עַֽל־הָעַמּ֜וּד כַּמִּשְׁפָּ֗ט וְהַשָּׂרִ֤ים וְהַחֲצֹֽצְרוֹת֙ אֶל־הַמֶּ֔לֶךְ וְכָל־עַ֤ם הָאָ֙רֶץ֙ שָׂמֵ֔חַ וְתֹקֵ֖עַ בַּחֲצֹֽצְר֑וֹת וַתִּקְרַ֤ע עֲתַלְיָה֙ אֶת־בְּגָדֶ֔יהָ וַתִּקְרָ֖א קֶ֥שֶׁר קָֽשֶׁר׃ ס

11:14   וְהַחֲצֹֽצְרוֹת

Four times   ד   Mp

2 Kgs 11:14; 2 Chr 23:13; 29:27; 82:92

Mm   וְהַחצצרות ד   *four times* הַחֲצֹֽצְרוֹת

2 Kgs 11:14   ותרא
And its companion (2 Chr 23:13)   וחבירו
2 Chr 29:27   להמזבח
2 Chr 29:28   והשיר משורר

Com.: The Masorah notes the *four* occurrences of this lemma with the def. article, to distinguish them from its two occurrences without the def. article (וַחֲצֹֽצְרוֹת) at Num 31:6 and 2 Chr 13:12.

11:14   וְכָל־עַם

Mm   וכל עם ז   *seven times* וְכָל־עַם

1–5   Josh 11:7   ויבא יהושע
      Josh 8:3   ויקם
      Josh 10:7   ויעל יהושע
      2 Sam 19:41   וכמהן עבר עמו
      2 Kgs 11:14   ותרא
6–7   And its companion (2 Chr 23:13)   וחבירו
      Jer 34:19   שרי יהודה

Com.: The Masorah notes the *seven* occurrences of this lemma with a ו cj., to distinguish them from its more numerous occurrences (21x) without a cj.

| 11:14 | וַתִּקַע |

| *Twice* | ב֗ | Mp |

2 Kgs 11:14; 2 Chr 23:13 (וַתּוֹקַע)

| וַתִּקַע *twice, once defective and once plene* | ותקע ב֗ חד חס֗ וחד מל | Mm |

וְתָקַע בַּחֲצֹצְרוֹת *of Kings* (2 Kgs 11:14)   ותקע בחצצרות דמלכי
וְתוֹקַע בַּחֲצֹצְרוֹת *of Chronicles* (2 Chr 23:13)   (ותוקע) [ותקע] בחצצרות דדברי ימים

And once (וְכִתְקֹעַ): Isa 18:3   וחד (ובתקע) [כתקע] שופר (השמיעו) [תשמעו]

Com.: The Masorah notes the *two* occurrences of this lemma in these parallel passages, and the Mm additionally notes the infin. form with a prep. (וְכִתְקֹעַ) at Isa 18:3.

The Mp of 2 Chr 23:13 (וַתּוֹקַע) correctly reads *unique plene*.

The addition in the Mm *of Kings* to the catchwords וְתָקַע בַּחֲצֹצְרוֹת of 2 Kgs 11:14 is to distinguish that reference from its parallel in 2 Chr 23:13. Similarly, the addition *of Chronicles* to the phrase וְתוֹקַע בַּחֲצֹצְרוֹת of 2 Chr 23:13 is to distinguish that reference from its parallel in 2 Kgs 11:14.

| 11:14 | עֲתַלְיָה |

| *Seven times* | ז֗ | Mp |

Com.: See directly above at **2 Kgs 11:1**.

---

2 KINGS 11:15

וַיְצַו יְהוֹיָדָע הַכֹּהֵן אֶת־שָׂרֵי הַמֵּאיוֹת ׀ פְּקֻדֵי הַחַיִל וַיֹּאמֶר אֲלֵיהֶם הוֹצִיאוּ אֹתָהּ אֶל־מִבֵּית לַשְּׂדֵרֹת וְהַבָּא אַחֲרֶיהָ הָמֵת בֶּחָרֶב כִּי אָמַר הַכֹּהֵן אַל־תּוּמַת בֵּית יְהוָה׃

| 11:15 | הַמֵּאיוֹת |

| Read הַמֵּאוֹת | המאות ק֗ | Mp |

Com.: See directly above at **2 Kgs 11:4**.

M^L, contrary to M (המאיות), reads the *kǝtîb* with a י before the א (המיאות); see Breuer, *The Biblical Text*, 126).

Both M^C and M^A read הַמֵּאיוֹת. M^A has a *qǝrê* הַמֵּאוֹת, whereas the Mp of M^C reads *superfluous* י.

11:15   לְשִׂדְרֹת

Twice defective   ב֗ חס֗   Mp

Com.: See **1 Kgs 6:9**.

---

2 KINGS 11:16

וַיָּשִׂמוּ לָהּ יָדַיִם וַתָּבוֹא דֶּרֶךְ־מְבוֹא הַסּוּסִים בֵּית הַמֶּלֶךְ וַתּוּמַת שָׁם׃ ס

11:16   וַיָּשִׂמוּ

Four times defective   ד֗ חס֗   Mp

Com.: See **Josh 10:27**.

11:16   וַתּוּמַת

Unique   ל֗   Mp

Com.: The Masorah notes the *sole* occurrence of this lemma (*hophal, she was put to death*), to distinguish it from the form וַיְמִיתוּהָ (*hiphil* plus sfx., *they put her to death*) that occurs in the parallel text of 2 Chr 23:15.

---

2 KINGS 11:18

וַיָּבֹאוּ כָל־עַם הָאָרֶץ בֵּית־הַבַּעַל וַיִּתְּצֻהוּ אֶת־מִזְבְּחֹתָו וְאֶת־צְלָמָיו שִׁבְּרוּ הֵיטֵב וְאֵת מַתָּן כֹּהֵן הַבַּעַל הָרְגוּ לִפְנֵי הַמִּזְבְּחוֹת וַיָּשֶׂם הַכֹּהֵן פְּקֻדּוֹת עַל־בֵּית יְהוָה׃

11:18   וַיִּתְּצֻהוּ

Twice   ב֗   Mp

2 Kgs 11:18; **2 Chr 23:17**

Com.: The Masorah notes the *two* occurrences of this lemma, *one* here and *one* in the parallel passage at 2 Chr 23:17.

The Mp heading at 2 Chr 23:17 reads *unique and defective* is inexact since there is another occurrence of this lemma. The note there more precisely should have read *unique and defective in the book* (of Chronicles).

However, by noting that this lemma is *unique* and written defective ו, the Masorah at 2 Chr 13:17 is also implying (correctly) that this lemma does not occur elsewhere written plene ו.

Neither M^C nor M^A has a note on this lemma here.

11:18   מִזְבְּחֹתָו

Mp   מזבחתיו ק   מִזְבְּחֹתָיו Read

Com.: The *kətîb* (מזבחתו) without a י represents the archaic form of the 3rd masc. sg. sfx. to a pl. noun, whereas the *qərê* (מִזְבְּחֹתָיו) with a י represents the later form; see Cohen, *The Kethib and Qeri System*, 33.

This lemma is featured in a Masoretic list of *hapax legomena* in which a י is read though it is not written; see Frensdorff, *Ochlah*, §128, and Díaz-Esteban, *Sefer Oklah we-Oklah*, §112.

---

2 KINGS 11:19

וַיִּקַּח אֶת־שָׂרֵי הַמֵּאוֹת וְאֶת־הַכָּרִי וְאֶת־הָרָצִים וְאֵת | כָּל־עַם הָאָרֶץ וַיֹּרִידוּ אֶת־הַמֶּלֶךְ מִבֵּית יְהוָה וַיָּבוֹאוּ דֶרֶךְ־שַׁעַר הָרָצִים בֵּית הַמֶּלֶךְ וַיֵּשֶׁב עַל־כִּסֵּא הַמְּלָכִים:

11:19   הַכָּרִי

Mp   ל   *Unique*

11:19   וַיָּבוֹאוּ

Mp   ג מל   *Three times* plene

2 Kgs 11:19; Jer 8:16; 2 Chr 29:18

Com.: The Masorah notes the *three* occurrences of this lemma written plene first ו, to distinguish them from its more numerous occurrences (100+) written defective first ו (וַיָּבֹאוּ).

This distinction is implied in the Mm of Jer 8:16 where there is an addition *of Kings* to the catchword of the 2 Kgs 11:19 reference, to distinguish this reference from its parallel passage in 2 Chr 23:20, where the lemma appears as וַיָּבֹאוּ.

> ## 2 KINGS 11:20
> וַיִּשְׂמַ֤ח כָּל־עַם־הָאָ֙רֶץ֙ וְהָעִ֣יר שָׁקָ֔טָה וְאֶת־עֲתַלְיָ֖הוּ הֵמִ֣יתוּ בַחֶ֑רֶב בֵּ֖ית ﹀מֶֽלֶךְ׃ ס

11:20   שָׁקָ֔טָה

Twice   בׄ   Mp

2 Kgs 11:20; 2 Chr 23:21

Com.: The Masorah notes the *two* occurrences of this lemma in these parallel passages with a *qameṣ* under the ק (pausal), to distinguish them from its more numerous occurrences (5x) with a *šəwâ* (שְׁקָטָה).

11:20   ﹀מֶֽלֶךְ

Read   הַמֶּ֫לֶךְ   המלך ק̇   Mp

Com.: The *kətîb* (מלך), and the *qərê* (הַמֶּ֫לֶךְ) represent examples of the omission of a definite article; see Gordis, *The Biblical Text*, 147.

This lemma is featured in a Masoretic list of words where a ה at the beginning of a word is read, but not written; see the Mm at **2 Sam 23:9** *sub* גְּבֹרִים֯, Frensdorff, *Ochlah*, §165 & p. 37*, and Díaz-Esteban, *Sefer Oklah we-Oklah*, §90.

> ## 2 KINGS 12:1
> בֶּן־שֶׁ֥בַע שָׁנִ֖ים יְהוֹאָ֣שׁ בְּמָלְכֽוֹ׃ פ

12:1   יְהוֹאָ֣שׁ

Four times   דׄ   Mp

1–5   **2 Kgs 12:1**; 12:2; 12:3: 12:5; 12:7
6–10   2 Kgs 12:8; 12:19; 13:10; 13:25; 14:8
11–15   2 Kgs 14:9; 14:11; 14:13ᵃ; 14:13ᵇ; 14:15
16–17   2 Kgs 14:16; 14:17

Com.: The Mp heading here of *four times* is incorrect since there are *seventeen* occurrences of this lemma.

The Masorah notes the *seventeen* occurrences of this lemma written with the divine element יְהוֹ, to distinguish them from its more numerous occurrences (40x), written with the divine element יוֹ (יוֹאָשׁ); see below at **2 Kgs 12:20**.

Since there are no other Mp notes for this lemma and, since neither M^C nor M^A has a note here, it may well be that this note is misplaced and belongs on another king's name that occurs *four times*, such as יְהוֹזָבָד (see below at **2 Kgs 12:22**) or יוֹאָחָז (see **2 Kgs 14:1**).

---

2 KINGS 12:2

בִּשְׁנַת־שֶׁבַע לְיֵהוּא מָלַךְ יְהוֹאָשׁ וְאַרְבָּעִים שָׁנָה מָלַךְ בִּירוּשָׁלָ͏ִם וְשֵׁם אִמּוֹ צִבְיָה מִבְּאֵר שָֽׁבַע׃

12:2   צִבְיָה

Three times   גׄ   Mp

2 Kgs 12:2; 1 Chr 8:9 (צִבְיָא); 2 Chr 24:1

Com.: The Masorah notes the *three* occurrences of this lemma, *twice* written with a ה and *once* with an א, to distinguish them from its *two* occurrences with a different pointing (צְבִיָּה) in Cant 4:5 and 7:4.

---

2 KINGS 12:3

וַיַּעַשׂ יְהוֹאָשׁ הַיָּשָׁר בְּעֵינֵי יְהוָה כָּל־יָמָיו אֲשֶׁר הוֹרָהוּ יְהוֹיָדָע הַכֹּהֵֽן׃

12:3   הוֹרָהוּ

Unique   לׄ   Mp

---

2 KINGS 12:5

וַיֹּאמֶר יְהוֹאָשׁ אֶל־הַכֹּהֲנִים כֹּל כֶּסֶף הַקֳּדָשִׁים אֲשֶׁר־יוּבָא בֵית־יְהוָה כֶּסֶף עוֹבֵר אִישׁ כֶּסֶף נַפְשׁוֹת עֶרְכּוֹ כָּל־כֶּסֶף אֲשֶׁר יַעֲלֶה עַל לֶב־אִישׁ לְהָבִיא בֵּית יְהוָֽה׃

12:5   יוּבָא

Five times   הׄ   Mp

1–5   **Lev 6:23**; 11:32; 2 Kgs 12:5; 12:17; Jer 10:9

Com.: The Masorah notes the *five* occurrences of the sg. form of this lemma, to distinguish them from its *sole* occurrence in the pl. (יוּבָאוּ) in Jer 27:22.

12:5   עֹובֵר

Eight times plene   ח̇ מל̇   Mp

1–5   **2 Kgs 12:5**; <u>Isa 60:15</u>; **Jer 13:24**; 18:16; Zeph 2:15
6–8   Zeph 3:6; **Ps 144:4**; **Esth 3:3**

Com.: The Masorah notes the *eight* occurrences of this lemma written plene ו, to distinguish them from its more numerous occurrences (35x) written defective ו (עָבַר).

This enumeration does not include the *six* occurrences of this lemma in Ezekiel.

The Mp headings at Jer 13:24 and Ps 144:4 read *eight times plene and similarly all of Ezekiel (apart from once)*, and the Mm at <u>Isa 60:15</u> also adds this note about the occurrences in Ezekiel.

The Mp heading at Esth 3:3 correctly reads *twice plene in the Writings*.

12:5   עֶרְכּוֹ

Three times   ג̇   Mp

Exod 40:4; 2 Kgs 12:5; <u>Job 41:4</u>

Com.: The Masorah notes the *three* occurrences of this lemma, possibly to distinguish them from its *sole* occurrence with the prep. כ (כְּעֶרְכּוֹ) at 2 Kgs 23:35, or from its *sole* occurrence with a fem. sfx. (עֶרְכָּהּ) at Job 28:13.

---

2 KINGS 12:6

יִקְחוּ לָהֶם הַכֹּהֲנִים אִישׁ מֵאֵת מַכָּרוֹ וְהֵם יְחַזְּקוּ אֶת־בֶּדֶק הַבַּיִת לְכֹל אֲשֶׁר־יִמָּצֵא שָׁם בָּדֶק: פ

12:6   מֵאֵת מַכָּרוֹ

Unique   ל̇   Mp

12:6   לְכֹל אֲשֶׁר־יִמָּצֵא

Unique   ל̇   Mp

Com.: The Masorah notes the *sole* occurrence of this lemma with the prep. ל, to distinguish it from its *sole* occurrence with the prep. ב (בְּכֹל אֲשֶׁר־יִמָּצֵא) at Deut 21:17.

2 KINGS

2 KINGS 12:7

וַיְהִ֗י בִּשְׁנַ֨ת עֶשְׂרִ֤ים וְשָׁלֹשׁ֙ שָׁנָ֣ה לַמֶּ֣לֶךְ יְהוֹאָ֔שׁ לֹֽא־חִזְּק֥וּ הַכֹּהֲנִ֖ים אֶת־בֶּ֥דֶק הַבָּֽיִת׃

12:7   חִזְּק֥וּ

Four times   דּ   Mp

Com.: See **Judg 9:24**.

2 KINGS 12:8

וַיִּקְרָא֩ הַמֶּ֨לֶךְ יְהוֹאָ֜שׁ לִיהוֹיָדָ֤ע הַכֹּהֵן֙ וְלַכֹּ֣הֲנִ֔ים וַיֹּ֣אמֶר אֲלֵהֶ֔ם מַדּ֛וּעַ אֵינְכֶ֥ם מְחַזְּקִ֖ים אֶת־בֶּ֣דֶק הַבָּ֑יִת וְעַתָּ֗ה אַל־תִּקְחוּ־כֶ֙סֶף֙ מֵאֵ֣ת מַכָּרֵיכֶ֔ם כִּֽי־לְבֶ֥דֶק הַבַּ֖יִת תִּתְּנֻֽהוּ׃

12:8   וְלַכֹּהֲנִים

Five times   ה   Mp

1–5   **2 Kgs 12:8**; Jer 33:18; **Neh 2:16**; **2 Chr 35:14**[a]; 35:14[b]

וְלַכֹּהֲנִים *five times*   ולכהנים ה   Mm

1–5   2 Kgs 12:8   ויקרא המלך יהואש
       Jer 33:18   לא יכרת איש
       2 Chr 35:14[a]   ואחר הכינו להם
       Twice in the verse (2 Chr 35:14[b])   שנים בפסוקה
       Neh 2:16   והסגנים

Com.: The Masorah notes the *five* occurrences of this lemma with a ו cj., to distinguish them from its more numerous occurrences (23x) without a cj.

12:8   אֲלֵהֶם

Thirteen times defective in the book   יג חס בסיפ   Mp

Com.: See **1 Kgs 12:16**.

12:8   מַכָּרֵיכֶם

Unique   ל   Mp

2 KINGS 12:9

וַיֵּאֹ֣תוּ הַכֹּהֲנִ֑ים לְבִלְתִּ֣י קְחַת־כֶּ֗סֶף מֵאֵת֙ הָעָ֔ם וּלְבִלְתִּ֥י חַזֵּ֖ק אֶת־בֶּ֥דֶק הַבָּֽיִת׃

12:9 חַזֵּק

Four times ד Mp

Deut 1:38; **2 Kgs 12:9**; **Nah 2:2**; Neh 6:9

חַזֵּק *four times* (ויחזק) [חזק] ד Mm

Deut 1:38   יהושע בן נון העמד לפניך
Neh 6:9   ועתה חזק את ידי
2 Kgs 12:9   ולבלתי
Nah 2:2   חזק מתנים

Com.: The Masorah notes the *four* occurrences of this lemma, which is both an imper. (Deut 1:38, Nah 2:2, and Neh 6:9), and an infin. cstr. (here).

2 KINGS 12:10

וַיִּקַּ֞ח יְהוֹיָדָ֤ע הַכֹּהֵן֙ אֲר֣וֹן אֶחָ֔ד וַיִּקֹּ֥ב חֹ֖ר בְּדַלְתּ֑וֹ וַיִּתֵּ֣ן אֹתוֹ֩ אֵ֨צֶל הַמִּזְבֵּ֜חַ בַּיָּמִ֗ין בְּבוֹא־אִישׁ֙ בֵּ֣ית יְהֹוָ֔ה וְנָתְנוּ־שָׁ֤מָּה הַכֹּֽהֲנִים֙ שֹׁמְרֵ֣י הַסַּ֔ף אֶת־כָּל־הַכֶּ֖סֶף הַמּוּבָ֥א בֵית־יְהֹוָֽה׃

12:10 וַיִּקֹּב

Twice ב Mp

Lev 24:11; 2 Kgs 12:10

12:10 חֹר

Twice ב Mp

2 Kgs 12:10; **Ezek 8:7**

| חֹר *twice* and defective | חר ב̇ וחס̇ | Mm |

2 Kgs 12:10   ויקב חר בדלתו
Ezek 8:7   ויבא אתי

Com.: By noting that this lemma occurs *twice* and written defective ו, the Masorah is also implying (correctly) that this lemma does not occur elsewhere written plene ו.

12:10   בִּימִין

| Read מִימָין | מימין ק̇ | Mp |

Com.: The *kətîb* (בימין) and the *qərê* (מִימָין) represent examples of interchanges between the letters ב and מ; see Gordis, *The Biblical Text*, 144.

This lemma is featured in a Masoretic list of words that have a ב read as a מ; see Frensdorff, *Ochlah*, §154, and Díaz-Esteban, *Sefer Oklah we-Oklah*, §141.

12:10   בְּבוֹא

| *Nine times* plene | ט מל | Mp |

Com.: See **2 Kgs 5:18**.

---

2 KINGS 12:11

וַיְהִי כִּרְאוֹתָם כִּי־רַב הַכֶּסֶף בָּאָרוֹן וַיַּעַל סֹפֵר הַמֶּלֶךְ וְהַכֹּהֵן הַגָּדוֹל וַיָּצֻרוּ וַיִּמְנוּ אֶת־הַכֶּסֶף הַנִּמְצָא בֵית־יְהוָה:

12:11   סֹפֵר הַמֶּלֶךְ

| *Unique* | ל̇ | Mp |

Com.: The Masorah notes the *sole* occurrence of הַמֶּלֶךְ with סֹפֵר written defective ו, to distinguish it from its *sole* occurrence with סֹפֵר written plene ו (סוֹפֵר הַמֶּלֶךְ) in the parallel text 2 Chr 24:11.

12:11   וְהַכֹּהֵן הַגָּדוֹל

| *Twice* | ב̇ | Mp |

Lev 21:10; 2 Kgs 12:11

	Mm	וְהַכֹּהֵן הַגָּדוֹל בׄ	*twice* וְהַכֹּהֵן הַגָּדוֹל
Lev 21:10		מֵאֶחָיו אֲשֶׁר יוּצַק עַל רֹאשׁוֹ	
<u>2 Kgs 12:11</u>		וַיַּעַל (סוֹפֵר) [סֵפֶר] הַמֶּלֶךְ	

Com.: The Masorah notes the *two* occurrences of this lemma with a ו cj., to distinguish them from its more numerous occurrences (16x) without a cj.

In M^L there is a לׄ in the margin beside the בׄ of this lemma, which does not appear to have a corresponding lemma.

2 KINGS 12:12

וְנָתְנוּ אֶת־הַכֶּסֶף הַמְתֻכָּן עַל־יַד עֹשֵׂי הַמְּלָאכָה הַמֻּפְקָדִים בֵּית יְהוָה וַיּוֹצִיאֻהוּ לְחָרָשֵׁי הָעֵץ וְלַבֹּנִים הָעֹשִׂים בֵּית יְהוָה:

12:12   הַמְתֻכָּן

Unique   לׄ   Mp

12:12   יַד

Read יָדֵי   ידי קׄ   Mp

Com.: The *kǝtîb* (יד), and the *qǝrê* (יָדֵי) are examples of *kǝtîb/qǝrê* variations in the sg. and pl.; see Gordis, *The Biblical Text*, 136–37.

This lemma is featured in a Masoretic list of words where a י at the end of the word is not written but is read; see Frensdorff, *Ochlah*, §126, and Díaz-Esteban, *Sefer Oklah we-Oklah*, §110.

12:12   הַמֻּפְקָדִים

Read הַמֻּפְקָדִים   המפקדים קׄ   Mp

Com.: The *kǝtîb* (הפקדים, *qal passive*), and the *qǝrê* (הַמֻּפְקָדִים, *hophal*) are examples of *kǝtîb/qǝrê* forms occurring in different conjugations with identical meanings; see Gordis, *The Biblical Text*, 133–34.

This lemma is featured in a Masoretic list of words where a מ, not written in the text, should be read; see the Mm at <u>1 Sam 20:38</u> *sub* הַחֵצִי

12:12   וְלַבֹּנִים

Five times defective   ה̇ חס̇   Mp

1–5   **2 Kgs 12:12**; **22:6**; **Job 3:14** (הַבֹּנִים); **Ezra 3:10** (הַבֹּנִים); **2 Chr 34:11**

וְלַבֹּנִים *five times* defective in this and another form   ולבנים ה̇ חסיר בלישנ̇   Mm

1–5   2 Kgs 12:12   לחרשי
       2 Kgs 22:6   לחרשים
       Job 3:14   חרבות
       2 Chr 34:11   ויתנו (על יד) [לחרשים]
       Ezra 3:10   ויסדו

Com.: The Masorah notes the *five* occurrences of this lemma in various forms written defective ו, to distinguish them from its *four* occurrences written plene ו (הַבּוֹנִים/וְהַבּוֹנִים).

This distinction is implied in the Mp of Job 3:14, which reads *five times and once* וְהַבּוֹנִים, to distinguish הַבֹּנִים from its form written plene with a ו cj. וְהַבּוֹנִים in Neh 4:12.

In the catchwords for 2 Chr 34:11 the scribe's eye wandered to the previous verse where the same catchword וַיִּתְּנוּ occurs. He wrote וַיִּתְּנוּ עַל יַד instead of וַיִּתְּנוּ לֶחָרָשִׁים.

---

2 KINGS 12:13

וְלַגֹּדְרִים וּלְחֹצְבֵי הָאֶבֶן וְלִקְנוֹת עֵצִים וְאַבְנֵי מַחְצֵב לְחַזֵּק אֶת־בֶּדֶק בֵּית־יְהוָה וּלְכֹל אֲשֶׁר־יֵצֵא עַל־הַבַּיִת לְחָזְקָה׃

12:13   וְלִקְנוֹת

Twice, *once* defective and *once* plene   ב̇ חד חס̇ וחד מל̇   Mp

2 Kgs 12:13; 22:6 (וְלִקְנוֹת)

Com.: The Mp note here of *once* defective, and *once* plene (ו) form is incorrect since *both* occurrences of this lemma are written plene ו.

The Mp at 2 Kgs 22:6 just reads *twice* as do the Mp notes at both references in M^A. M^C has no note at either occurrence.

12:13   וּלְכֹל אֲשֶׁר

Three times   ג̇   Mp

2 Kgs 12:13; Jer 42:21; Ezek 44:14

Com.: The Masorah notes the *three* occurrences of this lemma with a ו cj., to distinguish them from its more numerous occurrences (18x) without a cj.

---

2 KINGS 12:14

אַ֣ךְ לֹא־יֵעָשֶׂ֞ה בֵּ֤ית יְהוָה֙ סִפּ֣וֹת כֶּ֔סֶף מְזַמְּר֧וֹת מִזְרָק֛וֹת חֲצֹצְר֖וֹת כָּל־כְּלִ֣י זָהָ֑ב וּכְלִי־כָ֑סֶף מִן־הַכֶּ֖סֶף הַמּוּבָ֥א בֵית־יְהוָֽה׃

12:14   יֵעָשֶׂה

Thirty-six times   לו̇   Mp

Com.: See **Judg 11:37**.

12:14   מְזַמְּרוֹת מִזְרָקוֹת

Unique   ל̇   Mp

Com.: The Masorah notes the *sole* occurrence of this lemma, an indef. *snuffers, basins*, to distinguish it from its *two* occurrences as a def. וְהַמְזַמְּרוֹת וְהַמִּזְרָקוֹת, *and the basins, and the snuffers* at 1 Kgs. 7:50 and 2 Chr 4:22.

12:14   כְּלִי זָהָב

Three times   ג̇   Mp

Exod 35:22; Num 31:50; 2 Kgs 12:14

Com.: The Masorah notes the *three* occurrences of זָהָב with כְּלִי (sg.), to distinguish them from its *two* occurrences with כְּלֵי (pl., כְּלֵי זָהָב) at 1 Sam 6:15 and 1 Chr 18:10.

2 KINGS 12:15

כִּי־לְעֹשֵׂי הַמְּלָאכָה יִתְּנֻהוּ וְחִזְּקוּ־בוֹ אֶת־בֵּית יְהוָה׃

12:15   יִתְּנֻהוּ

Unique defective   ל חס̇   Mp

Com.: The Mp heading here *of unique defective* (וֹ) is inexact since there is no occurrence of this lemma written plene וֹ. The note more precisely should have read *unique and defective*.

M^C, similar to M^L, reads *defective* וּ. M^C has no note here.

2 KINGS 12:16

וְלֹא יְחַשְּׁבוּ אֶת־הָאֲנָשִׁים אֲשֶׁר יִתְּנוּ אֶת־הַכֶּסֶף עַל־יָדָם לָתֵת לְעֹשֵׂי הַמְּלָאכָה כִּי בֶאֱמֻנָה הֵם עֹשִׂים׃

12:16   יְחַשְּׁבוּ

Twice   ב̇   Mp

2 Kgs 12:16; <u>Hos 7:15</u>

Com.: The Masorah notes the *two* occurrences of this lemma in the *piel*, to distinguish them from its *three* occurrences in the *hiphil* (יַחְשְׁבוּ).

12:16   בֶאֱמֻנָה

Five times defective   ה̇ חס̇   Mp

1–5   **Deut 32:20** (אֵמֻן); **1 Sam 26:23** (אֱמֻנָתוֹ); **<u>2 Kgs 12:16</u>**
        Isa 26:2 (אֱמֻנִים); **Ps 143:1** (בֶּאֱמֻנָתְךָ)

בֶאֱמֻנָה *five times* defective   באמנה ה̇ חס̇   Mm

1–5   Deut 32:20   בנים לא אמן בם
        1 Sam 26:23   את צדקתו ואת
        <u>2 Kgs 12:16</u>   כי באמנה הם עשים
        Isa 26:2   ויבא גוי צדיק
        Ps 143:1   באמנתך ענני

Com.: The Masorah notes the *five* occurrences of this lemma in various forms written defective ו, to distinguish them from its more numerous occurrences (11x) in various forms written plene ו (e.g., אֱמוּנָה).

The Mp heading at Isa 26:2 reads *six times defective* and probably includes Lam 4:5 (הָאֱמֻנִים).

The Mp headings at Deut 32:20 and Ps 143:1 both read *unique defective* in reference to their particular forms.

---

2 KINGS 12:17

כֶּסֶף אָשָׁם וְכֶסֶף חַטָּאוֹת לֹא יוּבָא בֵּית יְהוָה לַכֹּהֲנִים יִהְיוּ׃ פ

12:17 חַטָּאוֹת

Three times   גׄ   Mp

2 Kgs 12:17; Job 13:23 (וְחַטָּאות); **Neh 10:34** (וְלַחַטָּאות)

Mm   חטאות גׄ ומלׄ   חַטָּאוֹת *three times* and plene

2 Kgs 12:17   כסף אשם וכסף חטאות
Job 13:23   כמה לי עונות וחטאות
Neh 10:34   ללחם המערכת

Com.: The Masorah notes the *three* occurrences of this lemma in various forms written plene ו, to distinguish them from the more numerous occurrences (6x) in various forms of a parallel form written defective ו (e.g., חַטָּאת); see **2 Kgs 13:2**.

By noting in the Mm that this lemma occurs *three times* and plene ו, the Masorah is also implying (correctly) that this lemma does not occur elsewhere written defective.

12:17 יוּבָא

Five times   הׄ   Mp

Com.: See above at **2 Kgs 12:5**.

2 KINGS 12:18

אָ֣ז יַעֲלֶ֗ה חֲזָאֵל֙ מֶ֣לֶךְ אֲרָ֔ם וַיִּלָּ֥חֶם עַל־גַּ֖ת וַֽיִּלְכְּדָ֑הּ וַיָּ֤שֶׂם חֲזָאֵל֙ פָּנָ֔יו לַעֲל֖וֹת עַל־יְרוּשָׁלָֽ͏ִם׃

12:18   לַעֲל֖וֹת

Fourteen times   יד̇   Mp

Com.: See **1 Sam 9:14**.

2 KINGS 12:19

וַיִּקַּ֣ח יְהוֹאָ֣שׁ מֶֽלֶךְ־יְהוּדָ֡ה אֵ֣ת כׇּל־הַקֳּדָשִׁ֣ים אֲשֶׁר־הִקְדִּ֣ישׁוּ יְהוֹשָׁפָ֣ט וִיהוֹרָם֩ וַאֲחַזְיָ֨הוּ אֲבֹתָ֜יו מַלְכֵ֣י יְהוּדָ֗ה וְאֶת־קֳדָשָׁיו֙ וְאֵ֣ת כׇּל־הַזָּהָ֗ב הַנִּמְצָ֛א בְּאֹצְר֥וֹת בֵּית־יְהֹוָ֖ה וּבֵ֣ית הַמֶּ֑לֶךְ וַיִּשְׁלַ֗ח לַֽחֲזָאֵל֙ מֶ֣לֶךְ אֲרָ֔ם וַיַּ֖עַל מֵעַ֥ל יְרוּשָׁלָֽ͏ִם׃

12:19   קֳדָשָׁיו֙

Twice   ב̇   Mp

Num 5:10; **2 Kgs 12:19**

קֳדָשָׁיו֙ *twice*   קדשיו ב̇   Mm

Num 5:10   ואיש את קדשיו
2 Kgs 12:19   ויקח יהואש מלך יהודה

And *once* (וְקׇדָשָׁיו): 2 Chr 15:18   וחד ויבא את קדשי אביו וקדשיו בית

Com.: The Masorah notes the *two* occurrences of this lemma, and the Mm additionally notes its *sole* occurrence with a ו cj. (וְקׇדָשָׁיו) at 2 Chr 15:18.

12:19   וּבֵ֣ית הַמֶּ֑לֶךְ

Three times   ג̇   Mp

2 Kgs 12:19; **Hos 5:1**; 2 Chr 16:2

| Mm | וּבֵית הַמֶּלֶךְ ג | *three times* | וּבֵית הַמֶּלֶךְ |

2 Kgs 12:19   ויקח יהואש מלך יהודה
Hos 5:1   שמעו זאת הכהנים
2 Chr 16:2   ויצא אסא כסף וזהב מאצרות

Com.: The Masorah notes the *three* occurrences of this lemma with a ו cj., to distinguish them from its more numerous occurrences (38x) without a cj.

---

2 KINGS 12:20

וְיֶ֙תֶר֙ דִּבְרֵ֣י יוֹאָ֔שׁ וְכָל־אֲשֶׁ֖ר עָשָׂ֑ה הֲלוֹא־הֵ֣ם כְּתוּבִ֗ים עַל־סֵ֛פֶר דִּבְרֵ֥י הַיָּמִ֖ים לְמַלְכֵ֥י יְהוּדָֽה׃

12:20   יוֹאָשׁ

Sixteen times   יו̇   Mp

1–5   1 Kgs 22:26; 2 Kgs 11:2; **12:20; 12:21**; 13:9
6–10   2 Kgs 13:12; **13:13**ᵃ; 13:13ᵇ; **13:14; 13:25**
11–15 2 Kgs 14:1; **14:3; 14:17; 14:23**ᵃ; 14:23ᵇ
16   2 Kgs 14:27

Com.: The Mp heading here of *sixteen times* is inexact since there are *forty* occurrences of this lemma in the Bible. The note more precisely should have read, as the Mp heading at 2 Kgs 14:17 and 14:23ᵃ, *sixteen times in the book* (of Kings).

The Masorah notes the *sixteen* occurrences in Kings of the name Joash written as יוֹאָשׁ, to distinguish them from its *seventeen* occurrences written as יְהוֹאָשׁ; see directly above at **2 Kgs 12:1**.

The Mp heading to 2 Kgs 13:25 reads *sixteen times, and similarly all cases in the books of Judges, The Twelve, and Chronicles*. In these latter books the lemma occurs *twenty-four times,* making a total of *forty* occurrences throughout the Bible.

Neither Mᶜ nor Mᴬ has a note on this lemma here.

12:20   הֲלוֹא

Seventeen times plene in the book   יז̇ מל בסיפ̇   Mp

Com.: See **1 Kgs 2:42**.

2 KINGS 12:21

וַיָּקֻמוּ עֲבָדָיו וַיִּקְשְׁרוּ־קָשֶׁר וַיַּכּוּ אֶת־יוֹאָשׁ בֵּית מִלֹּא הַיּוֹרֵד סִלָּא׃

12:21   יוֹאָשׁ

Sixteen times   יו̇   Mp

Com.: See directly above at **2 Kgs 12:20**.

12:21   מִלֹּא

Twice defective   ב̇ חס̇   Mp

2 Sam 17:27; **2 Kgs 12:21**

Com.: The Masorah notes the *two* occurrences of this lemma written defective ו, to distinguish them from its *three* occurrences written plene ו.

The two forms of this lemma are homonyms, *one* (here) is part of the place name בֵּית מִלֹּא *Beth-Millo*, and the other at 2 Sam 17:27 is part of the place name לֹא דְבָר *Lo debar* with the inseparable prefix מִ (מִלֹּא דְבָר).

2 KINGS 12:22

וְיוֹזָבָד בֶּן־שִׁמְעָת וִיהוֹזָבָד בֶּן־שֹׁמֵר ׀ עֲבָדָיו הִכֻּהוּ וַיָּמֹת וַיִּקְבְּרוּ אֹתוֹ עִם־אֲבֹתָיו בְּעִיר דָּוִד וַיִּמְלֹךְ אֲמַצְיָה בְנוֹ תַּחְתָּיו׃ פ

12:22   שִׁמְעָת

Twice   ב̇   Mp

2 Kgs 12:22; 2 Chr 24:26

Com.: The Masorah notes the *two* occurrences of this lemma in the parallel passages of 2 Kings and 2 Chronicles.

In M^L this lemma has no circellus, and the note has been placed in the right column one line below the text.

12:22   וִיהוֹזָבָד

Four times   ד   Mp

2 Kgs 12:22; **1 Chr 26:4** (יְהוֹזָבָד); 2 Chr 17:18 (יְהוֹזָבָד); **24:26**

Com.: The Masorah notes the *four* occurrences of this lemma written with the divine element יְהוֹ, to distinguish them from its more numerous occurrences (10x) written with the divine element יוֹ (יוֹזָבָד/וְיוֹזָבָד).

12:22   אֲמַצְיָה

Nine times   ט   Mp

1–5   **2 Kgs 12:22**, 13:12; **14:8; 15:1; Amos 7:10**
6–9   **Amos 7:12**; 7:14; **1 Chr 4:34; 6:30**

Com.: The Masorah notes the *nine* occurrences of this lemma written with a final יָה, to distinguish them from its more numerous occurrences (26x) with a final יָהוּ (אֲמַצְיָהוּ); see Ognibeni, *'Oklah*, §50.

---

2 KINGS 13:2

וַיַּעַשׂ הָרַע בְּעֵינֵי יְהוָה וַיֵּלֶךְ אַחַר חַטֹּאת יָרָבְעָם בֶּן־נְבָט אֲשֶׁר־הֶחֱטִיא אֶת־יִשְׂרָאֵל לֹא־סָר מִמֶּנָּה׃

13:2   חַטֹּאת

Six times defective   ו חס   Mp

1–5   **Num 5:6**; **2 Kgs 13:2**; 2 Kgs 13:6 (מֵחַטֹּאת)*; **24:3** (בְּחַטֹּאת); Jer 50:20
6   **Ezek 18:14**

Com.: The Masorah notes the *six* occurrences of this lemma in various forms written defective ו, to distinguish them from its more numerous occurrences in various forms written plene ו (e.g., חַטָּאוֹת); see **2 Kgs 12:17**.

*M^L, contrary to M (מֵחַטֹּאת), has only *five* occurrences of this lemma since it writes the form at 2 Kgs 13:6 plene ו (מֵחַטֹּאוֹת); see Breuer, *The Biblical Text*, 127.

The Mp heading at Num 5:6 enumerates only *five* occurrences, and the Mm at Num 5:6 similarly lists only *five* sets of catchword including 2 Kgs 13:6 as being defective, but mistakenly excluding 2 Kgs 13:2 from its list; for further discussion of this discrepancy, see Breuer, *The Biblical Text*, 125, n. 33.

M[A], as M[L], reads here *six times* defective, but M[C] reads *five times defective* (in the Prophets); see Castro, *El codice*, 3:243.

2 KINGS 13:4
וַיְחַל יְהוֹאָחָז אֶת־פְּנֵי יְהוָה וַיִּשְׁמַע אֵלָיו יְהוָה כִּי רָאָה אֶת־לַחַץ יִשְׂרָאֵל כִּי־לָחַץ אֹתָם מֶלֶךְ אֲרָם:

13:4   וַיְחַל

Four times   ד׳   Mp

Com.: See **1 Kgs 13:6**.

2 KINGS 13:5
וַיִּתֵּן יְהוָה לְיִשְׂרָאֵל מוֹשִׁיעַ וַיֵּצְאוּ מִתַּחַת יַד־אֲרָם וַיֵּשְׁבוּ בְנֵי־יִשְׂרָאֵל בְּאָהֳלֵיהֶם כִּתְמוֹל שִׁלְשׁוֹם:

13:5   כִּתְמוֹל שִׁלְשׁוֹם

Three times in the Prophets   ג׳ בנבי   Mp

Josh 4:18; 1 Sam 21:6 (כִּתְמוֹל שִׁלְשֹׁם); **2 Kgs 13:5**

כִּתְמוֹל שִׁלְשׁוֹם *three times* in the Prophets, and their references   כתמול שלשום ג׳ בנביא וסימנהון   Mm

Josh 4:18   וישבו מי הירדן
1 Sam 21:6   כי אם אשה עצרה
2 Kgs 13:5   ויתן יהוה

Com.: The Masorah notes the *three* occurrences of this lemma in the Prophets, to distinguish them from its *three* occurrences elsewhere in the Bible.

2 KINGS 13:6

אַ֣ךְ לֹא־סָ֠רוּ מֵחַטֹּ֨אות בֵּית־יָרָבְעָ֧ם אֲשֶׁר־הֶחֱטִי אֶת־יִשְׂרָאֵ֖ל בָּ֣הּ הָלָ֑ךְ וְגַם֙ הָאֲשֵׁרָ֔ה עָמְדָ֖ה בְּשֹׁמְרֽוֹן׃

13:6   הֶחֱטִי

Mp¹   החטיא ק   הֶחֱטִיא Read

Mp²   ב֫ חס   *Twice* defective

2 Kgs 13:6; Jer 32:35 (החטי, *kətîb*)

Com.: In the first Mp, the *kətîb* (החטי) represents an archaic orthography where only one of two adjoining and identical letters is written; see Gordis, *The Biblical Text*, 95. Here the adjoining letter is א, which is the first letter of the following word אֶת.

In the second Mp, the Masorah notes the *two* occurrences of this lemma written defective א, to distinguish them from its more numerous occurrences (18x) written plene א (הֶחֱטִיא).

Neither Mᶜ nor Mᴸ has a *kətîb*/*qərê* here. Mᴬ reads *twice defective* א, and Mᶜ reads *defective* א.

In Mᴸ there are two Mp notes but only one circellus.

13:6   עָמְדָה

Mp   ד֗   *Four times*

Gen 30:9; **2 Kgs 13:6**; Ps 26:12; Qoh 2:9

Com.: The Masorah notes the *four* occurrences of this lemma without a ו cj., to distinguish them from its *sole* occurrence with a cj. at 1 Kgs 1:2.

This lemma is featured in a Masoretic list of words that occur *five* times, *four* times without ו cj. and *once* with a ו cj.; see Frensdorff, *Ochlah*, §17.

2 KINGS 13:7

כִּי לֹא הִשְׁאִיר לִיהוֹאָחָז עָם כִּי אִם־חֲמִשִּׁים פָּרָשִׁים וַעֲשָׂרָה רֶכֶב וַעֲשֶׂרֶת אֲלָפִים רַגְלִי כִּי אִבְּדָם מֶלֶךְ אֲרָם וַיְשִׂמֵם כֶּעָפָר לָדֻשׁ׃

13:7 עָם

Seventeen times יז Mp

1–5   Num 23:9; 23:24; Deut 4:33; **Judg 9:36**; 9:37
6–10   **2 Kgs 13:7**; **15:10**; Isa 42:6; Ezek 33:31; **Joel 2:16**
11–15 Ps 18:44; **62:9**; **72:4**; **Prov 14:28**; Job 34:20
16–17 **Esth 3:8**; **1 Chr 17:21**

עָם *seventeen times* עם יז Mm

1–5	Num 23:9	הן
	Num 23:24	הן
	Deut 4:33	השמע
	Judg 9:36	יורד
	Judg 9:37	יורדים
6–10	2 Kgs 13:7	ליהואחז
	לִפְדוֹת *of Chronicles* (1 Chr 17:21)	לפדות דדברי ימים
	Esth 3:8	ודתיהם
	Joel 2:16	אספו
	Ps 18:44	תפלטני
11–15	Isa 42:6	ואצרך
	Ps 62:9	בטחו בו
	Ezek 33:31	אליך
	2 Kgs 15:10	ויכהו
	Ps 72:4	ישפט עניי
16–17	Job 34;20	יגעשו
	Prov 14:28	הדרת מלך

And similarly every <*zaqep,*> *'atnaḥ,*   וכל <זקף> אתנ' וסוף פסוק דכותהון
and *sôp pasûq*

Com.: The Masorah notes the *seventeen* occurrences of עָם written with a *qameṣ*, to distinguish them from its more numerous (100+) occurrences with a *pataḥ* (עַם).

This enumeration does not include the *twenty* occurences of this lemma with a *zaqep*, *'atnaḥ*, or *sôp pasûq*.

The additional notation *of Chronicles* to the 1 Chr 17:21 reference is to distinguish that reference from its parallel in 2 Sam 7:23 where the lemma occurs as לְעָם.

Notes on the Mp headings highlighted above.

Judg 9:36	*Seventeen times with a qameṣ and similarly with every ʾatnaḥ, qabbalah and sôp pasûq* apart from *twice* (Ruth 2:11 and 2 Chr 1:9, when it occurs as עָם). In this heading the term *qabbalah* (קבל) appears in place of *zaqep*; for a discussion of this term, see *BHQ, Judges*, 21*.
2 Kgs 13:7; 15:10; Esth 3:8	*Seventeen times.*
Joel 2:16	*Seventeen times and similarly with every ʾatnaḥ, and sôp pasûq.*
Ps 62:9	*Sixteen times with a qameṣ.* Probably a graphic error of יו *sixteen* for יז *seventeen.*
Ps 72:4	*Seventeen times with a qameṣ.*
Prov 14:28	*Sixteen times and similarly similarly every zaqep, ʾatnaḥ, and sôp pasûq.* Probably a graphic error of יו *sixteen* for יז *seventeen.*
1 Chr 17:21	*Sixteen times with a qameṣ and similarly with every ʾatnaḥ, and sôp pasûq.* Probably a graphic error of יו *sixteen* for יז *seventeen.*

13:7   לָדֹשׁ

Twice, once defective and once plene   ב֗ חד חס וח̇ מל   Mp

2 Kgs 13:7; Hos 10:11 (לָדוֹשׁ)

Com.: The Masorah notes the *two* occurrences of this lemma, *one* written defective ו (here), and *one* written plene ו (Hos 10:11).

---

2 KINGS 13:8

וְיֶ֨תֶר דִּבְרֵ֤י יְהוֹאָחָז֙ וְכָל־אֲשֶׁ֣ר עָשָׂ֔ה וּגְבוּרָת֑וֹ הֲלוֹא־הֵ֣ם כְּתוּבִ֗ים עַל־סֵ֛פֶר דִּבְרֵ֥י הַיָּמִ֖ים לְמַלְכֵ֥י יִשְׂרָאֵֽל׃

13:8   הֲלוֹא

Seventeen times plene in the book   יז̇ מל בסיפ̇   Mp

Com.: See **1 Kgs 2:42**.

2 KINGS 13:9

וַיִּשְׁכַּב יְהוֹאָחָז עִם־אֲבֹתָיו וַיִּקְבְּרֻהוּ בְּשֹׁמְרוֹן וַיִּמְלֹךְ יוֹאָשׁ בְּנוֹ תַּחְתָּיו: פ

13:9   וַיִּקְבְּרֻהוּ בְּשֹׁמְרוֹן

Unique   ל   Mp

Com.: The Masorah notes the *sole* occurrence of בְּשֹׁמְרוֹן with וַיִּקְבְּרֻהוּ (*qal*), to distinguish it from its *two* occurrences with וַיִּקָּבֵר (*niphal*, וַיִּקָּבֵר בְּשֹׁמְרוֹן) at **1 Kgs 16:28** and 2 Kgs 14:16.

2 KINGS 13:10

בִּשְׁנַת שְׁלֹשִׁים וָשֶׁבַע שָׁנָה לְיוֹאָשׁ מֶלֶךְ יְהוּדָה מָלַךְ יְהוֹאָשׁ בֶּן־יְהוֹאָחָז עַל־יִשְׂרָאֵל בְּשֹׁמְרוֹן שֵׁשׁ עֶשְׂרֵה שָׁנָה:

13:10   מָלַךְ יְהוֹאָשׁ

Unique   ל   Mp

1–2   2 Kgs 12:2; **13:10**

Com.: The Mp heading here of *unique* is incorrect since there are *two* occurrences of this lemma.

Neither M^C nor M^A has a note on this lemma here.

2 KINGS 13:11

וַיַּעֲשֶׂה הָרַע בְּעֵינֵי יְהוָה לֹא סָר מִכָּל־חַטֹּאות יָרָבְעָם בֶּן־נְבָט אֲשֶׁר־הֶחֱטִיא אֶת־יִשְׂרָאֵל בָּהּ הָלָךְ:

13:11   וַיַּעֲשֶׂה הָרַע

Three times   ג̇   Mp

Com.: See **2 Kgs 3:2**.

13:11   בָּהּ הָלָךְ

Unique at the end of a verse   ל בסו פס   Mp

Com.: In contrast to v.6 where this phrase is in the middle of the verse.

2 KINGS 13:12

וְיֶ֨תֶר דִּבְרֵ֤י יוֹאָשׁ֙ וְכָל־אֲשֶׁ֣ר עָשָׂ֔ה וּגְב֣וּרָת֔וֹ אֲשֶׁ֣ר נִלְחַ֔ם עִ֖ם אֲמַצְיָ֣ה מֶֽלֶךְ־יְהוּדָ֑ה הֲלוֹא־הֵ֣ם כְּתוּבִ֗ים עַל־סֵ֛פֶר דִּבְרֵ֥י הַיָּמִ֖ים לְמַלְכֵ֥י יִשְׂרָאֵֽל׃

13:12   נִלְחַם

Twelve times   יב   Mp

Com.: See **Judg 9:17**.

2 KINGS 13:13

וַיִּשְׁכַּ֤ב יוֹאָשׁ֙ עִם־אֲבֹתָ֔יו וְיָרָבְעָ֖ם יָשַׁ֣ב עַל־כִּסְא֑וֹ וַיִּקָּבֵ֤ר יוֹאָשׁ֙ בְּשֹׁ֣מְר֔וֹן עִ֖ם מַלְכֵ֥י יִשְׂרָאֵֽל׃ פ

13:13   יוֹאָשׁ[1]

Sixteen times   יו   Mp

Com.: See **2 Kgs 12:20**.

13:13   יָשַׁב

Fifteen times   יה   Mp

Com.: See **1 Sam 27:7**.

2 KINGS 13:14

וֶאֱלִישָׁע֙ חָלָ֣ה אֶת־חָלְי֔וֹ אֲשֶׁ֥ר יָמ֖וּת בּ֑וֹ וַיֵּ֨רֶד אֵלָ֜יו יוֹאָ֣שׁ מֶֽלֶךְ־יִשְׂרָאֵ֗ל וַיֵּ֤בְךְּ עַל־פָּנָיו֙ וַיֹּאמַ֔ר אָבִ֣י ׀ אָבִ֔י רֶ֥כֶב יִשְׂרָאֵ֖ל וּפָרָשָֽׁיו׃

13:14   יוֹאָשׁ

Sixteen times   יו   Mp

Com.: See **2 Kgs 12:20**.

2 Kings 13:15

וַיֹּ֤אמֶר לוֹ֙ אֱלִישָׁ֔ע קַ֖ח קֶ֣שֶׁת וְחִצִּ֑ים וַיִּקַּ֥ח אֵלָ֖יו קֶ֥שֶׁת וְחִצִּֽים׃

13:15   וַיִּקַּח אֵלָיו

Unique   ל   Mp

2 Kings 13:17

וַיֹּ֗אמֶר פְּתַ֧ח הַחַלּ֛וֹן קֵ֖דְמָה וַיִּפְתָּ֑ח וַיֹּ֤אמֶר אֱלִישָׁע֙ יְרֵ֔ה וַיּ֕וֹר וַיֹּ֗אמֶר חֵץ־תְּשׁוּעָ֤ה לַֽיהוָה֙ וְחֵ֣ץ תְּשׁוּעָ֣ה בַֽאֲרָ֔ם וְהִכִּיתָ֧ אֶת־אֲרָ֛ם בַּאֲפֵ֖ק עַד־כַּלֵּֽה׃

13:17   פְּתַח

Four times   ד   Mp

2 Kgs 13:17; Zech 11:1; Prov 31:8; **31:9**

פְּתַח *four times,* and their references   פתח ד וסימנהון   Mm

2 Kgs 13:17   פתח החלון קדמה
Zech 11:1   פתח לבנון דלתיך
Prov 31:8   פתח פיך לאלם
Prov 31:9   שפט צדק

Com.: The Masorah notes the *four* occurrences of this lemma pointed with a *šəwâ*, possibly to distinguish them from its more numerous occurrences with different pointing such as פֶּתַח (107x) or פָּתַח (9x).

13:17   וַיִּפְתָּח

Unique with *qameṣ*   ל   Mp

Com.: The Masorah notes the *sole* occurrence of this lemma with a *qameṣ*, to distinguish it from its more numerous occurrences (12x) with a *pataḥ* (וַיִּפְתַּח).

13:17   יְרֵה

Unique   ל   Mp

13:17	וַיּוֹר		
	Unique	לֹ	Mp

13:17	וְהִכִּיתָ		
	Five times accented (*milraʿ*)	ה̇ בטע	Mp

1–5   **Deut 20:13; Judg 6:16; <u>1 Sam 15:3</u>** (וְהִכִּיתָה); 2 Kgs 9:7 (וְהִכִּיתָה); **13:17**

Com.: The Masorah notes the *five* occurrences of this lemma accented *milraʿ*, to distinguish them from its *two* occurrences accented *milʿêl* at Exod 17:6 and 1 Sam 23:2.

The Mp heading at Judg 6:16 reads *twice with the accent* referring to the *two* occurrences of this lemma with the accent *mêrǝḵâ* (וְהִכִּיתָ) there and at Deut 20:13.

The headings at 1 Sam 15:3 and 2 Kgs 9:7 read *three times plene* referring to the *three* occurrences of this lemma written plene final ה, the third occurrence being that at Jer 5:3 which does not have the ו cj.

13:17	כַּלֵּה		
	Nine times written ה	ט̇ כת ה̇	Mp

1–5   1 Sam 3:12 (וְכַלֵּה); **<u>2 Kgs 13:17</u>; 13:19**; Ps 59:14ᵃ; 59:14ᵇ
6–9   Ps 74:11; Ezra 9:14; 2 Chr 24:10 (לְכַלֵּה); 31:1(לְכַלֵּה)

כַּלֵּה *nine times* written ה, and their references	כלה ט̇ כת ה̇ וסימנהון	Mm

1–5	1 Sam 3:12	אקים אל עלי
	<u>2 Kgs 13:17</u>	באפק עד כלה
	2 Kgs 13:19	אז הכית את ארם
	2 Chr 31:1	(את אפרים) [ובאפרים] ומנשה
	Ps 59:14ᵃ	כלה בחמה
6–9	*Twice* in the verse (Ps 59:14ᵇ)	שנים בפסוקה
	Ps 74:11	מקרב חיקך
	Ezra 9:14	הלוא תאנף בנו
	2 Chr 24:10	וישליכו לארון

<And *once*> (לְכַלֵּא): Dan 9:24   <וחד> לכלא הפשע

Com.: The Masorah notes the *nine* occurrences of this lemma in various forms written with a ה, and *one* written with an א.

The Mp and Mm headings in M^A read *ten times*, and the Mm there lists catchwords for all *ten* forms with an additional note at the end of *nine written* ה *and one written* א.

M^C does not have a note here.

2 KINGS 13:19

וַיִּקְצֹ֨ף עָלָ֜יו אִ֣ישׁ הָאֱלֹהִ֗ים וַיֹּ֙אמֶר֙ לְהַכּ֤וֹת חָמֵ֣שׁ אוֹ־שֵׁ֣שׁ פְּעָמִ֔ים אָ֛ז הִכִּ֥יתָ אֶת־אֲרָ֖ם עַד־כַּלֵּ֑ה וְעַתָּ֕ה שָׁלֹ֥שׁ פְּעָמִ֖ים תַּכֶּ֥ה אֶת־אֲרָֽם: ס

13:19   כַּלֵּה

Nine times written ה   ט כת ה   Mp

Com.: See directly above at **2 Kgs 13:17**.

2 KINGS 13:21

וַיְהִ֞י הֵ֣ם ׀ קֹבְרִ֣ים אִ֗ישׁ וְהִנֵּה֙ רָא֣וּ אֶֽת־הַגְּד֔וּד וַיַּשְׁלִ֥יכוּ אֶת־הָאִ֖ישׁ בְּקֶ֣בֶר אֱלִישָׁ֑ע וַיֵּ֜לֶךְ וַיִּגַּ֤ע הָאִישׁ֙ בְּעַצְמ֣וֹת אֱלִישָׁ֔ע וַיְחִ֖י וַיָּ֥קָם עַל־רַגְלָֽיו: פ

13:21   וַיְהִ֞י

Nine times with the accent (*geršayim*) in the book   ט בטע בסיפ   Mp

Com.: See **1 Kgs 3:18**.

13:21   וַיַּשְׁלִ֥יכוּ

וַיַּשְׁלִ֥יכוּ *four times* plene, and their references   וישליכו ד מל וסימנהון   Mm

Exod 7:12   וישליכו איש מטהו
וַיַּשְׁלִ֥יכוּ אֹתָ֖הּ *of the King of Ai* (Josh 8:29)   וישליכו (אתה) [אותה] דמלך העי
Judg 8:25   וישליכו שמה איש
2 Kgs 13:21   בקבר אלישע

And similarly in all the Writings apart from   וכל כתיבי דכות בר מן
one וַיַּשְׁלִ֥כוּ אֶת־תּוֹרָתְךָ֖ *of Ezra*   חד וישלכו את תורתך דעזרא
(Neh 9:26)

Com.: The Masorah notes the *four* occurrences of this lemma in the Pentateuch and Prophets written plene י, to distinguish them from its *six* occurrences written defective י (וַיַּשְׁלִכוּ).

The Mm has an additional note that this lemma written plene י is also the norm (2x) in the Writings, apart from *one* case when it is written defective י (וַיַּשְׁלִכוּ) at Neh 9:26.

The addition *of the King of Ai* to the catchwords וַיַּשְׁלִיכוּ אוֹתָהּ of the Josh 8:29 reference is simply for reference since there is no other occurrence of these catchwords. Similarly, the addition of Ezra to the catchwords וַיַּשְׁלִכוּ אֶת תּוֹרָתְךָ of the Neh 9:26 is also just for reference since there is no other occurrence of these catchwords.

M^L, contrary to M (וַיַּשְׁלִכוּ), has a *fifth* occurrence of this lemma since it writes the form at 2 Sam 18:17 plene י (וַיַּשְׁלִיכוּ); see Breuer, *The Biblical Text*, 95. However, the Mp headings at Exod 7:12, Josh 8:29, Judg 8:25 and the Mm headings here and at Exod 7:12 all read *four times*, thus supporting the enumeration inherent in the text of M. This lemma occurs in the ms. in folio 211r, but the Mm note appears on the top right of the following folio 211v.

2 KINGS 13:23

וַיָּחָן יְהוָה אֹתָם וַיְרַחֲמֵם וַיִּפֶן אֲלֵיהֶם לְמַעַן בְּרִיתוֹ אֶת־אַבְרָהָם יִצְחָק וְיַעֲקֹב וְלֹא אָבָה הַשְׁחִיתָם וְלֹא־הִשְׁלִיכָם מֵעַל־פָּנָיו עַד־עָתָּה:

13:23   וַיְרַחֲמֵם

Unique   ל̇   Mp

13:23   אַבְרָהָם יִצְחָק וְיַעֲקֹב

Twice   ב̇   Mp

Exod 3:16; **2 Kgs 13:23**

אַבְרָהָם יִצְחָק וְיַעֲקֹב   אברהם יצחק ויעקב   Mm

Exod 3:16   לך ואספת את זקני
2 Kgs 13:23   ויחן יהוה אתם וירחמם ויפן

Com.: The Masorah notes the *two* occurrences of this lemma, to distinguish them from its more numerous occurrences (11x) that have ל prepositions (לְאַבְרָהָם לְיִצְחָק וּלְיַעֲקֹב).

Note that there is no number in the Mm heading.

13:23	וַיַּעֲקֹב		
Fourteen times	יֹ׳	Mp	

Com.: See **Josh 24:4**.

13:23	הַשְׁחִיתָם		
Unique with *pataḥ*	לֹ׳	Mp	

Com.: The Mp heading of *unique with pataḥ* is inexact since there is no other occurrence of this lemma with a different vowel (presumably *ḥîreq*). The note more precisely should have read *unique and with pataḥ*.

M^A correctly reads here *unique*, whereas M^C has no note.

13:23	עַד־עָתָּה		
Four times	ד׳	Mp	

Gen 32:5; **Deut 12:9**; 2 Sam 19:8; **2 Kgs 13:23**

עַד־עָתָּה *four times*	עד עתה ד׳	Mm

Gen 32:5	עם לבן (גרת) [גרתי] ואחר עד
2 Sam 19:8	(מנעוריך) [מנעריך]
Deut 12:9	כי לא באתם עד עתה אל המנוחה
2 Kgs 13:23	מעל פניו

Com.: The Masorah notes the *four* occurrences of this lemma without a ו cj., to distinguish them from its *five* occurrences with a cj. (וְעַד־עָתָּה); see Ognibeni, *'Oklah*, §162.

---

2 KINGS 13:25

וַיָּשָׁב יְהוֹאָשׁ בֶּן־יְהוֹאָחָז וַיִּקַּח אֶת־הֶעָרִים מִיַּד בֶּן־הֲדַד בֶּן־חֲזָאֵל אֲשֶׁר לָקַח מִיַּד יְהוֹאָחָז אָבִיו בַּמִּלְחָמָה שָׁלֹשׁ פְּעָמִים הִכָּהוּ יוֹאָשׁ וַיָּשֶׁב אֶת־עָרֵי יִשְׂרָאֵל: פ

13:25	יוֹאָשׁ		
Sixteen times, and similarly all cases in Judges, The Twelve, and Chronicles	יו׳ וכל שפטים ותרי עשר ודברי הימ׳ דכות	Mp	

Com.: See **2 Kgs 12:20**.

> ### 2 KINGS 14:1
> בִּשְׁנַת שְׁתַּ֗יִם לְיוֹאָ֤שׁ בֶּן־יוֹאָחָז֙ מֶ֣לֶךְ יִשְׂרָאֵ֔ל מָלַ֛ךְ אֲמַצְיָ֥הוּ בֶן־יוֹאָ֖שׁ מֶ֥לֶךְ יְהוּדָֽה׃

14:1   יוֹאָחָז

Four times   ד׳   Mp

2 Kgs 14:1; 2 Chr 34:8; 36:2; 36:4

Com.: The Masorah notes the *four* occurrences of this lemma written with the divine element יוֹ, to distinguish them from its more numerous occurrences (19x) with the divine element יְהוֹ (יְהוֹאָחָז).

> ### 2 KINGS 14:2
> בֶּן־עֶשְׂרִ֨ים וְחָמֵ֤שׁ שָׁנָה֙ הָיָ֣ה בְמָלְכ֔וֹ וְעֶשְׂרִ֤ים וָתֵ֙שַׁע֙ שָׁנָ֔ה מָלַ֖ךְ בִּירוּשָׁלָ֑͏ִם וְשֵׁ֣ם אִמּ֔וֹ יְהוֹעַדִּ֖ין מִן־יְרוּשָׁלָֽםִ׃

14:2   הָיָה בְמָלְכוֹ

Seven times   ז׳   Mp

Com.: See **2 Kgs 8:17**.

14:2   יְהוֹעַדִּין

Read   יְהוֹעַדָּן ק׳   יהועדין   Mp

Com.: The *ketib* (יהועדין) represents the writing of the י of the diphthong *ay* whereas the *qere* (יְהוֹעַדָּן) represents the contraction of this diphthong; see Gordis, *The Biblical Text*, 100, and Cohen, *The Kethib and Qeri System*, 135.

14:2   מִן־יְרוּשָׁלָם

Twice   ב׳   Mp

2 Kgs 14:2; 2 Chr 26:3

Com.: The Masorah notes the *two* occurrences of this lemma with the separable prep. מִן, to distinguish them from its more numerous occurrences (30x) written with the inseparable prep. (מִירוּשָׁלָם).

2 Kings 14:3

וַיַּ֧עַשׂ הַיָּשָׁ֛ר בְּעֵינֵ֥י יְהוָ֖ה רַ֑ק לֹ֣א כְדָוִ֣ד אָבִ֑יו כְּכֹ֧ל אֲשֶׁר־עָשָׂ֛ה יוֹאָ֥שׁ אָבִ֖יו עָשָֽׂה׃

14:3   יוֹאָשׁ

Sixteen times   יוֹ   Mp

Com.: See **2 Kgs 12:20**.

2 Kings 14:6

וְאֶת־בְּנֵ֥י הַמַּכִּ֖ים לֹ֣א הֵמִ֑ית כַּכָּת֣וּב בְּסֵ֣פֶר תּֽוֹרַת־מֹ֠שֶׁה אֲשֶׁר־צִוָּ֨ה יְהוָ֜ה לֵאמֹ֗ר לֹא־יוּמְת֨וּ אָב֤וֹת עַל־בָּנִים֙ וּבָנִים֙ לֹא־יוּמְת֣וּ עַל־אָב֔וֹת כִּ֛י אִם־אִ֥ישׁ בְּחֶטְא֖וֹ יָמֽוּת׃

14:6   וְאֶת־בְּנֵי

Ten times   י   Mp

Com.: See **Josh 10:4**.

14:6   בְּסֵפֶר תּוֹרַת מֹשֶׁה

Three times   ג   Mp

Com.: See **Josh 8:31**.

In M^L two circelli have been placed to include the preceding word כַּכָּתוּב (כַּכָּתוּב בְּסֵפֶר תּוֹרַת) there being no circellus on מֹשֶׁה. However, the phrase כַּכָּתוּב בְּסֵפֶר תּוֹרַת only occurs *twice*, whereas the phrase בְּסֵפֶר תּוֹרַת מֹשֶׁה occurs *three times*. M^A takes the lemma to be בְּסֵפֶר תּוֹרַת מֹשֶׁה, and, like M^L, has notes at all *three* occurrences of *three times*. M^C has no note here.

14:6   יָמוּת

Read   יוּמָת ק   Mp

Com.: The *kәtîb* (ימות, *qal*), and the *qәrê* (יומת, *hophal*) are examples of *kәtîb/qәrê* forms occurring in different conjugations with identical meanings; see Gordis, *The Biblical Text*, 133–34.

This lemma is featured in a Masoretic list of words in which two letters have been interchanged; see Frensdorff, *Ochlah*, §91, and Díaz-Esteban, *Sefer Oklah we-Oklah*, §73.

In M^L this lemma has no circellus.

> ### 2 KINGS 14:7
> הוּא־הִכָּ֨ה אֶת־אֱד֜וֹם בְּגֵיא־הַמֶּ֗לַח עֲשֶׂ֣רֶת אֲלָפִ֔ים וְתָפַ֥שׂ אֶת־הַסֶּ֖לַע בַּמִּלְחָמָ֑ה וַיִּקְרָ֤א אֶת־שְׁמָהּ֙ יָקְתְאֵ֔ל עַ֖ד הַיּ֥וֹם הַזֶּֽה: פ

14:7   הַמֶּ֔לַח

Read   מֶלַח   מלח ק   Mp

Com.: The *kǝtîb* (המלח), and the *qǝrê* (מֶלַח) represent examples of the omission of a definite article; see Gordis, *The Biblical Text*, 147.

This lemma is featured in a Masoretic list of words in which a ה at the beginning of a word is written but not read; see Frensdorff, *Ochlah*, §166, and Díaz-Esteban, *Sefer Oklah we-Oklah*, §91.

14:7   וַיִּקְרָ֤א אֶת־שְׁמָהּ

Twice   ב̇   Mp

Com.: See **1 Sam 7:12**.

14:7   יָקְתְאֵל

Unique   ל   Mp

Com.: The Masorah notes occurrence of this lemma without a ו cj., to distinguish it from its occurrence with a cj. at Josh 15:38.

> ### 2 KINGS 14:8
> אָ֣ז שָׁלַ֤ח אֲמַצְיָה֙ מַלְאָכִ֔ים אֶל־יְהוֹאָ֨שׁ בֶּן־יְהוֹאָחָ֧ז בֶּן־יֵה֛וּא מֶ֥לֶךְ יִשְׂרָאֵ֖ל לֵאמֹ֑ר לְכָ֖ה נִתְרָאֶ֥ה פָנִֽים:

14:8   אֲמַצְיָה

Nine times   ט̇   Mp

Com.: See **2 Kgs 12:22**.

2 KINGS 14:10

הִכֵּה הִכִּ֤יתָ אֶת־אֱדֹום֙ וּנְשָׂאֲךָ֣ לִבֶּ֔ךָ הִכָּבֵ֖ד וְשֵׁ֣ב בְּבֵיתֶ֑ךָ וְלָ֤מָּה תִתְגָּרֶה֙ בְּרָעָ֔ה וְנָ֣פַלְתָּ֔ה אַתָּ֖ה וִיהוּדָ֥ה עִמָּֽךְ׃

14:10   וּנְשָׂאֲךָ

Twice   ב׳   Mp

2 Kgs 14:10; 2 Chr 25:19

Com.: The Masorah notes the *two* occurrences of this lemma in the parallel passages of 2 Kings and 2 Chronicles.

14:10   תִתְגָּרֶה

Twice   ב׳   Mp

2 Kgs 14:10; 2 Chr 25:19

Com.: The Masorah notes the *two* occurrences of this lemma in the parallel passages of 2 Kings and 2 Chronicles.

14:10   וְנָפַלְתָּה

Unique plene   ל מל   Mp

Com.: The Masorah notes the *sole* occurrence of this lemma written plene ה, to distinguish it from its *sole* occurrence written without this ה (וְנָפַלְתָּ) in the parallel passage at 2 Chr 25:19.

2 KINGS 14:11

הִכֵּה הִכִּ֤יתָ אֶת־אֱדֹום֙ וּנְשָׂאֲךָ֣ לִבֶּ֔ךָ הִכָּבֵ֖ד וְשֵׁ֣ב בְּבֵיתֶ֑ךָ וְלָ֤מָּה תִתְגָּרֶה֙ בְּרָעָ֔ה וְנָ֣פַלְתָּ֔ה אַתָּ֖ה וִיהוּדָ֥ה עִמָּֽךְ׃

14:11   וַיִּתְרָאוּ

Twice   ב׳   Mp

2 Kgs 14:11; 2 Chr 25:21

Com.: The Masorah notes the *two* occurrences of this lemma in the parallel passages of 2 Kings and 2 Chronicles.

> **2 KINGS 14:12**
>
> וַיִּנָּ֣גֶף יְהוּדָ֔ה לִפְנֵ֖י יִשְׂרָאֵ֑ל וַיָּנֻ֖סוּ אִ֥ישׁ לְאֹהָלָֽיו׃

14:12   וַיִּנָּ֣גֶף

Mp   ז פסוק מן ז מלין כל מלה אית בהון יוד   *Seven* verses of *seven* words each of which contain the letter י

1–5   2 Sam 22:49; **2 Kgs 14:12**; Ezek 14:1; 30:19; Hos 6:2
6–10 Ps 3:6; 68:2; Job 7:13; Cant 1:2; 1 Chr 4:36;
11   2 Chr 25:22.

Com.: The Mp heading here of *seven verses of seven words each of which contain the letter* י is incorrect since there are *eleven* occurrences of this feature.

There is no Mm for this note in M^L, and the only other places it is found in the Mp are in *Miqra'ot Gedolot* at Hos 6:2 (same note as above), and at 2 Chr 25:22 where the note says that there are *ten verses with seven words each of which contain a* י; see Weiss, "A Puzzling Masoretic Note."

Neither M^C nor M^A has a note on this lemma here.

In M^L this lemma has no circellus.

14:12   לְאֹהָלָֽו

Mp   לאהליו ק   לְאֹהָלָֽיו Read

Mm   לאהלו בֿ חסירין וסימנהון   לְאֹהָלָֽו *twice* defective, and their references

2 Sam 18:17   ויקחו את אבשלום
(2 Kgs 14:12) *of Kings* וַיִּנָּ֣גֶף יְהוּדָ֔ה לִפְנֵ֖י   וינגף יהודה לפני דמלכ֯

Com.: The *kətîb* (לאהלו) without a י represents the archaic form of the 3rd masc. sg. sfx. to a pl. noun, whereas the *qərê* (לְאֹהָלָֽיו) with a י represents the later form; see Cohen, *The Kethib and Qeri System*, 33.

M^C, as M^L, has a *kətîb/qərê* here, but M^A reads *twice defective*.

The Mm notes the *two* occurrences of this lemma written defective י, to distinguish them from its more numerous occurrences (10x) written plene י (לְאֹהָלָיו).

This distinction is implied in the Mm note where the addition *of Kings* to the catchwords וַיִּנָּגֶף יְהוּדָה לִפְנֵי of the 2 Kgs 14:12 reference distinguishes that verse from its parallel in 2 Chr 25:22, where the lemma is written as לְאֹהָלָיו.

> ## 2 KINGS 14:13
> וְאֵת אֲמַצְיָהוּ מֶלֶךְ־יְהוּדָה בֶּן־יְהוֹאָשׁ בֶּן־אֲחַזְיָהוּ תָּפַשׂ יְהוֹאָשׁ מֶלֶךְ־יִשְׂרָאֵל בְּבֵית שֶׁמֶשׁ וַיָּבֹאוּ יְרוּשָׁלַ͏ִם וַיִּפְרֹץ בְּחוֹמַת יְרוּשָׁלַ͏ִם בְּשַׁעַר אֶפְרַיִם עַד־שַׁעַר הַפִּנָּה אַרְבַּע מֵאוֹת אַמָּה׃

14:13   וְאֵת אֲמַצְיָהוּ מֶלֶךְ יְהוּדָה

Mm	וְאֵת אמציהו מלך יהודה	King Amaziah of Judah (2 Kgs 14:13)
	‹וְאֶת־צדקיהו מלך יהודה›	‹King Zedekiah of Judah (Jer 34:21)›

The *first* has *təlîšâ* (וְאֵ֠ת), the *second* has *ḥaṭep̄* (וְאֶת־)   הראשון תלש והשני חטף

The *first* was displaced from kingship, but restored to kingship   הראשון נתלש מן הממלכות וחזר למלכות

‹The *second*›, Zedekiah, was snatched, from kingship and was not restored to kingship   ‹השני› צדקיהו נחטף מן המלכות ולא חזר למלכות

Com.: This Mm note is one of the few that are both descriptive as well as exegetical, and is concerned with the different fates of Amaziah and Zedekiah, kings of Judah.

The former was captured, but then released (2 Kgs 14:13–17; 2 Chr 25:23–25), while the latter was captured and exiled to Babylon where he died (2 Kgs 25:6–7; Jer 39:5–7; 52:9–11).

The difference between the fates of the two kings is illustrated by a comparison of the accents used to describe them in the formula *and X, King of Judah*. The restoration in the Mm is on the basis of the Mm in M^A at 2 Chr 25:23 *sub* וְאֵת אֲמַצְיָהוּ מֶלֶךְ יְהוּדָה.

In the case of Amaziah, with which the note begins, there is a *təlîšâ qəṭannâ* over the initial combination וְאֵת, thus וְאֵ֠ת אֲמַצְיָהוּ (2 Kgs 14:13; 2 Chr 25:23). With Zedekiah there is no accent, thus וְאֶת־צִדְקִיָּהוּ (Jer 34:21).

The descriptive part of the note says that the *first* phrase has a *təlîšâ* accent (תלש), the second phrase, represented by a *maqqēp̄*, has no accent – it is *ḥaṭep̄* (חטף), that is, it does not have a *gaʿyâ* or *meteḡ*.

The exegetical part of the note puns on these accents and remarks that *the first* (Amaziah) *was displaced* (נִתְלַשׁ) *from kingship, but restored to kingship; the second* (Zedekiah) *was snatched* (נֶחְטַף) *from kingship, and was not restored to kingship.*

Note that the accents *təlîšâ qəṭannâ* and *ʾazlâ gereš* have been written in the Mm note.

14:13 וַיָּבֹאוּ

Read וַיָּבֹא ק ויבאו Mp

Com.: The *kətîb* (ויבאו, *they came*), and the *qərê* (וַיָּבֹא, *he came*) represent variants of equal value; see Gordis, *The Biblical Text*, 151.

This lemma is featured in a Masoretic list of words where a ו at the end of a word is written but not read; see Frensdorff, *Ochlah*, §120, and Díaz-Esteban, *Sefer Oklah we-Oklah*, §106.

---

2 KINGS 14:14

וְלָקַח אֶת־כָּל־הַזָּהָב־וְהַכֶּסֶף וְאֵת כָּל־הַכֵּלִים הַנִּמְצְאִים בֵּית־יְהוָה וּבְאֹצְרוֹת בֵּית הַמֶּלֶךְ וְאֵת בְּנֵי הַתַּעֲרֻבוֹת וַיָּשָׁב שֹׁמְרוֹנָה׃

14:14 וְאֶת־בְּנֵי

Ten times י Mp

Com.: See **Josh 10:4**.

14:14 הַתַּעֲרֻבוֹת

Twice בּ Mp

2 Kgs 14:14; 2 Chr 25:24

Com.: The Masorah notes the *two* occurrences of this lemma in the parallel passages of 2 Kings and 2 Chronicles.

The Mp heading at 2 Chr 25:24 reads *twice and written* (this way).

14:14 שֹׁמְרוֹנָה

Three times ג Mp

Com.: See **1 Kgs 20:43**.

> **2 KINGS 14:15**
>
> וְיֶ֨תֶר דִּבְרֵ֥י יְהוֹאָ֜שׁ אֲשֶׁ֣ר עָשָׂ֗ה וּגְב֙וּרָתוֹ֙ וַאֲשֶׁ֣ר נִלְחַ֔ם עִ֖ם אֲמַצְיָ֣הוּ מֶֽלֶךְ־יְהוּדָ֑ה הֲלֹא־הֵ֣ם כְּתוּבִ֗ים עַל־סֵ֛פֶר דִּבְרֵ֥י הַיָּמִ֖ים לְמַלְכֵ֥י יִשְׂרָאֵֽל׃

14:15   נִלְחַם

Twelve times   יבׄ   Mp

1–5   **Num 21:26**; Judg 9:17; 11:25; <u>2 Sam 8:10</u>; **1 Kgs 14:19**
6–10   **2 Kgs 13:12**; <u>14:15</u>; Isa 30:32; Isa 63:10; **1 Chr 18:10**
11–12   **2 Chr 20:29**; 27:5

נִלְחָם *twelve times* with *pataḥ*   נלחם יב פת   Mm

1–5	Num 21:26	חשבון
	Judg 11:25	הטוב
	Judg 9:17	אשר
	<u>2 Sam 8:10</u>	בהדדעזר
	And its companion (1 Chr 18:10)	וחביר
6–10	יָרְבְעָם the *first* (occurrence) (1 Kgs 14:19)	ירבעם קדמי
	2 Kgs 13:12	יואש
	<u>2 Kgs 14:15</u>	יהואש
	Isa 30:32	ובמלחמות
	Isa 63:10	ויהפך
11–12	2 Chr 20:29	פחד
	2 Chr 27:5	ויחזק

Com.: The Masorah notes the *twelve* occurrences of this lemma with a *pataḥ* (perf.), to distinguish them from its more numerous occurrences (11x) with a *qameṣ* (נִלְחָם, ptcpl.); see Ognibeni, *'Oklah*, §182A.

This distinction is implied in the Mm lists of <u>2 Sam 8:10</u> and here, where there is an additional notation of the *first occurrence* to the catchword Jeroboam in the 1 Kgs 14:19 reference, to distinguish this reference from its *second occurrence* of this catchword in 2 Kgs 14:28 where the lemma appears as נִלְחָם.

In M^L the circellus has also mistakenly been placed between this lemma and the preceding word וַאֲשֶׁר, but that combination only occurs *twice*, at 1 Kgs 22:46 and here, so the note belongs only on נִלְחָם.

This lemma occurs in the ms. in folio 211v, but the Mm note appears on the bottom left of the following folio 212r.

> **2 KINGS 14:17**
> וַיְחִ֨י אֲמַצְיָ֤הוּ בֶן־יוֹאָשׁ֙ מֶ֣לֶךְ יְהוּדָ֔ה אַחֲרֵ֣י מ֔וֹת יְהוֹאָ֥שׁ בֶּן־יְהוֹאָחָ֖ז מֶ֣לֶךְ יִשְׂרָאֵ֑ל חֲמֵ֥שׁ עֶשְׂרֵ֖ה שָׁנָֽה׃

14:17   יוֹאָשׁ

Sixteen times in the book   יוֹ בסיפֿ   Mp

Com.: See **2 Kgs 12:20**.

14:17   אַחֲרֵי מוֹת

Three times   גׂ   Mp

Lev 16:1; **2 Kgs 14:17**; 2 Chr 25:25

Com.: The Masorah notes the *three* occurrences of this phrase with the accents *mûnaḥ* and *zaqep*, to distinguish them from occurrences with different accents such as *paštâ* and *mûnaḥ* (Gen 25:11; Judg 1:1; 2 Sam 1:1), *ṭipḥâ* and *mûnaḥ* (Gen 26:18; Ruth 2:11), *ṭəbîr* and *mêrəkâ* (Josh 1:1; 2 Chr 22:4), or *ṭipḥâ* and *mêrəkâ* (2 Kgs 1:1).

Neither M^C nor M^A has a note on this lemma here.

> **2 KINGS 14:19**
> וַיִּקְשְׁר֨וּ עָלָ֥יו קֶ֛שֶׁר בִּירוּשָׁלַ֖͏ִם וַיָּ֣נָס לָכִ֑ישָׁה וַיִּשְׁלְח֤וּ אַחֲרָיו֙ לָכִ֔ישָׁה וַיְמִתֻ֖הוּ שָֽׁם׃

14:19   לָכִישָׁה¹

Six times   וׂ   Mp

1–5   **Josh 10:31; <u>2 Kgs 14:19</u>ᵃ**; 14:19ᵇ; 18:14; 2 Chr 25:27ᵃ
6   **2 Chr 25:27**ᵇ

לָכִישָׁה *six times*   לכישה וׂ   Mm

1–5	Josh 10:31	ויעבר יהושע
	<u>2 Kgs 14:19</u>ᵃ	ויקשרו עליו
	Twice in it (2 Kgs 14:19ᵇ)	בׂ בו
	חִזְקִיָּה *of Kings* (2 Kgs 18:14)	(יחזקיה) [חזקיה] (דישעיה) [דמלכים]
	2 Chr 25:27ᵃ	ומעת אשר סר (אמציה) [אמציהו]
6	*Twice* in it (2 Chr 25:27ᵇ)	בׂ בו

Com.: The Masorah notes the *six* occurrences of this lemma with the locative ה, to distinguish them from its more numerous occurrences (13x) without this adverbial ending.

This distinction is implied in the Mm list in the additional note *of Kings* (incorrectly written as *of Isaiah*) to the 2 Kgs 18:14 reference which distinguishes that verse from its parallel in 2 Chr 32:9, where the lemma occurs as לָכִישׁ.

14:19   לְכִישָׁה²

Six times   ו̇   Mp

Com.: See directly above.

14:19   וַיְמִתֻהוּ

Three times defective   ג̇ חס̇   Mp

2 Sam 4:7; **18:15*; 2 Kgs 14:19**

וַיְמִתֻהוּ *three times* defective   וימתהו ג̇ חסירין   Mm

2 Sam 4:7   ויכהו (וימתהו) ויסירו
2 Sam 18:15   ויסבו עשרה נערים
וַיִּקְשְׁרוּ עָלָיו *of Kings* (2 Kgs 14:19)   ויקשרו עליו דמלכים

And *three times* written וַיְמִיתֻהוּ   ותלתה כת̇ (וימתהו) [וימיתהו]
(2 Chr 22:9; 25:27; 33:24)

Com.: The Masorah notes the *three* occurrences of this lemma written defective second י, and the Mm also notes its *three* occurrences written plene second י (וַיְמִיתֻהוּ).

The additional notation *of Kings* to the catchwords וַיִּקְשְׁרוּ עָלָיו of the 2 Kgs 14:19 reference is to distinguish that verse from its parallel in 2 Chr 25:27, where the lemma is written plene as וַיְמִיתֻהוּ.

*M^L, contrary to M (וַיְמִתֻהוּ), writes 2 Sam 18:15 plene second י (וַיְמִיתֻהוּ); see Breuer, *The Biblical Text*, 95. On the other hand, contra M (וַיְמִיתֻהוּ), it writes the form at 2 Chr 22:9 defective second י (וַיְמִתֻהוּ); see ibid, 380.

The Mp heading at 2 Sam 18:15 reads *six times, three defective* noting all *six* forms listed in the Mm above.

2 KINGS 14:21

וַיִּקְח֣וּ כָל־עַ֣ם יְהוּדָ֗ה אֶת־עֲזַרְיָ֔ה וְה֕וּא בֶּן־שֵׁ֥שׁ עֶשְׂרֵ֖ה שָׁנָ֑ה וַיַּמְלִ֤כוּ אֹתוֹ֙ תַּ֣חַת אָבִ֔יו אֲמַצְיָֽהוּ׃

14:21   והוא

Mp   וְהוּא ק׳   וְהוּא Read

Com.: The *kətîb* of M^L is illegible for this word in that the space for its four consonants is overcrowded, with the letters superimposed on each other. The *qərē* is written larger than usual in a darker ink, and untypically is vocalized. It may have come from the original scribe who, having made a copying error, corrected it in the margin.

2 KINGS 14:22

ה֣וּא בָּנָ֤ה אֶת־אֵילַת֙ וַיְשִׁבֶ֣הָ לִֽיהוּדָ֔ה אַחֲרֵ֥י שְׁכַֽב־הַמֶּ֖לֶךְ עִם־אֲבֹתָֽיו׃ פ

14:22   וַיְשִׁבֶהָ

Mp   ב֗ חד חס֗ וחד מל֗   *Twice, once* defective *and once* plene

2 Kgs 14:22 (וַיְשִׁבֶהָ); 2 Chr 26:2 (וַיְשִׁיבֶהָ)

Mm   מלכים   *(In) Kings:*
והשיבום מל֗   וְהֵשִׁיבוּם plene (1 Kgs 14:28)
וישבה חס֗   וַיְשִׁבֶהָ defective (2 Kgs 14:22)

דדבר הימ֗   *In Chronicles:*
והשבום חס֗   וְהֵשִׁבוּם defective (2 Chr 12:11)
וישיבה מל֗   וַיְשִׁיבֶהָ plene (2 Chr 26:2)

Com.: The Masorah notes the *two* occurrences of this lemma, *once* written defective י in Kings (וַיְשִׁבֶהָ, here), and *once* written plene י (וַיְשִׁיבֶהָ) in Chronicles (the parallel text, 2 Chr 26:2).

The Mm also notes the opposite phenomenon that the form וְהֵשִׁיבוּם is written plene י in Kings (1 Kgs 14:28), but defective י in Chronicles (וְהֵשִׁבוּם, 2 Chr 12:11).

2 KINGS 14:23

בִּשְׁנַת֩ חֲמֵשׁ־עֶשְׂרֵ֨ה שָׁנָ֜ה לַאֲמַצְיָ֣הוּ בֶן־יוֹאָ֣שׁ מֶ֣לֶךְ יְהוּדָ֗ה מָלַ֡ךְ יָרׇבְעָם֩ בֶּן־יוֹאָ֨שׁ מֶ֤לֶךְ יִשְׂרָאֵל֙ בְּשֹׁ֣מְר֔וֹן אַרְבָּעִ֥ים וְאַחַ֖ת שָׁנָֽה׃

14:23　יוֹאָשׁ¹

Sixteen times in the book　　יוֹ בסיפ　　Mp

Com.: See **2 Kgs 12:20**.

2 KINGS 14:24

וַיַּ֥עַשׂ הָרַ֖ע בְּעֵינֵ֣י יְהֹוָ֑ה לֹ֣א סָ֗ר מִכׇּל־חַטֹּאות֙ יָרׇבְעָ֣ם בֶּן־נְבָ֔ט אֲשֶׁ֥ר הֶחֱטִ֖יא אֶת־יִשְׂרָאֵֽל׃

14:24　מִכׇּל־חַטֹּאות

Twice　　ב̇　　Mp

2 Kgs 13:11; **14:24**

Com.: This lemma features in a Masoretic list showing how the phrase *from the sins* (of Jeroboam son of Nebat) is used in connection with various kings; see Frensdorff, *Ochlah*, §294, and Ognibeni, *'Oklah*, §128.

With Jehu (**2 Kgs 10:31**) and Menahem (**2 Kgs 15:18**), it is מֵעַל חַטֹּאות.

With Joash (2 Kgs 13:11) and Jeroboam (here), it is מִכׇּל חַטֹּאות

With Jehoahaz (2 Kgs 13:6), Zechariah (2 Kgs 15:9), and Pekahiah (2 Kgs 15:24), it is מֵחַטֹּאות.

2 KINGS 14:25

ה֗וּא הֵשִׁיב֙ אֶת־גְּב֣וּל יִשְׂרָאֵ֔ל מִלְּב֥וֹא חֲמָ֖ת עַד־יָ֣ם הָעֲרָבָ֑ה כִּדְבַ֤ר יְהֹוָה֙ אֱלֹהֵ֣י יִשְׂרָאֵ֔ל אֲשֶׁ֣ר דִּבֶּ֔ר בְּיַד־עַבְדּ֞וֹ יוֹנָ֤ה בֶן־אֲמִתַּי֙ הַנָּבִ֔יא אֲשֶׁ֖ר מִגַּ֥ת הַחֵֽפֶר׃

14:25　מִלְּבוֹא חֲמָת עַד יָם

Unique　　ל̇　　Mp

Com.: The Masorah notes the *sole* occurrence of מְלְבוֹא חֲמָת עַד with יָם, to distinguish it from its *two* occurrences with נַחַל (מִלְּבוֹא חֲמָת עַד נַחַל) at 1 Kgs 8:65 and 2 Chr 7:8.

In M^L only one circellus has been placed on מִלְּבוֹא חֲמָת but, since this phrase occurs more than once, it is most likely that the note should be extended to include עַד יָם as the longer phrase מִלְּבוֹא חֲמָת עַד יָם only occurs this once.

14:25   בֶּן־אֲמִתַּי

Unique   ל   Mp

1–2 **2 Kgs 14:25**; Jonah 1:1

Com.: The Mp heading of *unique* is inexact since there are *two* occurrences of this lemma. The note more precisely should have read *unique in the book*.

M^C has no note, and M^A is not extant here.

14:25   הַחֶפֶר

Unique   ל   Mp

---

2 KINGS 14:26

כִּי־רָאָה יְהוָה אֶת־עֳנִי יִשְׂרָאֵל מֹרֶה מְאֹד וְאֶפֶס עָצוּר וְאֶפֶס עָזוּב וְאֵין עֹזֵר לְיִשְׂרָאֵל׃

14:26   מֹרֶה

Five times defective   ה חס̇   Mp

1–5 Deut 11:30; 21:20 (וּמֹרֶה); **2 Kgs 14:26**; Ps 78:8 (וּמֹרֶה); **Prov 6:13**

Com.: The Masorah notes the *five* occurrences of this lemma written defective ו, to distinguish them from its more numerous occurrences (11x) written plene ו (מוֹרֶה/וּמוֹרֶה).

14:26   וְאֶפֶס עָזוּב

Unique   ל   Mp

Com.: The Masorah notes the *sole* occurrence of וְאֶפֶס with עָזוּב, to distinguish it from its *two* occurrences with עָצוּר (וְאֶפֶס עָצוּר) at Deut 32:36, and also in this verse.

14:26 וְאֵין עֹזֵר

Three times ג׳ Mp

1–5 **2 Kgs 14:26; Isa 63:5**; Ps 72:12; 107:12; **Lam 1:7** (עֹזֵר)
6 Dan 11:45 (עוֹזֵר)

וְאֵין עֹזֵר *six times*, and (their) references ואין עזר ו׳ וסימ׳ Mm

1–5 2 Kgs 14:26   כי ראה יהוה
      Isa 63:5   ואביט ואין עזר
      Ps 72:12   כי יציל
      Ps 107:12   ויכנע (בעֹ) [בעמל]
      Dan 11:45   ויטע אהלי
6   Lam 1:7   זכרה ירושלם

Com.: The Mp number here of *three times* is incorrect; it should be *six times* as correctly noted in the Mm here and in Isa 63:5, and in the headings of the other highlighted Mp notes.

The Masorah notes the *six* occurrences of this lemma with a ו cj., to distinguish them from its *sole* occurrence without a cj. at Ps 22:12.

M^C correctly reads *six times*, and M^A is not extant here.

In M^L on the top of folio 212r there is an additional fragment of this Masorah. The scribe started to write this note but, having run out of space, restarted the full note at the bottom right of the folio. The fragmentary text contains the lemma and two sets of catchwords, בְּיַד צָר (Lam 1:7) and וּבָא עַד (Dan 11:45).

2 KINGS 14:27
וְלֹא־דִבֶּר יְהוָה לִמְחוֹת אֶת־שֵׁם יִשְׂרָאֵל מִתַּחַת הַשָּׁמָיִם וַיּוֹשִׁיעֵם בְּיַד יָרָבְעָם בֶּן־יוֹאָשׁ׃

14:27 וַיּוֹשִׁיעֵם

Four times ד׳ Mp

Judg 3:9 (וַיּשִׁעֵם)*; **2 Kgs 14:27**; **Ps 106:8**; 106:10

Mm	ויושיעם ד	וַיּוֹשִׁיעֵם *four times*

Judg 3:9   עתניאל
Ps 106:8   למען שמו
2 Kgs 14:27 ירבעם
Ps 106:10   מיד שונא

The *first* is written וַיּוֹשִׁיעֵם and the   קדמיה ויושיעם כתב ותרי ויושיעם
second (= the rest) וַיֹּשִׁעֵם

(And *two* with a ו cj. וְיוֹשִׁיעֵם)
Ps 37:40   ויעזרם יהוה ויפלטם
Ps 145:19   רצון יראיו יעשה

Com.: The Masorah notes the *four* occurrences of this lemma with a ו consec., and the Mm notes its *two* occurrences with a ו cj. (וְיוֹשִׁיעֵם) at Ps 37:40 and 145:19.

*M^L, contrary to M (וַיֹּשִׁעֵם), writes Judg 3:9 plene ו (וַיּוֹשִׁיעֵם); see Breuer, *The Biblical Text*, 56),

The Mm note also observes that the *first* of these forms (at Judg 3:9) is written plene ו (וַיּוֹשִׁיעֵם), while the *rest* of the forms are written defective ו (וַיֹּשִׁעֵם).

Whereas the *first* part of this observation is true for M^L (but not for M, see above), the *second* part of this observation is neither true for M^L nor for M, since in both M^L and M the last three forms are written plene ו (וַיּוֹשִׁיעֵם).

Dotan/Reich *(Masora Thesaurus, ad loc.)* suggest that the Masorete intended to write "the first is written וַיֹּשִׁעֵם [= M]" but inadvertently mixed up with the terms "first" and "second (= the rest)."

---

2 KINGS 14:28

וְיֶ֩תֶר֩ דִּבְרֵ֨י יָרָבְעָ֜ם וְכָל־אֲשֶׁ֣ר עָשָׂ֗ה וּגְבוּרָת֤וֹ אֲשֶׁר־נִלְחָם֙ וַאֲשֶׁ֣ר הֵשִׁ֔יב אֶת־דַּמֶּ֛שֶׂק וְאֶת־חֲמָ֥ת לִיהוּדָ֖ה בְּיִשְׂרָאֵ֑ל הֲלֹא־הֵ֣ם כְּתוּבִ֗ים עַל־סֵ֛פֶר דִּבְרֵ֥י הַיָּמִ֖ים לְמַלְכֵ֥י יִשְׂרָאֵֽל׃

14:28   וְיֶ֩תֶר֩ דִּבְרֵ֨י

Mp	ד בטע	*Four times* with the accents (*təlîšâ qəṭannâ* and *ʾazlâ*)

1 Kgs 22:39; 2 Kgs 14:15; **14:28**; 2 Chr 36:8

Com.: The Masorah notes the *four* occurrences of וְיֶ֨תֶר with the accents *təlîšâ qəṭannâ* and *ʾazlâ*, to distinguish them from occurrences of וְיֶ֥תֶר with other accents such as *ʾazlâ* and *mêrəkâ* (**2 Kgs 10:34**), *ʾazlâ* and *mahpak* (**2 Kgs 21:17**) and *ṭəbîr* (**2 Kgs 15:36**; **16:19**).

This distinction is implied in the Mm to 1 Kgs 22:39 where there is an additional notation *of Chronicles* to the 2 Chr 36:8 reference, which distinguishes it from its parallel passage in 2 Kgs 24:5, where וְיֶ֥תֶר occurs with a *ṭəbîr* accent.

14:28   לִיהוּדָה בְּיִשְׂרָאֵל

Unique   ל   Mp

Com.: The Masorah notes the *sole* occurrence of לִיהוּדָה with בְּיִשְׂרָאֵל, to distinguish it from its *sole* occurrence with וְיִשְׂרָאֵל (לִיהוּדָה וְיִשְׂרָאֵל) at 2 Chr 16:11.

2 KINGS 15:1

בִּשְׁנַת עֶשְׂרִ֤ים וְשֶׁ֙בַע֙ שָׁנָ֔ה לְיָרָבְעָ֖ם מֶ֣לֶךְ יִשְׂרָאֵ֑ל מָלַ֛ךְ עֲזַרְיָ֥ה בֶן־אֲמַצְיָ֖ה מֶ֥לֶךְ יְהוּדָֽה׃

15:1   אֲמַצְיָה

Nine times   ט׳   Mp

Com.: See **2 Kgs 12:22**.

2 KINGS 15:2

בֶּן־שֵׁ֨שׁ עֶשְׂרֵ֤ה שָׁנָה֙ הָיָ֣ה בְמָלְכ֔וֹ וַחֲמִשִּׁ֤ים וּשְׁתַּ֙יִם֙ שָׁנָ֔ה מָלַ֖ךְ בִּירוּשָׁלָ֑͏ִם וְשֵׁ֣ם אִמּ֔וֹ יְכָלְיָ֖הוּ מִירוּשָׁלָֽ͏ִם׃

15:2   יְכָלְיָהוּ מִירוּשָׁלָ͏ִם

Unique   ל   Mp

Com.: The Masorah notes the occurrence of this lemma written this way, to distinguish it from its *sole* occurrence in the parallel passage at 2 Chr 26:3 written as יְכָלְיָה מִן יְרוּשָׁלָ͏ִם.

> **2 KINGS 15:5**
> וַיְנַגַּע יְהוָה אֶת־הַמֶּלֶךְ וַיְהִי מְצֹרָע עַד־יוֹם מֹתוֹ וַיֵּשֶׁב בְּבֵית הַחָפְשִׁית וְיוֹתָם בֶּן־הַמֶּלֶךְ עַל־הַבַּיִת שֹׁפֵט אֶת־עַם הָאָרֶץ׃

15:5   וַיְנַגַּע יְהוָה

Twice   בׄ   Mp

Gen 12:17; **2 Kgs 15:5**

Com.: The Mp heading at Gen 12:17 contains the catchwords את המלך (אֶת־הַמֶּלֶךְ), which refer the reader back to this verse.

In M^L the circellus has been placed here only on וַיְנַגַּע, but it is on both words in M^C and in Gen 12:17.

15:5   מֹתוֹ

Three times defective   גׄ חס   Mp

Num 33:39 (בְּמֹתוֹ); Deut 34:7 (בְּמֹתוֹ); 2 Kgs 15:5

Com.: The Masorah notes the *three* occurrences of this lemma written defective ו, to distinguish them from its more numerous occurrences (14x) written plene ו (מוֹתוֹ/בְּמוֹתוֹ).

15:5   וַיֵּשֶׁב בְּבֵית הַחָפְשִׁית

(In) *Kings*:   מלכים   Mm
2 Kgs 15:5   וישב בבית החפשית

In *Chronicles*:   דדברי הימים
2 Chr 26:21   בית החפשית

And their *sîman* is   וסימנהון
Deut 4:3   עיניכם הראת את אשר

Com.: The Masorah notes *two* parallel phrases, *one* in 2 Kgs 15:5 and *one* in 2 Chr 26:21, the *first* one has the prep. בּ with בֵּית and the *second* does not.

The verse from Deut 4:3 is cited as the third verse *sîman* because it contains the elements of this difference, namely two phrases בְּבַעַל פְּעוֹר and בַּעַל פְּעוֹר, *one* with the prep. בּ and *one* without the prep., and occurring in the same order as in the two verses from Kings and Chronicles.

This lemma is featured in a wider list of parallel phrases, *all* of which are characterized by the *first* phrase occurring with the prep. ב with בַּיִת, and the *second* without; see the Mm at Esth 5:1 *sub* בְּבֵית הַמַּלְכוּת

This lemma occurs in the ms. in folio 212r, but the Mm note appears on the bottom right of the following folio 212v.

2 KINGS 15:6
וְיֶ֨תֶר דִּבְרֵ֤י עֲזַרְיָ֙הוּ֙ וְכָל־אֲשֶׁ֣ר עָשָׂ֔ה הֲלֹא־הֵ֣ם כְּתוּבִ֔ים עַל־סֵ֛פֶר דִּבְרֵ֥י הַיָּמִ֖ים לְמַלְכֵ֥י יְהוּדָֽה׃

15:6   עֲזַרְיָהוּ

Twice in the Prophets   ב̇ בנביא̇   Mp

Com.: See **1 Kgs 4:2**.

2 KINGS 15:7
וַיִּשְׁכַּ֤ב עֲזַרְיָה֙ עִם־אֲבֹתָ֔יו וַיִּקְבְּר֥וּ אֹת֛וֹ עִם־אֲבֹתָ֖יו בְּעִ֣יר דָּוִ֑ד וַיִּמְלֹ֛ךְ יוֹתָ֥ם בְּנ֖וֹ תַּחְתָּֽיו׃ פ

15:7   וַיִּקְבְּרוּ אֹתוֹ עִם

Twice in the book   ב̇ בסיפ̇   Mp

2 Kgs 12:22; **15:7**

Com.: The Masorah notes the *two* occurrences of this lemma in the book, to distinguish them from its *two* occurrences in the book of Chronicles at 2 Chron 25:28 and 26:23.

2 KINGS 15:8
בִּשְׁנַ֨ת שְׁלֹשִׁ֤ים וּשְׁמֹנֶה֙ שָׁנָ֔ה לַעֲזַרְיָ֖הוּ מֶ֣לֶךְ יְהוּדָ֑ה מָ֠לַךְ זְכַרְיָ֨הוּ בֶן־יָרָבְעָ֧ם עַל־יִשְׂרָאֵ֛ל בְּשֹׁמְר֖וֹן שִׁשָּׁ֥ה חֳדָשִֽׁים׃

15:8   זְכַרְיָהוּ

Four times in the Prophets   ד̇ בנביא̇   Mp

1–2   **2 Kgs 15:8; Isa 8:2**

Com.: The Mp heading here of *four times in the Prophets* is incorrect since there are only *two* occurrences of this lemma in the Prophets.

The Masorah notes the *two* occurrences of this lemma in the Prophets written with the divine element יָהוּ, to distinguish them from its more numerous occurrences (7x) in the Prophets without the divine element יָה (זְכַרְיָה); see Ognibeni, *'Oklah*, §59.

The Mp heading at Isa 8:2 correctly reads *twice in the Prophets*.

M^C reads here *twice* (in the Prophets), *and similarly all Chronicles apart from seven*. M^A is not extant here.

---

2 KINGS 15:10

וַיִּקְשֹׁר עָלָיו שַׁלֻּם בֶּן־יָבֵשׁ וַיַּכֵּהוּ קָבָלְ־עָם וַיְמִיתֵהוּ וַיִּמְלֹךְ תַּחְתָּיו׃

15:10   יָבֵשׁ

Six times defective   ו חסֿ   Mp

Com.: See **Judg 21:14**.

15:10   עָם

Seventeen times   יֹּז   Mp

Com.: See **2 Kgs 13:7**.

---

2 KINGS 15:11

וְיֶתֶר דִּבְרֵי זְכַרְיָה הִנָּם כְּתוּבִים עַל־סֵפֶר דִּבְרֵי הַיָּמִים לְמַלְכֵי יִשְׂרָאֵל׃

15:11   הִנָּם כְּתוּבִים

Five times in the Prophets   הֿ בנבֿ   Mp

Com.: See **1 Kgs 14:19**.

2 KINGS 15:12

הוּא דְבַר־יְהוָה אֲשֶׁר דִּבֶּר אֶל־יֵהוּא לֵאמֹר בְּנֵי רְבִיעִים יֵשְׁבוּ לְךָ עַל־כִּסֵּא יִשְׂרָאֵל וַיְהִי־כֵן: פ

15:12   רְבִיעִים

Mp   בׄ חד מל וחד חסׄ   *Twice, once* plene and *once* defective

2 Kgs 10:30 (רְבִעִים); **15:12** (רְבִיעִים)

Mm   (רביעים) [רביעים] בׄ חד מל וחד חסׄ   רְבִיעִים *twice, once* plene, *and once* defective

2 Kgs 15:12 (רְבִיעִים)   (ושבו) [ישבו] לך
2 Kgs 10:30 (רְבִעִים)   ישבו לך

Com.: The Masorah notes the *two* occurrences of this lemma, *one* written plene first י (here), and *one* written defective first י at 2 Kgs 10:30.

2 KINGS 15:13

שַׁלּוּם בֶּן־יָבֵישׁ מָלַךְ בִּשְׁנַת שְׁלֹשִׁים וָתֵשַׁע שָׁנָה לְעֻזִּיָּה מֶלֶךְ יְהוּדָה וַיִּמְלֹךְ יֶרַח־יָמִים בְּשֹׁמְרוֹן:

15:13   שַׁלּוּם

Mp   גׄ מל בנבׄי   *Three times* plene in the Prophets

2 Kgs 15:13; 15:14; 15:15

Com.: The Masorah notes the *three* occurrences of this lemma in the Prophets written plene ו, to distinguish them from its *five* occurrences in the Prophets written defective ו (שַׁלֻּם); see **2 Kgs 22:14**.

15:13   לְעֻזִּיָּה

Mp   דׄ   *Four times*

2 Kgs 15:13; 15:30 (עֻזִּיָּה); **1 Chr 6:9** (עֲזִיָּה); **11:44** (עֻזִּיָּא)

Mm   עזיה ד   עֲזִיָה *four times*

2 Kgs 15:13	שלום בן יביש
2 Kgs 15:30	ויקשר קשר
1 Chr 6:9	עזיה בנו
1 Chr 11:44	העשתרתי [עזיא] (עזיה)
The *last form* is written with an א	בתריה כת׳ א

And similarly *all* The Twelve and Ezra   וכל תרי עשר ועזרא דכות

Com.: The Masorah notes the *four* occurrences of this lemma written with the divine element יָה, to distinguish them from its more numerous occurrences (19x) written with the divine element יָהוּ (עֲזִיָהוּ/לְעֻזִּיָהוּ).

The Mm additionally notes that this lemma also occurs in The Twelve (*three times*) and Ezra (*twice*).

The Mp heading at 1 Chr 6:9 reads *four times and similarly all The Twelve*.

The Mp heading at 1 Chr 11:44 reads *unique written with an* א noting that its form עֲזִיא only occurs *once*.

15:13   יֶרַח־יָמִים

Mm   ירח ימים ב׳   יֶרַח־יָמִים *twice*

Deut 21:13	את אביה ואת אמה
2 Kgs 15:13	וימלך ירח ימים בשמרון

Com.: The Masorah notes the *two* occurrences of יָמִים with יֶרַח, to distinguish them from its *three* occurrences with חֹדֶשׁ (חֹדֶשׁ יָמִים).

---

2 KINGS 15:14

וַיַּעַל מְנַחֵם בֶּן־גָּדִי מִתִּרְצָה וַיָּבֹא שֹׁמְרוֹן וַיַּךְ אֶת־שַׁלּוּם בֶּן־יָבֵישׁ בְּשֹׁמְרוֹן וַיְמִיתֵהוּ וַיִּמְלֹךְ תַּחְתָּיו׃

15:14   שַׁלּוּם

Mp   ג׳ מל בנב   *Three times* plene in the Prophets

Com.: See directly above at **2 Kgs 15:13**.

2 Kings 15:16

אָ֣ז יַכֶּֽה־מְ֠נַחֵם אֶת־תִּפְסַ֨ח וְאֶת־כָּל־אֲשֶׁר־בָּ֤הּ וְאֶת־גְּבוּלֶ֙יהָ֙ מִתִּרְצָ֔ה כִּ֛י לֹ֥א פָתַ֖ח וַיַּ֑ךְ אֵ֛ת כָּל־הֶהָרוֹתֶ֖יהָ בִּקֵּֽעַ׃ פ

15:16   גְּבוּלֶ֙יהָ֙

Three times   גׄ   Mp

Com.: See **1 Sam 5:6**.

15:16   הֶהָרוֹתֶ֖יהָ

Unique   ל   Mp

Com.: This lemma is featured in a Masoretic list of words that contain both the accents *mêrĕkâ* and *ṭiphâ*; see the Mm at Lev 23:21 *sub* מוֹשְׁבֹתֵיכֶֽם.

2 Kings 15:17

בִּשְׁנַ֣ת שְׁלֹשִׁ֤ים וָתֵ֙שַׁע֙ שָׁנָ֔ה לַעֲזַרְיָ֖ה מֶ֣לֶךְ יְהוּדָ֑ה מָ֠לַךְ מְנַחֵ֨ם בֶּן־גָּדִ֤י עַל־יִשְׂרָאֵל֙ עֶ֣שֶׂר שָׁנִ֔ים בְּשֹׁמְרֽוֹן׃

15:17   בִּשְׁנַ֣ת שְׁלֹשִׁ֤ים

Unique with these accents (*ʾazlâ* and *mahpak*) in this section   ל בטע בעינ   Mp

Com.: The Masorah notes that this phrase with these accents (*ʾazlâ* and *mahpak*) occurs only *once* in this section concerning Menahem.

The same phrase and accents occurs in adjacent sections: in 2 Kgs 15:8 concerning Zechariah, and in 2 Kgs 15:13 concerning Shallum.

2 Kings 15:18

וַיַּ֥עַשׂ הָרַ֖ע בְּעֵינֵ֣י יְהוָ֑ה לֹ֣א סָ֗ר מֵעַ֤ל חַטֹּאות֙ יָרָבְעָ֣ם בֶּן־נְבָ֔ט אֲשֶׁר־הֶחֱטִ֖יא אֶת־יִשְׂרָאֵ֑ל כָּל־יָמָֽיו׃

15:18   מֵעַ֤ל חַטֹּאות

Twice   בׄ   Mp

Com.: See **2 Kgs 10:31**.

2 KINGS 15:20

וַיֹּצֵא֩ מְנַחֵ֨ם אֶת־הַכֶּ֜סֶף עַל־יִשְׂרָאֵ֗ל עַ֤ל כָּל־גִּבּוֹרֵי֙ הַחַ֔יִל לָתֵת֙ לְמֶ֣לֶךְ אַשּׁ֔וּר חֲמִשִּׁ֥ים שְׁקָלִ֛ים כֶּ֖סֶף לְאִ֣ישׁ אֶחָ֑ד וַיָּ֙שָׁב֙ מֶ֣לֶךְ אַשּׁ֔וּר וְלֹא־עָ֥מַד שָׁ֖ם בָּאָֽרֶץ׃

15:20   וַיֹּצֵא

Thirteen times defective   יג֯ חס֯   Mp

Com.: See **2 Kgs 10:22**.

15:20   גִּבּוֹרֵי הַחַיִל

Five times   ה֯   Mp

Com.: See **Josh 1:14**.

15:20   וְלֹא־עָמַד

Three times   ג֯   Mp

Gen 45:1; Josh 21:44; 2 Kgs 15:20

וְלֹא־עָמַד *three times*   ולא עמד ג֯   Mm

Gen 45:1   יוסף
2 Kgs 15:20   מנחם
Josh 21:44   (אביהם) [איביהם]

Com.: The Masorah notes the *three* occurrences of this lemma with a ו cj., to distinguish them from its *four* occurrences of this lemma without a cj.

2 KINGS 15:21

וְיֶ֛תֶר דִּבְרֵ֥י מְנַחֵ֖ם וְכָל־אֲשֶׁ֣ר עָשָׂ֑ה הֲלוֹא־הֵ֣ם כְּתוּבִ֗ים עַל־סֵ֛פֶר דִּבְרֵ֥י הַיָּמִ֖ים לְמַלְכֵ֥י יִשְׂרָאֵֽל׃

15:21   הֲלוֹא

Seventeen times plene in the book   יז֯ מל בסיפ֯   Mp

Com.: See **1 Kgs 2:42**.

2 Kings 15:23

בִּשְׁנַת חֲמִשִּׁים שָׁנָה לַעֲזַרְיָה מֶלֶךְ יְהוּדָה מָלַךְ פְּקַחְיָה בֶן־מְנַחֵם עַל־יִשְׂרָאֵל בְּשֹׁמְרוֹן שְׁנָתָיִם:

15:23   בִּשְׁנַת חֲמִשִּׁים שָׁנָה

Unique   ל   Mp

2 Kings 15:25

וַיִּקְשֹׁר עָלָיו פֶּקַח בֶּן־רְמַלְיָהוּ שָׁלִישׁוֹ וַיַּכֵּהוּ בְשֹׁמְרוֹן בְּאַרְמוֹן בֵּית־᮰מֶלֶךְ אֶת־אַרְגֹּב וְאֶת־הָאַרְיֵה וְעִמּוֹ חֲמִשִּׁים אִישׁ מִבְּנֵי גִלְעָדִים וַיְמִיתֵהוּ וַיִּמְלֹךְ תַּחְתָּיו:

15:25   שָׁלִישׁוֹ

Twice   בׄ   Mp

Com.: See **2 Kgs 9:25**.

15:25   ᮰מֶלֶךְ

Read   הַמֶּלֶךְ קׄ   המלך קׄ   Mp

Com.: The *katîb* (מלך), and the *qәrē* (הַמֶּלֶךְ) represent examples of the omission of a definite article; see Gordis, *The Biblical Text*, 147.

This lemma is featured in a Masoretic list of words where a ה is not written at the beginning of a word; see the Mm at **2 Sam 23:9** *sub* גִּבֹּרִים᮰, Frensdorff, *Ochlah*, §165, and Díaz-Esteban, *Sefer Oklah we-Oklah*, §90.

15:25   גִלְעָדִים

Unique   ל   Mp

2 Kings 15:26

וְיֶתֶר דִּבְרֵי פְקַחְיָה וְכָל־אֲשֶׁר עָשָׂה הִנָּם כְּתוּבִים עַל־סֵפֶר דִּבְרֵי הַיָּמִים לְמַלְכֵי יִשְׂרָאֵל: פ

15:26   הִנָּם כְּתוּבִים

Five times in the Prophets   הׄ בנב   Mp

Com.: See **1 Kgs 14:19**.

> ## 2 KINGS 15:28
> וַיַּעַשׂ הָרַע בְּעֵינֵי יְהוָה לֹא סָר מִן־חַטֹּאות יָרָבְעָם בֶּן־נְבָט אֲשֶׁר הֶחֱטִיא אֶת־יִשְׂרָאֵל׃

15:28   מִן־חַטֹּאות

Unique   ל̇   Mp

Com.: This lemma is featured in a Masoretic list of words preceded only *once* by the separable prep. מִן, whereas normally it is attached by the inseparable prep. מ; see Frensdorff, *Ochlah*, §196, and Ognibeni, *'Oklah*, §151.

> ## 2 KINGS 15:29
> בִּימֵי פֶּקַח מֶלֶךְ־יִשְׂרָאֵל בָּא תִּגְלַת פִּלְאֶסֶר מֶלֶךְ אַשּׁוּר וַיִּקַּח אֶת־עִיּוֹן וְאֶת־אָבֵל בֵּית־מַעֲכָה וְאֶת־יָנוֹחַ וְאֶת־קֶדֶשׁ וְאֶת־חָצוֹר וְאֶת־הַגִּלְעָד וְאֶת־הַגָּלִילָה כֹּל אֶרֶץ נַפְתָּלִי וַיַּגְלֵם אַשּׁוּרָה׃

15:29   אֶת

Seven verses that have the sequence   פסוק אית בהון ז̇   Mp
<אֶת>...וְאֶת...וְאֶת...וְאֶת...וְאֶת...<וְאֶת>   <ואת> את ואת ואת ואת ואת

1–5   Gen 36:6; Lev 8:2; **8:25**; Judg 1:31; 1 Kgs 9:15
6–7   **2 Kgs 15:29; 2 Chr 28:18**

Seven verses that have the sequence   פסוקין אית בהון ז̇   Mm
<אֶת>...וְאֶת...וְאֶת...וְאֶת...וְאֶת...<וְאֶת>   <ואת> את ואת ואת ואת ואת

1–5   Gen 36:6   ויקח עשו את נשיו
      Lev 8:2   קח את אהרן ואת בניו
      Lev 8:25   ויקח את החלב ואת האליה
      1 Kgs 9:15   וזה דבר המס
      Judg 1:31   אשר לא הוריש
6–7   2 Kgs 15:29   בימי פקח מלך
      2 Chr 28:18   ופלשתים פשטו

Com.: The Masorah notes the *seven* verses that have the sequence of אֶת followed by *six* occurrences of וְאֶת (אֶת...וְאֶת...וְאֶת...וְאֶת...וְאֶת...וְאֶת); see Jobin, *Concordance*, 94.

Both the Mp and Mm here have omitted the *sixth* וְאֶת from its sequence, but all *six* are found in the headings of the Mp notes at Lev 8:25 and 2 Chr 28:18.

The Mp at 2 Chr 28:18 list only *six* verses, which might have been thought to be the result of a graphic confusion of ו *six* and ז *seven*, except that its Mm also has the heading of *six*, and it lists only *six* references, omitting Judg 1:31.

In M^L this lemma has no circellus.

15:29	וְאֶת־יָנוֹחַ		
Unique		ל	Mp

15:29	וְאֶת־קֶדֶשׁ		
Unique		ל	Mp

Com.: The Masorah notes the *sole* occurrence of this lemma with a ו cj., to distinguish it from its *five* occurrences without a cj.

15:29	וְאֶת־הַגָּלִילָה		
Unique		ל	Mp

15:29	וַיַּגְלֵם		
Unique		ל	Mp

1–2 **2 Kgs 15:29**; 1 Chr 5:26

Com.: The Mp heading here of *unique* is incorrect since there is another occurrence of this lemma at 1 Chr 5:26.

The Masorah notes the *two* occurrences of this lemma (*hiphil* of גָּלָה with sfx., *he exiled them*), to distinguish it from its *sole* occurrence pointed as וַיִּגְלֹם (*qal* of גָּלַם, *he wrapped*) at **2 Kgs 2:8**.

M^C has no note, and M^A is not extant here.

15:29	אַשּׁוּרָה		
Six times		ו	Mp

1–5 **Gen 25:18**; <u>**2 Kgs 15:29**</u>; **17:6**; **17:23**; 18:11
6   Isa 19:23

		אשורה וֹ	Mm	אֲשׁוּרָה *six times*

1–5	Gen 25:18	וישכנו מחוילה
	2 Kgs 17:6	התשיעית להושע
	<u>2 Kgs 15:29</u>	בימי פקח מלך
	2 Kgs 18:11	ויגל מלך אשור
	2 Kgs 17:23	עד אשר
6	<Isa 19:23>	

Com.: The Masorah notes the *six* occurrences of this lemma with the locative ה, to distinguish them from its more numerous occurrences (100+) without this adverbial ending. This lemma occurs in the ms. in folio 213r, but the Mm note appears on the top left of the preceding folio 212v.

---

2 KINGS 15:30

וַיִּקְשָׁר־קֶ֠שֶׁר הוֹשֵׁ֨עַ בֶּן־אֵלָ֜ה עַל־פֶּ֣קַח בֶּן־רְמַלְיָ֗הוּ וַיַּכֵּ֙הוּ֙ וַיְמִיתֵ֔הוּ וַיִּמְלֹ֖ךְ תַּחְתָּ֑יו בִּשְׁנַת֙ עֶשְׂרִ֣ים לְיוֹתָ֔ם בֶּן־עֻזִּיָּֽה׃

15:30   וַיְמִיתֵהוּ

Eight times plene   ח̇ מל̇   Mp

1–5	**1 Kgs 13:24; 1 Kgs 16:10; 2 Kgs 15:10; 15:14; <u>15:30</u>**
6–8	**2 Kgs 23:29; 1 Chr 2:3; 10:14**

וַיְמִיתֵהוּ *eight times* plene   וימיתהו ח̇ מל̇   Mm

1–5	1 Kgs 13:24	וימצאהו
	1 Kgs 16:10	ויבא זמרי
	2 Kgs 15:14	ויעל מנחם
	2 Kgs 15:10	קבל עם
	2 Kgs 15:25	גלעדים
6–9	<u>2 Kgs 15:30</u>	ויקשר קשר (הוש) [הושע]
	1 Chr 2:3	ויהי
	2 Kgs 23:29	במגדו
	1 Chr 10:14	ולא דרש ביהוה וימיתהו

Com.: The Masorah notes the *eight* occurrences of this lemma written plene י, to distinguish them from occurrences written defective י as וַיְמִתֵהוּ.

M^L, contrary to M (וַיְמִתֵהוּ), has *two* more occurrences of this lemma since it writes the form plene (וַיְמִיתֵהוּ) at 1 Sam 17:50 and 2 Sam 21:17; see Breuer, *The Biblical Text*, 75 and 97.

It will be noticed that, despite its heading of *eight*, the Mm list here includes a *ninth* listing, that of 2 Kgs 15:25 which is, however, defective in M; see Breuer, *The Biblical Text*, 128.

However, all the Mp headings highlighted above, and the Mm heading read *eight times*, thus supporting the enumeration inherent in the text of M.

15:30	בִּשְׁנַת עֶשְׂרִים לְיוֹתָם
Unique	לׄ Mp

15:30	עֲזִיָּה
Four times	דׄ Mp

Com.: See directly above at **2 Kgs 15:13**.

---

2 KINGS 15:33

בֶּן־עֶשְׂרִים וְחָמֵשׁ שָׁנָה הָיָה בְמָלְכוֹ וְשֵׁשׁ־עֶשְׂרֵה שָׁנָה מָלַךְ בִּירוּשָׁלָ͏ִם וְשֵׁם אִמּוֹ יְרוּשָׁא בַּת־צָדוֹק׃

15:33	הָיָה בְמָלְכוֹ
Seven times	זׄ Mp

Com.: See **2 Kgs 8:17**.

15:33	יְרוּשָׁא
Twice, once written שָׁא *and once* written שָׁה	ב׳ חד כת שא וחד כת שה Mp

---

2 Kgs 15:33; 2 Chr 27:1 (יְרוּשָׁה)

ירושא *twice, once* written שָׁא *and once* written שָׁה	ירושא ב׳ חד כתב שא וחד כת שה Mm

2 Kgs 15:33 And its companion in Chronicles is written יְרוּשָׁה (2 Chr 27:1)	צדוק וחבירו דדברי הימים כת ירושה

Com.: The Masorah notes the *two* forms of this lemma appearing in the parallel passages of 2 Kgs 15:33 and 2 Chr 27:1. Here the lemma is written with an א (יְרוּשָׁא), but in Chronicles it is written with a ה (יְרוּשָׁה).

This lemma is featured in two Masoretic lists of words. One is in a list of doublets commencing with י; see Frensdorff, *Ochlah*, §66. The other is in a list of words occurring *once* with at the end with an א and *once* with a ה; see Frensdorff, *Ochlah*, §95, and Díaz-Esteban, *Sefer Oklah we-Oklah*, §78.

2 KINGS 15:36
וְיֶ֨תֶר דִּבְרֵ֤י יוֹתָם֙ אֲשֶׁ֣ר עָשָׂ֔ה הֲלֹא־הֵ֣ם כְּתוּבִ֗ים עַל־סֵ֛פֶר דִּבְרֵ֥י הַיָּמִ֖ים לְמַלְכֵ֥י יְהוּדָֽה׃

15:36   וְיֶ֨תֶר

Thirteen times with the accent (*ṭəbîr*)   יג בטע   Mp

Com.: See **1 Kgs 15:31**.

2 KINGS 15:37
בַּיָּמִ֣ים הָהֵ֔ם הֵחֵ֣ל יְהוָ֗ה לְהַשְׁלִ֙יחַ֙ בִּֽיהוּדָ֔ה רְצִ֥ין מֶֽלֶךְ־אֲרָ֖ם וְאֵ֥ת פֶּ֖קַח בֶּן־רְמַלְיָֽהוּ׃

15:37   לְהַשְׁלִ֙יחַ֙

Unique   ל   Mp

15:37   וְאֵ֥ת

וְאֵת *seven times* with the accent (*ṭipḥâ*)   ואת ז בטע מטע   Mm
where one is liable to err

1–5	<Gen 19:25>	
	Num 32:28	יהושע בן
	Isa 36:22	רבשקה
	2 Kgs 15:37	ואת פקח
	Ezek 3:2	המגלה
6–7	Zech 8:9	תחזקנה
	Neh 5:6	(מזעקתם הדברים) [את זעקתם ואת הדברים]

Com.: The Masorah notes the *seven* occurrences of וְאֵת with a *ṭipḥâ* accent, and observes that in these occurrences one is liable to err if one were to write וְאֵת in these cases with a *maqqep̄* (וְאֶת־) instead of a *ṭipḥâ*; see Ginsburg, 4, א, §1289, and Kelley et al., *The Masorah*, 135–36.

The heading of the Mm to Isa 36:22 reads *seven unusual cases* (מיחדים = מיחד) *with this accent* (*ṭipḥâ*).

15:37   וְאֵת פֶּקַח

Unique   ל   Mp

---

2 KINGS 15:38

וַיִּשְׁכַּב יוֹתָם עִם־אֲבֹתָיו וַיִּקָּבֵר עִם־אֲבֹתָיו בְּעִיר דָּוִד אָבִיו וַיִּמְלֹךְ אָחָז בְּנוֹ תַּחְתָּיו: פ

15:38   בְּעִיר דָּוִד אָבִיו

Four times in the book   ד בסיפ   Mp

Com.: See **1 Kgs 11:27**.

---

2 KINGS 16:2

בֶּן־עֶשְׂרִים שָׁנָה אָחָז בְּמָלְכוֹ וְשֵׁשׁ־עֶשְׂרֵה שָׁנָה מָלַךְ בִּירוּשָׁלָ͏ִם וְלֹא־עָשָׂה הַיָּשָׁר בְּעֵינֵי יְהוָה אֱלֹהָיו כְּדָוִד אָבִיו:

16:2   וְלֹא־עָשָׂה

Five times   ה   Mp

1–5   **2 Sam 19:25**ᵃ; 19:25ᵇ; **2 Kgs 16:2; Jonah 3:10**; 2 Chr 28:1

וְלֹא־עָשָׂה   ולא עשה   Mm¹

1–5   2 Sam 19:25ᵃ   ומפבשת בן
       Twice in the verse (2 Sam 19:25ᵇ)   שנים בפסוקה
       2 Kgs 16:2   בן עשרים שנה אחז
       And its companion (2 Chr 28:1)   וחבירו
       Jonah 3:10   וירא האלהים

Mm²	ולא עשה ה׳ וסימנהון	וְלֹא־עָשָׂה *five times*, and their references

1–5   2 Sam 19:25ᵃ   ומפבשת בן שאול
      הַיָּשָׁר *of Kings* (2 Kgs 16:2)   הישר דמלכים
      Jonah 3:10   וינחם האלהים על
      2 Sam 19:25ᵇ   שפמו
      הַיָּשָׁר *of Chronicles* (2 Chr 28:1)   הישר דדבר ימים

Com.: The Masorah notes the *five* occurrences of this lemma with a ו cj., to distinguish them from its *seven* occurrences without a cj.

The additions *of Kings* and *of Chronicles* to the catchword הַיָּשָׁר of the 2 Kgs 16:2 and 2 Chr 28:1 are simply to distinguish one from the other.

In the second Mm, a catchword is given for the second occurrence of this lemma in 2 Sam 19:25. Normally in these instances a notation "twice in the verse" is given, as is indeed the case in the first Mm.

This Mm occurs *twice* on fol. 213r, *once* at the top right without a number heading, and *once* at the bottom left with a number heading.

---

2 KINGS 16:3

וַיֵּלֶךְ בְּדֶרֶךְ מַלְכֵי יִשְׂרָאֵל וְגַם אֶת־בְּנוֹ הֶעֱבִיר בָּאֵשׁ כְּתֹעֲבוֹת הַגּוֹיִם אֲשֶׁר הוֹרִישׁ יְהוָה אֹתָם מִפְּנֵי בְּנֵי יִשְׂרָאֵל:

16:3   וַיֵּלֶךְ

Mp	ד׳ בטע׳	*Four times* with the accent (*zaqep gadôl*)

1 Kgs 13:24; 15:3; **2 Kgs 16:3**; 21:21

Mm	וילך ד׳ בטע׳ וסימנהון	וַיֵּלֶךְ *four times* with the accent (*zaqep gadôl*), and their references

1 Kgs 13:24   וימצאהו
1 Kgs 15:3   בכל חטאות
2 Kgs 16:3   בדרך
2 Kgs 21:21   (הגלולים) [הגללים]

Com.: Both the Mp and Mm headings of *four times etc.* are inexact since there are *three* additional occurrences of this lemma. The note more precisely should have read *four times etc. in the book*.

The Masorah notes these *four* occurrences of וַיֵּ֧לֶךְ in the book with the accent *zaqep gadôl*, to distinguish them from its more numerous occurrences (62x) in the book with other accents.

M^C has no note, and M^A is not extant here.

16:3   כְּתוֹעֲבוֹת

Nine times defective   ט֔ חס   Mp

1–5	**2 Kgs 16:3**; **21:11** (הַתּוֹעֵבוֹת); **Jer 44:4** (הַתּוֹעֵבָה)
	Ezra 9:1 (הַתּוֹעֵבוֹת); **9:14** (כְּתוֹעֲבֹתֵיהֶם)*;
6–9	**2 Chr 28:3**; 34:33 (הַתּוֹעֵבוֹת)*; **36:8** (וְתֹעֲבֹתָיו); **36:14** (תֹּעֲבוֹת)

Com.: The Masorah notes the *nine* occurrences of this lemma in various forms written defective first ו, to distinguish them from its more numerous occurrences (15x) in various forms written plene first ו (תּוֹעֵבוֹת); see also the Mm at 2 Chr 33:2 *sub* כְּתוֹעֲבוֹת.

M^L, contrary to M (כְּתֹעֲבֹתֵיהֶם and הַתּוֹעֵבוֹת), has only *seven* occurrences of this lemma since it writes the forms at Ezra 9:1 and 2 Chr 34:33 plene first ו (כְּתוֹעֲבֹתֵיהֶם and הַתּוֹעֵבוֹת); see Breuer, *The Biblical Text*, 347 and 387. However, the Mp headings here and at Jer 44:4 and 2 Chr 36:8 read *nine times*, thus supporting the enumeration inherent in the text of M.

Notes on the Mp headings highlighted above.

2 Kgs 16:3; Jer 44:4	*Nine times defective.* Includes all the references.
2 Kgs 21:11 (הַתּוֹעֵבוֹת)	*Three times written like this.* Refers to the *three* writings of this form here, and at Ezra 9:14 and 2 Chr 34:33.
Ezra 9:14 (הַתּוֹעֵבוֹת)	*Four times written like this.* Refers to forms with the def. article (the *three* occurrences of הַתּוֹעֵבוֹת and הַתּוֹעֵבָה of Jer 44:4); see Breuer, *The Biblical Text*, 191.
2 Chr 28:3 (כְּתוֹעֲבוֹת)	*Unique written like this.* Inexact since there are *two* occurrences of this form, but only *one* in Chronicles. More precisely the heading should have read *unique written like this in the book*.
2 Chr 36:8	*Nine times defective in this and other forms.* Includes all the references.
2 Chr 36:14 (תֹּעֲבוֹת)	*Three times written like this.* Refers to the *three* writings of this lemma ending in וֹת with עֲ (not עֵ) at 2 Kgs 16:3 (כְּתוֹעֲבוֹת), 2 Chr 28:3 (כְּתוֹעֲבוֹת), and 2 Chr 36:14 (תֹּעֲבוֹת).

> **2 Kings 16:5**
> אָ֣ז יַעֲלֶ֣ה רְצִ֣ין מֶֽלֶךְ־אֲ֠רָם וּפֶ֨קַח בֶּן־רְמַלְיָ֧הוּ מֶֽלֶךְ־יִשְׂרָאֵ֛ל יְרוּשָׁלַ֖͏ִם לַמִּלְחָמָ֑ה וַיָּצֻ֣רוּ עַל־אָחָ֔ז וְלֹ֥א יָכְל֖וּ לְהִלָּחֵֽם׃

16:5   עַל־אָחָז

Unique   ל̇   Mp

Com.: The Masorah notes the *sole* occurrence of this lemma with עַל, to distinguish it from its occurrence with אֶל (אֶל־אָחָז) at Isa 7:10.

This lemma is featured in a Masoretic list of words occurring *once* with a preceding אֶל (Isa 7:10), and *once* with a preceding עַל (here); see Frensdorff, *Ochlah*, §2, and Díaz-Esteban, *Sefer Oklah we-Oklah*, §2.

> **2 Kings 16:6**
> בָּעֵ֣ת הַהִ֗יא הֵ֠שִׁיב רְצִ֨ין מֶֽלֶךְ־אֲרָ֤ם אֶת־אֵילַת֙ לַֽאֲרָ֔ם וַיְנַשֵּׁ֥ל אֶת־הַיְּהוּדִ֖ים מֵֽאֵיל֑וֹת וַֽאֲרַמִּים֙ בָּ֣אוּ אֵילַ֔ת וַיֵּ֣שְׁבוּ שָׁ֔ם עַ֖ד הַיּ֥וֹם הַזֶּֽה׃ פ

16:6   וַיְנַשֵּׁל

Unique   ל̇   Mp

16:6   וַאֲרַמִּים

Mp   ואדומים ק   וַאֲדוּמִים Read

Com.: The *kətîb* (וארמים, *and Arameans*), and the *qərê* (וַאֲדוּמִים, *and Edomites*) are examples of *kətîb*/*qərê* variations where the *kətîb* is generally regarded as preferable; see Gordis, *The Biblical Text*, 148–49.

This lemma is featured in a Masoretic list of *four* words that are written with a ר but read with a ד; see the Mm at Prov 19:19 *sub* גֶּרֶל, Frensdorff, *Ochlah*, §122, and Díaz-Esteban, *Sefer Oklah we-Oklah*, §147.

2 KINGS 16:7

וַיִּשְׁלַ֣ח אָחָ֡ז מַלְאָכִ֡ים אֶל־תִּ֠גְלַת פְּלֶ֨סֶר מֶֽלֶךְ־אַשּׁ֤וּר לֵאמֹר֙ עַבְדְּךָ֣ וּבִנְךָ֣ אָ֔נִי עֲלֵ֨ה וְהוֹשִׁעֵ֜נִי מִכַּ֣ף מֶֽלֶךְ־אֲרָ֗ם וּמִכַּף֙ מֶ֣לֶךְ יִשְׂרָאֵ֔ל הַקּוֹמִ֖ים עָלָֽי׃

16:7   פְּלֶסֶר

Unique   ל   Mp

Com.: The Masorah notes the *sole* occurrence of this lemma without an א, to distinguish it from its *two* occurrences with an א (פִּלְאֶסֶר) at 2 Kgs 15:29 and 16:10.

This lemma is featured in a Masoretic list of words where an א, normally in the word, is omitted; see the Mm to 1 Chr 12:39 *sub* שָׂרִית, Frensdorff, *Oklah*, §199, and Ognibeni, *'Oklah*, §153.

16:7   וְהוֹשִׁעֵנִי

Twice   ב   Mp

2 Kgs 16:7; Ps 71:2 (וְהוֹשִׁיעֵנִי)

Com.: The Masorah notes the *two* occurrences of this lemma with a ו cj., to distinguish them from its more numerous occurrences (12x) without a cj. (הוֹשִׁיעֵנִי).

16:7   הַקּוֹמִים

Unique   ל   Mp

2 KINGS 16:9

וַיִּשְׁמַ֤ע אֵלָיו֙ מֶ֣לֶךְ אַשּׁ֔וּר וַיַּעַל֩ מֶ֨לֶךְ אַשּׁ֤וּר אֶל־דַּמֶּ֨שֶׂק֙ וַֽיִּתְפְּשֶׂ֔הָ וַיַּגְלֶ֖הָ קִ֑ירָה וְאֶת־רְצִ֖ין הֵמִֽית׃

16:9   וַיִּתְפְּשֶׂהָ

Unique   ל   Mp

16:9   וַיַּגְלֶהָ

Unique   ל   Mp

16:9	קִירָה		
Twice	ב׳	Mp	

2 Kgs 16:9; Amos 1:5

16:9	וְאֶת־רְצִין		
Unique	ל׳	Mp	

Com.: The Masorah notes the *sole* occurrence of this lemma with a ו cj., to distinguish it from its occurrence without a ו cj. at Isa 8:6.

> ### 2 KINGS 16:10
>
> וַיֵּלֶךְ הַמֶּלֶךְ אָחָז לִקְרַאת תִּגְלַת פִּלְאֶסֶר מֶלֶךְ־אַשּׁוּר דּוּמֶשֶׂק וַיַּרְא אֶת־הַמִּזְבֵּחַ אֲשֶׁר בְּדַמָּשֶׂק וַיִּשְׁלַח הַמֶּלֶךְ אָחָז אֶל־אוּרִיָּה הַכֹּהֵן אֶת־דְּמוּת הַמִּזְבֵּחַ וְאֶת־תַּבְנִיתוֹ לְכָל־מַעֲשֵׂהוּ:

16:10	דּוּמֶשֶׂק		
Unique and plene	ל׳ ומל׳	Mp	

Com.: By noting that this lemma is *unique* and written plene ו, the Masorah is also implying (correctly) that this lemma does not occur elsewhere written plene.

This lemma is featured in a Masoretic list of words occurring only *once* in which their first and last letters are in reverse alphabetical order (אתב״ש); see Frensdorff, *Ochlah*, §38, and Díaz-Esteban, *Sefer Oklah we-Oklah*, §39.

16:10	לְכָל־מַעֲשֵׂהוּ		
Unique	ל׳	Mp	

> ### 2 KINGS 16:11
>
> וַיִּבֶן אוּרִיָּה הַכֹּהֵן אֶת־הַמִּזְבֵּחַ כְּכֹל אֲשֶׁר־שָׁלַח הַמֶּלֶךְ אָחָז מִדַּמֶּשֶׂק כֵּן עָשָׂה אוּרִיָּה הַכֹּהֵן עַד־בּוֹא הַמֶּלֶךְ־אָחָז מִדַּמָּשֶׂק:

16:11	כְּכֹל אֲשֶׁר־שָׁלַח		
Unique	ל׳	Mp	

2 Kings 16:12

וַיָּבֹא הַמֶּ֙לֶךְ֙ מִדַּמֶּ֔שֶׂק וַיַּ֥רְא הַמֶּ֖לֶךְ אֶת־הַמִּזְבֵּ֑חַ וַיִּקְרַ֥ב הַמֶּ֛לֶךְ עַל־הַמִּזְבֵּ֖חַ וַיַּ֥עַל עָלָֽיו׃

16:12   וַיִּקְרַב

Five times   הֹ   Mp

Com.: See **1 Sam 17:48**.

2 Kings 16:13

וַיַּקְטֵ֤ר אֶת־עֹֽלָתוֹ֙ וְאֶת־מִנְחָת֔וֹ וַיַּסֵּ֖ךְ אֶת־נִסְכּ֑וֹ וַיִּזְרֹ֛ק אֶת־דַּֽם־הַשְּׁלָמִ֥ים אֲשֶׁר־ל֖וֹ עַל־הַמִּזְבֵּֽחַ׃

16:13   וַיַּסֵּךְ

Three times   גֹ   Mp

Com.: See **2 Sam 23:16**.

2 Kings 16:14

וְאֵ֨ת הַמִּזְבַּ֣ח הַנְּחֹ֘שֶׁת֮ אֲשֶׁ֣ר לִפְנֵ֣י יְהוָה֒ וַיַּקְרֵ֗ב מֵאֵת֙ פְּנֵ֣י הַבַּ֔יִת מִבֵּין֙ הַמִּזְבֵּ֔חַ וּמִבֵּ֖ין בֵּ֣ית יְהוָ֑ה וַיִּתֵּ֥ן אֹת֛וֹ עַל־יֶ֥רֶךְ הַמִּזְבֵּ֖חַ צָפֽוֹנָה׃

16:14   הַמִּזְבַּח

Twice   בֹ   Mp

2 Kgs 16:14; 23:17

Com.: This lemma is featured in a Masoretic list of doublets starting with הַ; see Frensdorff, *Ochlah*, §64, and Díaz-Esteban, *Sefer Oklah we-Oklah*, §65.

In M^L the circellus has mistakenly been placed on the more common form הַמִּזְבֵּחַ (100+) that occurs later in the verse.

16:14   מֵאֵת פְּנֵי

Five times   הֹ   Mp

1–5   Gen 27:30; **Exod 10:11**; Lev 10:4; **2 Kgs 16:14**; Job 2:7

Com.: The Masorah notes the *five* occurrences of פְּנֵי with מֵאֵת, to distinguish them from its *two* occurrences with מֵעִם פְּנֵי (מֵעִם פְּנֵי) at Gen 44:29 and Job 1:12.

This distinction is implied in the Mm note at Lev 10:4 in the additional notation to the Job 2:7 reference, which distinguishes it from its parallel passage in Job 1:12, where the lemma occurs as מֵעִם פְּנֵי.

16:14   וּמִבֵּין בֵּית יְהוָה

Unique   ל   Mp

---

2 KINGS 16:15

וַיְצַוֵּהוּ הַמֶּלֶךְ־אָחָז אֶת־אוּרִיָּה הַכֹּהֵן לֵאמֹר עַל הַמִּזְבֵּחַ הַגָּדוֹל הַקְטֵר אֶת־עֹלַת־הַבֹּקֶר וְאֶת־מִנְחַת הָעֶרֶב וְאֶת־עֹלַת הַמֶּלֶךְ וְאֶת־מִנְחָתוֹ וְאֵת עֹלַת כָּל־עַם הָאָרֶץ וּמִנְחָתָם וְנִסְכֵּיהֶם וְכָל־דַּם עֹלָה וְכָל־דַּם־זֶבַח עָלָיו תִּזְרֹק וּמִזְבַּח הַנְּחֹשֶׁת יִהְיֶה־לִּי לְבַקֵּר׃

16:15   וַיְצַוֵּהוּ

Read   וַיְצַוֶּה   ויצוה ק   Mp

Com.: The *kətîb* (ויצוהו, *he commanded him*), and the *qərê* (וַיְצַוֶּה, *he commanded*) represent variants of equal value; see Gordis, *The Biblical Text*, 151.

This lemma is featured in a Masoretic list of words where a ו is written but not read; see Frensdorff, *Ochlah*, §120, and Díaz-Esteban, *Sefer Oklah we-Oklah*, §106.

16:15   הַמִּזְבֵּחַ הַגָּדוֹל

Unique   ל   Mp

16:15   וְכָל־דָּם¹

Four times   ד   Mp

Lev 3:17; 7:26; **2 Kgs 16:15**ᵃ; 16:15ᵇ

| | Mm | וכל דם ד׳ | וְכָל־דָּם *four times* |

Lev 3:17 — חקת עולם לדרתיכם
Lev 7:26 — וכל דם לא תאכלו
2 Kgs 16:15ª — ויצוה המלך אחז את אוריה
Twice in the verse (2 Kgs 16:15ᵇ) — שנים בפסו׳

Com.: The Masorah notes the *four* occurrences of this lemma with a ו cj., to distinguish them from its *three* occurrences without a cj.

16:15   וְכָל־דָּם²

Four times   ד׳   Mp

Com.: See directly above.

16:15   וּמִזְבַּח הַנְּחֹשֶׁת

Twice   ב׳   Mp

2 Kgs 16:15; 2 Chr 1:5

| | Mm | ומזבח הנחשת ב׳ *twice* | וּמִזְבַּח הַנְּחֹשֶׁת |

2 Kgs 16:15 — ומזבח הנחשת יהיה לי לבקר
2 Chr 1:5 — ומזבח הנחשת אשר עשה בצלאל

Com.: The Masorah notes the *two* occurrences of this lemma with a ו cj., to distinguish them from its more numerous occurrences (6x) without a cj.

16:15   לְבַקֵּר

Twice   ב׳   Mp

2 Kgs 16:15; Prov 20:25

Com.: The Masorah notes the *two* occurrences of this lemma without a ו cj., to distinguish them from its *sole* occurrence with a cj. (וּלְבַקֵּר) at Ps 27:4.

This lemma is featured in a Masoretic list of words occurring *three times*, *twice* without a ו cj. and *once* with it (Ps 27:4); see Frensdorff, *Ochlah*, §13, and Díaz-Esteban, *Sefer Oklah we-Oklah*, §14.

2 KINGS 16:17

וַיְקַצֵּץ֩ הַמֶּ֨לֶךְ אָחָ֜ז אֶת־הַמִּסְגְּר֣וֹת הַמְּכֹנ֗וֹת וַיָּ֤סַר מֵֽעֲלֵיהֶם֙ וְאֶת־הַכִּיֹּ֔ר וְאֶת־הַיָּ֣ם הוֹרִ֔ד מֵעַ֛ל הַבָּקָ֥ר הַנְּחֹ֖שֶׁת אֲשֶׁ֣ר תַּחְתֶּ֑יהָ וַיִּתֵּ֣ן אֹת֔וֹ עַ֖ל מַרְצֶ֥פֶת אֲבָנִֽים׃

16:17   הַמִּסְגְּרוֹת

Five times plene   ה מלֿ   Mp

1–5   **2 Sam 22:46** (מִמִּסְגְּרוֹתָם); **1 Kgs 7:29**; 7:32 (לַמִּסְגְּרוֹת)
       2 Kgs 16:17; Ps 18:46 (מִמִּסְגְּרוֹתֵיהֶם)

הַמִּסְגְּרוֹת *five times* plene   המסגרות ה מלֿ   Mm

1–5   1 Kgs 7:29   ועל המסגרות אשר
       1 Kgs 7:32   וארבעת האופנים למתחת
       2 Kgs 16:17   ויקצץ המלך אחז
       2 Sam 22:46   (ויחגרו) [ויחגרו] ממסגרותם
       Ps 18:46   ויחגרו ממסגרותיהם

Com.: The Masorah notes the *five* occurrences of this lemma in various forms written plene ו, to distinguish them from its *five* occurrences in various forms written defective ו (e.g., מִסְגֶּרֶת).

The Mp at 2 Sam 22:46 reads *unique* for its particular form (מִמִּסְגְּרוֹתָם).

16:17   הַמְּכֹנוֹת

Unique written like this   לֿ כתֿ כן   Mp

16:17   וְאֶת

Read את קֿ   את   Mp

Com.: The *kətîb* (ואת) and the *qərê* (אֶת) represent variant forms where the *qərê* is preferable to the *kətîb*; see Gordis, *The Biblical Text*, 152.

This lemma is featured in a Masoretic list of words where a ו is written at the beginning of a word but is not read; see Frensdorff, *Ochlah*, §118, and Díaz-Esteban, *Sefer Oklah we-Oklah*, §104.

16:17   הַכִּיֹּר

Mp   ב׳ חס׳ בנבי׳   *Twice* defective in the Prophets

Com.: See **1 Kgs 7:30**.

2 KINGS 16:18

וְאֶת־מִיסַ֨ךְ הַשַּׁבָּ֜ת אֲשֶׁר־בָּ֣נוּ בַבַּ֗יִת וְאֶת־מְב֤וֹא הַמֶּ֙לֶךְ֙ הַֽחִיצ֔וֹנָה הֵסֵ֖ב בֵּ֣ית יְהוָ֑ה מִפְּנֵ֖י מֶ֥לֶךְ אַשּֽׁוּר׃

16:18   מִיסַךְ

Mp   מוּסַךְ ק׳   Read מוּסַךְ

Com.: The *kǝtîb* (מיסך) and the *qǝrê* (מוסך) represent examples of interchanges between original initial ו and initial י verbs; see Gordis, *The Biblical Text*, 130.

16:18   הַחִיצוֹנָה

Mp   ל׳ בטע׳   *Unique* accented (*milʿêl*)

Com.: The Masorah notes the *sole* occurrence of this lemma accented *milʿêl*, to distinguish it from its more numerous occurrences (13x) accented *milraʿ*.

This lemma is featured in a Masoretic list of words that normally occur with an ultimate accent, but does occur *once* (as הַחִיצוֹנָה here) with a penultimate one; see Frensdorff, *Ochlah*, §372.

2 KINGS 16:19

וְיֶ֛תֶר דִּבְרֵ֥י אָחָ֖ז אֲשֶׁ֣ר עָשָׂ֑ה הֲלֹא־הֵ֣ם כְּתוּבִ֗ים עַל־סֵ֛פֶר דִּבְרֵ֥י הַיָּמִ֖ים לְמַלְכֵ֥י יְהוּדָֽה׃

16:19   וְיֶ֛תֶר דִּבְרֵי...אֲשֶׁר עָשָׂה

Mp   ו׳   *Six times*

1–5   <u>1 Kgs 16:27</u>; 2 Kgs 1:18; 14:15; 15:36; **16:19**
6   **2 Kgs 21:25**

Com.: The Masorah notes the *six* occurrences where וְיֶ֫תֶר דִּבְרֵי is followed by a king's name and then by אֲשֶׁ֣ר עָשָׂ֔ה, to distinguish them from its more numerous occurrences (19x) where וְיֶ֫תֶר דִּבְרֵי is followed by a king's name and then by וְכָל־אֲשֶׁ֣ר עָשָׂ֔ה (וְיֶ֫תֶר דִּבְרֵי...וְכָל־אֲשֶׁ֣ר עָשָׂ֔ה); see Dotan/Reich, *Masora Thesaurus, ad loc.*

In M^L the circellus has been placed only on the words וְיֶ֫תֶר דִּבְרֵי, which phrase occurs over *forty times*. However, the Mm to 1 Kgs 16:27 and the Mp to 2 Kgs 21:25 indicate that the note refers to the larger phrase וְיֶ֫תֶר דִּבְרֵי...אֲשֶׁ֣ר עָשָׂ֔ה that occurs with the *six* kings Omri, Ahaziah, Jehoash, Jotham, Ahaz, and Amon.

2 KINGS 17:3

עָלָ֣יו עָלָ֗ה שַׁלְמַנְאֶ֙סֶר֙ מֶ֣לֶךְ אַשּׁ֔וּר וַיְהִי־ל֤וֹ הוֹשֵׁ֙עַ֙ עֶ֔בֶד וַיָּ֥שֶׁב ל֖וֹ מִנְחָֽה׃

17:3   וַיָּ֥שֶׁב

Twenty-five times   כֹּה   Mp

Com.: See **Judg 17:3**.

2 KINGS 17:4

וַיִּמְצָא֩ מֶֽלֶךְ־אַשּׁ֨וּר בְּהוֹשֵׁ֜עַ קֶ֗שֶׁר אֲשֶׁ֨ר שָׁלַ֤ח מַלְאָכִים֙ אֶל־ס֣וֹא מֶֽלֶךְ־מִצְרַ֔יִם וְלֹא־הֶעֱלָ֥ה מִנְחָ֖ה לְמֶ֣לֶךְ אַשּׁ֑וּר כְּשָׁנָ֣ה בְשָׁנָ֔ה וַֽיַּעַצְרֵ֙הוּ֙ מֶ֣לֶךְ אַשּׁ֔וּר וַיַּאַסְרֵ֖הוּ בֵּ֥ית כֶּֽלֶא׃

17:4   בְּהוֹשֵׁ֜עַ

Twice   בּ   Mp

2 Kgs 17:4; Hos 1:2

Com.: The Masorah notes the *two* occurrences of this lemma with the prep. בּ, to distinguish it from its *five* occurrences with the prep. ל (לְהוֹשֵׁ֣עַ), *one* of which occurs in v. 6.

17:4   וְלֹא־הֶעֱלָ֥ה

Unique   ל   Mp

17:4   כְּשָׁנָ֣ה

Unique   ל   Mp

Com.: The Masorah notes the *sole* occurrence of this lemma with the prep. כְּ, to distinguish it from its more numerous occurrences (14x) with the prep. בְּ, one of which occurs in this verse.

This lemma is featured in a Masoretic list of words occurring only *once* that start with a כְּ; see Frensdorff, *Ochlah*, §19.

17:4	וַיַּעַצְרֵהוּ		
Unique		ל	Mp

17:4	בֵּית כֶּלֶא		
Three times		גׄ	Mp

(מִבֵּית כֶּלֶא) Isa 42:7; **2 Kgs 17:4**; 25:27 (מִבֵּית כֶּלֶא)

בֵּית כֶּלֶא *three times* in similar forms   בית כלא גׄ בליש   Mm

2 Kgs 17:4   ויעצרהו מלך
2 Kgs 25:27   נשא אויל מרדך
Isa 42:7   להוציא ממסגר אסיר

Com.: The Masorah notes the *three* occurrences of this lemma without the def. article, to distinguish them from its *four* occurrences with the def. article (בֵּית הַכֶּלֶא/לְבֵית הַכֶּלֶא).

---

2 KINGS 17:6

בִּשְׁנַת הַתְּשִׁיעִית לְהוֹשֵׁעַ לָכַד מֶלֶךְ־אַשּׁוּר אֶת־שֹׁמְרוֹן וַיֶּגֶל אֶת־יִשְׂרָאֵל אַשּׁוּרָה וַיֹּשֶׁב אֹתָם בַּחְלַח וּבְחָבוֹר נְהַר גּוֹזָן וְעָרֵי מָדָי׃ פ

17:6	בִּשְׁנַת הַתְּשִׁיעִית		
Twice		בׄ	Mp

Mm	בשנת התשיעית בֿ	twice	בִּשְׁנַת *הַתְּשִׁיעִית

[להושיע] (להושיע)   2 Kgs 17:6
ויהי ‹בשנת› התשיעית דצדקיהו   וַיְהִי בִּשְׁנַת הַתְּשִׁיעִית of Zedekiah (2 Kgs 25:1)

Com.: The Masorah notes the *two* occurrences of הַתְּשִׁיעִית with בִּשְׁנַת (cstr.), to distinguish them from its *three* occurrences with בַּשָּׁנָה (בַּשָּׁנָה הַתְּשִׁיעִית). The additional notation "of Zedekiah" to the 2 Kgs 25:1 reference is to distinguish that verse from the occurrence of this lemma in 2 Kgs 17:6 with Hoshea.

*M^L, contrary to M (הַתְּשִׁעִית), writes the *second* word of this lemma plene first י (הַתְּשִׁיעִית); see Breuer, *The Biblical Text*, 129.

M^C reads the second word as הַתְּשִׁעִית, but has no note, and M^A is not extant here.

In M^L the circellus has been placed only on הַתְּשִׁיעִית, but as is clear from its Mm the note belongs on both words.

17:6   אַשּׁוּרָה

Six times   ו̇   Mp

Com.: See **2 Kgs 15:29**.

17:6   וַיֹּשֶׁב

Four times   דֿ   Mp

2 Kgs 17:6; **17:24**; Ps 107:36 (וַיּוֹשֶׁב); **2 Chr 8:2** (וַיּוֹשֶׁב)

Com.: The Masorah notes the *four* occurrences of this lemma accented *mil'êl*, to distinguish them from its *sole* occurrence accented *milra'* (וַיּוֹשֵׁב) at Gen 47:11.

> **2 KINGS 17:8**
> וַיֵּלְכוּ בְּחֻקּוֹת הַגּוֹיִם אֲשֶׁר הוֹרִישׁ יְהוָה מִפְּנֵי בְּנֵי יִשְׂרָאֵל וּמַלְכֵי יִשְׂרָאֵל אֲשֶׁר עָשׂוּ׃

17:8   וּמַלְכֵי יִשְׂרָאֵל

Unique   לֿ   Mp

Com.: The Masorah notes the *sole* occurrence of this lemma with a ו cj., to distinguish it from its more numerous occurrences (19x) without a cj.

2 KINGS 17:9

וַיְחַפְּאוּ בְנֵי־יִשְׂרָאֵל דְּבָרִים אֲשֶׁר לֹא־כֵן עַל־יְהוָה אֱלֹהֵיהֶם וַיִּבְנוּ לָהֶם בָּמוֹת בְּכָל־עָרֵיהֶם מִמִּגְדַּל נוֹצְרִים עַד־עִיר מִבְצָר:

17:9 וַיְחַפְּאוּ

Unique ל Mp

17:9 לֹא־כֵן

Nineteen times יט Mp

Com.: See **2 Sam 20:21.**

2 KINGS 17:10

וַיַּצִּבוּ לָהֶם מַצֵּבוֹת וַאֲשֵׁרִים עַל כָּל־גִּבְעָה גְבֹהָה וְתַחַת כָּל־עֵץ רַעֲנָן:

17:10 וַיַּצִּבוּ

Twice defective ב חס Mp

Com.: See **2 Sam 18:17**.

2 KINGS 17:11

וַיְקַטְּרוּ־שָׁם בְּכָל־בָּמוֹת כַּגּוֹיִם אֲשֶׁר־הֶגְלָה יְהוָה מִפְּנֵיהֶם וַיַּעֲשׂוּ דְּבָרִים רָעִים לְהַכְעִיס אֶת־יְהוָה:

17:11 וַיְקַטְּרוּ־שָׁם

Unique ל Mp

Com.: The Masorah notes the *sole* occurrence of וַיְקַטְּרוּ with שָׁם, to distinguish it from its *four* occurrences with לֵאלֹהִים (וַיְקַטְּרוּ לֵאלֹהִים/וַיְקַטְּרוּ בוֹ לֵאלֹהִים).

17:11 כַּגּוֹיִם

Three times ג Mp

Deut 8:20; 2 Kgs 17:11; Ezek 20:32

Mm¹	כגוים ג̇	*three times* כַּגּוֹיִם
	אשר יהוה מאביד (מפניהם) [מפניכם]	Deut 8:20
	ויקטרו שם בכל במות	2 Kgs 17:11
	על רוחכם	Ezek 20:32

Mm²	כגוים ג̇ וסימנהון	*three times*, and their references כַּגּוֹיִם
	מאביד מפניכם	Deut 8:20
	אשר (נגלה) [הגלה] יהוה	2 Kgs 17:11
	נהיה	Ezek 20:32

Com.: The Masorah notes the *three* occurrences of this lemma with the prep. כְּ, to distinguish them from its more numerous occurrences (74x) with the prep. בְּ (בַּגּוֹיִם).

This Mm occurs *twice*, once (Mm¹) on the bottom left of fol. 213v, and *once* (Mm²) on the bottom right of fol. 214r.

	דְּבָרִים רָעִים	17:11
Mp	ל̇	*Unique*

Com.: The Masorah notes the *sole* occurrence of this lemma in the pl., to distinguish it from its more numerous occurrences (5x) in the sg. (דְּבָר רָע).

---

2 KINGS 17:12

וַיַּעַבְדוּ הַגִּלֻּלִים אֲשֶׁר אָמַר יְהוָה לָהֶם לֹא תַעֲשׂוּ אֶת־הַדָּבָר הַזֶּה׃

	אֲשֶׁר אָמַר יְהוָה לָהֶם	17:12
Mp	ג̇	*Three times*

Exod 6:26; **2 Kgs 17:12**; **Ps 106:34**

Mm	אשר אמר יהוה להם ג̇	*three times* אֲשֶׁר אָמַר יְהוָה לָהֶם
	הוא אהרן ומשה	Exod 6:26
	ויעבדו (את הגלולים) [הגללים]	2 Kgs 17:12
	את העמים	Ps 106:34

Com.: The Masorah notes the *three* occurrences of this lemma with the rel. pron. אֲשֶׁר, to distinguish them from its *sole* occurrence with the cj. כִּי (כִּי אָמַר יְהוָה לָהֶם) at Num 26:65.

The Mp heading at Ps 106:34 reads *four times*, and includes the *four* occurrences of this phrase, *three* with אֲשֶׁר and *one* with כִּי.

---

2 Kings 17:13

וַיָּ֣עַד יְהוָ֡ה בְּיִשְׂרָאֵ֣ל וּבִיהוּדָ֡ה בְּיַד֩ כָּל־נְבִיאֵ֨י כָל־חֹזֶ֜ה לֵאמֹ֗ר שֻׁ֤בוּ מִדַּרְכֵיכֶ֣ם הָרָעִים֙ וְשִׁמְרוּ֙ מִצְוֺתַ֣י חֻקּוֹתַ֔י כְּכָל־הַתּוֹרָ֕ה אֲשֶׁ֥ר צִוִּ֖יתִי אֶת־אֲבֹתֵיכֶ֑ם וַאֲשֶׁר֙ שָׁלַ֣חְתִּי אֲלֵיכֶ֔ם בְּיַ֖ד עֲבָדַ֥י הַנְּבִיאִֽים׃

17:13   וַיָּ֣עַד

Twice   בׄ   Mp

2 Kgs 17:13; Zech 3:6

Com.: The Masorah notes the *two* occurrences of this lemma written with a ד, possibly to distinguish it from its *three* occurrences written with a ר (וַיָּ֣עַר).

17:13   וַיָּ֣עַד יְהוָ֡ה

וַיָּ֣עַד יְהוָ֡ה *twice*, and their references   ויעד יהוה בׄ וסימנהון   Mm

2 Kgs 17:13   בישראל וביהודה
Zech 3:6 (וַיַּ֣עַד מַלְאַ֣ךְ יְהוָ֔ה)   [ביהושע] (יהושע)

Com.: The Masorah notes the *two* occurrences of this lemma, possibly, to distinguish them from the *two* occurrences of וַיָּ֣עַר יְהוָ֡ה at Hag 1:14 and 2 Chr 21:16.

17:13   וּבִיהוּדָ֡ה

וּבִיהוּדָ֡ה *five times*   וביהודה הׄ   Mm

1–5   Josh 19:34   אזנות
        2 Kgs 17:13   ויעד יהוה
        הִשְׁלִכוּ of *Kings* (2 Kgs 24:20)   דמלכים [השלכו] (השליכו)
        Zech 14:21   והיה כל סיר
        דִּרְשׁוּ of *Chronicles* (2 Chr 34:21)   דדברי הימים [דרשו] (דרושל)

Com.: The Masorah notes the *five* occurrences of this lemma with a ו cj., to distinguish them from its more numerous occurrences (47x) written without a cj.

The addition *of Kings* to the catchword of the 2 Kgs 24:20 reference is to distinguish that verse from its parallel in Jer 52:3, where the lemma appears as וִיהוּדָה.

The addition *of Chronicles* to the catchword of the 2 Chr 34:21 reference is to distinguish that verse from its parallel in 2 Kgs 22:13, where the lemma appears as יְהוּדָה.

17:13   נְבִיאָו

Mp   נביאי קֿ   נְבִיאֵי Read

Com.: The *kətîb* (נביאו, *his prophets*), and the *qərê* (נְבִיאֵי, *prophets of*) are examples of *kətîb/qərê* variations where the *kətîb* is generally regarded as preferable; see Gordis, *The Biblical Text*, 148–49.

This lemma is featured in a Masoretic list of words that are written with a ו at the end but read with a י; see the Mm at Dan 3:19 *sub* אשתנו; Frensdorff, *Ochlah*, §136, and Díaz-Esteban, *Sefer Oklah we-Oklah*, §120.

17:13   שָׁבוּ

Mp   הֿ בטע   *Five times* with the accents (*gereš* and *təlîšâ gədôlâ*)

1–5   Gen 5:29 (זֶֿה); Lev 10:4 (קִרְבֹֿו); **2 Kgs 17:13**
Ezek 48:10 (וּלְאֵֿלֶּה); Zeph 2:15 (זֹֿאת)

Com.: The Masorah notes the *five* forms that have the *two* accents *gereš* and *təlîšâ gədôlâ*.

The Mp heading at Ezek 48:10 reads *three times* and deals, not with the accents on the word וּלְאֵלֶּה, but with the fact that this word occurs *three times*.

17:13   מִצְוֹתַי חֻקֹּתַי

Mp   גֿ   *Three times*

Gen 26:5; **1 Kgs 9:6** (חֻקֹּתַי); **2 Kgs 17:13**

| Mm | מצוֹתי חקוֹתי ג׳ וסימנהון | *three times*, and their references | מִצְוֹתַי חֻקּוֹתַי |

Gen 26:5	עקב אשר שמע אברהם
1 Kgs 9:6	אם שוב (תשובון) [תשבון]
2 Kgs 17:13	ויעד יהוה

Com.: The Masorah notes the *three* occurrences of מִצְוֹתַי with חֻקּוֹתַי, to distinguish them from its *sole* occurrence with חֻקֹּתַי וְחֻקֹּתַי (מִצְוֹתַי וְחֻקֹּתַי) at 1 Kgs 11:34.

17:13 אֲבֹתֵיכֶם

| Mp | ל חס בסיפ | *Unique* defective in the book |

Com.: The heading of this note is inexact since there are no occurrences of this lemma written plene י in the book; see the Mm to 1 Sam 12:7 *sub* אֲבוֹתֵיכֶם. The note more precisely should have read *unique and defective in the book*.

M^C has no note, and M^A is not extant here.

---

2 KINGS 17:14

וְלֹא שָׁמֵעוּ וַיַּקְשׁוּ אֶת־עָרְפָּם כְּעֹרֶף אֲבוֹתָם אֲשֶׁר לֹא הֶאֱמִינוּ בַּיהוָה אֱלֹהֵיהֶם:

17:14 כְּעֹרֶף

| Mp | ל | *Unique* |

Com.: This lemma is featured in a Masoretic list of words that occur *once* with beginning with a כ (here), and *once* with a ב (Gen 49:8); see the Mm at Ezek 42:11 *sub* וּכְמִשְׁפְּטֵיהֶן, Frensdorff, *Ochlah*, §4, and Díaz-Esteban, *Sefer Oklah we-Oklah*, §4.

---

2 KINGS 17:15

וַיִּמְאֲסוּ אֶת־חֻקָּיו וְאֶת־בְּרִיתוֹ אֲשֶׁר כָּרַת אֶת־אֲבוֹתָם וְאֵת עֵדְוֺתָיו אֲשֶׁר הֵעִיד בָּם וַיֵּלְכוּ אַחֲרֵי הַהֶבֶל וַיֶּהְבָּלוּ וְאַחֲרֵי הַגּוֹיִם אֲשֶׁר סְבִיבֹתָם אֲשֶׁר צִוָּה יְהוָה אֹתָם לְבִלְתִּי עֲשׂוֹת כָּהֶם:

17:15 עֵדְוֺתָיו

| Mp | ה | *Five times* |

Com.: See **1 Kgs 2:3**.

17:15	וַיֶּהְבָּלוּ

Twice	ב֗	Mp

2 Kgs 17:15; Jer 2:5

17:15	סְבִיבֹתָם

Three times	ג֗	Mp

2 Kgs 17:15; **Ezek 28:24**; 28:26 (מִסְּבִיבוֹתָם)

Mm	סביבתם ג̇ ב̇ חסירין וחד מל וסימנהון	סְבִיבֹתָם *three times*, *twice* defective and *once* plene, and their references

2 Kgs 17:15	ואחרי הגוים
Ezek 28:24	סלון ממאיר
Ezek 28:26	השאטים

Com.: The Masorah notes the *three* occurrences of this lemma in various forms with this sfx. (תָם), to distinguish them from its *five* occurrences with the alternate sfx. תֵיהֶם (סְבִיבוֹתֵיהֶם/סְבִיבֹתֵיהֶם).

The Mp heading at Ezek 28:26 reads *unique* since the form that occurs there (מִסְּבִיבוֹתָם) only occurs *once*.

17:15	כָּהֶם

Unique	ל֗	Mp

Com.: This lemma is featured in two Masoretic lists. One is in a list of words that occur *once* with a final ם, and *once* wih a final ן; see Frensdorff, *Ochlah*, §12, and Díaz-Esteban, *Sefer Oklah we-Oklah*, §12.

The other is in a list of words that occur only *once* beginning with a כ; see Frensdorff, *Ochlah*, §19, and Díaz-Esteban, *Sefer Oklah we-Oklah*, §20.

2 KINGS 17:16

וַיַּעַזְב֗וּ אֶת־כָּל־מִצְוֺת֙ יְהוָ֣ה אֱלֹהֵיהֶ֔ם וַיַּעֲשׂ֥וּ לָהֶ֛ם מַסֵּכָ֖ה שְׁנֵ֣ים עֲגָלִ֑ים וַיַּעֲשׂ֣וּ אֲשֵׁירָ֗ה וַיִּֽשְׁתַּחֲווּ֙ לְכָל־צְבָ֣א הַשָּׁמַ֔יִם וַיַּעַבְד֖וּ אֶת־הַבָּֽעַל:

17:16   אֶת כָּל־מִצְוֺת יְהוָה

Three times   ג̇   Mp

Num 15:39; 2 Kgs 17:16; Neh 10:30

Com.: The Masorah notes the *three* occurrences of this lemma with אֶת, to distinguish them from its more numerous occurrences (9x) without כָּל (אֶת מִצְוֺת יְהוָה).

The circelli have been placed on the *four* words כָּל־מִצְוֺת יְהוָה אֱלֹהֵיהֶם which only occur *once*, but as indicated by the heading of the Mm at Num 15:39, the note should be on the highlighted phrase אֶת כָּל־מִצְוֺת יְהוָה, which does occur *three* times.

17:16   שְׁנֵים

Read   שְׁנֵי   שני קר   Mp

Com.: The *kətîb* (שנים), and the *qərê* (שְׁנֵי) represent examples where the *kətîb* and the *qərê* fluctuate between cstr. and absol. forms of the numerals; see Gordis, *The Biblical Text*, 143.

This lemma is featured in a Masoretic list of words written with a final ם that is not read; see Frensdorff, *Ochlah*, §156, and Díaz-Esteban, *Sefer Oklah we-Oklah*, §142.

17:16   אֲשֵׁירָה

Three times plene   ג̇ מל   Mp

Deut 7:5 (וַאֲשֵׁירֵיהֶם); 2 Kgs 17:16; Mic 5:13 (אֲשֵׁירֶיךָ)

Com.: The Masorah notes the *three* occurrences of this lemma in various forms written plene י, to distinguish them from its *seven* occurrences in various forms written defective ׳ (e.g., אֲשֵׁרָה).

The Mp heading at Mic 5:13 mistakenly reads *fourteen times plene*, but both M^C and M^A read there *unique plene*.

2 KINGS 17:17

וַיַּעֲבִ֜ירוּ אֶת־בְּנֵיהֶ֤ם וְאֶת־בְּנֽוֹתֵיהֶם֙ בָּאֵ֔שׁ וַיִּקְסְמ֥וּ קְסָמִ֖ים וַיְנַחֵ֑שׁוּ וַיִּֽתְמַכְּר֗וּ לַעֲשׂ֥וֹת הָרַ֛ע בְּעֵינֵ֥י יְהוָ֖ה לְהַכְעִיסֽוֹ׃

17:17   וַיִּֽתְמַכְּר֗וּ

Unique   ל   Mp

2 KINGS 17:18

וַיִּתְאַנַּ֨ף יְהוָ֤ה מְאֹד֙ בְּיִשְׂרָאֵ֔ל וַיְסִרֵ֖ם מֵעַ֣ל פָּנָ֑יו לֹ֣א נִשְׁאַ֔ר רַ֛ק שֵׁ֥בֶט יְהוּדָ֖ה לְבַדּֽוֹ׃

17:18   וַיְסִרֵ֖ם

Twice and defective   ב̇ וחס̇   Mp

1 Sam 17:39; **2 Kgs 17:18**

Com.: By noting that the *two* occurrences of this lemma are both written defective י, the Masorah is also implying (correctly) that this lemma does not occur elsewhere written plene.

2 KINGS 17:19

גַּם־יְהוּדָ֕ה לֹ֣א שָׁמַ֔ר אֶת־מִצְוֹ֖ת יְהוָ֣ה אֱלֹהֵיהֶ֑ם וַיֵּ֣לְכ֔וּ בְּחֻקּ֥וֹת יִשְׂרָאֵ֖ל אֲשֶׁ֥ר עָשֽׂוּ׃

17:19   גַּם

Unique at the beginning (of a verse) in the book   ל ראש בסיפ̇   Mp

Com.: The Masorah notes the *sole* occurrence of this lemma in the book at the beginning of a verse without a ו cj., to distinguish it from its more numerous occurrences (16x) in the book at the beginning of a verse with a ו cj.

2 KINGS 17:20

וַיִּמְאַ֨ס יְהוָ֜ה בְּכָל־זֶ֣רַע יִשְׂרָאֵ֗ל וַיְעַנֵּם֙ וַֽיִּתְּנֵ֖ם בְּיַד־שֹׁסִ֑ים עַ֛ד אֲשֶׁ֥ר הִשְׁלִיכָ֖ם מִפָּנָֽיו׃

17:20   וַיְעַנֵּם֙

Unique   ל   Mp

17:20   הִשְׁלִיכָם מִפָּנָיו

Unique   ל   Mp

Com.: The Masorah notes the *sole* occurrence of הִשְׁלִיכָם with מִפָּנָיו, to distinguish it from its *sole* occurrence with מֵעַל פָּנָיו (הִשְׁלִיכָם מֵעַל פָּנָיו) at 2 Kgs 13:23.

---

2 KINGS 17:21

כִּי־קָרַע יִשְׂרָאֵל מֵעַל בֵּית דָּוִד וַיַּמְלִיכוּ אֶת־יָרָבְעָם בֶּן־נְבָט וַיַּדָּא יָרָבְעָם אֶת־יִשְׂרָאֵל מֵאַחֲרֵי יְהוָה וְהֶחֱטִיאָם חֲטָאָה גְדוֹלָה:

17:21   וַיַּדָּא

Read   וַיַּדַּח ק   וידח   Mp

---

twice   וַיַּדַּח   וידח ב   Mm

2 Kgs 17:21	ירבעם את ישראל
2 Chr 21:11	את יהודה

Com.: The *kətîb* (וידא, *he caused to drive away*), and the *qərê* (וַיַּדַּח, *he caused to stray*) represent variants of equal value; see Gordis, *The Biblical Text*, 151.

The Mm notes the *two* occurrences of the *qərê* וַיַּדַּח, possibly to avoid confusion with the *kətîb* form וידא.

---

2 KINGS 17:22

וַיֵּלְכוּ בְּנֵי יִשְׂרָאֵל בְּכָל־חַטֹּאות יָרָבְעָם אֲשֶׁר עָשָׂה לֹא־סָרוּ מִמֶּנָּה:

17:22   חַטֹּאות יָרָבְעָם

Five times lacking   בֶּן־נְבָט   ה חס בן נבט   Mp

Com.: See **1 Kgs 14:16**.

> **2 KINGS 17:23**
> עַד אֲשֶׁר־הֵסִיר יְהוָה אֶת־יִשְׂרָאֵל מֵעַל פָּנָיו כַּאֲשֶׁר דִּבֶּר בְּיַד כָּל־עֲבָדָיו הַנְּבִיאִים וַיִּגֶל יִשְׂרָאֵל מֵעַל אַדְמָתוֹ אַשּׁוּרָה עַד הַיּוֹם הַזֶּה: פ

17:23   בְּיַד כָּל־עֲבָדָיו הַנְּבִיאִים

Unique   לׄ   Mp

Com.: The Masorah notes the *sole* occurrence of this lemma with כָּל, to distinguish it from its *three* occurrences without כָּל (בְּיַד עֲבָדָיו הַנְּבִיאִים).

In M^L there are only *two* circelli on this *four-word* phrase: one on בְּיַד כָּל and one on עֲבָדָיו הַנְּבִיאִים. With *four-* or *five-word* phrases it is not unusual for only *two* circelli to be given; see **Josh 1:6** and *passim*.

17:23   וַיִּגֶל

Four times   דׄ   Mp

2 Kgs 17:23; 25:21; **Jer 52:27**; Job 36:10

ויגל *four times* וַיִּגֶל   ד׳   Mm

2 Kgs 17:23   אדמתו
2 Kgs 25:21   מעל אדמתו
Jer 52:27   יהודה
Job 36:10   אזנם

Com.: The Masorah notes the *four* occurrences of this lemma with a ו consec., to distinguish them from its *sole* occurrence with a ו cj. (וְיִגֶל) at Job 36:15.

17:23   אַשּׁוּרָה

Six times   וׄ   Mp

Com.: See **2 Kgs 15:29**.

2 KINGS 17:24

וַיָּבֵ֣א מֶֽלֶךְ־אַשּׁ֡וּר מִבָּבֶ֡ל וּ֠מִכּ֠וּתָה וּמֵעַוָּ֤א וּמֵֽחֲמָת֙ וּסְפַרְוַ֔יִם וַיֹּ֙שֶׁב֙ בְּעָרֵ֣י שֹׁמְר֔וֹן תַּ֖חַת בְּנֵ֣י יִשְׂרָאֵ֑ל וַיִּֽרְשׁוּ֙ אֶת־שֹׁ֣מְר֔וֹן וַיֵּשְׁב֖וּ בְּעָרֶֽיהָ׃

17:24   וּמִכּוּתָה

Unique   ל   Mp

17:24   וַיֹּשֶׁב

Four times   ד   Mp

2 Kgs 17:6; **17:24**; Ps 107:36 (וַיּוֹשֶׁב); **2 Chr 8:2** (וַיּוֹשֶׁב)

וַיֹּשֶׁב *four times*, and their references   וישב ד וסימנהון   Mm

2 Kgs 17:6   להושע
2 Kgs 17:24   בני ישראל
                 {וישב אתם בבלה}
<2 Chr 8:2>
Ps 107:36   (וישב) [ויושב] שם רעבים

And *once* (וַיּוֹשֶׁב):
Gen 47:11   וחד ויושב יוסף

Com.: The Masorah notes the *four* occurrences of this lemma accented *milʿēl*, and the Mm additionally notes its *sole* occurrence accented *milraʿ* (וַיּוֹשֶׁב) at Gen 47:11.

In place of catchwords for the 2 Chr 8:2 reference are catchwords that do not occur anywhere in the Bible.

17:24   וַיִּרְשׁוּ

Four times defective   ד חס   Mp

Com.: See **Josh 12:1**.

> ## 2 KINGS 17:25
> וַיְהִ֞י בִּתְחִלַּ֣ת שִׁבְתָּ֣ם שָׁ֗ם לֹ֤א יָֽרְאוּ֙ אֶת־יְהוָ֔ה וַיְשַׁלַּ֨ח יְהוָ֤ה בָּהֶם֙ אֶת־הָ֣אֲרָי֔וֹת וַיִּֽהְי֥וּ הֹרְגִ֖ים בָּהֶֽם׃

17:25 בִּתְחִלַּ֣ת

Six times   ו   Mp

1–5   **2 Sam 21:9** (qərê); **2 Kgs 17:25**; Amos 7:1; Ruth 1:22; Dan 9:23
6   Ezra 4:6

Com.: The Masorah notes the *six* occurrences of this lemma with the prep. בְּ, to distinguish them from its *three* occurrences without this preposition.

17:25 וַיְשַׁלַּ֨ח

Twenty-two times   כב   Mp

Com.: See **Judg 2:6**.

> ## 2 KINGS 17:26
> וַיֹּאמְר֗וּ לְמֶ֣לֶךְ אַשּׁוּר֮ לֵאמֹר֒ הַגּוֹיִ֗ם אֲשֶׁ֤ר הִגְלִ֙יתָ֙ וַתּ֙וֹשֶׁב֙ בְּעָרֵ֣י שֹׁמְר֔וֹן לֹ֣א יָֽדְע֔וּ אֶת־מִשְׁפַּ֖ט אֱלֹהֵ֣י הָאָ֑רֶץ וַיְשַׁלַּח־בָּ֣ם אֶת־הָאֲרָי֗וֹת וְהִנָּם֙ מְמִיתִ֣ים אוֹתָ֔ם כַּאֲשֶׁ֛ר אֵינָ֥ם יֹדְעִ֖ים אֶת־מִשְׁפַּ֥ט אֱלֹהֵ֥י הָאָֽרֶץ׃

17:26 וַתּ֙וֹשֶׁב֙

Unique and plene   ל ומל   Mp

Com.: By noting that this lemma is *unique* and written plene ו, the Masorah is also implying (correctly) that this lemma does not occur elsewhere written defective.

17:26 וַיְשַׁלַּ֨ח

Twenty-two times   כב   Mp

Com.: See **Judg 2:6**.

17:26	מְמִיתִים
Twice	בֿ Mp

2 Kgs 17:26; **Jer 26:15** (מְמִתִים)

Com.: The Masorah notes the *two* occurrences of this lemma without a prep., to distinguish them from its *sole* occurrence with a prep. (לְמְמִתִים) at Job 33:22.

---

2 KINGS 17:27

וַיְצַו מֶלֶךְ־אַשּׁוּר לֵאמֹר הֹלִיכוּ שָׁמָּה אֶחָד מֵהַכֹּהֲנִים אֲשֶׁר הִגְלִיתֶם מִשָּׁם וְיֵלְכוּ וְיֵשְׁבוּ שָׁם וְיֹרֵם אֶת־מִשְׁפַּט אֱלֹהֵי הָאָרֶץ׃

17:27	הֹלִיכוּ שָׁמָּה
Three times	גֿ Mp

2 Kgs 17:27; **Jer 40:4** (לָלֶכֶת שָׁמָּה); Qoh 9:10 (הֹלֵךְ שָׁמָּה)

Com.: The Masorah notes the *three* occurrences of the verb הָלַךְ in various forms with שָׁמָּה, to distinguish them from its more numerous occurrences (7x) of this verb in various forms with שָׁם (e.g., וַיֵּלֶךְ שָׁם).

These *three* references are the ones that are given in the Mm in M^A at Jer 40:4. However, it is noteworthy that יֵלְכוּ שָׁמָּה of Ezek 1:20 is not included in this list; see Dotan/Reich, *Masora Thesaurus, ad loc.*

In M^L the circellus has been placed just on הֹלִיכוּ, which only occurs here. The note more properly should be on the *two* words הֹלִיכוּ שָׁמָה, see above.

17:27	מֵהַכֹּהֲנִים
Four times	דֿ Mp

2 Kgs 17:27; 17:28; **Ezra 3:12**; 2 Chr 29:34

Com.: The Masorah notes the *four* occurrences of this lemma with the inseparable prep. מ, to distinguish them from its *two* occurrences with the separable prep. מִן at Jer 1:1 and Neh 11:10.

17:27	וַיֵּלְכוּ		
Twice	ב׳	Mp	

Com.: See **2 Kgs 6:22**.

17:27	וַיֵּשְׁבוּ		
Twice	ב׳	Mp	

1–4   **Gen 34:21**; Gen 34:23; 2 Kgs 17:27; Ezek 33:31

Com.: The Mp heading here of *twice* is inexact since there are *four* occurrences of this lemma, as is correctly noted in the Mp headings to the Gen 34:21 and 34:23. The heading more precisely should have read *twice in the Prophets*.

The Masorah notes the *four* occurrences of this lemma with a ו cj., to distinguish them from its more numerous occurrences (55x) with a ו consec. (וַיֵּשְׁבוּ); see Ognibeni, *'Oklah*, §3R.

M^C correctly reads here *four times rapê* (that is, with a ו cj.), but M^A is not extant here.

---

2 KINGS 17:29

וַיִּהְיוּ עֹשִׂים גּוֹי גּוֹי אֱלֹהָיו וַיַּנִּיחוּ ׀ בְּבֵית הַבָּמוֹת אֲשֶׁר עָשׂוּ הַשֹּׁמְרֹנִים גּוֹי גּוֹי בְּעָרֵיהֶם אֲשֶׁר הֵם יֹשְׁבִים שָׁם׃

17:29	גּוֹי גּוֹי[1]		
Twice	ב׳	Mp	

2 Kgs 17:29[a]; 17:29[b]

Com.: The Masorah notes the *two* occurrences of this lemma גּוֹי גּוֹי in the same verse.

17:29	בְּבֵית הַבָּמוֹת		
Twice	ב׳	Mp	

2 Kgs 17:29; 17:32

17:29	הַשֹּׁמְרֹנִים		
Unique	ל׳	Mp	

17:29 ²גּוֹי גּוֹי

2 Kgs 17:29ᵃ; 17:29ᵇ

Four times   ד׳   Mp

Com.: The Mp heading reads *four times*, but there are only *two* occurrences of this lemma גּוֹי גּוֹי, and *both* are in the same verse; see directly above.

Dotan/Reich (*Masora Thesaurus*, ad loc.) suggest that the note belongs only on the first גּוֹי, and that a necessary additional phrase *in the verse* should be added because there are other occurrences of גּוֹי in the book (thus, *four times in the verse*).

Mᶜ has no note, and Mᴬ is not extant here.

---

2 KINGS 17:30

וְאַנְשֵׁי בָבֶ֡ל עָשׂוּ֙ אֶת־סֻכּ֣וֹת בְּנ֔וֹת וְאַנְשֵׁי־כ֖וּת עָשׂ֣וּ אֶת־נֵֽרְגַ֑ל וְאַנְשֵׁ֥י חֲמָ֖ת עָשׂ֥וּ אֶת־אֲשִׁימָֽא׃

17:30   וְאַנְשֵׁי

Four times at the beginning of a verse   ד׳ ראש פסוק   Mp

Gen 13:13; Exod 22:30; 2 Kgs 17:30ᵃ; Ezek 39:14

Com.: The Masorah notes the *four* occurrences of this lemma that occur at the beginning of a verse with a ו cj., to distinguish them from its more numerous occurrences (18x) that occur at the beginning of a verse without a ו cj.

The Mp heading at Ezek 39:14 reads *eighteen times*, and the Mm there lists all *eighteen* occurrences of this word, not just those at the beginning of a verse; see **2 Sam 2:17**.

17:30   כוּת

Unique   ל׳   Mp

17:30   אֲשִׁימָא

Unique and written with א   ל וכת׳ א   Mp

Com.: By noting that this lemma is *unique* and written with א, the Masorah is also implying (correctly) that this lemma does not occur elsewhere written with a ה.

> ## 2 KINGS 17:31
> וְהָעַוִּים עָשׂוּ נִבְחַז וְאֶת־תַּרְתָּק וְהַסְפַרְוִים שֹׂרְפִים אֶת־בְּנֵיהֶם בָּאֵשׁ לְאַדְרַמֶּלֶךְ וַעֲנַמֶּלֶךְ אֱלֹהּ סְפָרְיִם:

17:31   וְהָעַוִּים

Four times   דֿ   Mp

Deut 2:23; Josh 13:3; 18:23; **2 Kgs 17:31**

17:31   וְהַסְפַרְוִים

Unique   לֿ   Mp

17:31   לְאַדְרַמֶּלֶךְ

Unique   לֿ   Mp

Com.: The Masorah notes the *sole* occurrence of this lemma with the prep. לְ, to distinguish it from its *two* occurrences with a ו cj. (וְאַדְרַמֶּלֶךְ) at 2 Kgs 19:37 and Isa 37:38.

17:31   אֱלֹהּ

Read אֱלֹהֵי   אלהי קֿ   Mp

Com.: The *kǝtîb* (אלה), and the *qǝrê* (אֱלֹהֵי) are examples of *kǝtîb/qǝrê* variations, where a word ending in a י is read even though it is not written; see Frensdorff, *Ochlah*, §126, Díaz-Esteban, *Sefer Oklah we-Oklah*, §110, and Gordis, *The Biblical Text*, 97.

This lemma also occurs in a Masoretic list of words that occur *three times* written the same way, but each time are read differently; see Frensdorff, *Ochlah*, §93, and Díaz-Esteban, *Sefer Oklah we-Oklah*, §76.

17:31   סְפָרְיִם

Read סְפַרְוָיִם   ספרוים קֿ   Mp

Com.: The *kǝtîb* (ספרים) and the *qǝrê* (סְפַרְוָיִם), represent variations in proper names; see Gordis, *The Biblical Text*, 157.

2 KINGS 17:32

וַיִּהְיוּ יְרֵאִים אֶת־יְהוָה וַיַּעֲשׂוּ לָהֶם מִקְצוֹתָם כֹּהֲנֵי בָמוֹת וַיִּהְיוּ עֹשִׂים לָהֶם בְּבֵית הַבָּמוֹת׃

17:32   כֹּהֲנֵי בָמוֹת

Three times   גׄ   Mp

Com.: See **1 Kgs 13:33**.

2 KINGS 17:33

אֶת־יְהוָה הָיוּ יְרֵאִים וְאֶת־אֱלֹהֵיהֶם הָיוּ עֹבְדִים כְּמִשְׁפַּט הַגּוֹיִם אֲשֶׁר־הִגְלוּ אֹתָם מִשָּׁם׃

17:33   כְּמִשְׁפַּט

Five times   הׄ   Mp

Com.: See **Judg 18:7**.

2 KINGS 17:34

עַד הַיּוֹם הַזֶּה הֵם עֹשִׂים כַּמִּשְׁפָּטִים הָרִאשֹׁנִים אֵינָם יְרֵאִים אֶת־יְהוָה וְאֵינָם עֹשִׂים כְּחֻקֹּתָם וּכְמִשְׁפָּטָם וְכַתּוֹרָה וְכַמִּצְוָה אֲשֶׁר צִוָּה יְהוָה אֶת־בְּנֵי יַעֲקֹב אֲשֶׁר־שָׂם שְׁמוֹ יִשְׂרָאֵל׃

17:34   כַּמִּשְׁפָּטִים

Unique   לׄ   Mp

17:34   כַּמִּשְׁפָּטִים הָרִאשֹׁנִים

Unique   לׄ   Mp

17:34   וְכַתּוֹרָה

Twice   בׄ   Mp

2 Kgs 17:34; Ezra 10:3

Com.: The Masorah notes the *two* occurrences of this lemma with the prep. כ, to distinguish it from its *sole* occurrence with the prep. ב (וּבַתּוֹרָה) at 2 Chr 31:21.

The Mp heading at Ezra 10:3 reads *unique* but, since this lemma occurs *twice*, more precisely it should have read *unique in the book* (of Ezra).

> ### 2 KINGS 17:35
> וַיִּכְרֹ֨ת יְהוָ֤ה אִתָּם֙ בְּרִ֔ית וַיְצַוֵּ֣ם לֵאמֹ֔ר לֹ֥א תִֽירְא֖וּ אֱלֹהִ֣ים אֲחֵרִ֑ים וְלֹא־תִשְׁתַּחֲו֣וּ לָהֶ֔ם וְלֹ֥א תַעַבְד֖וּם וְלֹ֥א תִזְבְּח֥וּ לָהֶֽם׃

17:35   וַיְצַוֵּ֣ם

Mp   ד   *Four times*

Com.: See **2 Kgs 11:5**.

17:35   לֹ֥א

Mp   ט פסוק אית בהון לא ולא ולא   *Nine* verses with the sequence לֹא...וְלֹא...וְלֹא

Com.: See **Josh 23:7**.

In M^L this lemma has no circellus.

17:35   לֹ֥א תִֽירְא֖וּ אֱלֹהִ֣ים

Mp   ל   *Unique*

Com.: The Masorah notes the *sole* occurrence of this lemma without a ו cj., to distinguish it from its *two* occurrences with a cj. (וְלֹ֥א תִֽירְא֖וּ אֱלֹהִ֣ים) in vv. 37 and 38.

In M^L only one circellus has been placed on תִֽירְא֖וּ אֱלֹהִ֣ים, which occurs *three times*. The note should be extended to include the previous word לֹא since the longer phrase לֹ֥א תִֽירְא֖וּ אֱלֹהִ֣ים only occurs this *once*.

> ### 2 KINGS 17:37
> וְאֶת־הַחֻקִּ֨ים וְאֶת־הַמִּשְׁפָּטִ֜ים וְהַתּוֹרָ֤ה וְהַמִּצְוָה֙ אֲשֶׁ֣ר כָּתַ֣ב לָכֶ֔ם תִּשְׁמְר֥וּן לַעֲשׂ֖וֹת כָּל־הַיָּמִ֑ים וְלֹ֥א תִֽירְא֖וּ אֱלֹהִ֥ים אֲחֵרִֽים׃

17:37   וְאֶת־הַחֻקִּ֨ים

Mp   ד   *Four times*

Deut 7:11; **17:19**; **2 Kgs 17:37**; **Neh 1:7**

Mm	וְאֶת־הַחֻקִּים ד׳ *four times*	וְאֶת־הַחֻקִּים

Deut 7:11	ושמרת את המצוה
Deut 17:19	והיתה עמו וקרא בו
2 Kgs 17:37	ואת המשפטים
Neh 1:7	חבל חבלנו לך ולא

Com.: The Masorah notes the *four* occurrences of this lemma with a ו cj., to distinguish them from its *five* occurrences without a cj.

17:37   וְהַתּוֹרָה וְהַמִּצְוָה

Twice   ב׳   Mp

Exod 24:12; 2 Kgs 17:37

Mm	וְהַתּוֹרָה וְהַמִּצְוָה *twice*	וְהַתּוֹרָה וְהַמִּצְוָה

Exod 24:12	עלה אלי ההרה והיה שם
2 Kgs 17:37	ואת החקים ואת המשפטים

Com.: The Masorah notes the *two* occurrences of וְהַמִּצְוָה with וְהַתּוֹרָה, to distinguish them from its *sole* occurrence with הַתּוֹרָה (הַתּוֹרָה וְהַמִּצְוָה) at 2 Chr 14:3.

The first word of this lemma is featured in a Masoretic list of doublets that start with וה; see Frensdorff, *Ochlah*, §63, and Díaz-Esteban, *Sefer Oklah we-Oklah*, §64.

17:37   תִּשְׁמְרוּן

Five times   ה׳   Mp

1–5   **Deut 6:17; 8:1; 11:22; 12:1; 2 Kgs 17:37**

Mm	תשמרון ה׳ *five times*	תִּשְׁמְרוּן

1–5	Deut 8:1	כל המצוה
	Deut 6:17	(שמר) [שמור] תשמרון
	Deut 11:22	כי אם שמר
	Deut 12:1	אלה החקים
	2 Kgs 17:37	ואת החקים

Com.: The Masorah notes the *five* occurrences of this lemma with a paragogic נ, to distinguish them from its more numerous occurrences (17x) written without this נ (תִּשְׁמְרוּן); see Ognibeni, *'Oklah*, §71.

17:37   וְלֹא תִירָאוּ

Twice   בֿ   Mp

2 Kgs 17:37; 17:38

Com.: The Masorah notes the *two* occurrence of this lemma with a ו cj., to distinguish it from its *four* occurrences without a cj., *one* of which occurs in v. 35.

2 KINGS 17:38

וְהַבְּרִית אֲשֶׁר־כָּרַתִּי אִתְּכֶם לֹא תִשְׁכָּחוּ וְלֹא תִירְאוּ אֱלֹהִים אֲחֵרִים׃

17:38   וְלֹא תִירָאוּ

Twice   בֿ   Mp

Com.: See directly above at **2 Kgs 17:37**.

2 KINGS 17:39

כִּי אִם־אֶת־יְהוָה אֱלֹהֵיכֶם תִּירָאוּ וְהוּא יַצִּיל אֶתְכֶם מִיַּד כָּל־אֹיְבֵיכֶם׃

17:39   מִיַּד כָּל־אֹיְבֵיכֶם

Unique   ל   Mp

Com.: The Masorah notes the *sole* occurrence of this lemma with כָּל, to distinguish it from its *sole* occurrence without כָּל (מִיַּד אֹיְבֵיכֶם) at 1 Sam 12:11.

2 KINGS 17:40

וְלֹא שָׁמֵעוּ כִּי אִם־כְּמִשְׁפָּטָם הָרִאשׁוֹן הֵם עֹשִׂים׃

17:40   כְּמִשְׁפָּטָם הָרִאשׁוֹן

Unique   ל   Mp

2 Kings 17:41

וַיִּהְי֣וּ ׀ הַגּוֹיִ֣ם הָאֵ֗לֶּה יְרֵאִים֙ אֶת־יְהוָ֔ה וְאֶת־פְּסִֽילֵיהֶ֖ם הָי֣וּ עֹֽבְדִ֑ים גַּם־בְּנֵיהֶ֣ם ׀ וּבְנֵ֣י בְנֵיהֶ֗ם כַּאֲשֶׁ֤ר עָשׂוּ֙ אֲבֹתָ֔ם הֵ֣ם עֹשִׂ֔ים עַ֖ד הַיּ֥וֹם הַזֶּֽה׃ פ

17:41   וְאֶת־פְּסִילֵיהֶם

Mp   ל   *Unique*

17:41   אֲבֹתָם

Mp   ג̇ חס̇ בנב̇   *Three times* defective in the Prophets

Com.: See **1 Kgs 9:9**.

2 Kings 18:1

וַֽיְהִ֗י בִּשְׁנַ֣ת שָׁלֹ֔שׁ לְהוֹשֵׁ֥עַ בֶּן־אֵלָ֖ה מֶ֣לֶךְ יִשְׂרָאֵ֑ל מָלַ֛ךְ חִזְקִיָּ֥ה בֶן־אָחָ֖ז מֶ֥לֶךְ יְהוּדָֽה׃

18:1   חִזְקִיָּה

Mp   יב̇   *Twelve times*

1–5   **2 Kgs 18:1**; <u>18:10</u> (לְחִזְקִיָּה); 18:13; 18:14ᵃ; **18:14ᵇ**
6–10   2 Kgs 18:15; 18:16ᵃ; **18:16ᵇ**; **Zeph 1:1**; Prov 25:1
11–12 **Neh 7:21** (לְחִזְקִיָּה); <u>10:18</u>

Com.: The Masorah notes the *twelve* occurrences of חִזְקִיָּה written with the divine element יָה, to distinguish them from its more numerous occurrences (100+) written with the divine element יָהוּ (חִזְקִיָּהוּ).

The Mp at Zeph 1:1 and Prov 15:1, and the Mm headings at <u>Zeph 1:1</u> and <u>Neh 10:18</u>, read *three times* for the *three* occurrences of חִזְקִיָּה (with and without the prep. לְ) outside of 2 Kgs 18:1–17.

The Mp and Mm at <u>2 Kgs 18:10</u> (לְחִזְקִיָּה), and the Mp at Neh 7:21 (לְחִזְקִיָּה), read *twice* for the *two* occurrences of this lemma with the prep. לְ.

The enumerations given in the various Mp headings in Mᴸ do not take into account the form with the ו cj. at 1 Chr 3:23 (וְחִזְקִיָּה), which would constitute a *thirteenth* occurrence; see Breuer, *The Biblical Text*, 131.

> ## 2 KINGS 18:2
> בֶּן־עֶשְׂרִ֨ים וְחָמֵ֤שׁ שָׁנָה֙ הָיָ֣ה בְמָלְכ֔וֹ וְעֶשְׂרִ֤ים וָתֵ֙שַׁע֙ שָׁנָ֔ה מָלַ֖ךְ בִּירוּשָׁלָ֑͏ִם וְשֵׁ֣ם אִמּ֔וֹ אֲבִ֖י בַּת־זְכַרְיָֽה׃

18:2   הָיָ֣ה בְמָלְכ֔וֹ

Seven times   ז̇   Mp

Com.: See **2 Kgs 8:17**.

18:2   אֲבִ֖י

Unique as name of a woman   ל שם אתה   Mp

Com.: The Masorah notes the *sole* occurrence of this lemma as the name of a woman, to distinguish it from all other occurrences (75x) meaning *father of*, and to distinguish it from its occurrence as אֲבִיָּה in the parallel text at 2 Chr 29:1.

> ## 2 KINGS 18:4
> ה֣וּא ׀ הֵסִ֣יר אֶת־הַבָּמ֗וֹת וְשִׁבַּר֙ אֶת־הַמַּצֵּבֹ֔ת וְכָרַ֖ת אֶת־הָאֲשֵׁרָ֑ה וְכִתַּת֩ נְחַ֨שׁ הַנְּחֹ֜שֶׁת אֲשֶׁר־עָשָׂ֣ה מֹשֶׁ֗ה כִּ֣י עַד־הַיָּמִ֤ים הָהֵ֙מָּה֙ הָי֤וּ בְנֵֽי־יִשְׂרָאֵל֙ מְקַטְּרִ֣ים ל֔וֹ וַיִּקְרָא־ל֖וֹ נְחֻשְׁתָּֽן׃

18:4   הַמַּצֵּבֹ֔ת

Unique defective   ל חס̇   Mp

Com.: The Masorah notes the *unique* occurrence of this lemma written defective ו, to distinguish it from its *three* occurrences written plene ו (הַמַּצֵּבוֹת).

18:4   וְכִתַּת֩

Unique   ל   Mp

Com.: The Masorah notes the *sole* occurrence of this lemma with a ו cj., to distinguish it from its occurrence without a cj. at 2 Chr 34:7.

18:4   נְחַ֨שׁ

Three times   ג̇   Mp

Num 21:9ª; 21:9ᵇ; 2 Kgs 18:4

| נָחָשׁ *three times* | נחש ג׳ | Mm |

Num 21:9[a]	ויעש משה נחש נחשת
Twice in the verse (Num 21:9[b])	שנים בפסוקה
2 Kgs 18:4	וכתת נחש הנחשת

| And *once* (נִחֵשׁ): Num 23:23 | וחד כי לא נחש (ביע׳) [ביעקב] |

Com.: The Masorah notes the *three* occurrences of this lemma pointed as נָחָשׁ, to which the Mm adds *one* occurrence pointed as נִחֵשׁ, to distinguish them from the more numerous occurrences (20x) of this lemma pointed as נָחָשׁ.

18:4   הָהֵמָּה

Twelve times   יב׳   Mp

1–5	Num 9:7; **2 Kgs 18:4**; Jer 3:16; **3:18**; Jer 5:18
6–10	**Jer 14:15**; 50:4; Joel 3:2; 4:1; Zech 8:23
11–12	Zech 14:15; **Neh 13:15**

Com.: The Masorah notes the *twelve* occurrences of this lemma (a demon. adj.) written with a final ה, to distinguish them from its more numerous occurrences (46x) written without this ה (הָהֵם).

18:4   נְחֻשְׁתָּן

Unique   ל׳   Mp

---

2 KINGS 18:5

בַּיהוָה אֱלֹהֵי־יִשְׂרָאֵל בָּטָח וְאַחֲרָיו לֹא־הָיָה כָמֹהוּ בְּכֹל מַלְכֵי יְהוּדָה וַאֲשֶׁר הָיוּ לְפָנָיו׃

18:5   וַאֲשֶׁר הָיוּ לְפָנָיו

Unique   ל׳   Mp

Com.: The Masorah notes the *sole* occurrence of this lemma with a ו cj., to distinguish it from its *two* occurrences without a cj. at 1 Kgs 16:33 and 2 Kgs 17:2.

The second word of this lemma is featured in a Masoretic list of words which occur only *once* with a preceding וַאֲשֶׁר; see Frensdorff, *Ochlah*, §254.

2 KINGS 18:6

וַיִּדְבַּק֙ בַּֽיהוָ֔ה לֹא־סָ֖ר מֵאַחֲרָ֑יו וַיִּשְׁמֹר֙ מִצְוֺתָ֔יו אֲשֶׁר־צִוָּ֥ה יְהוָ֖ה אֶת־מֹשֶֽׁה׃

18:6   וַיִּשְׁמֹר֙ מִצְוֺתָ֔יו

Unique   ל   Mp

2 KINGS 18:7

וְהָיָ֤ה יְהוָה֙ עִמּ֔וֹ בְּכֹ֥ל אֲשֶׁר־יֵצֵ֖א יַשְׂכִּ֑יל וַיִּמְרֹ֥ד בְּמֶֽלֶךְ־אַשּׁ֖וּר וְלֹ֥א עֲבָדֽוֹ׃

18:7   וְהָיָ֤ה יְהוָה֙

וְהָיָה יְהוָה *six times*   [i̇] (i̇) יהוה [והיה] (יהיה)   Mm

1–5	Gen 28:21	ושבתי בשלום
	Judg 2:18	וכי הקים יהוה
	1 Sam 24:16	והיה יהוה לדין ושפט
	2 Kgs 18:7	והיה יהוה עמו בכל
	Jer 17:7	ברוך הגבר אשר
6	Zech 14:9	והיה יי למלך... ביום ההוא

Com.: The Masorah notes the *six* occurrences of this lemma with a ו cj., to distinguish them from its *three* occurrences without a cj.

2 KINGS 18:8

הֽוּא־הִכָּ֧ה אֶת־פְּלִשְׁתִּ֛ים עַד־עַזָּ֖ה וְאֶת־גְּבוּלֶ֑יהָ מִמִּגְדַּ֥ל נוֹצְרִ֖ים עַד־עִ֥יר מִבְצָֽר׃ פ

18:8   גְּבוּלֶ֑יהָ

Three times   ג̇   Mp

Com.: See **1 Sam 5:6**.

2 Kings 18:10

וַֽיִּלְכְּדֻ֗הָ מִקְצֵה֙ שָׁלֹ֣שׁ שָׁנִ֔ים בִּשְׁנַת־שֵׁ֛שׁ לְחִזְקִיָּ֖ה הִ֣יא שְׁנַת־תֵּ֗שַׁע לְהוֹשֵׁ֙עַ֙ מֶ֣לֶךְ יִשְׂרָאֵ֔ל נִלְכְּדָ֖ה שֹׁמְרֽוֹן׃

18:10   וַֽיִּלְכְּדֻ֗הָ

Five times   הֿ   Mp

Com.: See **Josh 8:19**.

18:10   לְחִזְקִיָּה

Twice   בֿ   Mp

2 Kgs 18:10; **Neh 7:21**

לְחִזְקִיָּה   *twice*   לחזקיה בֿ   Mm

2 Kgs 18:10   בשנת שש לחזקיה
The *second occurrence* of בְּנֵי אָטֵר (Neh 7:21)   בני אטר בתרי

And in the rest of the Bible it is לִיחִזְקִיָּה   ושאר קרייה ליחזקיה

Com.: The Masorah notes the *two* occurrences of this lemma written with the divine element יָה, to distinguish it from its *sole* occurrence written with the divine element יָהוּ (לְחִזְקִיָּהוּ) at Isa 38:9.

The Mm also notes the occurrence of this lemma written as לִיחִזְקִיָּה at Ezra 2:16 [= the rest of the Bible!], to distinguish it from its *two* occurrences with the divine element יָהוּ (לִיחִזְקִיָּהוּ) at 2 Chr 32:23 and 27.

The additional notation in the Mm *of the second occurrence* to the catchwords בְּנֵי אָטֵר of the Neh 7:21 reference distinguishes this verse containing לְחִזְקִיָּה from the *first occurrence* of the catchwords בְּנֵי אָטֵר in Ezra 2:16, where the lemma occurs as לִיחִזְקִיָּה.

> ### 2 KINGS 18:11
> וַיֶּ֣גֶל מֶֽלֶךְ־אַשּׁ֡וּר אֶת־יִשְׂרָאֵל֮ אַשּׁ֒וּרָה֒ וַיַּנְחֵ֣ם בַּחְלַ֣ח וּבְחָב֔וֹר נְהַ֥ר גּוֹזָ֖ן וְעָרֵ֥י מָדָֽי׃

18:11   וַיַּנְחֵ֣ם

Seven times   ז֗   Mp

Com.: See **1 Sam 22:4**.

> ### 2 KINGS 18:12
> עַ֣ל ׀ אֲשֶׁ֣ר לֹֽא־שָׁמְע֗וּ בְּקוֹל֙ יְהוָ֣ה אֱלֹֽהֵיהֶ֔ם וַיַּעַבְרוּ֙ אֶת־בְּרִית֔וֹ אֵ֚ת כָּל־אֲשֶׁ֣ר צִוָּ֔ה מֹשֶׁ֖ה עֶ֣בֶד יְהוָ֑ה וְלֹ֥א שָׁמְע֖וּ וְלֹ֥א עָשֽׂוּ׃ פ

18:12   כָּל־אֲשֶׁ֣ר צִוָּ֔ה מֹשֶׁ֖ה

Unique   ל֗   Mp

Com.: The Masorah notes the *sole* occurrence of this lemma without the prep. כ, to distinguish it from its *two* occurrences with this prep. (כְּכָל אֲשֶׁר צִוָּה מֹשֶׁה) at **Josh 4:10** and 1 Chr 6:34. In M^L there are only *two* circelli on this *four-word* phrase; see **Josh 1:6** and *passim*.

18:12   וְלֹ֥א עָשֽׂוּ

Five times   ה֗   Mp

Com.: See **Judg 8:35**.

> ### 2 KINGS 18:13
> וּבְאַרְבַּע֩ עֶשְׂרֵ֨ה שָׁנָ֜ה לַמֶּ֣לֶךְ חִזְקִיָּ֗ה עָלָ֞ה סַנְחֵרִ֤יב מֶֽלֶךְ־אַשּׁוּר֙ עַ֣ל כָּל־עָרֵ֧י יְהוּדָ֛ה הַבְּצֻר֖וֹת וַֽיִּתְפְּשֵֽׂם׃

18:13   וּבְאַרְבַּע֩

Twice   ב֗   Mp

Gen 14:5; 2 Kgs 18:13

Com.: The Masorah notes the *two* occurrences of this lemma with a ו cj., to distinguish it from its *five* occurrences without a cj.

This lemma is featured in two Masoretic lists. One is in a list of doublets occuring at the beginning of a verse with a prefixed ו; see Frensdorff, *Ochlah*, §172, and Ognibeni, *'Oklah*, §96.

The other is in list of doublets beginning with וב; see Frensdorff, *Ochlah*, §62, and Díaz-Esteban, *Sefer Oklah we-Oklah*, §63.

2 KINGS 18:14

וַיִּשְׁלַח חִזְקִיָּה מֶלֶךְ־יְהוּדָה אֶל־מֶלֶךְ־אַשּׁוּר ׀ לָכִישָׁה ׀ לֵאמֹר ׀ חָטָאתִי שׁוּב מֵעָלַי אֵת אֲשֶׁר־תִּתֵּן עָלַי אֶשָּׂא וַיָּשֶׂם מֶלֶךְ־אַשּׁוּר עַל־חִזְקִיָּה מֶלֶךְ־יְהוּדָה שְׁלֹשׁ מֵאוֹת כִּכַּר־כֶּסֶף וּשְׁלֹשִׁים כִּכַּר זָהָב:

18:14   לָכִישָׁה

Six times   ו̇   Mp

Com.: See **Josh 10:31**.

18:14   חִזְקִיָּה²

Twelve times   יב̇   Mp

Com.: See **2 Kgs 18:1**.

2 KINGS 18:15

וַיִּתֵּן חִזְקִיָּה אֶת־כָּל־הַכֶּסֶף הַנִּמְצָא בֵית־יְהוָה וּבְאֹצְרוֹת בֵּית הַמֶּלֶךְ:

18:15   אֶת־כָּל־הַכֶּסֶף

Unique   ל̇   Mp

1–4   Gen 47:14; 1 Kgs 15:18; 2 Kgs 12:10; **18:15**

Com.: The Mp heading here of *unique* is incorrect since there are *four* occurrences of this lemma.

The Masorah notes the *four* occurrences of this lemma with כָּל, to distinguish them from its more numerous occurrences (28x) without כָּל (אֶת הַכֶּסֶף).

Neither M^C nor M^A has a note on this lemma here.

> ## 2 Kings 18:16
> בָּעֵת הַהִיא קִצַּץ חִזְקִיָּה אֶת־דַּלְתוֹת הֵיכַל יְהוָה וְאֶת־הָאֹמְנוֹת אֲשֶׁר צִפָּה חִזְקִיָּה מֶלֶךְ יְהוּדָה וַיִּתְּנֵם לְמֶלֶךְ אַשּׁוּר: פ

18:16	קִצַּץ		
Unique		ל	Mp

18:16	הָאֹמְנוֹת		
Unique		ל	Mp

18:16	חִזְקִיָּה²		
Twelve times		יב	Mp

Com.: See **2 Kgs 18:1**.

> ## 2 Kings 18:17
> וַיִּשְׁלַח מֶלֶךְ־אַשּׁוּר אֶת־תַּרְתָּן וְאֶת־רַב־סָרִיס | וְאֶת־רַב־שָׁקֵה מִן־לָכִישׁ אֶל־הַמֶּלֶךְ חִזְקִיָּהוּ בְּחֵיל כָּבֵד יְרוּשָׁלִָם וַיַּעֲלוּ וַיָּבֹאוּ יְרוּשָׁלַם וַיַּעֲלוּ וַיָּבֹאוּ וַיַּעַמְדוּ בִּתְעָלַת הַבְּרֵכָה הָעֶלְיוֹנָה אֲשֶׁר בִּמְסִלַּת שְׂדֵה כוֹבֵס:

18:17	מִן־לָכִישׁ		
Unique		ל	Mp

Com.: The Masorah notes the *sole* occurrence of this lemma with the separable prep. מִן, to distinguish it from its *four* occurrences with the inseparable prep. מ (מִלָּכִישׁ).

This lemma is featured in a Masoretic list of words where a word normally joined by the inseparable prep. מ occurs *once* with the separable prep. מִן; see Frensdorff, *Ochlah*, §196, and Ognibeni, *'Oklah*, §151.

18:17	בְּחֵיל כָּבֵד		
Twice		ב	Mp

2 Kgs 18:17; Isa 36:2

Com.: The Masorah notes the *two* occurrences in these parallel texts of כָּבֵד with בְּחֵיל (cstr.), to distinguish them from its *two* occurrences with בְּחַיִל כָּבֵד, absol.) at 1 Kgs 10:2 and 2 Chr 9:1.

18:17   אֲשֶׁר בִּמְסִלַּת

Unique   ל   Mp

Com.: The Masorah notes the occurrence of בִּמְסִלַּת with אֲשֶׁר, to distinguish it from its *sole* occurrence without אֲשֶׁר in the parallel passage at Isa 36:2.

18:17   כּוֹבֵס

Three times   ג   Mp

2 Kgs 18:17 (כֹּבֵס)*; **Isa 7:3**; **36:2**

| כּוֹבֵס *three times, once* defective and *twice* plene | (כבס) [כובס] ג חד חס וב׳ מל | Mm |

<2 Kgs 18:17>
Isa 7:3   אל מסלת שדה
בִּמְסִלַּת *of Isaiah* (Isa 36:2)   במסלת דישעיהו

Com.: The Masorah notes that this word occurs *three* times, *once* defective ו (here) and *twice* plene ו (at Isa 7:3 and 36:2).

*M^L, contrary to M (כֹּבֵס), writes the form here plene ו (כּוֹבֵס); see Breuer, *The Biblical Text*, 131. However, both the heading of the Mm here as well as the additional note in the Mm is only fully understandable with M's text.

In the Mm, the additional notation *of Isaiah* to the catchword בִּמְסִלַּת of the Isaiah reference contrasts that reference with its plene form of the lemma (כּוֹבֵס) with its parallel in our text (2 Kgs 18:17), which for the contrast to work, must be written defective (כֹּבֵס) exactly as in M.

M^A reads here כֹּבֵס, whereas M^C, as M^L, reads כּוֹבֵס, and both of them have Mp notes of *three times*.

---

2 KINGS 18:18

וַיִּקְרְאוּ אֶל־הַמֶּלֶךְ וַיֵּצֵא אֲלֵהֶם אֶלְיָקִים בֶּן־חִלְקִיָּהוּ אֲשֶׁר עַל־הַבָּיִת וְשֶׁבְנָה הַסֹּפֵר וְיוֹאָח בֶּן־אָסָף הַמַּזְכִּיר׃

18:18   אֲלֵהֶם

Twelve times defective in the book   יב חס בסי׳   Mp

Com.: The Mp heading of *twelve times defective in the book* is incorrect since there are *thirteen* occurrences of this lemma in the book; see **1 Kgs 12:16**.

M^A correctly reads here *thirteen times defective in the book*. M^C has no note here.

2 KINGS 18:19

וַיֹּ֤אמֶר אֲלֵהֶם֙ רַב־שָׁקֵ֔ה אִמְרוּ־נָ֖א אֶל־חִזְקִיָּ֑הוּ כֹּֽה־אָמַ֞ר הַמֶּ֣לֶךְ הַגָּדוֹל֙ מֶ֣לֶךְ אַשּׁ֔וּר מָ֧ה הַבִּטָּח֛וֹן הַזֶּ֖ה אֲשֶׁ֥ר בָּטָֽחְתָּ׃

18:19	הַבִּטָּח֛וֹן		
Twice	ב֗		Mp

2 Kgs 18:19; Isa 36:4

Com.: The Masorah notes the *two* occurrences of this lemma in these parallel passages with the def. article, to distinguish it from its occurrence without this def. article (בִּטָּחוֹן) at Qoh 9:4.

2 KINGS 18:20

אָמַ֗רְתָּ אַךְ־דְּבַר־שְׂפָתַ֛יִם עֵצָ֥ה וּגְבוּרָ֖ה לַמִּלְחָמָ֑ה עַתָּה֙ עַל־מִ֣י בָטַ֔חְתָּ כִּ֥י מָרַ֖דְתָּ בִּֽי׃

18:20	אָמַ֗רְתָּ		
Three times at the beginning of a verse	ג֗ רא פֿ		Mp

2 Kgs 18:20; Jer 45:3; 2 Chr 25:19

אָמַ֗רְתָּ *three times* at the beginning of a verse, and their references	(אמרתי) [אמרת] ג֗ ראש פסוקין וסימנהון	Mm¹

2 Kgs 18:20   (אמרתי) [אמרת] אך דבר שפתים
Jer 45:3   אמרת אוי נא לי כי יסף
of Chronicles (2 Chr 25:19) אָמַ֗רְתָּ הִנֵּ֤ה הִכִּ֙יתָ֙   אמרת הנה (הבית) [הכית] דדברי הימ׳

Com.: This Masorah notes the *three* occurrences of this lemma at the beginning of a verse to distinguish them from the more numerous occurrences (12x) at the beginning of a verse of the first pers. אָמַרְתִּי.

The addition *of Chronicles* to the catchwords אָמַרְתָּ הִנֵּה הִכִּיתָ of the 2 Chr 25:19 reference is solely to identify this Chronicles verse since these catchwords do not occur anywhere else.

		Mm²	מלכים	*In Kings*
אמרת אך דבר שפתים		(אָמַרְתָּ)	2 Kgs 18:20	

			ישעיה	*In Isaiah*
אמרתי אך דבר שפתים		(אָמַרְתִּי)	Isa 36:5	

And *one* verse is the *sîman*   וחד פסוק סימן

Gen 26:9   ויקרא אבימלך ליצחק ויאמר אך
(אָמַרְתָּ...אָמַרְתִּי)   הנה אשתך היא ואיך אמרת... כי אמרתי

Com.: This second Masorah compares the *two* parallel phrases of 2 Kgs 18:20 and Isa 36:5, and notes their difference by means of a *third* verse *sîman*. Gen 26:9 serves as this *one* verse *sîman* to illustrate the difference between the *two* parallel phrases, in which the *first* has the verb אָמַרְתָּ, and the *second* אָמַרְתִּי; see Ognibeni, *'Oklah*, §117N.

2 KINGS 18:21

עַתָּ֡ה הִנֵּ֣ה בָטַ֣חְתָּ לְּךָ֡ עַל־מִשְׁעֶנֶת֩ הַקָּנֶ֨ה הָרָצ֤וּץ הַזֶּה֙ עַל־מִצְרַ֔יִם אֲשֶׁ֨ר יִסָּמֵ֥ךְ אִישׁ֙ עָלָ֔יו וּבָ֥א בְכַפּ֖וֹ וּנְקָבָ֑הּ כֵּ֚ן פַּרְעֹ֣ה מֶֽלֶךְ־מִצְרַ֔יִם לְכָֽל־הַבֹּטְחִ֖ים עָלָֽיו׃

18:21   הָרָצוּץ

Twice   בׄ   Mp

2 Kgs 18:21; Isa 36:6

Com.: The Masorah notes the *two* occurrences of this lemma in these parallel passages with the def. article, to distinguish it from its *sole* occurrence without this article (רָצוּץ) at Isa 42:3.

18:21   וּנְקָבָה

Twice   ב֗   Mp

2 Kgs 18:21; Isa 36:6

Com.: The Masorah notes the *two* occurrences of this lemma in the parallel passages of 2 Kings and Isaiah.

---

2 KINGS 18:22

וְכִי־תֹאמְר֣וּן אֵלַ֔י אֶל־יְהוָ֥ה אֱלֹהֵ֖ינוּ בָּטָ֑חְנוּ הֲלוֹא־ה֗וּא אֲשֶׁ֨ר הֵסִ֤יר חִזְקִיָּ֙הוּ֙ אֶת־בָּמֹתָ֣יו וְאֶת־מִזְבְּחֹתָ֔יו וַיֹּ֤אמֶר לִֽיהוּדָה֙ וְלִיר֣וּשָׁלִַ֔ם לִפְנֵי֙ הַמִּזְבֵּ֣חַ הַזֶּ֔ה תִּֽשְׁתַּחֲו֖וּ בִּירוּשָׁלָֽםִ:

18:22   תֹאמְר֣וּן

Nine times   ט֗   Mp

Com.: See **1 Sam 11:9**.

18:22   הֲלוֹא

Seventeen times plene in the book   יז מל בסי   Mp

Com.: See **1 Kgs 2:42**.

18:22   לִֽיהוּדָה וְלִירוּשָׁלִַם

Four times   ד֗   Mp

2 Kgs 18:22; Isa 36:7; 2 Chr 11:14; 32:12

Com.: The Masorah notes the *four* occurrences of this lemma with an initial ל, to distinguish them from its *sole* occurrence without this initial ל (יְהוּדָ֖ה וְלִירוּשָׁלִָ֑ם) at Jer 4:3.

18:22   וְלִירוּשָׁלִַם

Eight times   ח֗   Mp

1–5   **2 Kgs 18:22**; Isa 36:7; 41:27; **Jer 4:3**; 4:10
6–8   Jer 4:11; **2 Chr 11:14**; **32:12**

Mm	וליׁרושלם ח֗	*eight times* וְלִירוּשָׁלַםִ
1–5	נירו	Jer 4:3
	הׁשא הׁשאת	Jer 4:10
	יאמר	Jer 4:11
	ראשון	Isa 41:27
	ליהודה	2 Kgs 18:22
6–8	וחבירו	And its companion (Isa 36:7)
	(הלוא) [הלא] הוא	2 Chr 32:12
	כי עזבו	2 Chr 11:14

Com.: The Masorah notes the *eight* occurrences of this lemma with a ו cj., to distinguish them from its more numerous occurrences (30x) without a cj.

18:22 תִּשְׁתַּחֲווּ בִּירוּשָׁלָםִ

Mp	לׄ	*Unique*

Com.: The Masorah notes the occurrence of תִּשְׁתַּחֲווּ with בִּירוּשָׁלָםִ, to distinguish it from its occurrence without בִּירוּשָׁלָםִ in the parallel passage at Isa 36:7.

---

2 KINGS 18:24

וְאֵיךְ תָּשִׁיב אֵת פְּנֵי פַחַת אַחַד עַבְדֵי אֲדֹנִי הַקְּטַנִּים וַתִּבְטַח לְךָ עַל־מִצְרַיִם לְרֶכֶב וּלְפָרָשִׁים:

18:24 וְאֵיךְ

Mp	ג׳ ראש פסו	*Three times* at the beginning of a verse

2 Kgs 18:24; Isa 36:9; Job 21:34

Mm	ואיך ג׳ ראש פסוק	וְאֵיךְ *three times* at the beginning of a verse
	תשיב	2 Kgs 18:24
	וחבירו	And its companion (Isa 36:9)
	תנחמוני הבל	Job 21:34

Com.: The Masorah notes the *three* occurrences of this lemma at the beginning of a verse with a ו cj., to distinguish them from its more numerous occurrences (14x) at the beginning of a verse without a cj.

This lemma is featured in a Masoretic list of words that occur *three times* at the beginning of a verse with a preceding ו but which normally occur at the beginning of a verse without this ו; see Frensdorff, *Ochlah*, §173, and Ognibeni, *'Oklah*, §97.

18:24 תָּשִׁיב

תָּשִׁיב *ten times*   תשיב י҃   Mm

1–5	Gen 24:6	השמר
	Deut 24:13	העבוט
	Judg 5:29	חכמות
	2 Kgs 18:24	ואיך
	And its companion (Isa 36:9)	וחבירו
6–10	Isa 58:13	משבת
	Ps 89:44	חרבו
	Ps 74:11	וימינך
	Job 15:13	אל אל
	Lam 3:64	גמול יהוה כמעשה

Com.: The Masorah notes the *ten* occurrences of this lemma in the *hiphil*, to distinguish them from its more numerous occurrences (33x) in the *qal* (תָּשׁוּב); see Ognibeni, *'Oklah*, §3G.

18:24 אֶחָד

Twenty-five times   כ҃ה   Mp

Com.: See **1 Sam 9:3**.

---

2 KINGS 18:25

עַתָּה הֲמִבַּלְעֲדֵי יְהוָה עָלִיתִי עַל־הַמָּקוֹם הַזֶּה לְהַשְׁחִתוֹ יְהוָה אָמַר אֵלַי עֲלֵה עַל־הָאָרֶץ הַזֹּאת וְהַשְׁחִיתָהּ׃

18:25 עַתָּה

Twenty-five times at the beginning of a verse   כ҃ה ראש פסו   Mp

Com.: See **1 Sam 15:3**.

18:25	הֲמִבַּלְעֲדֵי

Three times   ג̇   Mp

2 Kgs 18:25; Isa 36:10; Jer 44:19

Com.: The Masorah notes the *three* occurrences of this lemma with an interrog. הֲ, to distinguish them from its more numerous occurrences (8x) without an interrogative.

18:25	עַל־הַמָּקוֹם

Three times   ג̇   Mp

2 Kgs 18:25; 22:20; Jer 19:3

Com.: The Masorah notes the *three* occurrences of הַמָּקוֹם with עַל, to distinguish them from its more numerous occurrences (44x) with אֶל (אֶל הַמָּקוֹם).

This enumeration does not include the *four* occurrences of this lemma when it is followed by וְעַל־יֹשְׁבָיו.

The distinction between עַל־הַמָּקוֹם and אֶל הַמָּקוֹם is implied in the Mp heading at 2 Kgs 22:20 and the additonal Mm note at Jer 19:3. These notes read *three times and similarly every occurrence with* וְעַל־יֹשְׁבָיו, *apart from one*. The *one* exception that provides the contrast is at 2 Kgs 22:16, where the lemma occurs as אֶל הַמָּקוֹם.

18:25	לְהַשְׁחִתוֹ

Seven times defective   ז̇ חס   Mp

Com.: See **2 Sam 11:1**.

2 KINGS 18:26

וַיֹּ֣אמֶר אֶלְיָקִ֣ים בֶּן־חִ֠לְקִיָּהוּ וְשֶׁבְנָ֨ה וְיוֹאָ֜ח אֶל־רַב־שָׁקֵ֗ה דַּבֶּר־נָ֤א אֶל־עֲבָדֶ֙יךָ֙ אֲרָמִ֔ית כִּ֥י שֹׁמְעִ֖ים אֲנָ֑חְנוּ וְאַל־תְּדַבֵּ֤ר עִמָּ֙נוּ֙ יְהוּדִ֔ית בְּאָזְנֵ֣י הָעָ֔ם אֲשֶׁ֖ר עַל־הַחֹמָֽה׃

18:26   וַיֹּאמֶר אֶלְיָקִים

Twice   ב֫   Mp

2 Kgs 18:26; Isa 36:11

The circellus has been placed only on אֶלְיָקִים, but since this name occurs *eleven* times it is probable that the lemma was meant to include the previous word since the phrase וַיֹּאמֶר אֶלְיָקִים only occurs *twice*.

18:26   וְשֶׁבְנָה

Twice written with ה   ב֫ כת֫ ה֫   Mp

2 Kgs 18:18; **18:26**

וְשֶׁבְנָה *twice* written with ה, and their references   ושבנה ב כת ה וסימנהון   Mm

2 Kgs 18:18   ויקראו אל המלך
<u>2 Kgs 18:26</u>   ויאמר אליקים בן חלקיהו

Com.: The Masorah notes the *two* occurrences of this lemma written with a ה, to distinguish them from its more numerous occurrences (5x) written with an א (וְשֶׁבְנָא).

18:26   בְּאָזְנֵי

Thirty-seven times   לז֫   Mp

Com.: See **Josh 20:4**.

2 KINGS 18:27

וַיֹּאמֶר אֲלֵיהֶם רַב־שָׁקֵה הַעַל אֲדֹנֶיךָ וְאֵלֶיךָ שְׁלָחַנִי אֲדֹנִי לְדַבֵּר אֶת־הַדְּבָרִים הָאֵלֶּה הֲלֹא עַל־הָאֲנָשִׁים הַיֹּשְׁבִים עַל־הַחֹמָה לֶאֱכֹל אֶת־חֹרֵיהֶם וְלִשְׁתּוֹת אֶת־שֵׁינֵיהֶם עִמָּכֶם׃

18:27   הַעַל

Twice   ב̇   Mp

2 Kgs 18:27; Neh 2:19

Com.: The Masorah notes the *two* occurrences of this form accented *milraʿ*, to distinguish them from its *eight* occurrences accented *milʿêl*; see Ognibeni, *ʾOklah*, §8X.

At Neh 2:19 the Mp, which reads *twice accented* (*milraʿ*), contains the catchword אדניך (אֲדֹנֶיךָ) referring the reader back to this verse.

This lemma is featured in two Masoretic lists. One is in a list of interrogatives preceding words beginning with א or ע; see the Mm at Isa 36:12 *sub* הַאֵל.

The other is in a Masoretic list of doublets that begin with ה (here and Neh 2:19); see Frensdorff, *Ochlah*, §64, and Díaz-Esteban, *Sefer Oklah we-Oklah*, §65.

18:27   וְאֵלֶיךָ

Three times   ג̇   Mp

<u>Gen 4:7</u>; **2 Kgs 18:27**; <u>Isa 36:12</u>

Com.: The Masorah notes the *three* occurrences of this lemma with a ו cj., to distinguish them from its more numerous occurrences (200+) without a cj.

The Mm heading at <u>Gen 4:7</u> reads *three times and plene* indicating that the lemma does not appear elsewhere written defective as, for example, is the case with other forms of this preposition אֵלוֹ, אֲלֵכֶם, אֲלֵהֶם, and וַאֲלֵהֶם.

18:27   עַל־הָאֲנָשִׁים

Five times   ה̇   Mp

1–5   Exod 5:9; **2 Kgs 18:27**; <u>Isa 36:12</u>; <u>Zeph 1:12</u>; <u>1 Chr 19:5</u>

Com.: The Masorah notes the *five* occurrences of this lemma with עַל, to distinguish them from its *four* occurrences with אֶל (אֶל הָאֲנָשִׁים); see Ognibeni, *ʾOklah*, §280, no 106.

18:27   חֲרֵיהֶם

Mp   צואתם ק   Read צוֹאָתָם

Com.: The *kətîb* (חריהם), and the *qərê* (צוֹאָתָם) both meaning *their excrement* are examples of *kətîb/qərê* variations, where the reader is enjoined to substitute the *kətîb* because it was thought to be too coarse; see Gordis, *The Biblical Text*, 86.

18:27   שֵׁינֵיהֶם

Mp   מימי רגליהם ק   Read מֵימֵי רַגְלֵיהֶם

Com.: The *kətîb* (שיניהם, *their urine*), and the *qərê* (מֵימֵי רַגְלֵיהֶם, lit. *waters of their legs = their urine*) are examples of *kətîb/qərê* variations where the reader is enjoined to substitute the *kətîb* because it was thought to be too coarse; see Gordis, *The Biblical Text*, 86.

---

2 KINGS 18:28

וַיַּעֲמֹד רַב־שָׁקֵה וַיִּקְרָא בְקוֹל־גָּדוֹל יְהוּדִית וַיְדַבֵּר וַיֹּאמֶר שִׁמְעוּ דְּבַר־הַמֶּלֶךְ הַגָּדוֹל מֶלֶךְ אַשּׁוּר׃

18:28   יְהוּדִית

Mp   ז̇   *Seven times*

1–5   **Gen 26:34**; 2 Kgs 18:26; **18:28**; Isa 36:11; 36:13
6–7   Neh 13:24; **2 Chr 32:18**

Com.: The Masorah notes the *seven* occurrences of this lemma with a fem. ending, to distinguish them from its *seven* occurrences with a masc. ending (יְהוּדִי).

18:28   הַמֶּלֶךְ הַגָּדוֹל

Mp   ד̇   *Four times*

2 Kgs 18:19; **18:28**; Isa 36:4; 36:13

Com.: The Masorah notes the *four* occurrences of this lemma, a def. *the great king*, to distinguish them from its *three* occurrences as an indefin. מֶלֶךְ גָּדוֹל *a great king*.

The Mp headings here and at Isa 36:4 correctly read *four times*, but the one at Isa 36:13 mistakenly reads *five times*.

In M^L the circellus has been placed on the words דְּבַר־הַמֶּלֶךְ. But since this phrase occurs *nine times* it is more likely that the circellus should have been placed on הַמֶּלֶךְ הַגָּדוֹל, which occurs only *four times*.

2 KINGS 18:29

כֹּה אָמַר הַמֶּלֶךְ אַל־יַשִּׁא לָכֶם חִזְקִיָּהוּ כִּי־לֹא יוּכַל לְהַצִּיל אֶתְכֶם מִיָּדוֹ:

18:29   יַשִּׁא

Five times   הֿ   Mp

1–5   **2 Kgs 18:29** (יַשִּׁא)*; Isa 36:14 (יַשִּׁא); **Ps 55:16** (יַשִּׁי, *qerê*)
      Ps 89:23 (יַשִּׁיא)*; **2 Chr 32:15** (יַשִּׁיא)

Com.: The Masorah notes the *five* occurrences of this form, *two* of which are written plene י (Ps 89:23 and 2 Chr 32:15), *two* written defective י (2 Kgs 18:29 and Isa 36:14) and *one* written defective א (Ps 55:16).

*M^L, contrary to M (יַשִּׁא), reads the lemma here plene י (יַשִּׁיא); see Breuer, *The Biblical Text*, 132. On the other hand, contra M (יַשִּׁיא), it reads Ps 89:23 defective י (יַשִּׁא); see ibid, 262.

The Mp heading at 2 Chr 32:15 (יַשִּׁיא) reads *five times, twice plene*, which conforms to the text of M, rather than M^L.

Both M^C and M^A read here יַשִּׁא. The Mp at M^A reads *twice defective* (for the forms here and at Isa 36:14), whereas that at M^C reads, as M^L, *five times*.

2 KINGS 18:30

וְאַל־יַבְטַח אֶתְכֶם חִזְקִיָּהוּ אֶל־יְהוָה לֵאמֹר הַצֵּל יַצִּילֵנוּ יְהוָה וְלֹא תִנָּתֵן אֶת־הָעִיר הַזֹּאת בְּיַד מֶלֶךְ אַשּׁוּר:

18:30   יַבְטַח

Twice   בֿ   Mp

2 Kgs 18:30; Isa 36:15

Com.: The Masorah notes the *two* occurrences of this lemma in these parallel passagaes in the *hiphil*, to distinguish them from its more numerous occurrences (5x) in the *qal* (יִבְטַח).

This distinction is implied in the headings of the Mp and Mm notes here in M^A, which read *twice with pataḥ* (בַּ) and (ב פתֿ), thereby assuming a contrast with a form with a different vowel under the י, which can only be a *ḥîreq* (and thus a *qal*). M^C has no note here.

18:31 וְלֹא תִנָּתֵן

Twice   בׄ   Mp

2 Kgs 18:30; Jer 39:17

Com.: The Masorah notes the *two* occurrences of this lemma with a ו cj., to distinguish it from its *three* occurrences without a cj., *one* of which occurs in the parallel passage at Isa 36:15.

---

2 KINGS 18:31

אַל־תִּשְׁמְע֖וּ אֶל־חִזְקִיָּ֑הוּ כִּי֩ כֹ֨ה אָמַ֜ר מֶ֣לֶךְ אַשּׁ֗וּר עֲשֽׂוּ־אִתִּ֤י בְרָכָה֙ וּצְא֣וּ אֵלַ֔י וְאִכְל֤וּ אִישׁ־גַּפְנוֹ֙ וְאִ֣ישׁ תְּאֵנָת֔וֹ וּשְׁת֖וּ אִ֥ישׁ מֵי־בוֹרֽוֹ׃

18:31   בוֹרוֹ

Twice, once plene   בׄ חד מל   Mp

2 Kgs 18:31 (ברׄו)*; **Isa 36:16** (בוֹרׄו)

Com.: The Masorah notes the *two* occurrences of this lemma, *one* written plene first ו in the parallel passage at Isa 36:16, and *one* written defective first ו (here).

*M^L, contrary to M (ברׄו), writes the lemma here plene first ו (בוֹרׄו); see Breuer, *The Biblical Text*, 132. Nevertheless, the Mp note here and at Isa 36:16, which reads *unique plene*, is only understandable with the text of M.

Both M^C and M^A read here ברׄו. The Mp at M^A correctly *unique defective*, and the Mp at M^C more expansively also correctly reads: *twice, once defective, and once plene*.

---

2 KINGS 18:32

עַד־בֹּאִ֞י וְלָקַחְתִּ֤י אֶתְכֶם֙ אֶל־אֶ֣רֶץ כְּאַרְצְכֶ֔ם אֶ֤רֶץ דָּגָן֙ וְתִיר֔וֹשׁ אֶ֥רֶץ לֶ֖חֶם וּכְרָמִ֑ים אֶ֣רֶץ זֵ֤ית יִצְהָר֙ וּדְבַ֔שׁ וִֽחְי֖וּ וְלֹ֣א תָמֻ֑תוּ וְאַֽל־תִּשְׁמְעוּ֙ אֶל־חִזְקִיָּ֔הוּ כִּֽי־יַסִּ֤ית אֶתְכֶם֙ לֵאמֹ֔ר יְהוָ֖ה יַצִּילֵֽנוּ׃

18:32   זֵית יִצְהָר

Unique   לׄ   Mp

18:32   וִחְיוּ

Seven times   זׄ   Mp

1–5   Gen 42:18; **2 Kgs 18:32**; Jer 27:12; 27:17; Ezek 18:32
6–8   Amos 5:4; 5:6; Prov 9:6

Com.: The heading of the Mp here of *seven times* is incorrect since there are *eight* occurrences of this lemma.

The Masorah notes the *eight* occurrences of this lemma pointed this way, to distinguish them from its *two* forms pointed as וְחָיו at Num 4:19 and Zech 10:9; see Ginsburg, 4, ח, §172.

In their *Thesaurus*, Dotan/Reich suggest two ways in which this number might be explained: (1) that Amos 5:4 and 5:6 were originally taken as *one* reference because of the closely associated catchwords (דְּרָשׁוּנִי and (דְּרָשׁוּ); (2) that the *seven* includes only the *seven* references in Prophets and Writings (thus excluding Gen 42:18); see Dotan/Reich, *Masora Thesaurus, ad loc.*

Neither M^C nor M^A has a note on this lemma here.

---

2 KINGS 18:36

וְהֶחֱרִישׁוּ הָעָם וְלֹא־עָנוּ אֹתוֹ דָּבָר כִּי־מִצְוַת הַמֶּלֶךְ הִיא לֵאמֹר לֹא תַעֲנֻהוּ׃

18:36   וְהֶחֱרִישׁוּ

Unique   ל   Mp

Com.: The Masorah notes the *sole* occurrence of this lemma, to distinguish it from its *two* occurrences of the form וַיַּחֲרִישׁוּ at Isa 36:21 and Neh 5:8.

18:36   תַעֲנֻהוּ

Twice   בֿ   Mp

2 Kgs 18:36; Isa 36:21

Com.: The Masorah notes the *two* occurrences of this lemma, *one* here and *one* in the parallel passage at Isa 36:21.

---

2 KINGS 18:37

וַיָּבֹא אֶלְיָקִים בֶּן־חִלְקִיָּה אֲשֶׁר־עַל־הַבַּיִת וְשֶׁבְנָא הַסֹּפֵר וְיוֹאָח בֶּן־אָסָף הַמַּזְכִּיר אֶל־חִזְקִיָּהוּ קְרוּעֵי בְגָדִים וַיַּגִּדוּ לוֹ דִּבְרֵי רַב־שָׁקֵה׃

18:37   חִלְקִיָּה

Eleven times   יֿא   Mp

1–5   **2 Kgs 18:37; 22:8; 22:10; 22:12; Jer 29:3**
6–10   **1 Chr 5:39**ᵃ; 5:39ᵇ (וְחִלְקִיָּה); **6:30; 9:11;** 2 Chr 35:8
11   *All* Ezra-Neh

Com.: The Masorah notes the *eleven* occurrences of this lemma written with the divine element יָה, to distinguish them from its more numerous (19x) occurrences written with the divine element יָהוּ (חִלְקִיָּהוּ).

The *five* occurrences in Ezra-Neh (Ezra 7:1; Neh 8:4, וְחִלְקִיָּה; 11:11; 12:7; 12:21, לְחִלְקִיָּה) are treated as *one* reference.

Some Mp headings (1 Chr 5:39ª, 6:30 and 9:11) exclude the Ezra-Neh references in their count and read *ten times and similarly all Ezra-Neh*.

The heading at 1 Chr 9:11 of *seven times* is a graphic error of ז *seven* for י *for ten*.

18:37   קְרוּעֵי

Twice plene   ב׳ מל   Mp

2 Kgs 18:37; Isa 36:22

Com.: The Masorah notes the *two* occurrences of this lemma in these parallel passages written plene ו, to distinguish them from its occurrence written defective ו (קְרֻעֵי) at 2 Sam 13:31.

18:37   וַיַּגִּדוּ

Four times defective   ד׳ חס   Mp

Gen 26:32; 45:26; 2 Kgs 7:15; **18:37**

Com.: The Masorah notes the *four* occurrences of this lemma written defective second י, to distinguish them from its more numerous occurrences (23x) written plene second י (וַיַּגִּידוּ).

This enumeration does not include the *seventeen* occurrences of this lemma in Judges (3x) and Samuel (14x).

The Mp heading at Gen 45:26 *four times and similarly all Judges and Samuel, apart from two.*

The Mm heading to Gen 26:32 reads *four times*, but at the end of the listings the note adds *and similarly all occurrences <in Judges> and Samuel apart from two* (1 Sam 11:9 and **14:33**).

2 KINGS 19:1

וַיְהִ֗י כִּשְׁמֹ֙עַ֙ הַמֶּ֣לֶךְ חִזְקִיָּ֔הוּ וַיִּקְרַ֖ע אֶת־בְּגָדָ֑יו וַיִּתְכַּ֣ס בַּשָּׂ֔ק וַיָּבֹ֖א בֵּ֥ית יְהוָֽה׃

19:1   וַיִּתְכַּ֣ס בַּשָּׂ֔ק

Twice   ב׳   Mp

2 Kgs 19:1; Isa 37:1

Com.: The Masorah notes the *two* occurrences of this lemma, *one* here and *one* in the parallel passage at Isa 37:1.

2 KINGS 19:2

וַיִּשְׁלַ֡ח אֶת־אֶלְיָקִ֣ים אֲשֶׁר־עַל־הַבַּ֩יִת֩ וְשֶׁבְנָ֨א הַסֹּפֵ֜ר וְאֵת֙ זִקְנֵ֣י הַכֹּהֲנִ֔ים מִתְכַּסִּ֖ים בַּשַּׂקִּ֑ים אֶל־יְשַֽׁעְיָ֥הוּ הַנָּבִ֖יא בֶּן־אָמֽוֹץ׃

19:2   וְאֵת֙ זִקְנֵ֣י

Three times   ג׳   Mp

Com.: See **2 Sam 17:15**.

2 KINGS 19:3

וַיֹּאמְר֣וּ אֵלָ֗יו כֹּ֚ה אָמַ֣ר חִזְקִיָּ֔הוּ יוֹם־צָרָ֧ה וְתוֹכֵחָ֛ה וּנְאָצָ֖ה הַיּ֣וֹם הַזֶּ֑ה כִּ֣י בָ֤אוּ בָנִים֙ עַד־מַשְׁבֵּ֔ר וְכֹ֥חַ אַ֖יִן לְלֵדָֽה׃

19:3   וְתוֹכֵחָ֛ה

Twice   ב׳   Mp

2 Kgs 19:3; Isa 37:3

Com.: The Masorah notes the *two* occurrences of this lemma in these parallel passages with a ו cj., to distinguish it from its *sole* occurrence without a cj. at Hos 5:9.

וְכֹחַ אַיִן		19:3

Twice	בׄ	Mp

2 Kgs 19:3; Isa 37:3

Com.: The Masorah notes the *two* occurrences of this lemma, *one* here and *one* in the parallel passage at Isa 37:3.

---

2 KINGS 19:4

אוּלַ֡י יִשְׁמַע֩ יְהוָ֨ה אֱלֹהֶ֜יךָ אֵ֣ת ׀ כָּל־דִּבְרֵ֣י רַב־שָׁקֵ֗ה אֲשֶׁר֩ שְׁלָח֨וֹ מֶלֶךְ־אַשּׁ֤וּר ׀ אֲדֹנָיו֙ לְחָרֵף֙ אֱלֹהִ֣ים חַ֔י וְהוֹכִ֙יחַ֙ בַּדְּבָרִ֔ים אֲשֶׁ֥ר שָׁמַ֖ע יְהוָ֣ה אֱלֹהֶ֑יךָ וְנָשָׂ֣אתָ תְפִלָּ֔ה בְּעַ֥ד הַשְּׁאֵרִ֖ית הַנִּמְצָאָֽה׃

		19:4	אֶת כָּל

The first case	Mm	קדמייה
Kings		מלכים
2 Kgs 19:4 (אֶת כָּל)		אולי ישמע יהוה אלהיך את כל דברי רב שקה
2 Kgs 19:16 (אֶת)		הטה יהוה אזנך ושמע פקח יהוה עיניך
		וראה ושמע את דברי סנחריב
One verse is the *sîman*		וחד פסוק סימנם
Exod 30:27 (וְאֶת כָּל...אֶת)		ואת השלחן ואת כל כליו

The second case		תיניני
Isaiah		ישעיה
Isa 37:4 (אֶת)		אולי ישמע יהוה אלהיך את דברי רבשקה
Isa 37:17 (אֶת כָּל)		הטה יהוה אזנך ושמע פקח יהוה עינך
		וראה ושמע את כל דברי סנחריב
One verse is the *sîman*		וחד פסוק סימנׄ
Exod 31:8 (וְאֶת...וְאֶת כָּל)		ואת השלחן (ואת כל כליו) [ואת כליו]
		ואת המנרה הטהרה ואת כל כליה

Com.: The Masorah compares two sets of *two* parallel phrases containing the sequence אֶת and אֶת כָּל, *one* set consisting of 2 Kgs 19:4 and 19:16, and the *other* set consisting of Isa 34:4 and 34:17, and notes their differences by means of a *third-verse sîman*.

The *first* third-verse *sîman*, that of Exod 30:27, indicates the order of the sequence אֶת כָּל and אֶת in the *two* passages in Kings, and the *second* third-verse *sîman*, that of Exod 31:8, indicates the reverse order of אֶת and אֶת כָּל in the parallel passages in Isaiah.

For ease of reference we have placed the phrases קדמייה *the first case* and תיניי *the second case* at the beginning of their respective notes though in the ms. they occur at the end of their notes.

---

2 KINGS 19:6

וַיֹּאמֶר לָהֶם יְשַׁעְיָהוּ כֹּה תֹאמְרוּן אֶל־אֲדֹנֵיכֶם כֹּה ׀ אָמַר יְהוָה אַל־תִּירָא מִפְּנֵי הַדְּבָרִים אֲשֶׁר שָׁמַעְתָּ אֲשֶׁר גִּדְּפוּ נַעֲרֵי מֶלֶךְ־אַשּׁוּר אֹתִי:

19:6   וַיֹּאמֶר לָהֶם

Twenty-four times   כ̇ד̇   Mp

Com.: See **Josh 4:5**.

19:6   תֹאמְרוּן

Nine times   ט̇   Mp

Com.: See **1 Sam 11:9**.

19:6   גִּדְּפוּ

Three times   ג̇   Mp

2 Kgs 19:6; <u>Isa 37:6</u>; **Ezek 20:27**

> **2 KINGS 19:7**
> הִנְנִי נֹתֵן בּוֹ רוּחַ וְשָׁמַע שְׁמוּעָה וְשָׁב לְאַרְצוֹ וְהִפַּלְתִּיו בַּחֶרֶב בְּאַרְצוֹ׃

19:7   וְהִפַּלְתִּיו

Twice   בׄ   Mp

2 Kgs 19:7; Isa 37:7

Com.: The Masorah notes the *two* occurrences of this lemma, *one* here and *one* in the parallel passage at Isa 37:7.

> **2 KINGS 19:9**
> וַיִּשְׁמַע אֶל־תִּרְהָקָה מֶלֶךְ־כּוּשׁ לֵאמֹר הִנֵּה יָצָא לְהִלָּחֵם אִתָּךְ וַיָּשָׁב וַיִּשְׁלַח מַלְאָכִים אֶל־חִזְקִיָּהוּ לֵאמֹר׃

19:9   אֶל־תִּרְהָקָה

Unique   לׄ   Mp

In *Kings* (2 Kgs 19:9)   דמלכים   Mm
     אֶל־תִּרְהָקָה   אל תרהקה
     הִנֵּה יָצָא   הנה יצא
     וַיָּשָׁב וַיִּשְׁלַח   וישב וישלח

In *Isaiah* (Isa 37:9)   דישעיה
     עַל־תִּרְהָקָה   על תרהקה
     יָצָא   חס הנה
     וַיִּשְׁמַע וַיִּשְׁלַח   וישמע וישלח

Com.: The Masorah compares *two* parallel verses, *one* in Kings (2 Kgs 19:9) and *one* in Isaiah (Isa 37:9) and indicates *three* areas of differences in the verses.

The *first* is that Kings reads אֶל־תִּרְהָקָה, whereas Isaiah has עַל־תִּרְהָקָה.

The *second* is that Kings reads הִנֵּה יָצָא, whereas Isaiah just reads יָצָא without הִנֵּה (indicated in the note by חס הנה, that is, lacking הִנֵּה).

The *third* point of difference is that Kings reads וַיָּשָׁב וַיִּשְׁלַח, whereas Isaiah reads וַיִּשְׁמַע וַיִּשְׁלַח.

The first part of the note is featured in a Masoretic list of words occurring *once* with אֶל, and *once* with עַל; see Frensdorff, *Ochlah*, §2.

---

2 KINGS 19:10

כֹּה תֹאמְרוּן אֶל־חִזְקִיָּהוּ מֶלֶךְ־יְהוּדָה לֵאמֹר אַל־יַשִּׁאֲךָ אֱלֹהֶיךָ אֲשֶׁר אַתָּה בֹּטֵחַ בּוֹ לֵאמֹר לֹא תִנָּתֵן יְרוּשָׁלַ͏ִם בְּיַד מֶלֶךְ אַשּׁוּר:

19:10   תֹאמְרוּן

Nine times   ט   Mp

Com.: See **1 Sam 11:9**.

19:10   יַשִּׁאֲךָ

Twice   ב   Mp

2 Kgs 19:10; Isa 37:10

Com.: The Masorah notes the *two* occurrences of this lemma, *one* here and *one* in the parallel passage at Isa 37:10.

---

2 KINGS 19:12

הַהִצִּילוּ אֹתָם אֱלֹהֵי הַגּוֹיִם אֲשֶׁר שִׁחֲתוּ אֲבוֹתַי אֶת־גּוֹזָן וְאֶת־חָרָן וְרֶצֶף וּבְנֵי־עֶדֶן אֲשֶׁר בִּתְלַאשָּׂר:

19:12   אֲבוֹתַי

Seven times plene   ז מל   Mp

Com.: See **1 Kgs 21:4**.

19:12   עֶדֶן

Four times   ד   Mp

2 Kgs 19:12; Isa 37:12; Ezek 27:23 (וְעֶדֶן); **Amos 1:5**

Com.: The Masorah notes the *four* occurrences of this lemma in various forms with a *səḡōl* under the ע, to distinguish them from its more numerous occurrences (16x) in various forms written with a *ṣerê* (e.g., עֵדֶן).

This lemma is featured in a Masoretic list of words that occur *four times, three times* without a ו cj., and *once* with a cj.; see Frensdorff, *Ochlah*, §15.

In M^L the circellus has been placed here and in Isa 37:12 on the phrase וּבְנֵי־עֶדֶן, but since this phrase occurs only *twice* it is most likely that note refers solely to עֶדֶן, which does occur *four times*.

19:12   בִּתְלַאשָׂר

Twice   בׄ   Mp

2 Kgs 19:12; Isa 37:12 (בִּתְלָשָׂר)

Mm	בתלאשר בׄ חד מל וחד חס	בִּתְלַאשָׂר *twice, once* plene, *and once* defective
	ורצף ובני עדן אשר דמלכים	וְרֶצֶף וּבְנֵי־עֶדֶן אֲשֶׁר *of Kings* (2 Kgs 19:12)
	וחבירו דישעיה	And its companion in Isaiah (Isa 37:12)
	בתלשר כתב	בִּתְלָשָׂר *is written*

Com.: The Masorah notes the *two* occurrences of this lemma, *one* written plene א (here), and *one* written defective א in the parallel passage Isa 37:12.

The addition *of Kings* to the catchwords of the 2 Kgs 19:12 is to distinguish this verse from its parallel in Isa 37:12, which writes the lemma בִּתְלַאשָׂר defective as בִּתְלָשָׂר.

This lemma occurs in the ms. in folio 216r, but the Mm note appears on the top right of the preceding folio 215v.

---

2 KINGS 19:14

וַיִּקַּח חִזְקִיָּהוּ אֶת־הַסְּפָרִים מִיַּד הַמַּלְאָכִים וַיִּקְרָאֵם וַיַּעַל בֵּית יְהוָה וַיִּפְרְשֵׂהוּ חִזְקִיָּהוּ לִפְנֵי יְהוָה: פ

19:14   וַיִּקְרָאֵם

Mm	דמלכים	*In Kings*
ויקראם	(וַיִּקְרָאֵם)	2 Kgs 19:14
ביד מלאכיך	(בְּיַד מַלְאָכֶיךָ)	2 Kgs 19:23

		(In) *Isaiah*	ישעיהו
	Isa 37:14	(וַיִּקְרָאֵ֖הוּ)	ויקראהו
	Isa 37:24	(בְּיַ֥ד עֲבָדֶ֖יךָ)	ביד עבדיך

Com.: The Masorah notes *two* differences between parallel passages in the books of Kings (in this chapter) and Isaiah (at Isaiah 37).

The *first* difference is that 2 Kgs 19:14 reads וַיִּקְרָאֵ֖ם, whereas Isa 37:14 reads וַיִּקְרָאֵ֖הוּ.

The *second* difference is that 2 Kgs 19:23 reads בְּיַ֥ד מַלְאָכֶ֖יךָ, whereas Isa 37:24 reads בְּיַ֥ד עֲבָדֶ֖יךָ.

This lemma occurs in the ms. in folio 216r, but the Mm note appears on the top right of the preceding folio 215v.

---

2 KINGS 19:15

וַיִּתְפַּלֵּ֨ל חִזְקִיָּ֜הוּ לִפְנֵ֥י יְהוָה֮ וַיֹּאמַר֒ יְהוָ֞ה אֱלֹהֵ֤י יִשְׂרָאֵל֙ יֹשֵׁ֣ב הַכְּרֻבִ֔ים אַתָּה־ה֤וּא הָֽאֱלֹהִים֙ לְבַדְּךָ֔ לְכֹ֖ל מַמְלְכ֣וֹת הָאָ֑רֶץ אַתָּ֣ה עָשִׂ֔יתָ אֶת־הַשָּׁמַ֖יִם וְאֶת־הָאָֽרֶץ׃

19:15		הַכְּרֻבִים		
Twelve times defective and similarly in *all* the Torah			יֿבֿ חס̇ וכל אור דכות	Mp

Com.: See **1 Sam 4:4**.

19:15		אֶת־הַשָּׁמַיִם וְאֶת־הָאָרֶץ		
Thirteen times			יֿגֿ	Mp

1–5	Gen 1:1; **Exod 20:11; 31:17; Deut 4:26; 30:19**
6–10	**Deut 31:28; 2 Kgs 19:15; Isa 37:16;** Jer 23:24; **32:17**
11–13	Hag 2:6; **2:21**; 2 Chr 2:11

Com.: The Masorah notes the *thirteen* occurrences when הַשָּׁמַיִם and הָאָרֶץ are both preceded by אֶת, to distinguish them from the *two* occurrences when they are not (הַשָּׁמַיִם וְהָאָרֶץ) at Gen 2:1 and 2:4.

In M^L only one circellus has been placed here, and at Deut 30:19 and 31:28, over the phrase אֶת־הַשָּׁמַיִם but, since this phrase occurs *seventeen times* (in the above list plus Deut 11:17; 28:12; Hos 2:23, and Neh 9:6), it is most likely that the note refers to the full phrase אֶת־הַשָּׁמַיִם וְאֶת־הָאָרֶץ which does occur only *thirteen times*, the catchwords of which are listed in the Mm at Hag 2:21.

2 KINGS 19:16

הַטֵּה יְהוָה ׀ אָזְנְךָ֙ וּֽשֲׁמָ֔ע פְּקַ֧ח יְהוָ֛ה עֵינֶ֖יךָ וּרְאֵ֑ה וּשְׁמַ֗ע אֵ֚ת דִּבְרֵ֣י סַנְחֵרִ֔יב אֲשֶׁ֣ר שְׁלָח֔וֹ לְחָרֵ֖ף אֱלֹהִ֥ים חָֽי׃

19:16   אָזְנְךָ

Thirteen times   יג   Mp

1–5   **2 Kgs 19:16**; Isa 37:17; Ps 17:6; 31:3; 71:2
6–10   Ps 86:1; 88:3; Prov 22:17; Ruth 4:4; Lam 3:56
11–13 Dan 9:18; Neh 1:6; 1:11

Com.: The Masorah notes the *thirteen* occurrences of this lemma with a *šəwâ* under the נ, to distinguish them from its *eight* occurrences pointed with a *səḡôl* (אָזְנֶךָ).

19:16   וּשֲׁמָע

Five times   ה   Mp

1–5   **Num 23:18; Deut 5:27; 2 Kgs 19:16; Isa 37:17** (וּשְׁמָע); **Dan 9:18**

Com.: The Masorah notes the *five* occurrences of this lemma with a *qameṣ* under the מ, to distinguish them from its more numerous occurrences (9x) with a *pataḥ* (וּשְׁמַע).

This distinction is implied in the Mp heading of Num 23:18, which reads *five times with qameṣ* (ה) thereby assuming a contrast with a form with a different vowel under the מ, which can only be a *pataḥ*.

2 KINGS 19:17

אָמְנָ֖ם יְהוָ֑ה הֶחֱרִ֜יבוּ מַלְכֵ֥י אַשּׁ֛וּר אֶת־הַגּוֹיִ֖ם וְאֶת־אַרְצָֽם׃

19:17   וְאֶת־אַרְצָם

Three times   ג   Mp

Com.: See **Josh 10:42**.

2 Kings 19:18

וְנָתְנוּ אֶת־אֱלֹהֵיהֶם בָּאֵשׁ כִּי לֹא אֱלֹהִים הֵמָּה כִּי אִם־מַעֲשֵׂה יְדֵי־אָדָם עֵץ וָאֶבֶן וַיְאַבְּדוּם׃

19:18   וַיְאַבְּדוּם

Twice   בׄ   Mp

2 Kgs 19:18; Isa 37:19

Com.: The Masorah notes the *two* occurrences of this lemma, *one* here and *one* in the parallel passage at Isa 37:19.

2 Kings 19:19

וְעַתָּה יְהוָה אֱלֹהֵינוּ הוֹשִׁיעֵנוּ נָא מִיָּדוֹ וְיֵדְעוּ כָּל־מַמְלְכוֹת הָאָרֶץ כִּי אַתָּה יְהוָה אֱלֹהִים לְבַדֶּךָ׃ ס

19:19   וְעַתָּה יְהוָה אֱלֹהֵינוּ

Three times   גׄ   Mp

2 Kgs 19;19; Isa 37:20; Dan 9:15 (וְעַתָּה אֲדֹנָי אֱלֹהֵינוּ)

Com.: The Masorah notes the *three* occurrences of this lemma with the 1st pers. pl. sfx., to distinguish them from its *three* occurrences without this sfx. (וְעַתָּה יְהוָה אֱלֹהִים).

In M^L only one circellus has been placed on יְהוָה אֱלֹהֵינוּ but, since this phrase occurs many more than *three times*, it is most likely that, with M^A, the note should include the previous word וְעַתָּה since the longer phrase וְעַתָּה יְהוָה אֱלֹהֵינוּ only occurs *three times*.

19:19   וְיֵדְעוּ

Eleven times   יאׄ   Mp

Com.: See **1 Sam 17:46**.

19:19   יְהוָה אֱלֹהִים

Five times written (this way) in the Prophets   הׄ כת בנביא   Mp

Com.: See **2 Sam 7:25**.

2 KINGS 19:20

וַיִּשְׁלַח֙ יְשַֽׁעְיָ֣הוּ בֶן־אָמ֔וֹץ אֶל־חִזְקִיָּ֖הוּ לֵאמֹ֑ר כֹּֽה־אָמַ֞ר יְהוָ֣ה אֱלֹהֵ֣י יִשְׂרָאֵ֗ל אֲשֶׁ֧ר הִתְפַּלַּ֛לְתָּ אֵלַ֖י אֶל־סַנְחֵרִ֥ב מֶֽלֶךְ־אַשּׁ֖וּר שָׁמָֽעְתִּי׃

19:20　סַנְחֵרִב

Unique defective　ל חס　Mp

Com.: The Masorah notes the *sole* occurrence of this lemma written defective י, to distinguish it from its more numerous occurrences (12x) written plene י (סַנְחֵרִיב).

2 KINGS 19:21

זֶ֣ה הַדָּבָ֔ר אֲשֶׁר־דִּבֶּ֥ר יְהוָ֖ה עָלָ֑יו בָּזָ֨ה לְךָ֜ לָעֲגָ֣ה לְךָ֗ בְּתוּלַת֙ בַּת־צִיּ֔וֹן אַחֲרֶ֙יךָ֙ רֹ֣אשׁ הֵנִ֔יעָה בַּ֖ת יְרוּשָׁלָֽםִ׃

19:21　בָּזָה

Eight times　ח　Mp

1–5　**Num 15:31; 2 Kgs 19:21;** Isa 37:22; Ezek 17:16; 17:19
6–8　**Ps 22:25;** 69:34; 102:18

Com.: The Masorah notes the *eight* occurrences of this lemma. The additional notes to the Mm at Isa 37:22 and Ps 69:34 also mention that this lemma occurs *once* with a ו cj. (וּבָזָה) at Ezek 17:18.

2 KINGS 19:22

אֶת־מִ֤י חֵרַ֙פְתָּ֙ וְגִדַּ֔פְתָּ וְעַל־מִ֖י הֲרִימ֣וֹתָ קּ֑וֹל וַתִּשָּׂ֥א מָר֛וֹם עֵינֶ֖יךָ עַל־קְד֥וֹשׁ יִשְׂרָאֵֽל׃

19:22　וְעַל־מִי

Four times　ד　Mp

1 Sam 17:28; **2 Kgs 19:22;** Isa 37:23; Job 25:3

| וְעַל־מִי four times, and their references | וְעַל מִי ד׳ וסימנהון | Mm |

2 Kgs 19:22 — הרימות
And its companion (Isa 37:23) — וחבירו
1 Sam 17:28 — נטשת
Job 25:3 — אורהו

Com.: The Masorah notes the *four* occurrences of this lemma with a ו cj., to distinguish them from its more numerous occurrences (8x) without a cj.

19:22 הֲרִימוֹתָ

Three times ג׳ Mp

2 Kgs 19:22; **Isa 37:23** (הֲרִימוֹתָה); **Ps 89:43**

Com.: The Masorah notes the *three* occurrences of this lemma, *two* are written defective ה (here and Ps 89:43), and *one* is written plene ה (Isa 37:23).

The Mp heading at **Isa 37:23** reads *twice*, but the note there may involve the phrase הֲרִימוֹתָ קוֹל, which only occurs *twice*; see Dotan/Reich, *Masora Thesaurus*, ad loc.

19:22 עַל־קָדוֹשׁ

Twice ב׳ Mp

2 Kgs 19:22; Isa 31:1

Com.: The Masorah notes the *two* occurrences of קָדוֹשׁ with עַל, to distinguish them from its *three* occurrences with אֶל (אֶל־קָדוֹשׁ), *one* of which occurs in the parallel text Isa 37:23.

This lemma is also featured in a Masoretic list of doublets beginning with עַל; see Frensdorff, *Ochlah*, §87, and Díaz-Esteban, *Sefer Oklah we-Oklah*, §156D.

---

2 KINGS 19:23

בְּיַד מַלְאָכֶיךָ חֵרַפְתָּ ׀ אֲדֹנָי וַתֹּאמֶר בְּרֹכֶב רִכְבִּי אֲנִי עָלִיתִי מְרוֹם הָרִים יַרְכְּתֵי לְבָנוֹן וְאֶכְרֹת קוֹמַת אֲרָזָיו מִבְחוֹר בְּרֹשָׁיו וְאָבוֹאָה מְלוֹן קִצֹּה יַעַר כַּרְמִלּוֹ:

19:23 בְּרֹכֶב

Read בְּרֹב ק ברב ק Mp

Com.: The *kətîb* (ברכב, *with a chariot*), and the *qərê* (בְּרֹב, *with much*) represent variant forms where the *qərê* is preferable to the *kətîb*; see Gordis, *The Biblical Text*, 152.

19:23   וָאֶכְרֹת

Twice   בֿ   Mp

2 Kgs 19:23; Isa 37:24

Com.: The Masorah notes the *two* occurrences of this lemma in these parallel passages with a ו cj., to distinguish it from its *four* occurrences without a cj.

19:23   מִבְחוֹר

Twice   בֿ   Mp

Com.: See **2 Kgs 3:19**.

19:23   וְאָבוֹאָה

Four times   דֿ   Mp

Gen 29:21; 2 Kgs 19:23; Ps 43:4; 2 Chr 1:10

וְאָבוֹאָה *four times*   ואבואה דֿ   Mm

Gen 29:21   כי מלאו
2 Kgs 19:23   מלון
Ps 43:4   אל מזבח
2 Chr 1:10   ואצאה

Com.: The Masorah notes the *four* occurrences of this lemma with the cohortative ה, to distinguish them form it more numerous occurrences (9x) without this cohortative (וְאָבוֹא).

The additional notes to the Mm at Gen 29:21 and Ps 43:4 also mention that this lemma occurs *once* without a ו cj. (אָבֹאָה) at **Judg 15:1**.

According to Ginsburg (4, ב, §129), in fixing the instances with ו cj. at *five*, the Masorah militates against the ancient reading here of וְאָבוֹאָה (see *BHS*, *ad loc*).

19:23	מָלוֹן
Twice	ב׳ Mp

2 Kgs 19:23; Jer 9:1

Com.: The Masorah notes the *two* occurrences of this lemma in the cstr., to distinguish it from its *sole* occurrence in the absol. (מָלוֹן) at Isa 10:29.

19:23	קִצֹּה
Three times	ג׳ Mp

2 Kgs 19:23; Isa 37:24 (קִצוֹ); Dan 11:45 (קִצּוֹ)

Com.: The Masorah notes the *three* occurrences of this lemma, *two* are written with a ו (Isa 37:24 and Dan 11:45) and *one* with a ה (here).

M^C and M^A have a *kǝtîb* (קצה) and *qǝrê* (קִצּוֹ) here, see also *BHS ad loc*.

---

2 KINGS 19:24

אֲנִי קַרְתִּי וְשָׁתִיתִי מַיִם זָרִים וְאַחְרִב בְּכַף־פְּעָמַי כֹּל יְאֹרֵי מָצוֹר׃

19:24	וְאַחְרִב
Twice	ב׳ Mp

2 Kgs 19:24; Isa 37:25

Com.: The Masorah notes the *two* occurrences of this lemma written defective י, *one* here and *one* in the parallel passage at Isa 37:25.

The heading for the Mm at Isa 37:25 reads *twice and defective* (י), thus implying (correctly) that this lemma does not occur elsewhere written defective י.

> ## 2 Kings 19:25
> הֲלֹא־שָׁמַעְתָּ לְמֵרָחוֹק אֹתָהּ עָשִׂיתִי לְמִימֵי קֶדֶם וִיצַרְתִּיהָ עַתָּה הֲבֵיאתִיהָ וּתְהִי לַהְשׁוֹת גַּלִּים נִצִּים עָרִים בְּצֻרוֹת:

19:25   לְמֵרָחוֹק

Eight times   ח׳   Mp

Com.: See **2 Sam 7:19**.

19:25   לְמִימֵי

Twice   ב׳   Mp

2 Kgs 19:25; Mal 3:7

Com.: The Masorah notes the *two* occurrences of this lemma with the prep. ל, to distinguish them from its numerous occurrences (18x) without this preposition, one of which occurs in the parallel passage Isa 37:26.

19:25   הֲבֵיאתִיהָ

Twice   ב׳   Mp

2 Kgs 19:25; Isa 37:26 (הֲבֵאתִיהָ)

Com.: The Masorah notes the *two* occurrences of this lemma in the parallel passages of 2 Kings and Isaiah.

This lemma is featured in a Masoretic list of doublets beginning with ה or הֲ; see Frensdorff, *Ochlah*, §64.

19:25   וּתְהִי

וּתְהִי *fourteen times*   ותהי יד׳   Mm

1–5	Gen 24:51	אשה
	Lev 15:24	נדתה
	Num 23:10	אחריתי
	1 Sam 18:21ª	למוקש
	Twice in it (1 Sam 18:21ᵇ)	ב׳ בו

6–10	1 Sam 18:17	פלשתים
	1 Kgs 1:2	סכנת
	2 Kgs 19:25	להשות
	Isa 30:8	ליום אחרון
	Isa 37:26	להשאות
11–14	Ruth 2:12	משכרתך
	Job 6:10	עוד
	Job 13:5	לכם לחכמה
	Job 21:2	תנחומתיכם

Com.: The Masorah notes the *fourteen* occurrences of this lemma with a ו cj., to distinguish them from its more numerous occurrences (87x) with a ו consec. (וַתְּהִי); see Ognibeni, *'Oklah*, §18D.

This distinction is implied in the headings of the Mp at Lev 15:24 and Job 6:10 and of the Mm at Gen 24:51, which read *fourteen times rapê*, thereby assuming a contrast with forms which are *dageš*, that is, ו consec. forms.

19:25   להשות

Unique   לׄ   Mp

Com.: The Masorah notes the *sole* occurrence of this lemma without an א, to distinguish it from its *sole* occurrence with an א (לְהַשְׁאוֹת) at Isa 37:26.

This lemma is featured in *two* Masoretic lists. One is in a list of words where an א, normally in the word, is omitted; see the Mm to 1 Chr 12:39 *sub* שְׁרִית, Frensdorff, *Ochlah*, §199, and Ognibeni, *'Oklah*, §153.

The other is in a list of word pairs, where one of the pairs has an א and the other does not; see the Mm to Gen 44:29 *sub* וּקְרָהוּ, Frensdorff, *Ochlah*, §201, and Ognibeni, *'Oklah*, §155.

19:25   נִצִּים

Three times   גׄ   Mp

Exod 2:13; **2 Kgs 19:25**; Isa 37:26

Com.: The Masorah notes the *three* occurrences of this lemma, possibly to protect them from other readings such as נצורים in the Isaiah Qumran scroll in the parallel passage at Isa 37:26; see *BHS ad loc*.

2 KINGS 19:26

וְיֹשְׁבֵיהֶן קִצְרֵי־יָד חַתּוּ וַיֵּבֹשׁוּ הָיוּ עֵשֶׂב שָׂדֶה וִירַק דֶּשֶׁא חֲצִיר גַּגּוֹת וּשְׁדֵפָה לִפְנֵי קָמָה:

19:26   וְיֹשְׁבֵיהֶן

Twice   בׄ   Mp

2 Kgs 19:26; Isa 37:27

Com.: The Masorah notes the *two* occurrences of this lemma, *one* here and *one* in the parallel passage at Isa 37:27.

19:26   חַתּוּ וַיֵּבֹשׁוּ

Unique   לׄ   Mp

Com.: The Masorah notes the *sole* occurrence of this lemma, to distinguish it from the *sole* occurrence of the phrase חַתּוּ וָבֹשׁוּ in the parallel passage of Isa 37:27.

19:26   וַיֵּבֹשׁוּ

Twice   בׄ   Mp

2 Kgs 19:26; Ps 109:28

Com.: The Masorah notes the *two* occurrences of this lemma with a ו consec., to distinguish it from its *five* occurrences with a ו cj. (וְיֵבֹשׁוּ).

19:26   עֵשֶׂב שָׂדֶה

Twice   בׄ   Mp

2 Kgs 19:26; Isa 37:27

Com.: The Masorah notes the *two* occurrences in these parallel passages of עֵשֶׂב with שָׂדֶה, to distinguish it from its *four* occurrences with הַשָּׂדֶה (עֵשֶׂב הַשָּׂדֶה).

2 Kings 19:27

וְשִׁבְתְּךָ֛ וְצֵאתְךָ֥ וּבֹאֲךָ֖ יָדָ֑עְתִּי וְאֵ֖ת הִתְרַגֶּזְךָ֥ אֵלָֽי׃

19:27   הִתְרַגֶּזְךָ

Four times   ד׳   Mp

2 Kgs 19:27; 19:28; Isa 37:28; 37:29

Com.: The Masorah notes the *four* occurrences of this lemma, *two* of them in successive verses in Kings (here and v. 28), and *two* of them in successive verses in Isaiah (Isa 37:28 and 29).

2 Kings 19:28

יַ֚עַן הִתְרַגֶּזְךָ֣ אֵלַ֔י וְשַׁאֲנַנְךָ֖ עָלָ֣ה בְאָזְנָ֑י וְשַׂמְתִּ֨י חַחִ֜י בְּאַפֶּ֗ךָ וּמִתְגִּי֙ בִּשְׂפָתֶ֔יךָ וַהֲשִׁבֹתִ֕יךָ בַּדֶּ֖רֶךְ אֲשֶׁר־בָּ֥אתָ בָּֽהּ׃

19:28   הִתְרַגֶּזְךָ

Four times   ד׳   Mp

Com.: See directly above at **2 Kgs 19:27**

19:28   וּמִתְגִּי

Twice   ב׳   Mp

2 Kgs 19:28; Isa 37:29

Com.: The Masorah notes the *two* occurrences of this lemma, *one* here and *one* in the parallel passage at Isa 37:29.

19:28   וַהֲשִׁבֹתִיךָ

Three times   ג׳   Mp

Gen 28:15; **2 Kgs 19:28**; Isa 37:29 (וַהֲשִׁיבֹתִיךָ)

	Mm	וְהֲשִׁבֹתִיךָ גֹ	וַהֲשִׁבֹתִיךָ *three times*

Gen 28:15   אל האדמה
2 Kgs 19:28 בדרך
Isa 37:29   בדרך

Com.: The Masorah notes the *three* occurrences of this lemma with a 2nd pers. sfx., to distinguish them from its more numerous occurrences (7x) with a 3rd pers. pl. sfx. (וַהֲשִׁבֹתִים).

---

2 KINGS 19:29

וְזֶה־לְּךָ הָאוֹת אָכוֹל הַשָּׁנָה סָפִיחַ וּבַשָּׁנָה הַשֵּׁנִית סָחִישׁ וּבַשָּׁנָה הַשְּׁלִישִׁית זִרְעוּ וְקִצְרוּ וְנִטְעוּ כְרָמִים וְאִכְלוּ פִרְיֵם:

19:29   וְזֶה

Mp	כֹּג רֹא פֹּס	*Twenty-three times* at the beginning of a verse

Com.: See **1 Sam 2:34**.

19:29   הַשְּׁלִישִׁית

Mp	ט מֹל	*Nine times* plene

Com.: See **1 Kgs 6:6**.

---

2 KINGS 19:31

כִּי מִירוּשָׁלִַם תֵּצֵא שְׁאֵרִית וּפְלֵיטָה מֵהַר צִיּוֹן קִנְאַת יְהוָה ֯ ֯ ֯ תַּעֲשֶׂה־זֹּאת: ס

19:31   ֯ ֯

Mp	צבאות קרי ולא כתב	צְבָאוֹת is read but not written

Com.: The form צְבָאוֹת is read, although only the first two vowels are written.

This is one of *ten* cases where words are read though not written; see the Mm to Jer 50:29 *sub* לָהּ and Ruth 3:5 *sub* אֵלַי, Frensdorff, *Ochlah*, §97, and Díaz-Esteban, *Sefer Oklah we-Oklah*, §80.

There is also another tradition that knows of *eleven* cases of this phenomenon; see Martín-Contreras, "The Phenomenon," 77–87.

2 Kings 19:32

לָכֵן כֹּה־אָמַר יְהוָה אֶל־מֶלֶךְ אַשּׁוּר לֹא יָבֹא אֶל־הָעִיר הַזֹּאת וְלֹא־יוֹרֶה שָׁם חֵץ וְלֹא־יְקַדְּמֶנָּה מָגֵן וְלֹא־יִשְׁפֹּךְ עָלֶיהָ סֹלְלָה׃

19:32   לָכֵן כֹּה־אָמַר יְהוָה

Twenty times   כ׳   Mp

1–5	**2 Kgs 19:32**; Isa 29:22; 37:33; Jer 6:21; 11:11
6–10	Jer 11:21; 14:15; 15:19; 18:13; 22:18
11–15	**Jer 23:38**; 28:16; 29:32; 32:28; 34:17
16–20	Jer 36:30; 51:36; Amos 7:17; Mic 2:3; Zech 1:16

לָכֵן כֹּה־אָמַר יְהוָה   *twenty times*   לכן כה אמר יהוה כ׳   Mm

1–5	2 Kgs 19:32	אל מלך אשור
	And its companion (Isa 37:33)	וחבירו
	Jer 6:21	(ומכשלים) [מכשלים]
	Jer 11:11	הנני מביא אליהם
	Jer 11:21	על אנשי ענתות
6–10	Jer 14:15	על (הנביאים) [הנבאים] בשמי
	Jer 15:19	(ואם) [אם] תשוב ואשיבך
	Jer 18:13	שאלו נא בגוים
	Jer 22:18	אל יהויקים
	Jer 23:38	יען אמרכם
11–15	Jer 28:16	הנני משלחך
	Jer 29:32	על (שמע יהוה בחלמי) [שמעיה הנחלמי]
	Jer 32:28	הנני נתן את העיר
	Jer 34:17	אתם לא שמעתם אלי
	Jer 36:30	על יהויקים
16–20	Jer 51:36	הנני רב את ריבך
	Isa 29:22	אל בית יעקב
	Amos 7:17	(אשיתך) [אשתך] בעיר
	Mic 2:3	חשב
	Zech 1:16	ברחמים

And *once* (וְלָכֵן): 2 Kgs 1:4   וחד ולכן כה אמר יהוה המטה

Com.: The Masorah notes the *twenty* occurrences of this lemma where the Tetragrammaton is not followed by אֱלֹהֵי יִשְׂרָאֵל or צְבָאוֹת, צְבָאוֹת אֱלֹהֵי יִשְׂרָאֵל, אֱלֹהִים to distinguish them from its more numerous cases (40x) where the Tetragrammaton is followed by these additions.

The Mp heading at Jer 23:38 reads *twenty-one times* to include the *sole* occurrence of this lemma with a ו cj. at **2 Kgs 1:4**.

19:32   לֹא

Mp	ט׳ פסוק לא ולא ולא	*Nine* verses in which there is the sequence לֹא...וְלֹא...וְלֹא

Com.: See **Josh 23:7**.

In Mᴸ this lemma has no circellus.

2 KINGS 19:33

בַּדֶּרֶךְ אֲשֶׁר־יָבֹא בָּהּ יָשׁוּב וְאֶל־הָעִיר הַזֹּאת לֹא יָבֹא נְאֻם־יְהוָה׃

19:33   בַּדֶּרֶךְ אֲשֶׁר־יָבֹא

Mp   ל   *Unique*

Com.: The Masorah notes the *sole* occurrence of בַּדֶּרֶךְ אֲשֶׁר with יָבֹא, to distinguish it from its *two* occurrences with בָּא (בַּדֶּרֶךְ אֲשֶׁר בָּא) at 1 Kgs 13:10 and Isa 37:34.

This lemma is featured in the Mm at Isa 37:34 where these *two* parallel phrases are listed.

2 KINGS 19:34

וְגַנּוֹתִי אֶל־הָעִיר הַזֹּאת לְהוֹשִׁיעָהּ לְמַעֲנִי וּלְמַעַן דָּוִד עַבְדִּי׃

19:34   וְגַנּוֹתִי אֶל־הָעִיר

Mp   ל   *Unique*

Com.: The Masorah notes the *sole* occurrence of this lemma with אֶל, to distinguish it from its *three* occurrences with עַל (וְגַנּוֹתִי עַל־הָעִיר), one of which occurs in the parallel passage Isa 37:35.

This lemma is featured in various Mm notes *sub* עַל־הָעִיר; see **Judg 9:33** and **2 Sam 12:28**.

2 KINGS 19:35

וַיְהִי֮ בַּלַּ֣יְלָה הַהוּא֒ וַיֵּצֵ֣א ׀ מַלְאַ֣ךְ יְהוָ֗ה וַיַּךְ֙ בְּמַחֲנֵ֣ה אַשּׁ֔וּר מֵאָ֛ה שְׁמוֹנִ֥ים וַחֲמִשָּׁ֖ה אָ֑לֶף וַיַּשְׁכִּ֣ימוּ בַבֹּ֔קֶר וְהִנֵּ֥ה כֻלָּ֖ם פְּגָרִ֥ים מֵתִֽים׃

19:35   שְׁמוֹנִ֥ים

Mp   ו֗ מל וכל דבר ימי דכות ב֗ מ֗ א֗   *Six times* plene and similarly *all* Chronicles except *one*

Com.: See **Judg 3:30**.

2 KINGS 19:37

וַיְהִ֣י ה֗וּא מִֽשְׁתַּחֲוֶ֜ה בֵּ֣ית ׀ נִסְרֹ֣ךְ אֱלֹהָ֗יו וְֽאַדְרַמֶּ֨לֶךְ וְשַׂרְאֶ֤צֶר הִכֻּ֣הוּ בַחֶ֔רֶב וְהֵ֥מָּה נִמְלְט֖וּ אֶ֣רֶץ אֲרָרָ֑ט וַיִּמְלֹ֛ךְ אֵֽסַר־חַדֹּ֥ן בְּנ֖וֹ תַּחְתָּֽיו׃ פ

19:37   נִסְרֹ֣ךְ

Mp   ב֗   *Twice*

2 Kgs 19:36; Isa 37:38

Com.: The Masorah notes the *two* occurrences of this lemma, *one* here and *one* in the parallel passage at Isa 37:38.

19:37   ֖וֹ

Mp   בניו קרי ולא כת   בָּנָ֖יו is read but not written

Com.: The form בָּנָ֖יו is read, although only the vowels are written.

This is one of *ten* cases where words are read though not written; see the Mm to <u>Jer 50:29</u> *sub* לָהּ and <u>Ruth 3:5</u> *sub* אֵלַי, Frensdorff, *Ochlah*, §97, and Díaz-Esteban, *Sefer Oklah we-Oklah*, §80.

There is also another tradition that knows of *eleven* cases of this phenomenon; see Martín-Contreras, "The Phenomenon," 77–87.

19:37   אֲרָרָט

Four times   ד̇   Mp

Gen 8:4; 2 Kgs 19:37; Isa 37:38; Jer 51:27 (אֲרָרַט)

Com.: The Masorah notes the *four* occurrences of this lemma, *three times* written with a *qameṣ* under the second ר, and *once* with *a pataḥ* (אֲרָרַט).

---

2 KINGS 20:2
וַיַּסֵּב אֶת־פָּנָיו אֶל־הַקִּיר וַיִּתְפַּלֵּל אֶל־יְהוָה לֵאמֹר:

20:2   וַיִּתְפַּלֵּל אֶל־יְהוָה לֵאמֹר

Unique   ל̇   Mp

Com.: The Masorah notes the *sole* occurrence of וַיִּתְפַּלֵּל אֶל־יְהוָה with לֵאמֹר, to distinguish it from its *three* occurrences of this phrase with וַיֹּאמַר/וַיֹּאמֶר (וַיִּתְפַּלֵּל אֶל־יְהוָה וַיֹּאמַר), *one* of which occurs in the parallel passage Isa 38:2–3.

In M^L there are only *two* circelli on this *four-word* phrase: *one* on וַיִּתְפַּלֵּל אֶל and *one* on יְהוָה לֵאמֹר. With *four-* or *five-word* phrases it is not unusual for only *two* circelli to be given; see **Josh 1:6** and *passim*.

---

2 KINGS 20:3
אָנָּה יְהוָה זְכָר־נָא אֵת אֲשֶׁר הִתְהַלַּכְתִּי לְפָנֶיךָ בֶּאֱמֶת וּבְלֵבָב שָׁלֵם וְהַטּוֹב בְּעֵינֶיךָ עָשִׂיתִי וַיֵּבְךְּ חִזְקִיָּהוּ בְּכִי גָדוֹל: ס

20:3   אָנָּה

Six times written with ה   ו̇ כת̇ ה   Mp

1–5   **2 Kgs 20:3**; Isa 38:3; Jon 1:14; 4:2; Ps 116:4
6   **Ps 116:16**

| אָנָה *six times* written with ה | אנה ו כת ה | Mm |

1–5   2 Kgs 20:3   את אשר התהלכתי
      Jonah 1:14   אל נא נאבדה בנפש
      Jonah 4:2   על כן קדמתי
      Isa 38:3   את אשר התהלכתי
      Ps 116:4   (מלמטה) [מלטה] נפשי
6   And the *one* after it (Ps 116:16)   ושל אחריו

And similarly all forms of אָנָה that are   וכל אנה רפ׳ דכותהון
rapê (are written with ה)

And similarly all forms of אָנָה in   וכל אנה בלש ארמית דכות
Aramaic (are written with ה)

Com.: The Masorah notes the *six* occurrences of this lemma written with a ה, to distinguish them from its *seven* occurrences written with an א (אָנָּא).

The Masorah also notes that all forms of אָנָה that are *rapê*, that is, without a *dāḡēš* in the נ, and all forms of אָנָה (1st pers. pron.) in Aramaic are written with ה.

20:3   וְהַטּוֹב

| *Four times* | ד׳ | Mp |

Deut 6:18; 2 Kgs 20:3; Isa 38:3; Lam 3:38

| וְהַטּוֹב *four times* | והטוב ד׳ | Mm |

Deut 6:18   ועשית הישר והטוב
2 Kgs 20:3   זכר נא
And its companion (Isa 38:3)   וחבירו
Lam 3:38   מפי עליון לא תצא

Com.: The Masorah notes the *four* occurrences of this lemma with a ו cj., to distinguish them from its more numerous occurrences (46x) without a cj.

The heading of the Mm at Isa 38:3 reads *four times and plene* (ו), thus also implying (correctly) that this lemma does not occur elsewhere written defective ו.

2 KINGS 20:4

וַיְהִ֣י יְשַׁעְיָ֔הוּ לֹ֣א יָצָ֔א הָעִ֖יר הַתִּֽיכֹנָ֑ה וּדְבַר־יְהוָ֔ה הָיָ֥ה אֵלָ֖יו לֵאמֹֽר׃

20:4	וַיְהִ֣י יְשַׁעְיָ֔הוּ
Unique	ל	Mp

20:4	הָעִ֖יר
Read חָצֵר ק	חצר ק	Mp

Com.: The *kətîb* (הָעִיר, *the city*), and the *qərê* (חָצֵר, [*the middle*] *court*) represent variants of equal value; see Gordis, *The Biblical Text*, 151.

20:4	וּדְבַר־יְהוָה
Seven times	ז	Mp

Com.: See **1 Sam 3:1**.

2 KINGS 20:5

שׁ֣וּב וְאָמַרְתָּ֞ אֶל־חִזְקִיָּ֣הוּ נְגִיד־עַמִּ֗י כֹּֽה־אָמַ֞ר יְהוָ֗ה אֱלֹהֵי֙ דָּוִ֣ד אָבִ֔יךָ שָׁמַ֙עְתִּי֙ אֶת־תְּפִלָּתֶ֔ךָ רָאִ֖יתִי אֶת־דִּמְעָתֶ֑ךָ הִנְנִי֙ רֹ֣פֵא לָ֔ךְ בַּיּוֹם֙ הַשְּׁלִישִׁ֔י תַּעֲלֶ֖ה בֵּ֥ית יְהוָֽה׃

20:5	רֹ֣פֵא לָ֔ךְ
Unique	ל	Mp

2 KINGS 20:6

וְהֹסַפְתִּ֣י עַל־יָמֶ֗יךָ חֲמֵ֤שׁ עֶשְׂרֵה֙ שָׁנָ֔ה וּמִכַּ֤ף מֶֽלֶךְ־אַשּׁוּר֙ אַצִּ֣ילְךָ֔ וְאֵ֖ת הָעִ֣יר הַזֹּ֑את וְגַנּוֹתִי֙ עַל־הָעִ֣יר הַזֹּ֔את לְמַעֲנִ֖י וּלְמַ֥עַן דָּוִ֖ד עַבְדִּֽי׃

20:6	וְהֹסַפְתִּ֣י
Four times	ד	Mp

2 Kgs 20:6; **Ps 71:14** (וְהוֹסַפְתִּי); **2:9** (וְהוֹסַפְתִּי); **Qoh 1:16** (וְהוֹסַפְתִּי)

Com.: The Masorah notes the *four* occurrences of this lemma, *three* times written plene וֹ and *once* (here) written defective וּ.

This lemma is featured in a Masoretic list of doublets commencing with וה; see Frensdorff, *Ochlah*, §63, and Díaz-Esteban, *Sefer Oklah we-Oklah*, §64.

20:6 וְאֶת־הָעִיר

Eight times   ח֗   Mp

1–5   **Judg 1:8**; 18:27; <u>2 Kgs 20:6</u>; Isa 38:6; **Jer 19:11**
6–8   **Jer 23:39**; 26:6; 38:23

וְאֶת־הָעִיר   *eight times*   ואת העיר ח֗   Mm

1–5	Judg 1:8 — וילחמו בני יהודה
	Judg 18:27 — והמה לקחו את אשר
	וְהֹסַפְתִּי עַל־יָמֶיךָ *of Kings* (2 Kgs 20:6) — והספתי על ימיך דמלכים
	וּמִכַּף מֶלֶךְ־אַשּׁוּר *of Isaiah* (Isa 38:6) — ומכף מלך אשור דישעיה
	Jer 26:6 — ונתתי את הבית
6–8	Jer 19:11 — ככה אשבר
	Jer 23:39 — ונטשתי אתכם
	Jer 38:23 — ואת כל נשיך ואת בניך

Com.: The Masorah notes the *eight* occurrences of this lemma with a ו cj., to distinguish them from its more numerous occurrences (46x) without a cj.

The additional notation *of Kings* in the Mm to the catchwords of the 2 Kgs 20:6 reference is simply to distinguish that verse from its parallel in Isa 38:6. Similarly the additonal notation *of Isaiah* to the catchwords of the Isa 38:6 reference is simply to distinguish that verse from its parallel here.

2 KINGS 20:8

וַיֹּאמֶר חִזְקִיָּהוּ אֶל־יְשַׁעְיָהוּ מָה אוֹת כִּי־יִרְפָּא יְהוָה לִי וְעָלִיתִי בַּיּוֹם הַשְּׁלִישִׁי בֵּית יְהוָה׃

20:8   יִרְפָּא

Three times   ג֗   Mp

<u>2 Kgs 20:8</u>; **Isa 30:26**; Lam 2:13

Mm	יֹרפּא ג̇	יְרְפָּא *three times*

2 Kgs 20:8   מה אות
Isa 30:26   ומחץ מכתו
Lam 2:13   כי גדול

Com.: The Masorah notes the *three* occurrences of this lemma in the *qal*, to distinguish them from its *two* occurrences in the *piel* (יְרְפָּא) at Exod 21:19 and Zech 11:16.

2 KINGS 20:9

וַיֹּאמֶר יְשַׁעְיָהוּ זֶה־לְּךָ הָאוֹת מֵאֵת יְהוָה כִּי יַעֲשֶׂה יְהוָה אֶת־הַדָּבָר אֲשֶׁר דִּבֵּר הָלַךְ הַצֵּל עֶשֶׂר מַעֲלוֹת אִם־יָשׁוּב עֶשֶׂר מַעֲלוֹת:

20:9   אִם־יָשׁוּב

Mp	ב̇	*Twice*

2 Kgs 20:9; **Jer 8:4**

Mm	אם ישוב ב̇	אִם־יָשׁוּב *twice*

2 Kgs 20:9   אם ישוב עשר מעלות
Jer 8:4   ואמרת (אלהם) [אליהם] כה אמר יהוה

And *once* (וְאִם־יָשׁוּב): Lev 14:43   וחד ואם ישוב הנגע

Com.: The Masorah notes the *two* occurrences of this lemma in the sg. to prevent it being read as אִם־יָשׁוּבוּ at Jer 8:4, as is attested in the *qərê* of eastern mss. (see *BHS ad loc*, and Ginsburg, 4, א, §753).

The Mm also notes that this lemma occurs with a ו cj. at Lev 14:43.

2 KINGS 20:10

וַיֹּאמֶר יְחִזְקִיָּהוּ נָקֵל לַצֵּל לִנְטוֹת עֶשֶׂר מַעֲלוֹת לֹא כִי יָשׁוּב הַצֵּל אֲחֹרַנִּית עֶשֶׂר מַעֲלוֹת:

20:10   יְחִזְקִיָּהוּ

Mp	ג בנב̇	*Three times* in the Prophets

2 Kgs 20:10; **Isa 1:1**; **Jer 15:4**

Com.: The Masorah notes the *three* occurrences of this lemma in the Prophets with an initial יְ, to distinguish them from its more numerous occurrences (68x) in the Prophets without this initial יְ (חִזְקִיָּהוּ); see Ginsburg, 4, ח, §122, and Ognibeni, *'Oklah*, §41B.

This distinction is implied in the Mp at Isa 1:1, which read*s three times in the Prophets and similarly all Chronicles apart from five* (which have חִזְקִיָּהוּ). The Mm at Isa 1:1 reads the same, but with the additional information about Chronicles coming at the end of its note.

20:10   אֲחֹרַנִּית

Seven times   ז̇   Mp

Com.: See **1 Sam 4:18.**

---

2 KINGS 20:11

וַיִּקְרָא יְשַׁעְיָהוּ הַנָּבִיא אֶל־יְהוָה וַיָּשֶׁב אֶת־הַצֵּל בַּמַּעֲלוֹת אֲשֶׁר יָרְדָה בְּמַעֲלוֹת אָחָז אֲחֹרַנִּית עֶשֶׂר מַעֲלוֹת׃
פ

20:11   וַיָּשֶׁב

Twenty-five times   כה̇   Mp

Com.: See **Judg 17:3.**

20:11   בַּמַּעֲלוֹת

Unique   ל̇   Mp

1–2   **2 Kgs 20:11; Isa 38:8**

Com.: The Mp heading of *unique* is inexact since there are *two* occurrences of this lemma in these parallel passages. The note more precisely should have read *unique in the book.*

The Mp heading at Isa 38:8 correctly reads *twice.*

The Masorah notes the *two* occurrences of this lemma in the absol., to distinguish them from its *two* occurrences in the cstr. (בְּמַעֲלוֹת) in the same verses.

This lemma is featured in a Masoretic list of words occurring *three times, twice* without the ו cj., and *once* with it (Ezek 40:49); see Frensdorff, *Ochlah*, §13, and Díaz-Esteban, *Sefer Oklah we-Oklah*, §14.

M^A correctly reads *twice,* whereas M^C has no note here.

20:11   בְּמַעֲלוֹת

Twice   בֿ   Mp

2 Kgs 20:11; Isa 38:8

Com.: The Masorah notes the *two* occurrences of this lemma in these parallel passages in the cstr., to distinguish them from its *two* occurrences in the absol. (בַּמַּעֲלוֹת) in the same verses (2 Kgs 20:11 and Isa 38:8).

20:11   אֲחֹרַנִּית

Seven times   ז̇   Mp

Com.: See **1 Sam 4:18**.

---

2 KINGS 20:12

בָּעֵת הַהִיא שָׁלַח בְּרֹאדַךְ בַּלְאֲדָן בֶּן־בַּלְאֲדָן מֶלֶךְ־בָּבֶל סְפָרִים וּמִנְחָה אֶל־חִזְקִיָּהוּ כִּי שָׁמַע כִּי חָלָה חִזְקִיָּהוּ׃

20:12   בְּרֹאדַךְ

Superfluous א   יתיר א̇   Mp

Com.: This lemma is featured in a Masoretic list of words in which an א is written but not read; see the Mm to <u>Num 11:4</u> *sub* וְהָאסַפְסֻף; Frensdorff, *Ochlah*, §103, and Díaz-Esteban, *Sefer Oklah we-Oklah*, §86.

In M^L this lemma has no circellus.

---

2 KINGS 20:13

וַיִּשְׁמַע עֲלֵיהֶם חִזְקִיָּהוּ וַיַּרְאֵם אֶת־כָּל־בֵּית נְכֹתֹה אֶת־הַכֶּסֶף וְאֶת־הַזָּהָב וְאֶת־הַבְּשָׂמִים וְאֵת ׀ שֶׁמֶן הַטּוֹב וְאֵת בֵּית כֵּלָיו וְאֵת כָּל־אֲשֶׁר נִמְצָא בְּאוֹצְרֹתָיו לֹא־הָיָה דָבָר אֲשֶׁר לֹא־הֶרְאָם חִזְקִיָּהוּ בְּבֵיתוֹ וּבְכָל־מֶמְשַׁלְתּוֹ׃

20:13   נְכֹתֹה

Twice written like this   בֿ כת כן   Mp

2 Kgs 20:13; Isa 39:2 (*kǝtîb*)

Com.: The Masorah notes the *two* occurrences of this lemma in the parallel passages of 2 Kings and Isaiah.

M^C and M^A have a *kǝtîb* (נכתה) and *qǝrê* (נכֹתו) here, as does M^L in the Isa 39:2 reference.

20:13   וְאֶת ׀ שֶׁמֶן

Seven times   ז̇   Mp

1–5   **Exod 31:11; 35:14**; 35:15; **39:37; 39:38**
6–7   **Lev 8:2; 2 Kgs 20:13**

Com.: The Masorah notes the *seven* occurrences of this lemma without a def. article on שֶׁמֶן, to distinguish them from its *three* occurrences with a def. article (וְאֶת הַשֶּׁמֶן).

20:13   בְּאוֹצְרֹתָיו

Unique written like this   ל כת̇ כן   Mp

Com.: The Masorah notes the *sole* occurrence of this lemma written plene first ו, to distinguish it from its occurrence written defective first ו (בְּאֹצְרֹתָיו) in the parallel text in Isa 39:2.

---

2 KINGS 20:14

וַיָּבֹא יְשַׁעְיָהוּ הַנָּבִיא אֶל־הַמֶּלֶךְ חִזְקִיָּהוּ וַיֹּאמֶר אֵלָיו מָה אָמְרוּ ׀ הָאֲנָשִׁים הָאֵלֶּה וּמֵאַיִן יָבֹאוּ אֵלֶיךָ וַיֹּאמֶר חִזְקִיָּהוּ מֵאֶרֶץ רְחוֹקָה בָּאוּ מִבָּבֶל׃

20:14   וּמֵאַיִן

Five times   ה̇   Mp

1–5   **Josh 9:8; Judg 19:17; 2 Kgs 20:14; Isa 39:3**; Jonah 1:8

וּמֵאַיִן *five times*, and their references   ומאין ה̇ וסימנהון   Mm

1–5   Josh 9:8   יהושע
      Judg 19:17   האיש הזקן
      2 Kgs 20:14   (ישע̇) [ישעיהו]
      And its companion (Isa 39:3)   וחבירו
      Jonah 1:8   מה מלאכתך ומאין תבוא

Com.: The Masorah notes the *five* occurrences of this lemma with a ו cj., to distinguish them from its more numerous occurrences (14x) without a cj.

2 KINGS 20:15

וַיֹּ֕אמֶר מָ֥ה רָא֖וּ בְּבֵיתֶ֑ךָ וַיֹּ֣אמֶר חִזְקִיָּ֗הוּ אֵ֣ת כָּל־אֲשֶׁ֤ר בְּבֵיתִי֙ רָא֔וּ לֹֽא־הָיָ֣ה דָבָ֗ר אֲשֶׁ֧ר לֹֽא־הִרְאִיתִ֛ם בְּאוֹצְרֹתָֽי׃

20:15   הִרְאִיתִם

Twice   בֿ   Mp

2 Kgs 20:15; Isa 39:4 (הִרְאִיתִים)

Com.: The Masorah notes the *two* occurrences of this lemma, *one* written plene second י in the parallel text (Isa 39:4), and *one* written defective second י (here).

20:15   בְּאוֹצְרֹתָי

Three times   גֿ   Mp

Deut 32:34 (בְּאוֹצְרֹתָי); **2 Kgs 20:15**; Isa 39:4 (בְּאוֹצְרוֹתָי)

Com.: The Masorah notes the *three* occurrences of this lemma, *twice* written plene first ו (Deut 32:34 and Isa 39:4) and *once* written defective first ו (here).

2 KINGS 20:17

הִנֵּה֙ יָמִ֣ים בָּאִ֔ים וְנִשָּׂ֣א ׀ כָּל־אֲשֶׁ֣ר בְּבֵיתֶ֗ךָ וַאֲשֶׁ֨ר אָצְר֧וּ אֲבֹתֶ֛יךָ עַד־הַיּ֥וֹם הַזֶּ֖ה בָּבֶ֑לָה לֹֽא־יִוָּתֵ֥ר דָּבָ֖ר אָמַ֥ר יְהוָֽה׃

20:17   וְנִשָּׂא

Twelve times   יֿב   Mp

1–5   **Exod 25:28; 2 Kgs 20:17**; Isa 2:2; Isa 6:1; <u>Isa 39:6</u>
6–10   Isa 52:13; 57:7; 57:15; Jer 51:9; Amos 4:2
11–12   Mic 4:1; Dan 11:12

| | | וְנִשָּׂא *twelve times*, and their references | ונשא יֹבֿ וסימנהון | Mm |

1–5	Exod 25:28 הבדים
	2 Kgs 20:17 בביתך
	Jer 51:9 משפטה
	Isa 2:2 מגבעות
	Amos 4:2 בצנות
6–10	Mic 4:1 מגבעות
	Isa 6:1 על כסא רם
	Isa 52:13 הנה ישכיל עבדי ירום
	Isa 39:6 (ימין) [ימים]
	Isa 57:7 (גבוה) [גבה]
11–12	Isa 57:15 כי כה אמר
	Dan 11:12 ההמון

Com.: The Masorah notes the *twelve* occurrences of this lemma with a ו cj., to distinguish it from its *four* occurrences without a cj.; see **2 Sam 19:43**.

20:17   בָּבֶ֑לָה

Twenty-nine times   כֹּטֿ   Mp

1–5	**2 Kgs 20:17; 24:15**ᵃ; 24:15ᵇ; 24:16; **25:13**
6–9	**Isa 43:14;** Jer 20:4; **20:5**; 27:16 (מִבָּבֶ֑לָה); **27:18**
10–15	**Jer 27:20**; 27:22; **28:4; 29:1; 29:3**
16–20	Jer 29:4; **29:15; 29:20**; 39:7; 40:1
21–25	**Jer 40:7**; 52:11; **52:17**; Ezek 12:13; 17:12
26–29	Ezek 17:20; 2 Chr 33:11; 36:6; 36:10

Com.: The Masorah notes the *twenty-nine* occurrences of this lemma with the locative ה, to distinguish them from its more numerous occurrences (200+) without this adverbial ending.

---

2 KINGS 20:18

וּמִבָּנֶ֜יךָ אֲשֶׁ֧ר יֵצְא֣וּ מִמְּךָ֗ אֲשֶׁ֤ר תּוֹלִיד֙ יִקָּ֔חוּ וְהָיוּ֙ סָרִיסִ֔ים בְּהֵיכַ֖ל מֶ֥לֶךְ בָּבֶֽל׃

20:18   וּמִבָּנֶ֜יךָ

Twice   בֿ   Mp

2 Kgs 20:18; Isa 39:7

Com.: The Masorah notes the *two* occurrences of this lemma in these parallel passages with a ו cj., to distinguish it from its *sole* occurrence without a cj. at 1 Chr 17:11.

20:18 יָצְאוּ

Fourteen times   יד̇   Mp

Com.: See **Josh 8:5**.

20:18 יִקָּח

Read יִקָּחוּ   יקחו ק̇   Mp

Com.: The *kəṯîḇ* (יקח), and *qərê* (יִקָּחוּ) represent examples where the text, in accordance with older orthography, writes only one of two adjoining and identical vowel-letters; see Gordis, *The Biblical Text*, 96.

This lemma is featured in two Masoretic lists. One is in a list of words where a ו which is not written is read; see Frensdorff, *Ochlah*, §119, and Díaz-Esteban, *Sefer Oklah we-Oklah*, §105.

The other is in a list of occurrences of יִקָּחוּ; see the Mm at 2 Sam 23:6.

2 KINGS 20:19

וַיֹּאמֶר חִזְקִיָּ֙הוּ֙ אֶֽל־יְשַֽׁעְיָ֔הוּ ט֖וֹב דְּבַר־יְהוָ֣ה אֲשֶׁ֣ר דִּבַּ֑רְתָּ וַיֹּ֕אמֶר הֲל֛וֹא אִם־שָׁל֥וֹם וֶאֱמֶ֖ת יִהְיֶ֥ה בְיָמָֽי׃

20:19 הֲלוֹא

Seventeen times plene in the book   יז̇ מל בסיפ̇   Mp

Com.: See **1 Kgs 2:42**.

2 KINGS 20:20

וְיֶ֩תֶר דִּבְרֵ֙י חִזְקִיָּ֜הוּ וְכָל־גְּבוּרָת֗וֹ וַאֲשֶׁ֤ר עָשָׂה֙ אֶת־הַבְּרֵכָ֣ה וְאֶת־הַתְּעָלָ֔ה וַיָּבֵ֥א אֶת־הַמַּ֖יִם הָעִ֑ירָה הֲלֹא־הֵ֣ם כְּתוּבִ֗ים עַל־סֵ֛פֶר דִּבְרֵ֥י הַיָּמִ֖ים לְמַלְכֵ֥י יְהוּדָֽה׃

20:20 וַאֲשֶׁר עָשָׂה

Seven times   ז̇   Mp

Com.: See **Josh 24:17**.

20:20	וְאֶת־הַתְּעָלָה		
Unique		ל	Mp

Com.: The Masorah notes the *sole* occurrence of this lemma with a ו cj., to distinguish it from its *sole* occurrence without a cj. at 1 Kgs 18:35.

20:20	הָעִירָה		
Nine times		ט׳	Mp

1–5	Gen 44:13; Josh 6:20; 20:4; 2 Sam 17:17; **1 Kgs 14:12**
6–9	1 Kgs 20:2; **2 Kgs 20:20**; Ps 35:23; 1 Chr 19:15

הָעִירָה *nine times*	העירה ט׳	Mm

Gen 44:13	ויקרעו שמלתם
Josh 6:20	וירע העם
Josh 20:4	ונס אל אחת
2 Sam 17:17	להראות
1 Kgs 20:2	אחאב
2 Kgs 20:20	ויבא את המים
1 Kgs 14:12	ואת קומי
וּבְנֵי עַמּוֹן *of Chronicles* (1 Chr 19:15)	ובני עמון דדברי ימים
Ps 35:23	למשפטי

One (the last one) has the meaning of *wake up*	חד לשון עוררו

Com.: The Masorah notes the *nine* occurrences of the form הָעִירָה, *eight* of which refer have the locative ה, to distinguish them from its more numerous occurrences (300+) without this adverbial ה.

This distinction is implied in the Mm in the additional notation *of Chronicles* to the catch-words of the 1 Chr 19:15 reference, which distinguishes it from its parallel passage in 2 Sam 10:14 where the lemma occurs as הָעִיר.

The Masorah also notes that the occurrence in Ps 35:23 is a 2 sg. masc. emphatic impf. *hiphil* of the verbal root עוּר *to wake up*.

2 KINGS 21:1

בֶּן־שְׁתֵּ֨ים עֶשְׂרֵ֤ה שָׁנָה֙ מְנַשֶּׁ֣ה בְמׇלְכ֔וֹ וַחֲמִשִּׁ֤ים וְחָמֵשׁ֙ שָׁנָ֔ה מָלַ֖ךְ בִּירוּשָׁלָ֑͏ִם וְשֵׁ֣ם אִמּ֔וֹ חֶפְצִי־בָֽהּ׃

21:1   חֶפְצִי־בָֽהּ

Mp   ב֡   *Twice*

2 Kgs 21:1; Isa 62:4

Mm   חפצי בה ב֡ וסימנהון   חֶפְצִי־בָֽהּ *twice*, and their references

2 Kgs 21:1   ושם אמו חפצי בה
Isa 62:4   כי לך יקרא

Com.: The Masorah notes the *two* occurrences of this lemma, possibly to distinguish them from the occurrence of a similar form חֶפְצִי־בָ֫ם in Ps 16:3.

2 KINGS 21:3

וַיָּ֗שׇׁב וַיִּ֙בֶן֙ אֶת־הַבָּמ֔וֹת אֲשֶׁ֥ר אִבַּ֖ד חִזְקִיָּ֣הוּ אָבִ֑יו וַיָּ֨קֶם מִזְבְּחֹ֜ת לַבַּ֗עַל וַיַּ֤עַשׂ אֲשֵׁרָה֙ כַּאֲשֶׁ֤ר עָשָׂה֙ אַחְאָ֣ב מֶ֣לֶךְ יִשְׂרָאֵ֔ל וַיִּשְׁתַּ֙חוּ֙ לְכׇל־צְבָ֣א הַשָּׁמַ֔יִם וַיַּעֲבֹ֖ד אֹתָֽם׃

21:3   אִבַּ֖ד

Mp   ב֡   *Twice*

2 Kgs 21:3; Lam 2:9

Mm   אבד ב֡ וסימנהון   אִבַּ֖ד *twice*, and their references

2 Kgs 21:3   ויעש אשרה כאשר עשה
Lam 2:9   אבד ושבר

וֹ֤ ואבד ממנה   And *once* (וַאִבַּ֖ד): Jer 51:55

Com.: The Masorah notes the *two* occurrences of this lemma in the *piel*, to distinguish them from its more numerous occurrences (10x) in the *qal* (אָבַד), and from other forms pointed as אֹבֵד, אָבֵד, etc.; see Ginsburg, 4, א, §56.

The Mm additionally notes that this lemma occurs with a ו cj. at Jer 51:55.

21:3   מִזְבְּחֹת

Twice defective   ב̇ חס̇   Mp

2 Kgs 21:3; 21:4

Com.: The Mp heading of *twice defective* is inexact since there are *three* more occurrences of this lemma in the Torah. The note more precisely should have read *twice defective in the book*.

The Masorah notes the *two* occurrences of this lemma in the book written defective ו, to distinguish them from its *sole* occurrence in the book written plene ו (מִזְבְּחוֹת), which occurs in v. 5.

The Mp note in the next verse reads *twice defective, and similarly all the Torah* (Num 23:1, 23:14, and 23:29).

M^A reads *three times defective* (for the above *two* references and the *third* being the *three* Torah references taken as *one* reference; see Breuer, *The Biblical Text*, 134, n. 66). M^C has no note here.

---

2 KINGS 21:4
וּבָנָה מִזְבְּחֹת בְּבֵית יְהוָה אֲשֶׁר אָמַר יְהוָה בִּירוּשָׁלַםִ אָשִׂים אֶת־שְׁמִי׃

21:4   מִזְבְּחֹת

Twice defective, and similarly *all* the Torah   ב̇ חס̇ וכל אור כות   Mp

Com.: See directly above in v. 3.

21:4   בְּבֵית יְהוָה

Thirty-nine times   לט̇   Mp

Com.: See **1 Sam 1:7**.

2 KINGS 21:7

וַיָּ֕שֶׂם אֶת־פֶּ֥סֶל הָאֲשֵׁרָ֖ה אֲשֶׁ֣ר עָשָׂ֑ה בַּבַּ֗יִת אֲשֶׁ֨ר אָמַ֤ר יְהוָה֙ אֶל־דָּוִד֙ וְאֶל־שְׁלֹמֹ֣ה בְנ֔וֹ בַּבַּ֧יִת הַזֶּ֛ה וּבִירוּשָׁלִַ֗ם אֲשֶׁ֤ר בָּחַ֙רְתִּי֙ מִכֹּל֙ שִׁבְטֵ֣י יִשְׂרָאֵ֔ל אָשִׂ֥ים אֶת־שְׁמִ֖י לְעוֹלָֽם׃

21:7 וּבִירוּשָׁלִַם

Twenty-one times   כֹּא   Mp

Com.: See **2 Sam 5:5**.

2 KINGS 21:8

וְלֹ֣א אֹסִ֗יף לְהָנִיד֙ רֶ֣גֶל יִשְׂרָאֵ֔ל מִן־הָ֣אֲדָמָ֔ה אֲשֶׁ֥ר נָתַ֖תִּי לַאֲבוֹתָ֑ם רַ֣ק ׀ אִם־יִשְׁמְר֣וּ לַעֲשׂ֗וֹת כְּכֹל֙ אֲשֶׁ֣ר צִוִּיתִ֔ים וּלְכָל־הַתּוֹרָ֕ה אֲשֶׁר־צִוָּ֥ה אֹתָ֖ם עַבְדִּ֥י מֹשֶֽׁה׃

21:8 וְלֹא אֹסִיף

וְלֹא אֹסִיף *four times*, and their references   ולא אסיף ד וסימנהון   Mm

Gen 8:21, the *second* form in the verse   (וידח) [וירח] יהוה תיניני דפסוק
2 Kgs 21:8   להניד
2 Chr 33:8   להסיר
Job 40:5   אחת דברתי

Com.: The Masorah notes the *four* occurrences of this lemma with a ו cj., to distinguish them from its more numerous occurrences (9x) without a cj.

This distinction is implied in the additional notation of *the second form in the verse* to the Gen 8:21 reference, which distinguishes it from the first form of the phrase in the verse that does not have the ו cj.

21:8 אֹסִיף

Six times written like this   ו כת כן   Mp

1–5   **1 Kgs 12:14; 2 Kgs 21:8; Job 34:32; 2 Chr 10:11; 10:14**
6   2 Chr 33:8*

Com.: The Masorah notes the *six* occurrences of this lemma written defective ו, to distinguish them from its more numerous occurrences (10x) written plene ו as אוֹסִיף.

*M^L, contrary to M, reads 2 Chr 33:8 plene ו (אוֹסִיף); see Breuer, *The Biblical Text,* 338, 393. and thus has only *five* occurrences.

However, the enumeration inherent in the text of M is supported by the Mp heading here and at 2 Chr 10:11, which both read *six*, and by the Mp heading at 2 Chr 10:14, which reads *three times in the book* (thus assuming that 2 Chr 33:8 is written defective, and not plene as in M^L).

The Mp heading at 1 Kgs 12:14 correctly reads *twice written like this in the book* (there and here), and the Mp heading at Job 34:32 correctly reads *unique written like this in the book* (of Job).

21:8   עַבְדֵי מֹשֶׁה

Twice   בֿ   Mp

Num 12:7; **2 Kgs 21:8**

Com.: The Masorah notes the *two* occurrences of this lemma in this order, to distinguish them from its *three* occurrences in the reverse order (מֹשֶׁה עַבְדִּי).

---

2 KINGS 21:9

וְלֹא שָׁמֵעוּ וַיַּתְעֵם מְנַשֶּׁה לַעֲשׂוֹת אֶת־הָרָע מִן־הַגּוֹיִם אֲשֶׁר הִשְׁמִיד יְהוָה מִפְּנֵי בְּנֵי יִשְׂרָאֵל׃

21:9   לַעֲשׂוֹת אֶת־הָרָע

Three times   גֿ   Mp

2 Kgs 21:9; 2 Chr 33:9 (לַעֲשׂוֹת הָרָע)

Com.: The Mp notes *three* occurrences of this phrase with a *qameṣ* under the ר instead of an expected *pataḥ*. The problem is that there only *two* such occurrences (here and 2 Chr 33:9) where the *qameṣ* is unusual, that is, not lengthened to a *qameṣ* as it is with an *ʾatnaḥ* (Prov 2:14) or a *sop pasûq* (Qoh 4:17; 8:11).

The Mp heading at 2 Chr 33:9 reads רע *with all forms of the verb* עשה *has a pataḥ apart from seven cases when it has a qameṣ*; see also the Mm at Lev 27:10.

The Mp at M^A here reads *three times with qameṣ*. M^C has no note here.

> **2 KINGS 21:11**
> יַ֗עַן אֲשֶׁ֨ר עָשָׂ֜ה מְנַשֶּׁ֤ה מֶֽלֶךְ־יְהוּדָה֙ הַתֹּעֵבֹ֣ות הָאֵ֔לֶּה הֵרַ֕ע מִכֹּ֛ל אֲשֶׁר־עָשׂ֥וּ הָאֱמֹרִ֖י אֲשֶׁ֣ר לְפָנָ֑יו וַיַּחֲטִ֥א גַם־אֶת־יְהוּדָ֖ה בְּגִלּוּלָֽיו׃ פ

21:11 הַתֹּעֵבֹות

Three times written like this   ג֗ כת֗ כן   Mp

2 Kgs 21:1; Ezra 9:14; 2 Chr 34:33*

Com.: The Masorah notes the *three* occurrences of this lemma written defective first ו.

*M^L, contrary to M (הַתֹּעֵבֹות), has only *two* occurrences of this lemma because it writes the form at 2 Chr 34:33 plene first ו (הַתּוֹעֵבֹות); see Breuer, *The Biblical Text,* 387. However, the Mp heading here of *three times* supports the enumeration inherent in the text of M.

The Mp heading at Ezra 9:14 reads *four times defective*, and includes the *three* references listed above plus Jer 44:4 (הַתֹּעֵבָה); see ibid, 191.

At **2 Kgs 16:3** the Masorah notes all *nine* occurrences of this lemma written defective first ו in various forms.

21:11 הֵרַע

Four times   ד֗   Mp

Exod 5:23; **2 Kgs 21:11**; **Ps 74:3**; **Ruth 1:21**

Com.: The Mp heading here notes the *four* occurrences of this lemma

The Mp heading at Ps 74:3 reads *five times*, and includes the form of this lemma with the ו cj. at Josh 24:20. Similarly, the Mp heading at Ruth 1:21 reads *four times and once* והרע ושב (וְשָׁב וְהֵרַע, Josh 24:20).

This lemma is featured in a Masoretic list of words that occur *five times, four times* without a ו cj., and *once* with it (Josh 24:20); see Frensdorff, *Ochlah*, §17, and Díaz-Esteban, *Sefer Oklah we-Oklah*, §18.

21:11 וַיַּחֲטִא

Four times defective   ד֗ חס   Mp

Judg 20:16 (יַחֲטִא); **1 Kgs 16:2** (וַתַּחֲטִא); 21:22 (וַתַּחֲטִא); **2 Kgs 21:11**

Com.: The Masorah notes the *four* occurrences of this lemma in various forms written defective י, to distinguish them from the *sole* occurrence written plene י (תֶּחֱטָ֖יא) at Deut 24:4.

The Mp headings at 1 Kgs 16:2 (וַתַּחֲטִא) and 21:22 (וַתַּחֲטִא) both read *twice defective* referring to their specific forms.

This lemma (וַיַּחֲטִא) is featured in a Masoretic list of words that occur *twice*, *once* with a ו cj. and *once* without; see Frensdorff, *Ochlah*, §1, and Díaz-Esteban, *Sefer Oklah we-Oklah*, §1.

> **2 KINGS 21:12**
> לָכֵ֗ן כֹּֽה־אָמַ֤ר יְהוָה֙ אֱלֹהֵ֣י יִשְׂרָאֵ֔ל הִנְנִ֨י מֵבִ֤יא רָעָה֙ עַל־יְרוּשָׁלַ֣͏ִם וִֽיהוּדָ֔ה אֲשֶׁר֙ כָּל־שֹׁ֣מְעָ֔יו תִּצַּ֖לְנָה שְׁתֵּ֥י אָזְנָֽיו׃

21:12   לָכֵ֗ן כֹּֽה־אָמַ֤ר יְהוָה֙ אֱלֹהֵ֣י יִשְׂרָאֵ֔ל

Three times   ג̇   Mp

2 Kgs 21:12; Jer 23:2; **32:36**

Com.: The Masorah notes the *three* occurrences of this lemma with the initial word לָכֵ֗ן, to distinguish them from its more numerous occurrences (24x) without לָכֵ֗ן; see **1 Sam 10:18**.

21:12   יְרוּשָׁלַ֣͏ִם וִֽיהוּדָ֔ה

Ten times   י̇   Mp

1–3   **2 Kgs 21:12**; Isa 3:8; **Jer 40:1**

Com.: The Mp headings here and at Jer 40:1 of *ten times* are incorrect since there are only *three* occurrences of this lemma.

Dotan/Reich (*Masora Thesaurus, ad loc.*) suggest expanding the note to *ten times in this and similar forms* to include forms with prepositions as well as the ו cj. such as בִּירוּשָׁלַ͏ִם וִֽיהוּדָה, לִירוּשָׁלַ͏ִם וִֽיהוּדָה, etc. but there are only *nine* such forms. To solve this difficulty, they propose that the *two* phrases in Ezra 1:2 and 1:3 (בִּירוּשָׁלַ͏ִם אֲשֶׁר בִּיהוּדָה and לִירוּשָׁלַ͏ִם אֲשֶׁר בִּיהוּדָה) be included as the *tenth* form.

Neither M^C nor M^A has a note on this lemma here.

21:12 שֹׁמְעָיו

Mp   שמעה ק   שֹׁמְעָה Read

Com.: The *kətîb* (שמעיו), and the *qərê* (שֹׁמְעָה) both meaning *who hears it*, represent variants in gender; see Gordis, *The Biblical Text*, 139.

21:12 תִּצַּלְנָה

Mp   ב֗   *Twice*

2 Kgs 21:12; Jer 19:3

Mm   תצלנה ב֗   *twice* תִּצַּלְנָה

2 Kgs 21:12   כל שמעה <תצלנה> שתי (אזני) [אזניו]
Jer 19:3   שמעה תצלנה

Com.: The Masorah notes the *two* occurrences of this lemma, to distinguish it from its parallel form תִּצַּלֶינָה at 1 Sam 3:11.

This lemma occurs in the ms. in folio 217r, but the Mm note appears on the top right of the following folio 217v.

---

2 KINGS 21:13

וְנָטִיתִי עַל־יְרוּשָׁלַ͏ִם אֵת קָו שֹׁמְרוֹן וְאֶת־מִשְׁקֹלֶת בֵּית אַחְאָב וּמָחִיתִי אֶת־יְרוּשָׁלַ͏ִם כַּאֲשֶׁר־יִמְחֶה אֶת־הַצַּלַּחַת מָחָה וְהָפַךְ עַל־פָּנֶיהָ:

21:13 מִשְׁקֹלֶת

Mp   ל֗   *Unique*

Com.: This lemma is featured in a Masoretic list of doublets with different hierarchial vowels, in a list termed *mil'êl* and *milra'*; see Yeivin, *Introduction*, §132, p. 103. In this connection, the higher vowel, the *mil'êl*, is the vowel *ḥolem*, and the lower vowel, the *milra'*, is the vowel *qameṣ*. Thus מִשְׁקֹלֶת with the *ḥolem* is *mil'êl* (here), but לְמִשְׁקָלֶת with the *qameṣ* is *milra'* (Isa 28:17); see Frensdorff, *Ochlah*, §5, and Díaz-Esteban, *Sefer Oklah we-Oklah*, §5.

21:13	וּמָחִיתִי		
Twice	בׄ	Mp	

Gen 7:4; <u>**2 Kgs 21:13**</u>

Mm	וּמָחִיתִי בׄ ומל וסימנהון	וּמָחִיתִי *twice* and plene, and their references
	ומחיתי את כל היקום	Gen 7:4
	ומחיתי את ירושלם כאשר	<u>2 Kgs 21:13</u>

And *once* (מָחִיתִי): ומחד מחיתי כעב   Isa 44:22

Com.: The Masorah notes the *two* occurrences of this lemma with a ו cj., and the Mm additionally notes its *sole* occurrence without a cj. at Isa 44:22.

By noting in the Mm that both occurrences of this lemma are written plene י, the Masorah is thus implying (correctly) that this lemma does not occur elsewhere written defective י.

21:13	יִמְחֶה		
Unique	ל	Mp	

21:13	מָחָה וְהָפַךְ		
Unique	ל	Mp	

2 KINGS 21:15

יַעַן אֲשֶׁר עָשׂוּ אֶת־הָרַע בְּעֵינַי וַיִּהְיוּ מַכְעִסִים אֹתִי מִן־הַיּוֹם אֲשֶׁר יָצְאוּ אֲבוֹתָם מִמִּצְרַיִם וְעַד הַיּוֹם הַזֶּה׃

21:15	עָשׂוּ אֶת־הָרַע		
Seven times	זׄ	Mp	

Com.: See **Judg 3:7**.

In M^L the circellus has been placed only on the first two words but the note refers to the entire phrase עָשׂוּ אֶת־הָרַע.

21:15 וְעַד הַיּוֹם הַזֶּֽה

Three times   גׄ   Mp

Com.: See **2 Sam 7:6**.

---

2 KINGS 21:16

וְגַם֩ דָּ֨ם נָקִ֜י שָׁפַ֤ךְ מְנַשֶּׁה֙ הַרְבֵּ֣ה מְאֹ֔ד עַ֛ד אֲשֶׁר־מִלֵּ֥א אֶת־יְרוּשָׁלַ֖͏ִם פֶּ֣ה לָפֶ֑ה לְבַ֤ד מֵֽחַטָּאתוֹ֙ אֲשֶׁ֣ר הֶחֱטִ֣יא אֶת־יְהוּדָ֔ה לַעֲשׂ֥וֹת הָרַ֖ע בְּעֵינֵ֥י יְהוָֽה׃

21:16 פֶּ֣ה לָפֶ֑ה

Twice   בׄ   Mp

Com.: See **2 Kgs 10:21**.

---

2 KINGS 21:17

וְיֶ֨תֶר דִּבְרֵ֤י מְנַשֶּׁה֙ וְכָל־אֲשֶׁ֣ר עָשָׂ֔ה וְחַטָּאת֖וֹ אֲשֶׁ֣ר חָטָ֑א הֲלֹא־הֵ֣ם כְּתוּבִ֗ים עַל־סֵ֛פֶר דִּבְרֵ֥י הַיָּמִ֖ים לְמַלְכֵ֥י יְהוּדָֽה׃

21:17 וְיֶ֨תֶר דִּבְרֵ֤י

וְיֶ֨תֶר דִּבְרֵ֤י *five times* with the accents (*ʾazlâ* and *mahpak*), and their references   ויתר דברי הׄ בטעׄ וסימנהון   Mm

1–5   1 Kgs 15:7   אבים
     1 Kgs 16:27   עמרי
     2 Kgs 13:12   יואש
     2 Kgs 20:20   חזקיהו
     <u>2 Kgs 21:17</u>   מנשה

Com.: The Masorah notes the *five* occurrences of this phrase with the accents *ʾazlâ* and *mahpak* to distinguish them from occurrences of this phrase written with different accents such as *ʾazlâ* and *mêrəkâ* (**2 Kgs 10:34**), *təlîšâ qəṭannâ* and *ʾazlâ* (**2 Kgs 14:28**), *təbîr* and *mêrəkâ* (2 Kgs 15:36 and 16:19).

2 KINGS 21:18

וַיִּשְׁכַּב מְנַשֶּׁה עִם־אֲבֹתָיו וַיִּקָּבֵר בְּגַן־בֵּיתוֹ בְּגַן־עֻזָּא וַיִּמְלֹךְ אָמוֹן בְּנוֹ תַּחְתָּיו: פ

21:18   בְּגַן־בֵּיתוֹ

Unique   ל   Mp

Com.: The Masorah notes the occurrence of בֵּיתוֹ with בְּגַן, to distinguish it from the parallel text in 2 Chr 33:20 where בֵּיתוֹ occurs by itself.

21:18   עֻזָּא

Three times written with א in the Prophets   ג כת א בנבי   Mp

2 Sam 6:3 (וְעֻזָּא); **2 Kgs 21:18; 21:26**

Com.: The Masorah notes the *three* occurrences of this lemma written in the Prophets with an א, to distinguish them from its *four* occurrences written in the Prophets with a ה (עֻזָּה/בְּעֻזָּה).

M^L, contrary to M (עֻזָּה), has a *fourth* occurrence of this lemma since it writes the form at 2 Sam 6:6 with an א (עֻזָּא); see Breuer, *The Biblical Text*, 87. However, the Mp headings here and at 2 Kgs 21:26 and the Mm at 2 Sam 6:3, which gives catchwords for the above *three* references, support the enumeration inherent in the text of M.

2 KINGS 21:19

בֶּן־עֶשְׂרִים וּשְׁתַּיִם שָׁנָה אָמוֹן בְּמָלְכוֹ וּשְׁתַּיִם שָׁנִים מָלַךְ בִּירוּשָׁלָ͏ִם וְשֵׁם אִמּוֹ מְשֻׁלֶּמֶת בַּת־חָרוּץ מִן־יָטְבָה:

21:19   מְשֻׁלֶּמֶת

Unique   ל   Mp

21:19   מִן־יָטְבָה

Unique   ל   Mp

2 KINGS 21:22
וַיַּעֲזֹב אֶת־יְהוָה אֱלֹהֵי אֲבֹתָיו וְלֹא הָלַךְ בְּדֶרֶךְ יְהוָה׃

21:22   וְלֹא הָלַךְ

Three times   ג̇   Mp

Num 24:1; 1 Kgs 22:49; **2 Kgs 21:22**

Mm   ולא הלך ג̇   וְלֹא הָלַךְ *three times*

Num 24:1   כפעם בפעם לקראת
1 Kgs 22:49   יהושפט עשה אניות
2 Kgs 21:22   ויעזב את (כל) [יהוה]

Com.: The Masorah notes the *three* occurrences of this lemma with a ו cj., to distinguish them from its *three* occurrences without a cj.

2 KINGS 21:23
וַיִּקְשְׁרוּ עַבְדֵי־אָמוֹן עָלָיו וַיָּמִיתוּ אֶת־הַמֶּלֶךְ בְּבֵיתוֹ׃

21:23   וַיָּמִיתוּ

Unique   ל̇   Mp

Com.: The Masorah notes the *sole* occurrence of this lemma without a sfx., to distinguish it from its *two* occurrences with a sfx. (וַיְמִיתֻהוּ) at 2 Chr 25:27 and in the parallel passage of 2 Chr 33:24.

2 KINGS 21:24

וַיַּ֣ךְ עַם־הָאָ֗רֶץ אֵ֤ת כָּל־הַקֹּשְׁרִים֙ עַל־הַמֶּ֣לֶךְ אָמ֔וֹן וַיַּמְלִ֧יכוּ עַם־הָאָ֛רֶץ אֶת־יֹאשִׁיָּ֥הוּ בְנ֖וֹ תַּחְתָּֽיו׃

21:24   הַקֹּשְׁרִים

Twice   ב̇   Mp

2 Kgs 21:24; 2 Chr 33:25

Com.: The Masorah notes the *two* occurrences of this lemma in these parallel passages with the def. article, to distinguish them from its *sole* occurrence with the prep. ב (בְּקֹשְׁרִים) at **2 Sam 15:31**.

21:24   עַל־הַמֶּלֶךְ

עַל־הַמֶּלֶךְ *eight times*   על המלך ח̇   Mm

1–5	2 Kgs 21:24	ויך
	2 Chr 33:25	ויכו
	2 Kgs 11:11	ויעמדו
	2 Chr 23:10	ויעמד
	2 Kgs 25:11	ואת יתר
6–8	2 Kgs 11:8	והקפתם
	וַתֵּרֶא *of Chronicles* (2 Chr 23:13)	ותרא דדבר ימים
	Esth 1:16	ממוכן

And similarly all cases of וכל על המלך טוב דכות ב̇ מ̇ ג̇ עַל־הַמֶּלֶךְ טוֹב apart from *three*

Com.: The Masorah notes the *eight* occurrences of the phrase עַל־הַמֶּלֶךְ, to distinguish them from its more numerous occurrences (100+) with אֶל (אֶל־הַמֶּלֶךְ).

This distinction is implied in the Mm in the addition *of Chronicles* to the catchword of the 2 Chr 23:13 reference, to distinguish this verse from its parallel in 2 Kgs 11:14 where the lemma appears as אֶל־הַמֶּלֶךְ.

The Mm additionally notes that this lemma also occurs with טוֹב in the phrase עַל־הַמֶּלֶךְ טוֹב, apart from *three* cases when it is with אֶל (e.g., טוֹב אֶל הַמֶּלֶךְ); see the Mm at 2 Kgs 11:8.

2 KINGS 21:25
וְיֶ֙תֶר דִּבְרֵ֤י אָמוֹן֙ אֲשֶׁ֣ר עָשָׂ֔ה הֲלֹא־הֵ֣ם כְּתוּבִ֗ים עַל־סֵ֛פֶר דִּבְרֵ֥י הַיָּמִ֖ים לְמַלְכֵ֥י יְהוּדָֽה׃

21:25   וְיֶ֙תֶר דִּבְרֵ֤י...אֲשֶׁ֣ר עָשָׂ֔ה

Six times   ו֯   Mp

Com.: See **2 Kgs 16:19**.

In M^L the circellus has been placed only on the words אֲשֶׁ֣ר עָשָׂ֔ה, which phrase occurs over a *hundred times*, however, the Mm to 1 Kgs 16:27 and the Mp to 2 Kgs 16:19 indicate that the note refers to the larger phrase וְיֶ֙תֶר דִּבְרֵ֤י...אֲשֶׁ֣ר עָשָׂ֔ה that occurs with the *six* kings Omri, Ahaziah, Jehoash, Jotham, Ahaz, and Amon.

2 KINGS 21:26
וַיִּקְבֹּ֨ר אֹת֥וֹ בִקְבֻרָת֖וֹ בְּגַן־עֻזָּ֑א וַיִּמְלֹ֛ךְ יֹאשִׁיָּ֥הוּ בְנ֖וֹ תַּחְתָּֽיו׃ פ

21:26   וַיִּקְבֹּ֨ר אֹת֥וֹ

Twice   ב֯   Mp

Deut 34:6; 2 Kgs 21:26

    וַיִּקְבֹּ֨ר אֹת֥וֹ *twice*   ויקבר אתו ב֯   Mm

Deut 34:6   ויקבר אתו בגי בארץ מואב

2 Kgs 21:26   ויקבר אתו בקברתו

Com.: The Masorah notes the *two* occurrences of this lemma with a sg. verb, to distinguish it from its more numerous occurrences (15x) with a pl. verb (וַיִּקְבְּר֥וּ אֹת֖וֹ).

It is noteworthy that in M^L the letter ב in the word וַיִּקְבֹּ֨ר is written with *two* vowels, a *šəwâ* and *ḥolem* (וַיִּקְבְֹּר). The *šəwâ* would indicate an attempt to write the pl. (וַיִּקְבְּרוּ), whereas the *ḥolem* would indicate an attempt to write the sg. (וַיִּקְבֹּר).

This lemma is featured in a Masoretic list of words only occurring *twice* that commence with וי; see Frensdorff, *Ochlah*, §68, and Díaz-Esteban, *Sefer Oklah we-Oklah*, §69.

21:26 עֻזָּא

| Three times written with א in the Prophets | ג̇ כת̇ א̇ בנב̇ | Mp |

Com.: See directly above at **2 Kgs 21:18**.

---

2 KINGS 22:1
בֶּן־שְׁמֹנֶ֤ה שָׁנָה֙ יֹאשִׁיָּ֣הוּ בְמָלְכ֔וֹ וּשְׁלֹשִׁ֤ים וְאַחַת֙ שָׁנָ֔ה מָלַ֖ךְ בִּירוּשָׁלָ֑͏ִם וְשֵׁ֣ם אִמּ֔וֹ יְדִידָ֥ה בַת־עֲדָיָ֖ה מִבָּצְקַֽת׃

22:1 יְדִידָה

Unique ל̇ Mp

22:1 מִבָּצְקַת

Unique ל̇ Mp

---

2 KINGS 22:2
וַיַּ֥עַשׂ הַיָּשָׁ֖ר בְּעֵינֵ֣י יְהוָ֑ה וַיֵּ֗לֶךְ בְּכָל־דֶּ֙רֶךְ֙ דָּוִ֣ד אָבִ֔יו וְלֹא־סָ֖ר יָמִ֥ין וּשְׂמֹֽאול׃ פ

22:2 וַיֵּ֗לֶךְ בְּכָל־דֶּ֙רֶךְ֙

Three times ג̇ Mp

1 Kgs 16:26; 22:43; **2 Kgs 22:2**

| וַיֵּ֗לֶךְ בְּכָל־דֶּ֙רֶךְ֙ *three times* | וילך בכל דרך ג̇ | Mm |

1 Kgs 16:26   עמרי
1 Kgs 22:43   יהושפט
וַיַּ֥עַשׂ הַיָּשָׁ֖ר *of Josiah* (2 Kgs 22:2)   ויעש הישר דיאשיהו

Com.: The Masorah notes the *three* occurrences of this lemma concerning the *three* kings Omri, Jehoshaphat, and Josiah, to distinguish them from the *two* occurrences of the parallel phrase וַיֵּלֶךְ בְּדַרְכֵי said of kings Ahaz and also of Josiah at 2 Chr 28:2 and 34:2.

The additional notation *of Josiah* to the catchwords of the 2 Kgs 22:2 reference is meant to contrast that verse with its parallel in 2 Chr 34:2, where the lemma is written as וַיֵּלֶךְ בְּדַרְכֵי. But this additional notation does not provide a contrast since Josiah occurs in both passages. Most likely the phrase *of Kings* (דמלכים) was intended, as is the norm for such contrasts with Chronicles.

22:2   וְלֹא־סָר

Four times   ד̇   Mp

Com.: See **1 Kgs 15:5**.

---

2 KINGS 22:4

עֲלֵה אֶל־חִלְקִיָּהוּ הַכֹּהֵן הַגָּדוֹל וְיַתֵּם אֶת־הַכֶּסֶף הַמּוּבָא בֵּית יְהוָה אֲשֶׁר אָסְפוּ שֹׁמְרֵי הַסַּף מֵאֵת הָעָם׃

22:4   חִלְקִיָּהוּ הַכֹּהֵן הַגָּדוֹל

Four times   ד̇   Mp

2 Kgs 22:4; 22:8; 23:4; 2 Chr 34:9

Com.: The Masorah notes the *four* occurrences of חִלְקִיָּהוּ הַכֹּהֵן with the adj. הַגָּדוֹל, to distinguish them from its *four* occurrences without this adjective.

The circellus has been placed here and at 2 Kgs 22:8 only over the first two words but, since there are *eight* occurrences of חִלְקִיָּהוּ הַכֹּהֵן, the note must refer to the full phrase חִלְקִיָּהוּ הַכֹּהֵן הַגָּדוֹל, which only occurs *four* times. The correct indication with two circelli is present at 2 Kgs 23:4.

> ## 2 KINGS 22:5
>
> וְיִתְּנֻה עַל־יַד עֹשֵׂי הַמְּלָאכָה הַמֻּפְקָדִים בְּבֵית יְהוָה וְיִתְּנוּ אֹתוֹ לְעֹשֵׂי הַמְּלָאכָה אֲשֶׁר בְּבֵית יְהוָה לְחַזֵּק בֶּדֶק הַבָּיִת:

22:5   וְיִתְּנֻה

Read וְיִתְּנֻהוּ ק̇   ויתנהו   Mp

Com.: The *kǝṯîḇ* (ויתנה), and the *qǝrê* (יִתְּנֻהוּ) are examples of *kǝṯîḇ/qǝrê* variations, where a word ending in a ו is read even though it is not written; see Frensdorff, *Ochlah*, §119, Díaz-Esteban, *Sefer Oklah we-Oklah*, §105, and Gordis, *The Biblical Text*, 97.

22:5   בְּבֵית

Read בֵּית ק̇   בית   Mp

Com.: The *kǝṯîḇ* (בבית), and the *qǝrê* (בֵּית) are examples of *kǝṯîḇ/qǝrê* variations where a prep. is omitted; see Gordis, *The Biblical Text*, 143.

This lemma is featured in a Masoretic list of words written with a ב at the beginning of a word that is not read: see the Mm at **2 Sam 10:9** *sub* בְּיִשְׂרָאֵל, Frensdorff, *Ochlah*, §107, and Díaz-Esteban, *Sefer Oklah we-Oklah*, §89.

22:5   וְיִתְּנוּ

וְיִתְּנוּ *three times*   ויתנו ג̇   Mm

1 Kgs 18:23   לנו שנים פרים
2 Kgs 22:5   ויתנו אתו לעשי המלאכה
Dan 1:12   מן הזרעים

Com.: The Masorah notes the *three* occurrences of this lemma with a ו cj., to distinguish them from its more numerous occurrences (55x) with a ו consec. (וַיִּתְּנוּ); see Ognibeni, *'Oklah*, §5K.

This distinction is implied in the Mm notes at 1 Kgs 18:23 and Dan 1:12, where there is the additional notation *of Kings* to the 2 Kgs 22:5 reference, which distinguishes it from its parallel passage in 2 Chr 34:10, where the lemma occurs as וַיִּתְּנוּ.

2 KINGS 22:6
לֶחָרָשִׁים וְלַבֹּנִים וְלַגֹּדְרִים וְלִקְנוֹת עֵצִים וְאַבְנֵי מַחְצֵב לְחַזֵּק אֶת־הַבָּיִת:

22:6   וְלַבֹּנִים

Five times defective   ה֗ חס   Mp

Com.: See **2 Kgs 12:12**.

22:6   וְלִקְנוֹת

Twice   ב֗   Mp

Com.: See **2 Kgs 12:13**.

2 KINGS 22:8
וַיֹּאמֶר חִלְקִיָּהוּ הַכֹּהֵן הַגָּדוֹל עַל־שָׁפָן הַסֹּפֵר סֵפֶר הַתּוֹרָה מָצָאתִי בְּבֵית יְהוָה וַיִּתֵּן חִלְקִיָּה אֶת־הַסֵּפֶר אֶל־שָׁפָן וַיִּקְרָאֵהוּ:

22:8   חִלְקִיָּהוּ הַכֹּהֵן הַגָּדוֹל

Four times   ד֗   Mp

Com.: See **2 Kgs 22:4**.

22:8   בְּבֵית יְהוָה

Thirty-nine times   ל֗ט   Mp

Com.: See **1 Sam 1:7**.

22:8   חִלְקִיָּה

Eleven times   י֗א   Mp

Com.: See **2 Kgs 18:37**.

2 KINGS 22:9

וַיָּבֹא שָׁפָן הַסֹּפֵר אֶל־הַמֶּלֶךְ וַיָּשֶׁב אֶת־הַמֶּלֶךְ דָּבָר וַיֹּאמֶר הִתִּיכוּ עֲבָדֶיךָ אֶת־הַכֶּסֶף הַנִּמְצָא בַבַּיִת וַיִּתְּנֻהוּ עַל־יַד עֹשֵׂי הַמְּלָאכָה הַמֻּפְקָדִים בֵּית יְהוָה:

22:9　　וַיִּתְּנֻהוּ

Four times　　ד׳　　Mp

2 Kgs 22:9; **Ezek 19:9**; **2 Chr 24:8**; 34:17 (וַיִּתְּנוּהוּ)

וַיִּתְּנֻהוּ *four times*　　ד׳ [ויתנהו] (ויתנוהו)　　Mm

2 Kgs 22:9	התיכו עבדיך
2 Chr 34:17	ויתיכו
Ezek 19:9	בסוגר
2 Chr 24:8	ויעשו

The *second* form is plene　　תיני מל

Com.: The Masorah notes the *four* occurrences of this lemma with a ו consec., to distinguish them from its *sole* occurrence with a ו cj. (וַיִּתְּנָה) in v. 5.

The Mp heading at 2 Chr 24:8 reads *four times, three times defective and once plene*, and the Mm here notes that the plene form at 2 Chr 34:17 (וַיִּתְּנוּהוּ) is the second one in its list.

2 KINGS 22:10

וַיַּגֵּד שָׁפָן הַסֹּפֵר לַמֶּלֶךְ לֵאמֹר סֵפֶר נָתַן לִי חִלְקִיָּה הַכֹּהֵן וַיִּקְרָאֵהוּ שָׁפָן לִפְנֵי הַמֶּלֶךְ:

22:10　　חִלְקִיָּה

Eleven times　　יא׳　　Mp

Com.: See **2 Kgs 18:37**.

2 KINGS 22:12

וַיְצַו הַמֶּלֶךְ אֶת־חִלְקִיָּה הַכֹּהֵן וְאֶת־אֲחִיקָם בֶּן־שָׁפָן וְאֶת־עַכְבּוֹר בֶּן־מִיכָיָה וְאֵת ׀ שָׁפָן הַסֹּפֵר וְאֵת עֲשָׂיָה עֶבֶד־הַמֶּלֶךְ לֵאמֹר׃

22:12 חִלְקִיָּה

Eleven times יֹא̇ Mp

Com.: See **2 Kgs 18:37**.

22:12 מִיכָיָה

Five times ה̇ Mp

1–5 **2 Kgs 22:12**; **Neh 12:35**; 12:41; **2 Chr 13:2** (מִיכָיָהוּ); **17:7** (וּלְמִיכָיָהוּ)

מִיכָיָה *five times*   מיכיה ה̇ וסימנהון   Mm

1–5 עֲשָׂיָה *of Kings* (2 Kgs 22:12)   עשיה דמלכים
2 Chr 13:2   (שלש) [שלוש] שנים
2 Chr 17:7   לשריו
Neh 12:41   והכהנים
Neh 12:35   הכהנים

Com.: The Masorah notes the *five* occurrences of this lemma with the divine element יָה or יָהוּ, to distinguish them from its more numerous occurrences (32x) written just with the element ה (מִיכָה/לְמִיכָה).

This distinction is implied in the additional notation *of Kings* to the 2 Kgs 22:12 reference, which distinguishes it from its parallel passage in 2 Chr 34:20, where the lemma occurs as מִיכָה.

The Mp heading at 2 Chr 17:7 reads *unique* reflecting the *sole* occurrence of the form וּלְמִיכָיָהוּ.

2 Kings 22:13

לְכוּ֩ דִרְשׁ֨וּ אֶת־יְהוָ֜ה בַּעֲדִ֣י וּבְעַד־הָעָ֗ם וּבְעַד֙ כָּל־יְהוּדָ֔ה עַל־דִּבְרֵ֛י הַסֵּ֥פֶר הַנִּמְצָ֖א הַזֶּ֑ה כִּֽי־גְדוֹלָ֞ה חֲמַ֣ת יְהוָ֗ה אֲשֶׁר־הִ֤יא נִצְּתָה֙ בָ֔נוּ עַל֩ אֲשֶׁ֨ר לֹֽא־שָׁמְע֜וּ אֲבֹתֵ֗ינוּ עַל־דִּבְרֵי֙ הַסֵּ֣פֶר הַזֶּ֔ה לַעֲשׂ֕וֹת כְּכָל־הַכָּת֖וּב עָלֵֽינוּ׃

22:13 ¹עַל־דִּבְרֵ֛י

Ten times   ⁚   Mp

Com.: See **2 Sam 3:8**.

2 Kings 22:14

וַיֵּ֣לֶךְ חִלְקִיָּ֣הוּ הַ֠כֹּהֵן וַאֲחִיקָ֨ם וְעַכְבּ֜וֹר וְשָׁפָ֣ן וַעֲשָׂיָ֗ה אֶל־חֻלְדָּ֨ה הַנְּבִיאָ֜ה אֵ֣שֶׁת ׀ שַׁלֻּ֣ם בֶּן־תִּקְוָ֗ה בֶּן־חַרְחַס֙ שֹׁמֵ֣ר הַבְּגָדִ֔ים וְהִ֛יא יֹשֶׁ֥בֶת בִּירוּשָׁלַ֖͏ִם בַּמִּשְׁנֶ֑ה וַֽיְדַבְּר֖וּ אֵלֶֽיהָ׃

22:14 שַׁלֻּם

Three times defective   ג֜ חס   Mp

1–5   2 Kgs 15:10; **22:14;** **Jer 22:11**; 32:7; 35:4
6–10 **Ezra 10:24; Neh 7:45***; **1 Chr 4:25; 9:31** (לְשַׁלּוּם); 2 Chr 28:12
11   2 Chr 34:22

Com.: The Mp heading here of *three times* is incorrect since there are *eleven* occurrences of this lemma. Dotan/Reich (*Masora Thesaurus, ad loc.*) suggest that the circellus has been misapplied here and really belongs with the lemma אֹסִפְךָ in v. 20.

The Masorah notes the *eleven* occurrences of this lemma written defective וּ, to distinguish them from its more numerous occurrences (16x) written plene וּ (שַׁלּוּם/וְשַׁלּוּם); see **2 Kgs 15:13**.

*M^L, contrary to M (שַׁלֻּם), has only *ten* occurrences of this lemma since it writes the form at Neh 7:45 plene (שַׁלּוּם); see Breuer, *The Biblical Text*, 350.

However, the Mp heading at Jer 22:11 reads *eleven times defective*, and all *four* Mp headings in the Writings highlighted above read *six times defective* as does the heading to the Mm at 2 Chr 28:12. All these headings thus support the enumeration inherent in the text of M.

Neither M^C nor M^A has a note on this lemma here.

22:14   יֹשֶׁבֶת

Eight times defective   ח֗ חס   Mp

1–5   **Lev 15:23**; 2 Kgs 4:13; **22:14**; Jer 21:13; **48:18**
6–8   **Jer 51:35; Zech 1:11; 7:7**

יֹשֶׁבֶת *eight times* defective   ישבת ח֗ חס   Mm

1–5	Lev 15:23	אשר (היא) [הוא] ישבת עליו
	2 Kgs 4:13	ותאמר בתוך עמי
	יֹשֶׁבֶת בִּירוּשָׁלָֽםִ *of Kings* (2 Kgs 22:14)	ישבת בירושלם דמלכים
	Jer 21:13	ישבת העמק
	Jer 48:18	רדי מכבוד
6–8	Jer 51:35	חמסי ושארי
	Zech 7:7	בהיות ירושלם ישבת
	Zech 1:11	והנה כל הארץ ישבת

Com.: The Masorah notes the *eight* occurrences of this lemma written defective ו, to distinguish them from its more numerous occurrences (16x) written plene ו (יוֹשֶׁבֶת).

This distinction is implied in the additional notation *of Kings* to the 2 Kgs 22:14 reference, which distinguishes it from its parallel passage in 2 Chr 34:22, where the lemma is written plene ו as יוֹשֶׁבֶת.

The Mp heading at Jer 51:35 reads *twice defective*, but there are *three* occurrences of this lemma in Jeremiah.

> ## 2 KINGS 22:15
> וַתֹּאמֶר אֲלֵיהֶם כֹּה־אָמַר יְהוָה אֱלֹהֵי יִשְׂרָאֵל אִמְרוּ לָאִישׁ אֲשֶׁר־שָׁלַח אֶתְכֶם אֵלָֽי׃

22:15   וַתֹּאמֶר אֲלֵיהֶם

Unique in the Prophets   ל בנביא   Mp

Com.: The Masorah notes the *sole* occurrence in the Prophets of וַתֹּאמֶר with אֲלֵיהֶם, to distinguish it from its *four* occurrences in the Prophets with לָהֶם (וַתֹּאמֶר לָהֶם); see the Mm at 2 Chr 34:23 *sub* וַתֹּאמֶר לָהֶם.

2 KINGS 22:16

כֹּה אָמַר יְהוָה הִנְנִי מֵבִיא רָעָה אֶל־הַמָּקוֹם הַזֶּה וְעַל־יֹשְׁבָיו אֵת כָּל־דִּבְרֵי הַסֵּפֶר אֲשֶׁר קָרָא מֶלֶךְ יְהוּדָה׃

22:16   אֶל־הַמָּקוֹם הַזֶּה וְעַל־יֹשְׁבָיו

Unique   ל   Mp

Com.: The Masorah notes the *sole* occurrence of the phrase הַמָּקוֹם הַזֶּה וְעַל־יֹשְׁבָיו with אֶל, to distinguish it from its *four* occurrences with עַל (עַל־הַמָּקוֹם הַזֶּה וְעַל־יֹשְׁבָיו), *one* of which occurs in v. 19; see directly below at **2 Kgs 22:20**. In M^L there are only *three* circelli on this *five-word* phrase; see **Josh 1:6** and *passim*.

2 KINGS 22:17

תַּחַת | אֲשֶׁר עֲזָבוּנִי וַיְקַטְּרוּ לֵאלֹהִים אֲחֵרִים לְמַעַן הַכְעִיסֵנִי בְּכֹל מַעֲשֵׂה יְדֵיהֶם וְנִצְּתָה חֲמָתִי בַּמָּקוֹם הַזֶּה וְלֹא תִכְבֶּה׃

22:17   הַכְעִיסֵנִי

Six times written like this   ו כת   Mp

Com.: Six times written plene first י; see Ginsburg 2, ב, §413.

2 KINGS 22:18

וְאֶל־מֶלֶךְ יְהוּדָה הַשֹּׁלֵחַ אֶתְכֶם לִדְרֹשׁ אֶת־יְהוָה כֹּה תֹאמְרוּ אֵלָיו כֹּה־אָמַר יְהוָה אֱלֹהֵי יִשְׂרָאֵל הַדְּבָרִים אֲשֶׁר שָׁמָעְתָּ׃

22:18   כֹּה תֹאמְרוּ

Seven times   ז   Mp

Com.: See **1 Sam 18:25**.

22:18   כֹּה־אָמַר יְהוָה אֱלֹהֵי יִשְׂרָאֵל

Twenty-four times   כד   Mp

Com.: See **1 Sam 10:18**.

In some of the Mp references, there is only *one* circellus between *two* of the words in the phrase, e.g., at 1 Kgs 14:7 and here just on כֹּה־אָמַר; and at 2 Kgs 9:6 and Isa 37:21 just on אֱלֹהֵי יִשְׂרָאֵל.

> **2 KINGS 22:19**
>
> יַ֣עַן רַךְ־לְבָבְךָ֗ וַתִּכָּנַ֣ע ׀ מִפְּנֵ֣י יְהוָ֡ה בְּֽשָׁמְעֲךָ֩ אֲשֶׁ֨ר דִּבַּ֜רְתִּי עַל־הַמָּק֣וֹם הַזֶּ֗ה וְעַל־יֹֽשְׁבָיו֙ לִהְי֤וֹת לְשַׁמָּה֙ וְלִקְלָלָ֔ה וַתִּקְרַ֥ע אֶת־בְּגָדֶ֖יךָ וַתִּבְכֶּ֣ה לְפָנָ֑י וְגַ֧ם אָנֹכִ֛י שָׁמַ֖עְתִּי נְאֻם־יְהוָֽה׃

22:19   בְּשָׁמְעֲךָ

Twice   בׄ   Mp

2 Kgs 22:19; 2 Chr 34:27

Com.: The Masorah notes the *two* occurrences of this lemma in these parallel passages with the prep. בְּ, to distinguish it from its *sole* occurrence with the prep. כְּ (כְּשָׁמְעֲךָ) at 1 Chr 14:15.

22:19   וְגַם אָנֹכִי

Five times   הׄ   Mp

1–5   **Gen 21:26**; 1 Sam 1:28; 2 Sam 2:6; **2 Kgs 22:19**; Amos 4:7

In Kings   דמלכים   Mm   וגם אנכי שמעתי נאם יהוה
2 Kgs 22:19 (וְגַם אָנֹכִי)

In Chronicles   דדברי הימים   וגם אני שמעתי
2 Chr 34:27 (וְגַם אֲנִי)

And *one* verse is their *sîman*   וחד פסוק סימנהון
Isa 45:12 (אָנֹכִי...אֲנִי)   אנכי עשיתי ארץ ואדם עליה בראתי אני

Com.: The Mp notes the *five* occurrences of וְגַם with אָנֹכִי, to distinguish them from its more numerous occurrences (17x) with וְגַם אֲנִי (אֲנִי).

This distinction is implied in the Mm note at Gen 21:26 in the additional notation *of Kings* to the 2 Kgs 22:19 reference, which distinguishes it from its parallel passage in 2 Chr 34:27, where the lemma occurs as וְגַם אֲנִי.

The Mm compares the *two* parallel phrases of 2 Kgs 22:19 and 2 Chr 34:27 in which the first has the pron. אָנֹכִי and the second the pron. אֲנִי, and notes their difference by means of a *third-verse sîman*.

Isa 45:12 is cited as the *third-verse sîman* because it contains the elements of this difference, namely both pronouns occurring in the same order as in the two parallel verses, first אָנֹכִי and then אֲנִי.

2 Kings 22:20

לָכֵן֩ הִנְנִ֨י אֹֽסִפְךָ֜ עַל־אֲבֹתֶ֗יךָ וְנֶאֱסַפְתָּ֣ אֶל־קִבְרֹתֶיךָ֮ בְּשָׁלוֹם֒ וְלֹא־תִרְאֶ֣ינָה עֵינֶ֔יךָ בְּכֹל֙ הָֽרָעָ֔ה אֲשֶׁר־אֲנִ֥י מֵבִ֖יא עַל־הַמָּק֣וֹם הַזֶּ֑ה וַיָּשִׁ֥יבוּ אֶת־הַמֶּ֖לֶךְ דָּבָֽר׃

22:20   אֹסִפְךָ עַל

Three times   גׄ   Mp

2 Kgs 22:20; Isa 24:22; **Amos 3:9**

אֲסִיפָה עַל *three times*   אסיפה על גׄ   Mm

לָכֵן הִנְנִי אֹסִפְךָ *of Kings* (2 Kgs 22:20)	לכן הנני אספך דמלכים
Isa 24:22	ואספו אספה אסיר
Amos 3:9	ואמרו האספו
{Jer 4:5}	{ונבואה}

Com.: The Masorah notes the *three* occurrences the verb אָסַף in various forms with עַל, to distinguish them from its more numerous occurrences (31x) in various forms with אֶל (e.g., אֹסִפְךָ אֶל).

This distinction is implied here, and in the Mm note at Amos 3:9, in the additional notation *of Kings* to the 2 Kgs 22:20 reference, which distinguishes it from its parallel passage in 2 Chr 34:28, where the prep. occurs as אֶל.

In the Mm list, a catchword from Jer 4:5, where the form הֵאָסְפוּ occurs with אֶל, has mistakenly been added.

22:20   עַל־אֲבֹתֶיךָ

Twice   בׄ   Mp

Deut 30:9; **2 Kgs 22:20**

| Mm | על אבתיך ב׳ וסימנהון | עַל־אֲבֹתֶיךָ *twice*, and their references |

כאשר שש על (אבות) [אבתיך]   Deut 30:9
לָכֵן הִנְנִי אֹסִפְךָ עַל־אֲבֹתֶיךָ (2 Kgs 22:20) *of Kings*

Com.: The Masorah notes the *two* occurrences of אֲבֹתֶיךָ with עַל, to distinguish them from its *two* occurrences with אֶל (אֶל־אֲבֹתֶיךָ).

This distinction is implied in the additional notation *of Kings* to the 2 Kgs 22:20 reference, which distinguishes it from its parallel passage in 2 Chr 34:28 where the lemma occurs with the prep. אֶל.

This lemma is featured in a Masoretic list of pairs of words occurring *twice* with עַל and *twice* with אֶל; see Frensdorff, *Ochlah*, §88, and Díaz-Esteban, *Sefer Oklah we-Oklah*, §156E.

22:20   עַל־הַמָּקוֹם

| Mp | ג׳ וכל וישבי דכות ב׳ מ׳ א׳ | *Three times* and similarly all occurrences with וְעַל־יֹשְׁבָיו except *one* |

Com.: See **2 Kgs 18:25**.

---

2 KINGS 23:1

וַיִּשְׁלַח הַמֶּלֶךְ וַיַּאַסְפוּ אֵלָיו כָּל־זִקְנֵי יְהוּדָה וִירוּשָׁלָ͏ִם׃

23:1   וַיַּאַסְפוּ

| Mp | י׳ | *Ten times* |

Com.: See **1 Sam 5:8**.

---

2 KINGS 23:2

וַיַּעַל הַמֶּלֶךְ בֵּית־יְהוָה וְכָל־אִישׁ יְהוּדָה וְכָל־יֹשְׁבֵי יְרוּשָׁלַ͏ִם אִתּוֹ וְהַכֹּהֲנִים וְהַנְּבִיאִים וְכָל־הָעָם לְמִקָּטֹן וְעַד־גָּדוֹל וַיִּקְרָא בְאָזְנֵיהֶם אֶת־כָּל־דִּבְרֵי סֵפֶר הַבְּרִית הַנִּמְצָא בְּבֵית יְהוָה׃

23:2   וְכָל־יֹשְׁבֵי

| Mp | ח׳ | *Eight times* |

Com.: See **Josh 7:9**.

| 23:2 | וְהַכֹּהֲנִים וְהַנְּבִיאִים |

| Three times | גׄ | Mp |

2 Kgs 23:2; Zech 7:3 (הַכֹּהֲנִים...הַנְּבִיאִים); Neh 9:32 (וּלְכֹהֲנֵינוּ וְלִנְבִיאֵנוּ)

Com.: The Masorah notes the *three* occurrences, apart from Jeremiah, where forms of כֹּהֲנִים precede forms of נְבִיאִים; see Dotan/Reich, *Masora Thesaurus*, ad loc.

This lemma is featured in a Masoretic list of word pairs occurring only *once* where both parts of the pair have a ו cj.; see Frensdorff, *Ochlah*, §253.

| 23:2 | לְמִקָּטֹן וְעַד־גָּדוֹל |

| Twice | בׄ | Mp |

2 Kgs 23:2; Jer 42:8

Com.: The Masorah notes the *two* occurrences of this lemma with the prep. ל, to distinguish it from its more numerous occurrences (7x) without this preposition (מִקָּטֹן וְעַד־גָּדוֹל).

| 23:2 | בְּבֵית יְהוָה |

| Thirty-nine times | לֹט | Mp |

Com.: See **1 Sam 1:7**.

2 KINGS 23:3

וַיַּעֲמֹד הַמֶּלֶךְ עַל־הָעַמּוּד וַיִּכְרֹת אֶת־הַבְּרִית | לִפְנֵי יְהוָה לָלֶכֶת אַחַר יְהוָה וְלִשְׁמֹר מִצְוֹתָיו וְאֶת־עֵדְוֹתָיו וְאֶת־חֻקֹּתָיו בְּכָל־לֵב וּבְכָל־נֶפֶשׁ לְהָקִים אֶת־דִּבְרֵי הַבְּרִית הַזֹּאת הַכְּתֻבִים עַל־הַסֵּפֶר הַזֶּה וַיַּעֲמֹד כָּל־הָעָם בַּבְּרִית:

| 23:3 | אַחַר יְהוָה |

| Twice | בׄ | Mp |

Com.: See **1 Sam 12:14**.

| 23:3 | עֵדְוֹתָיו |

| Five times | הׄ | Mp |

See **1 Kgs 2:3.**

23:3	הַכְּתֻבִים		
Five times defective, and all the Torah		הֿ חסֿ וכל אורֿ	Mp

Com.: See <u>1 Kgs 11:41</u>.

23:3	בַּבְּרִית		
Five times		הֿ	Mp

| 1–5 | <u>1 Kgs 20:34</u>; <u>2 Kgs 23:3</u>; <u>Jer 34:10</u>; 2 Chr 15:12; 23:1 |

בַּבְּרִית *five times*, and their references	(עדותיו) [בברית] הֿ וסימנהון	Mm

1–5	<u>1 Kgs 20:34</u>	ואני בברית אשלחך
	<u>Jer 34:10</u>	וישמעו
	2 Chr 15:12	ויבאו בברית
	2 Chr 23:1	עמו בברית
	הַכְּתֻבִים *of Kings* (<u>2 Kgs 23:3</u>)	הכתבים דמלכים

Com.: The Masorah notes the *five* occurrences of this lemma with the def. prep. בַּ, to distinguish them from its *three* occurrences with the indef. prep. בְּ (בִּבְרִית); see <u>1 Sam 20:8</u>.

The contrast between the *two* forms is expressly stated in the Mm at <u>Jer 34:10</u>, which lists catchwords for all *eight* forms.

The heading of the Mm here of עדותיו (עֵדְוֺתָיו) is incorrect for this Mm note. The correct lemma heading בַּבְּרִית is given in the headings of the Mm notes at <u>1 Kgs 20:34</u> and <u>Jer 34:10</u>.

The addition *of Kings* to the catchword הַכְּתֻבִים of the 2 Kgs 23:3 reference is to distinguish that verse from its parallel in 2 Chr 34:31, which lacks the phrase containing בַּבְּרִית.

2 Kings 23:4

וַיְצַ֣ו הַמֶּ֡לֶךְ אֶת־חִלְקִיָּהוּ֩ הַכֹּהֵ֨ן הַגָּד֜וֹל וְאֶת־כֹּהֲנֵ֣י הַמִּשְׁנֶה֮ וְאֶת־שֹׁמְרֵ֣י הַסַּף֒ לְהוֹצִיא֙ מֵהֵיכַ֣ל יְהוָ֔ה אֵ֣ת כָּל־הַכֵּלִ֗ים הָֽעֲשׂוּיִם֙ לַבַּ֣עַל וְלָאֲשֵׁרָ֔ה וּלְכֹ֖ל צְבָ֣א הַשָּׁמָ֑יִם וַֽיִּשְׂרְפֵ֞ם מִח֤וּץ לִירוּשָׁלִַ֙ם֙ בְּשַׁדְמ֣וֹת קִדְר֔וֹן וְנָשָׂ֥א אֶת־עֲפָרָ֖ם בֵּֽית־אֵֽל׃

23:4   חִלְקִיָּ֙הוּ֙ הַכֹּהֵ֣ן הַגָּד֔וֹל

Four times   ד   Mp

Com.: See **2 Kgs 22:4**.

23:4   הָעֲשׂוּיִם

Unique   ל   Mp

Com.: This lemma is featured in two Masoretic lists. *One* is in a list of words containing *two* וs (the reading in *Ochlah* is הָעֲשׂוּוִם; see Frensdorff, *Ochlah*, §184). The *other* is in a list of words written with a ו but read as a י; see Frensdorff, *Ochlah*, §81.

2 Kings 23:5

וְהִשְׁבִּ֣ית אֶת־הַכְּמָרִ֗ים אֲשֶׁ֤ר נָֽתְנוּ֙ מַלְכֵ֣י יְהוּדָ֔ה וַיְקַטֵּ֤ר בַּבָּמוֹת֙ בְּעָרֵ֣י יְהוּדָ֔ה וּמְסִבֵּ֖י יְרוּשָׁלִָ֑ם וְאֶת־הַֽמְקַטְּרִ֣ים לַבַּ֗עַל לַשֶּׁ֤מֶשׁ וְלַיָּרֵ֙חַ֙ וְלַמַּזָּל֔וֹת וּלְכֹ֖ל צְבָ֥א הַשָּׁמָֽיִם׃

23:5   הַכְּמָרִים

Twice   ב   Mp

2 Kgs 23:5; Zeph 1:4

2 Kings 23:6

וַיֹּצֵ֣א אֶת־הָאֲשֵׁרָה֩ מִבֵּ֨ית יְהוָ֜ה מִח֤וּץ לִירוּשָׁלִַ֙ם֙ אֶל־נַ֣חַל קִדְר֔וֹן וַיִּשְׂרֹ֥ף אֹתָ֛הּ בְּנַ֥חַל קִדְר֖וֹן וַיָּ֣דֶק לְעָפָ֑ר וַיַּשְׁלֵךְ֙ אֶת־עֲפָרָ֔הּ עַל־קֶ֖בֶר בְּנֵ֥י הָעָֽם׃

23:6   וַיֹּצֵא

Thirteen times defective   יג חס   Mp

Com.: See **2 Kgs 10:22**.

23:6   לֶעָפָר

Three times   גׄ   Mp

Deut 9:21; **2 Kgs 23:6; 23:15**

Com.: The Masorah notes the *three* occurrences of this lemma with the indef. prep. לְ, to distinguish them from its *four* occurrences with the def. prep. לַ (לֶעָפָר).

2 KINGS 23:7

וַיִּתֹּץ אֶת־בָּתֵּי הַקְּדֵשִׁים אֲשֶׁר בְּבֵית יְהוָה אֲשֶׁר הַנָּשִׁים אֹרְגוֹת שָׁם בָּתִּים לָאֲשֵׁרָה׃

23:7   הַקְּדֵשִׁים

Twice   בׄ   Mp

Com.: See **1 Kgs 15:12**.

2 KINGS 23:8

וַיָּבֵא אֶת־כָּל־הַכֹּהֲנִים מֵעָרֵי יְהוּדָה וַיְטַמֵּא אֶת־הַבָּמוֹת אֲשֶׁר קִטְּרוּ־שָׁמָּה הַכֹּהֲנִים מִגֶּבַע עַד־בְּאֵר שָׁבַע וְנָתַץ אֶת־בָּמוֹת הַשְּׁעָרִים אֲשֶׁר־פֶּתַח שַׁעַר יְהוֹשֻׁעַ שַׂר־הָעִיר אֲשֶׁר־עַל־שְׂמֹאול אִישׁ בְּשַׁעַר הָעִיר׃

23:8   קִטְּרוּ־שָׁמָּה

Unique   לׄ   Mp

23:8   עַד־בְּאֵר

Unique   לׄ   Mp

Com.: The Masorah notes the *sole* occurrence of this lemma without a ו cj., to distinguish it from its more numerous occurrences (7x) with a cj. (וְעַד־בְּאֵר).

2 KINGS 23:9

אַךְ לֹא יַעֲלוּ כֹּהֲנֵי הַבָּמוֹת אֶל־מִזְבַּח יְהוָה בִּירוּשָׁלָ͏ִם כִּי אִם־אָכְלוּ מַצּוֹת בְּתוֹךְ אֲחֵיהֶם׃

23:9   כֹּהֲנֵי הַבָּמוֹת

Four times   דׄ   Mp

Com.: See **1 Kgs 12:32**.

| 23:9 | אֶל־מִזְבַּח |

| Twice | בֿ | Mp |

2 Kgs 23:9; **Ps 43:4**

| אֶל־מִזְבַּח *twice* | אל מזבח בֿ | Mm |

2 Kgs 23:9   אך לא יעלו כהני הבמות אל
Ps 43:4   ואבואה אל מזבח אלהים

Com.: The Masorah notes the *two* occurrences of מִזְבַּח with אֶל, to distinguish them from its more numerous occurrences (13x) with עַל (עַל מִזְבַּח). This lemma occur in the ms. on fol. 218v., but the Mm note appears on the top right of the preceding folio 218r.

> ### 2 KINGS 23:10
> וְטִמֵּא אֶת־הַתֹּפֶת אֲשֶׁר בְּגֵי בְנֵי־הִנֹּם לְבִלְתִּי לְהַעֲבִיר אִישׁ אֶת־בְּנוֹ וְאֶת־בִּתּוֹ בָּאֵשׁ לַמֹּלֶךְ׃

| 23:10 | בְנִי |

| Read בֵּן | בן קֿ | Mp |

Com.: The *kətîb* (בני), and the *qərê* (בֵּן) are examples of *kətîb/qərê* variations in the sg. and pl.; see Gordis, *The Biblical Text*, 136–37.

This lemma is featured in a Masoretic list of words in which a י is written at the end but is not read; see Frensdorff, *Ochlah*, §127, and Díaz-Esteban, *Sefer Oklah we-Oklah*, §111.

| 23:10 | וְאֶת־בִּתּוֹ |

| Twice | בֿ | Mp |

Com.: See **1 Sam 17:25**.

2 KINGS 23:11

וַיַּשְׁבֵּת אֶת־הַסּוּסִים אֲשֶׁר נָתְנוּ מַלְכֵי יְהוּדָה לַשֶּׁמֶשׁ מִבֹּא בֵית־יְהוָה אֶל־לִשְׁכַּת נְתַן־מֶלֶךְ הַסָּרִיס אֲשֶׁר בַּפַּרְוָרִים וְאֶת־מַרְכְּבוֹת הַשֶּׁמֶשׁ שָׂרַף בָּאֵשׁ:

23:11   וַיַּשְׁבֵּת

Twice   ב̇   Mp

2 Kgs 23:11; 2 Chr 16:5

Com.: The Masorah notes the *two* occurrences of this lemma in the *hiphil*, to distinguish them from its *two* occurrences in the *qal* (וַיִּשְׁבֹּת) at Gen 2:2 and **Josh 5:12**.

This distinction is implied in the Mp heading at 2 Chr 16:5, which reads *twice and twice* וישבת, which must represent וַיַּשְׁבֵּת because the only other form of וישבת (וַיִּשְׁבֹּת) occurs just *once* (Prov 22:10).

23:11   מִבֹּא

Unique defective   ל חס̇   Mp

Com.: The Masorah notes the *sole* occurrence of this lemma written defective ו, to distinguish it from its more numerous occurrences (5x) written plene ו (מָבוֹא); see **1 Sam 25:26**.

23:11   מַרְכְּבוֹת

Four times   ד̇   Mp

Exod 15:4 (מַרְכְּבֹת); **2 Kgs 23:12; Isa 22:18; Cant 6:12**

Com.: The Masorah notes the *four* occurrences of this lemma, of which *three* (2 Kgs 23:12, Isa 22:18 and Cant 6:12) are written plene ו and *one* (Exod 15:4) is written defective ו as מַרְכְּבֹת.

2 KINGS 23:13

וְאֶת־הַבָּמוֹת אֲשֶׁר ׀ עַל־פְּנֵי יְרוּשָׁלִַם אֲשֶׁר מִימִין לְהַר־הַמַּשְׁחִית אֲשֶׁר בָּנָה שְׁלֹמֹה מֶלֶךְ־יִשְׂרָאֵל לְעַשְׁתֹּרֶת ׀ שִׁקֻּץ צִידֹנִים וְלִכְמוֹשׁ שִׁקֻּץ מוֹאָב וּלְמִלְכֹּם תּוֹעֲבַת בְּנֵי־עַמּוֹן טִמֵּא הַמֶּלֶךְ:

23:13   וּלְמִלְכֹּם תּוֹעֲבַת

Unique   ל   Mp

2 Kings 23:14

וְשִׁבַּר֙ אֶת־הַמַּצֵּבֹ֔ות וַיִּכְרֹ֖ת אֶת־הָאֲשֵׁרִ֑ים וַיְמַלֵּ֥א אֶת־מְקֹומָ֖ם עַצְמֹ֥ות אָדָֽם׃

23:14 וַיְמַלֵּ֥א

Nine times   ט׳   Mp

Com.: See **Judg 17:5**.

2 Kings 23:15

וְגַ֨ם אֶת־הַמִּזְבֵּ֜חַ אֲשֶׁ֣ר בְּבֵֽית־אֵ֗ל הַבָּמָה֙ אֲשֶׁ֣ר עָשָׂ֡ה יָרָבְעָ֣ם בֶּן־נְבָט֩ אֲשֶׁ֨ר הֶחֱטִ֤יא אֶת־יִשְׂרָאֵל֙ גַּ֣ם אֶת־הַמִּזְבֵּ֧חַ הַה֛וּא וְאֶת־הַבָּמָ֖ה נָתָ֑ץ וַיִּשְׂרֹ֧ף אֶת־הַבָּמָ֛ה הֵדַ֥ק לְעָפָ֖ר וְשָׂרַ֥ף אֲשֵׁרָֽה׃

23:15   וְאֶת־הַבָּמָ֖ה

Unique   ל׳   Mp

Com.: The Masorah notes the *sole* occurrence of this lemma with a ו cj., to distinguish it from its *sole* occurrence without a cj. in this same verse.

This lemma is featured in a Masoretic list of words occurring in the same verse, *once* with a ו and *once* without a ו; see Frensdorff, *Ochlah*, §231.

23:15   לְעָפָ֖ר

Three times   ג׳   Mp

Com.: See directly above at **2 Kgs 23:6**.

2 Kings 23:17

וַיֹּ֕אמֶר מָ֚ה הַצִּיּ֣וּן הַלָּ֔ז אֲשֶׁ֖ר אֲנִ֣י רֹאֶ֑ה וַיֹּאמְר֨וּ אֵלָ֜יו אַנְשֵׁ֣י הָעִ֗יר הַקֶּ֤בֶר אִישׁ־הָאֱלֹהִים֙ אֲשֶׁר־בָּ֣א מִֽיהוּדָ֔ה וַיִּקְרָ֗א אֶת־הַדְּבָרִ֤ים הָאֵ֙לֶּה֙ אֲשֶׁ֣ר עָשִׂ֔יתָ עַ֥ל הַמִּזְבַּ֖ח בֵּֽית־אֵֽל׃

23:17   הַצִּיּ֣וּן

Unique   ל׳   Mp

Com.: The Masorah notes the *sole* occurrence of this lemma with the def. article, to distinguish it from its *sole* occurrence without this article at Ezek 39:15.

This lemma is featured in a Masoretic list of words occurring *twice*, *once* with a ה at the beginning (here), and *once* without (Ezek 39:15); see Frensdorff, *Ochlah*, §8, and Díaz-Esteban, *Sefer Oklah we-Oklah*, §8.

23:17   הַמִּזְבֵּחַ

Twice   בֿ   Mp

Com.: See **2 Kgs 16:14**.

2 KINGS 23:18

וַיֹּאמֶר הַנִּיחוּ לוֹ אִישׁ אַל־יָנַע עַצְמֹתָיו וַיְמַלְּטוּ עַצְמֹתָיו אֵת עַצְמוֹת הַנָּבִיא אֲשֶׁר־בָּא מִשֹּׁמְרוֹן׃

23:18   יָנַע

Unique   ל   Mp

In M^L the circellus has been misplaced on the following word עַצְמֹתָיו, which occurs more than *once* so it is most likely, as M^C and M^A read, that the note belongs with this lemma that only occurs this *once*.

2 KINGS 23:19

וְגַם אֶת־כָּל־בָּתֵּי הַבָּמוֹת אֲשֶׁר | בְּעָרֵי שֹׁמְרוֹן אֲשֶׁר עָשׂוּ מַלְכֵי יִשְׂרָאֵל לְהַכְעִיס הֵסִיר יֹאשִׁיָּהוּ וַיַּעַשׂ לָהֶם כְּכָל־הַמַּעֲשִׂים אֲשֶׁר עָשָׂה בְּבֵית־אֵל׃

23:19   כְּכָל־הַמַּעֲשִׂים

Twice   בֿ   Mp

1 Sam 8:8; 2 Kgs 23:19

Mm   ככל המעשים ב וסימנהון   כְּכָל־הַמַּעֲשִׂים *twice*, and their references

1 Sam 8:8   אשר עשו
2 Kgs 23:19   ויעש להם

Com.: The Masorah notes the *two* occurrences of this lemma with the prep. כ, to distinguish them from its *three* occurrences without this preposition.

2 KINGS 23:20

וַיִּזְבַּח אֶת־כָּל־כֹּהֲנֵי הַבָּמוֹת אֲשֶׁר־שָׁם עַל־הַמִּזְבְּחוֹת וַיִּשְׂרֹף אֶת־עַצְמוֹת אָדָם עֲלֵיהֶם וַיָּשָׁב יְרוּשָׁלָ͏ִם:

23:20   כֹּהֲנֵי הַבָּמוֹת

Four times   ד   Mp

Com.: See **1 Kgs 12:32**.

2 KINGS 23:22

כִּי לֹא נַעֲשָׂה כַּפֶּסַח הַזֶּה מִימֵי הַשֹּׁפְטִים אֲשֶׁר שָׁפְטוּ אֶת־יִשְׂרָאֵל וְכֹל יְמֵי מַלְכֵי יִשְׂרָאֵל וּמַלְכֵי יְהוּדָה:

23:22   נַעֲשָׂה

Eight times   ח   Mp

1–5   **Lev 7:9**; Judg 16:11; **1 Kgs 10:20**; **2 Kgs 23:22**; 23:23
6–8   **2 Chr 9:19**; **35:18**; 35:19

נַעֲשָׂה *eight times* with *qameṣ*   נעשה ח̇ קמץ   Mm

1–5	Lev 7:9	(במחרשת) [במרחשת]
	Judg 16:11	יאסרוני
	2 Chr 9:19	(ממלכת) [ממלכה]
	1 Kgs 10:20	ממלכות
	2 Chr 35:18	פסח
6–8	2 Chr 35:19	הפסח
	2 Kgs 23:22	כפסח
	2 Kgs 23:23	הפסח

And similarly *all* (occurrences in) Qoheleth   וכל קהלת ואסתר דכותהון קמצין
and Esther are with *qameṣ*

Com.: The Masorah notes the *eight* occurrences of this lemma written with *qameṣ* to distinguish them from its more numerous occurrences (33x). written with *səgôl* (נַעֲשֶׂה); see Ognibeni, *'Oklah*, §13G.

The Mm additionally notes that this lemma occurs (*twelve times*) in the books of Qoheleth and Esther.

The Mp headings here and at 2 Kgs 23:23 read *eight times*, but those at 1 Kgs 10:20, 2 Chr 35:18, 35:19, and the Mm heading here, more specifically read *eight times with qameṣ*.

The Mp heading at Lev 7:9 reads *eight times and similarly all the Megilloth* (חומש) *apart from two*. The *two* exceptions with *səḡōl* in the Megilloth are Cant 1:11 and 8:8.

23:22   הַשֹּׁפְטִים

Four times   ד   Mp

Deut 19:18; **2 Kgs 23:22**; Ruth 1:1; **2 Chr 19:6**

Mm   השפטים ד וחסירין וסימנהון   הַשֹּׁפְטִים *four times* and defective, and their references

Deut 19:18   ודרשו השפטים היטב והנה עד שקר
2 Kgs 23:22   כי לא נעשה כפסח הזה מימי
2 Chr 19:6   ויאמר אל השפטים
Ruth 1:1   ויהי בימי <שפט> השפטים

And *once* (וְהַשֹּׁפְטִים): Deut 19:17 *unique and defective*   וחד והשפטים אשר יהיו ל וחס

Com.: The Masorah notes the *four* occurrences of this lemma written defective ו with the def. article, and *one* occurrence of this lemma with a ו cj.

By noting that all *five* occurrences of this lemma are written defective ו, the Masorah is also implying (correctly) that this lemma does not occur elsewhere written plene.

This lemma is featured in a Masoretic list of words that occur *five times*, *four* times without a ו cj., and *once* with a cj. (Deut 19:17); see Frensdorff, Ochlah, §17, and Díaz-Esteban, *Sefer Oklah we-Oklah*, §18.

23:22   וְכֹל יְמֵי

Three times   ג   Mp

Josh 24:31; Judg 2:7; **2 Kgs 23:22**

וְכֹל יְמֵי *three times*, and their references   וכל ימי ג׳ וסימנהון   Mm

Josh 24:31   וכל ימי הזקנים אשר האריכו ימים
2 Kgs 23:22   השפטים אשר שפטו את ישראל
Judg 2:7   הזקנים

Com.: The Masorah notes the *three* occurrences of this lemma with a ו cj., to distinguish them from its more numerous occurrences (69x) without a cj.

2 KINGS 23:23

כִּי אִם־בִּשְׁמֹנֶה עֶשְׂרֵה שָׁנָה לַמֶּלֶךְ יֹאשִׁיָּהוּ נַעֲשָׂה הַפֶּסַח הַזֶּה לַיהוָה בִּירוּשָׁלָם׃

23:23   נַעֲשָׂה

Eight times   ח׳   Mp

Com.: See directly above at **2 Kgs 23:22**.

2 KINGS 23:24

וְגַם אֶת־הָאֹבוֹת וְאֶת־הַיִּדְּעֹנִים וְאֶת־הַתְּרָפִים וְאֶת־הַגִּלֻּלִים וְאֵת כָּל־הַשִּׁקֻּצִים אֲשֶׁר נִרְאוּ בְּאֶרֶץ יְהוּדָה וּבִירוּשָׁלַם בִּעֵר יֹאשִׁיָּהוּ לְמַעַן הָקִים אֶת־דִּבְרֵי הַתּוֹרָה הַכְּתֻבִים עַל־הַסֵּפֶר אֲשֶׁר מָצָא חִלְקִיָּהוּ הַכֹּהֵן בֵּית יְהוָה׃

23:24   הַשִּׁקֻּצִים

Three times defective   ג׳ חס׳   Mp

2 Kgs 23:24; **Zech 9:7** (וְשִׁקֻּצָיו); **Nah 3:6** (שִׁקֻּצִים)

הַשִּׁקֻּצִים *three times* defective, and their references   השקצים ג׳ חסירין וסימנהון   Mm

2 Kgs 23:24   וגם את האבות
Zech 9:7   (והסירתי) [והסרתי] דמיו
Nah 3:6   והשלכתי עליך (שקוצים) [שקצים]

Com.: The Masorah notes the *three* occurrences of this lemma in various forms written defective ו, to distinguish them from its more numerous occurrences (18x) in various forms written plene ו, (e.g., שִׁקּוּצֵיהֶם).

2 KINGS 23:25

וְכָמֹ֩הוּ֩ לֹֽא־הָיָ֨ה לְפָנָ֜יו מֶ֗לֶךְ אֲשֶׁר־שָׁ֤ב אֶל־יְהוָה֙ בְּכָל־לְבָב֤וֹ וּבְכָל־נַפְשׁוֹ֙ וּבְכָל־מְאֹד֔וֹ בְּכֹ֖ל תּוֹרַ֣ת מֹשֶׁ֑ה וְאַחֲרָ֖יו לֹֽא־קָ֥ם כָּמֹֽהוּ׃

23:25   מְאֹדוֹ

Unique   [ל]   Mp

Com.: This lemma has a circellus but no note. It only occurs once. Neither M^C nor M^A has a note here.

23:25   בְּכֹל תּוֹרַת

Unique   ל   Mp

Com.: The circellus has been placed on the phrase תּוֹרַת מֹשֶׁה but, since this phrase occurs seven times, it is most likely that the circellus should include the preceding word בְּכֹל as the phrase בְּכֹל תּוֹרַת occurs only this once. Neither M^C nor M^A has a note here.

2 KINGS 23:26

אַ֣ךְ ׀ לֹֽא־שָׁ֣ב יְהוָ֗ה מֵחֲר֤וֹן אַפּוֹ֙ הַגָּד֔וֹל אֲשֶׁר־חָרָ֥ה אַפּ֖וֹ בִּֽיהוּדָ֑ה עַ֚ל כָּל־הַכְּעָסִ֔ים אֲשֶׁ֥ר הִכְעִיס֖וֹ מְנַשֶּֽׁה׃

23:26   הַכְּעָסִים

Unique   ל   Mp

23:26   הִכְעִיסוֹ

Unique   ל   Mp

Com.: This lemma is featured in a Masoretic list of words occurring only *once* ending in a *ḥo-lem*; see Frensdorff, *Ochlah*, §33.

2 KINGS 23:27

וַיֹּ֣אמֶר יְהוָ֗ה גַּ֤ם אֶת־יְהוּדָה֙ אָסִיר֙ מֵעַ֣ל פָּנַ֔י כַּאֲשֶׁ֥ר הֲסִרֹ֖תִי אֶת־יִשְׂרָאֵ֑ל וּ֠מָאַסְתִּי אֶת־הָעִ֨יר הַזֹּ֤את אֲשֶׁר־בָּחַ֙רְתִּי֙ אֶת־יְר֣וּשָׁלִַ֔ם וְאֶת־הַבַּ֔יִת אֲשֶׁ֣ר אָמַ֔רְתִּי יִהְיֶ֥ה שְׁמִ֖י שָֽׁם׃

23:27   וְאֶת־הַבַּיִת

Five times   ה   Mp

Com.: See **1 Kgs 9:7**.

2 KINGS 23:29

בְּיָמָיו עָלָה פַּרְעֹה נְכֹה מֶלֶךְ־מִצְרַיִם עַל־מֶלֶךְ אַשּׁוּר עַל־נְהַר־פְּרָת וַיֵּלֶךְ הַמֶּלֶךְ יֹאשִׁיָּהוּ לִקְרָאתוֹ וַיְמִיתֵהוּ בִּמְגִדּוֹ כִּרְאֹתוֹ אֹתוֹ:

23:29   עַל־מֶלֶךְ

Nine times   ט׳   Mp

1–5   **2 Kgs 23:29**; 24:12; 25:20; **Isa 14:4**; Jer 25:12
6–9   **Ezek 28:12**; Dan 11:14; 11:25; 2 Chr 16:7

Com.: The Masorah notes the *nine* occurrences of this lemma with עַל, to distinguish them from its more numerous occurrences (37x) with אֶל מֶלֶךְ (אֶל מֶלֶךְ).

This distinction is implied in the Mm to **Ezek 28:12** in the additional notation *of Kings* to the 2 Kgs 25:20 reference, which distinguishes it from its parallel passage in Jer 52:26, where the lemma occurs as אֶל־מֶלֶךְ.

23:29   וַיְמִיתֵהוּ

Eight times plene   ח׳ מל   Mp

Com.: See **1 Kgs 13:24**

23:29   כִּרְאֹתוֹ

Twice, once defective   ב׳ חד חס׳   Mp

2 Kgs 6:21; <u>23:29</u>

כִּרְאֹתוֹ *twice* defective   כראתו ב׳ חסירין   Mm

2 Kgs 6:21   ויאמר מלך ישראל אל אלישע
<u>2 Kgs 23:29</u>   (וימתהו) [וימיתהו] במגדו כראתו

Com.: The Mp heading here of *twice, once defective* is incorrect. Both forms are defective as is correctly noted in the Mp to 2 Kgs 6:21, and in the heading of the Mm here.

The Masorah notes the *two* occurrences of this lemma written defective ו, to distinguish them from its *two* occurrences written plene ו (כִּרְאוֹתוֹ) at Gen 44:31 and Judg 11:35.

M^A correctly reads here *twice* defective, whereas M^C has no note.

> ### 2 KINGS 23:33
> וַיַּאַסְרֵ֣הוּ פַרְעֹ֣ה נְכֹ֡ה בְרִבְלָ֞ה בְּאֶ֣רֶץ חֲמָ֗ת בִּמְלֹךְ֙ בִּיר֣וּשָׁלִַ֔ם וַיִּתֶּן־עֹ֙נֶשׁ֙ עַל־הָאָ֔רֶץ מֵאָ֥ה כִכַּר־כֶּ֖סֶף וְכִכַּ֥ר זָהָֽב׃

23:33   בִּמְלֹךְ

Mp   ממלך קר   מִמְּלֹךְ Read

Com.: The *kətîb* (במלך), and the *qərê* (מִמְּלֹךְ) represent examples of interchanges between the letters ב and מ; see Gordis, *The Biblical Text*, 144.

This lemma is featured in a Masoretic list of words written with a ב but read as a מ; see Frensdorff, *Ochlah*, §154, and Díaz-Esteban, *Sefer Oklah we-Oklah*, §141.

> ### 2 KINGS 23:35
> וְהַכֶּ֣סֶף וְהַזָּהָ֗ב נָתַ֤ן יְהוֹיָקִים֙ לְפַרְעֹ֔ה אַ֚ךְ הֶעֱרִ֣יךְ אֶת־הָאָ֔רֶץ לָתֵ֥ת אֶת־הַכֶּ֖סֶף עַל־פִּ֣י פַרְעֹ֑ה אִ֣ישׁ כְּעֶרְכּ֗וֹ נָגַ֞שׂ אֶת־הַכֶּ֣סֶף וְאֶת־הַזָּהָ֗ב אֶת־עַם֙ הָאָ֔רֶץ לָתֵ֖ת לְפַרְעֹ֥ה נְכֹֽה׃ ס

23:35   וְהַכֶּסֶף וְהַזָּהָב

Mp   ב̇   *Twice*

2 Kgs 23:35; Ezra 8:28

Com.: The Masorah notes the *two* occurrences of וְהַזָּהָב with וְהַכֶּסֶף, to distinguish them from its more numerous occurrences (6x) with הַכֶּסֶף (הַכֶּסֶף וְהַזָּהָב).

23:35   הֶעֱרִיךְ

Mp   ל   *Unique*

23:35   כְּעֶרְכּוֹ

Mp   ל   *Unique*

Com.: This lemma is featured in three Masoretic lists. One is in a Mm listing all *four* forms of this lemma, *three* without a prep., and this *one* with a prep.; see the Mm at Job 41:4 *sub* עֶרְכּוֹ.

Another is in a list of words occurring only *once* that start with כ; see Frensdorff, *Ochlah*, §19.

A third is in a list of words occurring *twice*, once ending in a י (Ps 55:14), and once ending in a ו (here); see Frensdorff, *Ochlah*, §53, and **2 Sam 15:8**.

23:35   נָגַשׂ

Unique   ל   Mp

Com.: The Masorah notes the *sole* occurrence of this lemma in the perf., to distinguish it from its *three* occurrences in the present (נֹגֵשׂ).

---

2 KINGS 23:36

בֶּן־עֶשְׂרִ֨ים וְחָמֵ֤שׁ שָׁנָה֙ יְה֣וֹיָקִ֣ים בְּמָלְכ֔וֹ וְאַחַ֤ת עֶשְׂרֵה֙ שָׁנָ֔ה מָלַ֖ךְ בִּירוּשָׁלָ֑͏ִם וְשֵׁ֣ם אִמּ֔וֹ זְבִידָּ֥ה בַת־פְּדָיָ֖ה מִן־רוּמָֽה׃

23:36   זְבִידָּה

Read   זְבוּדָה קְ   זבודה   Mp

Com.: The *kətîb* (זבידה), and the *qərê* (זבודה) represent noun variants of the *qātîl/qātûl* type; see Gordis, *The Biblical Text*, 118.

This lemma is featured in a Masoretic list of words that has a י written in the middle of a word that is read as ו; see the Mm at <u>Num 1:16</u> *sub* קריאי, Frensdorff, *Ochlah*, §80, and Díaz-Esteban, *Sefer Oklah we-Oklah*, §71.

---

2 KINGS 24:2

וַיְשַׁלַּ֣ח יְהוָ֣ה ׀ בּ֡וֹ אֶת־גְּדוּדֵ֣י כַשְׂדִּים֩ וְאֶת־גְּדוּדֵ֨י אֲרָ֜ם וְאֵ֣ת ׀ גְּדוּדֵ֣י מוֹאָ֗ב וְאֵת֙ ׀ גְּדוּדֵ֣י בְנֵֽי־עַמּ֔וֹן וַיְשַׁלְּחֵ֥ם בִּֽיהוּדָ֖ה לְהַֽאֲבִיד֑וֹ כִּדְבַ֣ר יְהוָ֔ה אֲשֶׁ֣ר דִּבֶּ֔ר בְּיַ֖ד עֲבָדָ֥יו הַנְּבִיאִֽים׃

24:2   וַיְשַׁלַּח

Twenty-two times   כֿב   Mp

Com.: See **Judg 2:6**.

24:2   וַיְשַׁלְּחֵם

וַיְשַׁלְּחֵם *four times*, and their references   וישלחם ד וסימנהון   Mm

Gen 25:6   מעל יצחק בנו
Gen 26:31   מאתו (בש) [בשלום]
2 Kgs 6:23   ויכרה
<u>2 Kgs 24:2</u>   ביהודה להאבידו

Com.: The Mm heading here, and the Mp heading at Josh 22:6 of *four times*, is incorrect since there are *nine* occurrences of this lemma; see **Josh 22:6**.

The Masorah notes the *nine* occurrences in the *piel*, to distinguish them from its *four* occurrences of this form in the *qal* (וַיִּשְׁלָחֵם); see **Josh 8:9**.

Neither M^C nor M^A has a note on this lemma here.

2 KINGS 24:3

אַךְ ׀ עַל־פִּי יְהוָה הָיְתָה בִּיהוּדָה לְהָסִיר מֵעַל פָּנָיו בְּחַטֹּאת מְנַשֶּׁה כְּכֹל אֲשֶׁר עָשָׂה׃

24:3   בְּחַטֹּאת

Six times defective   ו חס   Mp

Com.: See **2 Kgs 13:2**.

2 KINGS 24:4

וְגַם דַּם־הַנָּקִי אֲשֶׁר שָׁפָךְ וַיְמַלֵּא אֶת־יְרוּשָׁלַ͏ִם דָּם נָקִי וְלֹא־אָבָה יְהוָה לִסְלֹחַ׃

24:4   דָּם הַנָּקִי

Three times   ג   Mp

Deut 19:13; **2 Kgs 24:4**; Jer 22:17

דָּם הַנָּקִי *three times*, and their references   דם הנקי ג׳ וסימנהון   Mm

Deut 19:13   ובערת דם הנקי
Jer 22:17   ועל דם הנקי
2 Kgs 24:4   אשר שפך

Com.: The Masorah notes the *three* occurrences of דָּם with הַנָּקִי, to distinguish it from its more numerous occurrences (9x) with נָקִי (דָּם נָקִי), *one* of which occurs in this verse.

24:4   שָׁפָךְ

Twice zaqep qameṣ   ב׳ זקף קמץ   Mp

Lev 17:4; 2 Kgs 24:4

Com.: The Masorah notes the *two* occurrences of this lemma with a *qameṣ* under the פ (due to the *zaqep̄* accent), to distinguish it from its *four* occurrences with a *pataḥ* (שְׁפַךְ).

This lemma is featured in a Masoretic list of doublets that occur exceptionally with *qameṣ*; see Frensdorff, *Ochlah*, §25, and Díaz-Esteban, *Sefer Oklah we-Oklah*, §26.

2 KINGS 24:7

וְלֹא־הֹסִ֨יף ע֜וֹד מֶ֤לֶךְ מִצְרַ֙יִם֙ לָצֵ֣את מֵֽאַרְצ֔וֹ כִּֽי־לָקַ֞ח מֶ֣לֶךְ בָּבֶ֗ל מִנַּ֤חַל מִצְרַ֙יִם֙ עַד־נְהַר־פְּרָ֔ת כֹּ֛ל אֲשֶׁ֥ר הָיְתָ֖ה לְמֶ֥לֶךְ מִצְרָֽיִם׃ פ

24:7   מִנַּ֤חַל

Four times   ד   Mp

Deut 3:8; Josh 12:1; <u>2 Kgs 24:7</u>; Ps 110:7

מִנַּ֤חַל *four times*, and their references   מנחל ד וסימנהון   Mm

Deut 3:8   (ארנון) [ארנן]
Josh 12:1   ארנון
<u>2 Kgs 24:7</u>   מצרים
Ps 110:7   בדרך ישתה

Com.: The Masorah notes the *four* occurrences of this lemma with the prep. מִ, to distinguish them from its more numerous occurrences (46x) without this preposition.

2 KINGS 24:8

בֶּן־שְׁמֹנֶ֤ה עֶשְׂרֵה֙ שָׁנָ֣ה יְהוֹיָכִ֣ין בְּמָלְכ֔וֹ וּשְׁלֹשָׁ֣ה חֳדָשִׁ֔ים מָלַ֖ךְ בִּירוּשָׁלָ֑͏ִם וְשֵׁ֣ם אִמּ֔וֹ נְחֻשְׁתָּ֥א בַת־אֶלְנָתָ֖ן מִירוּשָׁלָֽ͏ִם׃

24:8   נְחֻשְׁתָּ֥א

Unique   ל   Mp

2 KINGS 24:10

בָּעֵת הַהִיא עָלָה עַבְדֵי נְבֻכַדְנֶאצַּר מֶלֶךְ־בָּבֶל יְרוּשָׁלָ͏ִם וַתָּבֹא הָעִיר בַּמָּצֽוֹר׃

24:10   עָלָה

Read   עָלוּ   עלו ק   Mp

Com.: The *kətîb* (עלה, *he went up*), and the *qərê* (עָלוּ, *they went up*) are examples of *kətîb*/*qərê* variations in number; see Gordis, *The Biblical Text*, 138.

This lemma is featured in a Masoretic list of words ending in a ה but read as a ו; see the Mm at Lev 21:5 *sub* יִקְרְחָה, the Mm at Lam 4:17 *sub* עוֹדֵינָה, Frensdorff, *Ochlah*, §113, and Díaz-Esteban, *Sefer Oklah we-Oklah*, §95.

2 KINGS 24:11

וַיָּבֹא נְבוּכַדְנֶאצַּר מֶלֶךְ־בָּבֶל עַל־הָעִיר וַעֲבָדָיו צָרִים עָלֶֽיהָ׃

24:11   עַל־הָעִיר

	עַל־הָעִיר *seventeen times*	על העיר יֹז	Mm
1–5	Gen 34:25	כאבים	
	Deut 20:20	מצור	
	Judg 9:33	כזרח	
	2 Sam 12:28	וחנה	
	1 Kgs 20:12	בסכות	
6–10	2 Kgs 6:14	ויקפו	
	2 Kgs 10:5	והאמנים	
	2 Kgs 24:11	נבוכדנאצר	
	2 Kgs 25:4	ותבקע	
	And its companion (Jer 52:7)	(וחבי) [וחבירו]	
11–15	Jer 22:8	(ועמדו) [ועברו]	
	Jer 37:8	ונלחמו	
	Jer 32:29	הנלחמים	
	Jer 26:20	וגם איש	
	Ezek 10:2	וזרק	
16–17	Neh 11:9	ויואל	
	Neh 13:18	כה עשו	

And similarly every instance of וגנותי apart from *one*, the *first one* in Kings (2 Kgs 19:34)   וכל וגנותי דכותהון בֹ מֹ אֹ דמלכים קדמיה

Com.: The Masorah notes the *seventeen* occurrences of the phrase עַל־הָעִיר, to distinguish them from its slightly more numerous occurrences (21x) with the prep. אֶל (אֶל־הָעִיר).

This distinction is implied in the additional notation that the verbal form וְגַנּוֹתִי also occurs with the phrase עַל־הָעִיר with *one* exception, that of *the first one in Kings* (2 Kgs 19:34), where it occurs with אֶל (וְגַנּוֹתִי אֶל הָעִיר). In its *second* occurrence in Kings at 2 Kgs 20:6, the phrase as expected occurs with עַל (וְגַנּוֹתִי עַל הָעִיר).

2 KINGS 24:13

וַיּוֹצֵא מִשָּׁם אֶת־כָּל־אוֹצְרוֹת בֵּית יְהוָה וְאוֹצְרוֹת בֵּית הַמֶּלֶךְ וַיְקַצֵּץ אֶת־כָּל־כְּלֵי הַזָּהָב אֲשֶׁר עָשָׂה שְׁלֹמֹה מֶלֶךְ־יִשְׂרָאֵל בְּהֵיכַל יְהוָה כַּאֲשֶׁר דִּבֶּר יְהוָה׃

24:13   וַיּוֹצֵא

Twelve times plene   יֹב מל   Mp

1–5   **Gen 15:5; 24:53; 43:23; 48:12; Exod 19:17**
6–10   **Judg 6:19; <u>2 Kgs 24:13</u>; Jer 10:13; 50:25; 51:16***
11–12 **<u>Ps 136:11</u>; 2 Chr 23:14**

וַיּוֹצֵא *twelve times* plene   ויוצא יֹב מל   Mm

1–5   Gen 15:5   אתו החוצה
       Gen 24:53   העבד
       Gen 43:23   שלום
       Gen 48:12   יוסף
       Exod 19:17   המחנה
6–10   Judg 6:19   האלה
       <u>2 Kgs 24:13</u> משם
       Jer 50:25   פתח יהוה
       Jer 10:13   לקול תתו
       Jer 51:16*   לקול תתו
11–12 2 Chr 23:14   יהוידע
       <u>Ps 136:11</u>   מתוכם

Com.: The Masorah notes the *twelve* occurrences of this lemma written plene וֹ, to distinguish them from its *thirteen* occurrences written defective וֹ (וַיֹּצֵא); see <u>2 Sam 10:16</u>.

This distinction is implied in the additional notation in the Mm at <u>Ps 136:11</u> which, after listing the *twelve* plene forms, states that there are also *thirteen* defective forms making a total of *twenty-five* such forms in the Bible.

*M^L, contrary to M (וַיּוֹצֵא), has only *eleven* occurrences since it writes this lemma defective at Jer 51:16 (וַיֹּצֵא); see Breuer, *The Biblical Text*, 196. However, all the Mp headings highlighted above and the Mm heading here read *twelve times*, thus supporting the enumeration inherent in the text of M.

24:13   אוֹצְרוֹת

Eleven times plene   יא֫ מל֫   Mp

Com.: See **1 Kgs 14:26**^{b}.

---

2 KINGS 24:14

וְהִגְלָה אֶת־כָּל־יְרוּשָׁלַ͏ִם וְאֶת־כָּל־הַשָּׂרִים וְאֵת ׀ כָּל־גִּבּוֹרֵי הַחַיִל עֲשֶׂרֶה אֲלָפִים גּוֹלֶה וְכָל־הֶחָרָשׁ וְהַמַּסְגֵּר לֹא נִשְׁאַר זוּלַת דַּלַּת עַם־הָאָרֶץ׃

24:14   גִּבּוֹרֵי הַחַיִל

Five times with a *pataḥ*   ה֫   Mp

Com.: See **Josh 1:14**.

In M^L the circellus has been placed at Josh 1:14, 8:3, and here only on הַחַיִל, which occurs *fourteen times*. However, it belongs on both words, as is correctly indicated in M^A here, and in M^L in the Mp notes at 2 Kgs 15:20, and 1 Chr 12:9. M^C has no note here.

24:14   עֲשֶׂרֶה

Read   עֲשֶׂרֶת   עשרת קרי   Mp

Com.: The *kətîb* (עשרה), and the *qərê* (עֲשֶׂרֶת) represent examples where the *kətîb* and the *qərê* fluctuate between cstr. and absol. forms of the numerals; see Gordis, *The Biblical Text*, 143.

This lemma is featured in a Masoretic list of words where a ת is read that is not written; see the Mm to **Cant 4:9** sub בְּאַחַד, Frensdorff, *Ochlah*, §162, and Díaz-Esteban, *Sefer Oklah we-Oklah*, §148.

24:14   גּוֹלֶה

Five times plene   ה֫ מל֫   Mp

1–2   **2 Kgs 24:14**; **Prov 20:19**

| Mm | גולה ב׳ מל וסימנהון | גּוֹלֶה *twice* plene, and their references |

עשרת אלפים גולה   2 Kgs 24:14
גולה סוד הולך רכיל   Prov 20:19

Com.: The Mp heading here of *five times plene* (וֹ) is incorrect since, as the Mm indicates, there are only *two* occurrences that are written plene וֹ.

The Masorah notes the *two* occurrences of this lemma written plene וֹ, to distinguish it from its *three* occurrences, written defective ו (גֹּלָה/וְגֹלָה).

M^C, and the Mp heading at Prov 20:19, more exactly read just *five times* to include the *five* occurrences of this lemma, *three times* written defective (1 Sam 22:8^a; 22:8^b, and 2 Sam 15:19) and *twice* written plene (here and Prov 20:19); see **1 Sam 22:8**.

M^A reads as the Mm does here, *twice plene*.

This lemma is featured in a Masoretic list of words which occur *once* with a ו at the beginning but no ו in the middle (וְגֹלָה, 1 Sam 22:8^b), and *once* with a ו in the middle but no ו at the beginning (גּוֹלֶה); see Frensdorff, *Ochlah*, §248. But this Ochlah list does not take into account the fact that the form גּוֹלֶה occurs *twice* (here, and at Prov 20:19).

In M^L in the heading of the Mm an original ה has been overwritten with a ב.

24:14   דַּלַּת

Unique   ל   Mp

Com.: The Masorah notes the *sole* occurrence of this lemma without a ו cj., to distinguish it from its *sole* occurrence with a cj. at Cant 7:6.

---

2 KINGS 24:15

וַיֶּגֶל אֶת־יְהוֹיָכִין בָּבֶלָה וְאֶת־אֵם הַמֶּלֶךְ וְאֶת־נְשֵׁי הַמֶּלֶךְ וְאֶת־סָרִיסָיו וְאֵת אוּלֵי הָאָרֶץ הוֹלִיךְ גּוֹלָה מִירוּשָׁלַם בָּבֶלָה׃

24:15   בָּבֶלָה¹

Twenty-nine times   כ״ט   Mp

Com.: See **2 Kgs 20:17**.

24:15   אוּלֵי

Read אִילֵי קׄ   אילי קׄ   Mp

Com.: The *kǝtîb* (אולי), and the *qǝrê* (אִילֵי) are examples of *kǝtîb/qǝrê* variations where a ו in the middle of a word is read as a י; see Frensdorff, *Ochlah*, §81, Díaz-Esteban, *Sefer Oklah we-Oklah*, §72, and Gordis, *The Biblical Text*, 128.

---

2 KINGS 24:16

וְאֵת֩ כָּל־אַנְשֵׁ֨י הַחַ֜יִל שִׁבְעַ֣ת אֲלָפִ֗ים וְהֶחָרָ֤שׁ וְהַמַּסְגֵּר֙ אֶ֔לֶף גִּבּוֹרִ֖ים עֹשֵׂ֣י מִלְחָמָ֑ה וַיְבִיאֵ֧ם מֶֽלֶךְ־בָּבֶ֛ל גּוֹלָ֖ה בָּבֶֽלָה׃

24:16   אַנְשֵׁי הַחַיִל

Twice   בׄ   Mp

2 Kgs 24:16; **Qoh 12:3** (הֶחָיִל)

Com.: The Masorah notes the *two* occurrences of אַנְשֵׁי with הַחַיִל, to distinguish it from its more numerous occurrences (9x) with חַיִל (אַנְשֵׁי חַיִל).

Com.: Another circellus has been placed between the preceding word כָּל and אַנְשֵׁי, but the phrase כָּל־אַנְשֵׁי הַחַיִל only occurs *once*. However, it is most likely that the note was intended just for the phrase אַנְשֵׁי הַחַיִל as is marked here in M^A and in M^L at Qoh 12:3. M^C has no note here.

---

2 KINGS 24:17

וַיַּמְלֵ֧ךְ מֶֽלֶךְ־בָּבֶ֛ל אֶת־מַתַּנְיָ֥ה דֹדֹ֖ו תַּחְתָּ֑יו וַיַּסֵּ֥ב אֶת־שְׁמ֖וֹ צִדְקִיָּֽהוּ׃ פ

24:17   וַיַּמְלֵךְ

Five times   הׄ   Mp

1–5   2 Kgs 23:34; **24:17**; 1 Chr 23:1; 2 Chr 36:4; 36:10

Com.: The Masorah notes the *five* occurrences of this lemma in the *hiphil*, to distinguish them from its more numerous occurrences (81x) in the *qal* (וַיִּמְלֹךְ).

This distinction is implied in the Mp heading at 1 Chr 23:1, which reads *five times with ṣerê* (הׄ), which distinguishes this form from one with a different vowel, namely וַיִּמְלֹךְ.

> ## 2 KINGS 24:18
> בֶּן־עֶשְׂרִ֨ים וְאַחַ֤ת שָׁנָה֙ צִדְקִיָּ֣הוּ בְמָלְכ֔וֹ וְאַחַ֤ת עֶשְׂרֵה֙ שָׁנָ֔ה מָלַ֖ךְ בִּירוּשָׁלָ֑͏ִם וְשֵׁ֣ם אִמּ֔וֹ חֲמִיטַ֥ל בַּת־יִרְמְיָ֖הוּ מִלִּבְנָֽה׃

חֲמִיטַל 24:18

Mp¹ חמוטל ק׳ חֲמוּטַל Read

Five sets ה׳ זוגין Mp²

1 Gen 25:23 גיים (kətîb)/גּוֹיִם (qərê) and Ps 79:10 בגיים (kətîb)/בַּגּוֹיִם (qərê)

2 Judg 16:21 הָאֲסִירִים (kətîb)/הָאֲסוּרִים (qərê) and Judg 16:25 הָאֲסִירִים (kətîb)/הָאֲסוּרִים (qərê)

3 **2 Kgs 24:18** חמיטל (kətîb)/חֲמוּטַל (qərê) and Jer 52:1 חמיטל (kətîb)/חֲמוּטַל (qərê)

4 Jer 37:4 הכליא (kətîb)/הַכְּלוּא (qərê) and Jer 52:31 הכליא (kətîb)/הַכְּלוּא (qərê)

5 Ps 73:10 ישיב (kətîb)/יָשׁוּב (qərê) and 1 Chr 7:1 ישיב (kətîb)/יָשׁוּב (qərê)

Five sets of words that occur *twice* in which a י is written but read as a ו, and their references	ה׳ זוגין מן תרין תרין כת׳ יוד וקרי ו׳ וסימנהון	Mm
1 Judg 16:21 Judg 16:25	(כל) [בבית] (האסירים) [האסורים] (כל) [מבית] האסירים	
2 Gen 25:23 Ps 79:10	שני גיים בבטנך יודע (בגיים) [בגוים] לעינינו	
3 Jer 37:4 Jer 52:31	(מבית) [בית] {הסורים} (הכלוא) [הכליא] מבית הכליא	
4 חֲמִיטַל of Zedekiah (2 Kgs 24:18) חֲמוּטַל of Zedekiah (Jer 52:1)	(חמיטל) [חמוטל] דצדקיהו חמיטל דצדקיהו	
5 <Ps 73:10> <1 Chr 7:1>		

Com.: In the first Mp note, the *kǝtîb* (חמיטל) represents the archaic gen. ending *i* whereas the *qǝrê* (חֲמוּטַל) represents the archaic nom. ending *u*; see Gordis, *The Biblical Text*, 119.

In the second Mp note and in the Mm, the Masorah notes *five* sets of words that occur *twice*, in which a י is written but read as a ו; see Frensdorff, *Ochlah*, §138, and Díaz-Esteban, *Sefer Oklah we-Oklah*, §122.

In the Mm note, despite its correct heading, only *four* pairs are listed, that of Ps 73:10 and 1 Chr 7:1 (ישיב/ישוב) has been omittted.

The addition *of Zedekiah* to the 2 Kings 24:18 and Jer 52:1 references of the fourth pair is to distinguish these verses from the parallel verse with Jehoahaz in 2 Kgs 23:31 where חֲמוּטַל is both written and read.

This lemma has two Mp notes but only one circellus. This lemma occurs in the ms. in folio 219v, but the Mm note appears on the bottom left of the preceding folio 219r.

2 KINGS 24:20

כִּי ׀ עַל־אַף יְהוָה הָיְתָה בִּירוּשָׁלַם וּבִיהוּדָה עַד־הִשְׁלִכוֹ אֹתָם מֵעַל פָּנָיו וַיִּמְרֹד צִדְקִיָּהוּ בְּמֶלֶךְ בָּבֶל׃ ס

24:20   וּבִיהוּדָה

Five times   ה̇   Mp

1–5 **Josh 19:34**; 2 Kgs 17:13; **24:20**; Zech 14:21; 2 Chr 34:21

וּבִיהוּדָה *five times*   וביהודה ה̇   Mm

1–5	Josh 19:34	אזנות תבור
	2 Kgs 17:13	ויעד יהוה בישראל
	הִשְׁלִכוֹ אֹתָם *of Kings* (2 Kgs 24:20)	(השליכו) [השלכו] (אותם) [אתם] דמלכים
	Zech 14:21	והיה כל סיר
	2 Chr 34:21	לכו דרשו את יהוה

Com.: The Masorah notes the *five* occurrences of this lemma with a ו cj., to distinguish them from its more numerous occurrences (47x) written without a cj.

The addition *of Kings* to the catchword of the 2 Kgs 24:20 reference is to distinguish that verse from its parallel in Jer 52:3 where the lemma appears as וִיהוּדָה.

24:20 הִשְׁלִכוֹ

Unique defective   ל חס   Mp

Com.: The Masorah notes the *sole* occurrence of this lemma written defective י, to distinguish it from its *sole* occurrence written plene י in the parallel passage Jer 52:3.

> **2 KINGS 25:1**
> וַיְהִי בִשְׁנַת הַתְּשִׁיעִית לְמָלְכוֹ בַּחֹדֶשׁ הָעֲשִׂירִי בֶּעָשׂוֹר לַחֹדֶשׁ בָּא נְבֻכַדְנֶאצַּר מֶלֶךְ־בָּבֶל הוּא וְכָל־חֵילוֹ עַל־יְרוּשָׁלַםִ וַיִּחַן עָלֶיהָ וַיִּבְנוּ עָלֶיהָ דָּיֵק סָבִיב:

25:1   בִּשְׁנַת הַתְּשִׁיעִית

Twice   ב   Mp

Com.: See 2 Kgs 17:6.

25:1   הַתְּשִׁיעִית

Twice plene   ב מל   Mp

2 Kgs 25:1; Ezek 24:1

Com.: The Masorah notes *two* occurrences of this lemma הַתְּשִׁיעִית written plene first י, to distinguish them from *three* occurrences written defective first י (הַתְּשִׁעִית).

This distinction is implied in the additional notation in the Mm of Ezek 24:1 *of Kings* to the 2 Kgs 25:1 reference, which distinguishes it from its parallel passages in Jer 39:1 and 52:4, where the lemma occurs as הַתְּשִׁעִית.

M^L, contrary to M (הַתְּשִׁעִית), has a *third* occurrence of this lemma since it writes the form at 2 Kgs 17:6 plene first י (הַתְּשִׁיעִית); see Breuer, *The Biblical Text*, 129.

Nevertheless the Mp notes here and Ezek 24:1 read *twice plene*, and the Mm at Ezek 24:1 lists catchwords for only 2 Kgs 25:1 and Ezek 24:1, thus supporting the enumeration inherent in the text of M.

25:1   עָלֶיהָ וַיִּבְנוּ

Unique   ל   Mp

1–2   **2 Kgs 25:1**; Jer 52:4

Com.: The Mp heading of *unique* is inexact since there are *two* occurrences of this lemma, *once* here and *once* in the parallel passage at Jer 52:4. The note more precisely should have read *unique in the book*.

Neither M^C nor M^A has a note on this lemma here.

2 KINGS 25:3
בְּתִשְׁעָ֣ה לַחֹ֔דֶשׁ וַיֶּחֱזַ֥ק הָרָעָ֖ב בָּעִ֑יר וְלֹא־הָ֥יָה לֶ֖חֶם לְעַ֥ם הָאָֽרֶץ׃

25:3   וַיֶּחֱזַ֥ק

Fifteen times   ה֗ו   Mp

Com.: See **1 Sam 17:50**.

2 KINGS 25:4
וַתִּבָּקַ֣ע הָעִ֗יר וְכָל־אַנְשֵׁ֨י הַמִּלְחָמָ֤ה ׀ הַלַּ֨יְלָה֙ דֶּ֣רֶךְ שַׁ֔עַר ׀ בֵּ֤ין הַחֹמֹתַ֨יִם֙ אֲשֶׁר֙ עַל־גַּ֣ן הַמֶּ֔לֶךְ וְכַשְׂדִּ֥ים עַל־הָעִ֖יר סָבִ֑יב וַיֵּ֖לֶךְ דֶּ֥רֶךְ הָעֲרָבָֽה׃

25:4   וַתִּבָּקַ֣ע

Four times   ד֗   Mp

Num 16:31; 1 Kgs 1:40; <u>2 Kgs 25:4</u>; <u>Jer 52:7</u>

וַתִּבָּקַ֣ע *four times,* and their references   ותבקע ד וסימנהון   Mm

Num 16:31	ותבקע האדמה אשר
1 Kgs 1:40	ותבקע
<u>2 Kgs 25:4</u>	העיר וכל אנשי
<u>Jer 52:7</u>	ותבקע (העור) [העיר]

Com.: The Masorah notes the *four* occurrences of this lemma with a ו consec., to distinguish them from its *sole* occurrence without a ו (תִּבָּקַע) in Isa 59:5.

25:4   עַל־גַּן

Three times   ג̇   Mp

2 Kgs 25:4; Jer 52:7; Job 8:16 (וְעַל־גַּנָּתוֹ)

Com.: The Masorah notes the *three* occurrences of this lemma, *twice* in this form and *once* with a ו cj. and sfx.

The Mp to Job 8:16 reads *unique* reflecting the *sole* occurrence of its specific form (וְעַל־גַּנָּתוֹ).

2 KINGS 25:5

וַיִּרְדְּפוּ חֵיל־כַּשְׂדִּים אַחַר הַמֶּלֶךְ וַיַּשִּׂגוּ אֹתוֹ בְּעַרְבוֹת יְרֵחוֹ וְכָל־חֵילוֹ נָפֹצוּ מֵעָלָיו:

25:5   וַיַּשִּׂגוּ

Five times defective   ה̇ חס   Mp

Com.: See **1 Sam 30:8.**

2 KINGS 25:7

וְאֶת־בְּנֵי צִדְקִיָּהוּ שָׁחֲטוּ לְעֵינָיו וְאֶת־עֵינֵי צִדְקִיָּהוּ עִוֵּר וַיַּאַסְרֵהוּ בַנְחֻשְׁתַּיִם וַיְבִאֵהוּ בָּבֶל: ס

25:7   וְאֶת־בְּנֵי

Ten times   י̇   Mp

Com.: See **Josh 10:4**.

2 KINGS 25:8

וּבַחֹדֶשׁ הַחֲמִישִׁי בְּשִׁבְעָה לַחֹדֶשׁ הִיא שְׁנַת תְּשַׁע־עֶשְׂרֵה שָׁנָה לַמֶּלֶךְ נְבֻכַדְנֶאצַּר מֶלֶךְ־בָּבֶל בָּא נְבוּזַרְאֲדָן רַב־טַבָּחִים עֶבֶד מֶלֶךְ־בָּבֶל יְרוּשָׁלָ͏ִם:

25:8   וּבַחֹדֶשׁ

Five times at the beginning of a verse   ה̇ ראׁ פס   Mp

1–5   **Gen 8:14**; Num 28:16; 29:1; **2 Kgs 25:8**; Jer 52:12

Com.: The Masorah notes the *five* occurrences of this lemma at the beginning of a verse with a ו cj., to distinguish them from its *seven* occurrences at the beginning of a verse without a cj. (בַּחֹדֶשׁ); see Ginsburg, 4, ח, §55

2 KINGS 25:9

וַיִּשְׂרֹף אֶת־בֵּית־יְהוָה וְאֶת־בֵּית הַמֶּלֶךְ וְאֵת כָּל־בָּתֵּי יְרוּשָׁלִַם וְאֶת־כָּל־בֵּית גָּדוֹל שָׂרַף בָּאֵשׁ׃

25:9   וְאֵת כָּל־בֵּית

Nine times   ט׳   Mp

Com.: See **Josh 2:18**.

2 KINGS 25:10

וְאֶת־חוֹמֹת יְרוּשָׁלִַם סָבִיב נָתְצוּ כָּל־חֵיל כַּשְׂדִּים אֲשֶׁר רַב־טַבָּחִים׃

25:10   חוֹמֹת

Four times written (like this)   ד׳ כת׳   Mp

2 Kgs 25:10; **Jer 51:12**; **Lam 2:7**; **Neh 2:13** (בְּחוֹמֹת)

Com.: The Masorah here, and at Jer 51:12, notes the *four* occurrences of this lemma written defective second ו, to distinguish them from its *five* occurrences in various forms written plene second ו (e.g., חוֹמוֹת).

The Mp headings at Lam 2:7 and Neh 2:13 read *eight times*, noting the *eight* occurrences, apart from Jeremiah, of this lemma in various forms written plene and defective first and second ו; see the Mm to <u>Ezek 26:4</u> *sub* חמות, and Ognibeni, *'Oklah*, §171.

2 KINGS 25:11

וְאֵת יֶתֶר הָעָם הַנִּשְׁאָרִים בָּעִיר וְאֶת־הַנֹּפְלִים אֲשֶׁר נָפְלוּ עַל־הַמֶּלֶךְ וְאֵת יֶתֶר הֶהָמוֹן הֶגְלָה נְבוּזַרְאֲדָן רַב־טַבָּחִים׃

25:11   עַל־הַמֶּלֶךְ

Eight times   ח׳   Mp

Com.: See **2 Kgs 11:8**.

2 KINGS 25:12

וּמִדַּלַּת הָאָרֶץ הִשְׁאִיר רַב־טַבָּחִים לְכֹרְמִים וּלְיֹגְבִים:

25:12   וּמִדַּלַּת

Twice   בֿ   Mp

2 Kgs 25:12; Jer 40:7

Com.: The Masorah notes the *two* occurrences of this lemma in the sg., to distinguish them from its *two* occurrences in the pl. (וּמִדַּלּוֹת), *one* of which occurs in the parallel passage to this text at Jer 52:16, and the *other* occurs in the preceding verse (52:15).

This lemma is featured in a Mm note at Jer 52:16 illustrating the differences between the *two* parallel verses of 2 Kgs 25:12 and Jer 52:16. The Aramaic catchwords in this Mm are in the form of a mnemonic "(in the book of) Kings poverty is sg., (but in the book of) Jeremiah poverty is pl."; see Marcus, *Scribal Wit*, 99.

25:12   וּלְיֹגְבִים

Twice   בֿ   Mp

2 Kgs 25:12; Jer 52:16

2 KINGS 25:13

וְאֶת־עַמּוּדֵי הַנְּחֹשֶׁת אֲשֶׁר בֵּית־יְהוָה וְאֶת־הַמְּכֹנוֹת וְאֶת־יָם הַנְּחֹשֶׁת אֲשֶׁר בְּבֵית־יְהוָה שִׁבְּרוּ כַשְׂדִּים וַיִּשְׂאוּ אֶת־נְחֻשְׁתָּם בָּבֶלָה:

25:13   בְּבֵית יְהוָה

Thirty-nine times   לֿט   Mp

Com.: See **1 Sam 1:7**.

25:13   בָּבֶלָה

Twenty-nine times   כֿט   Mp

Com.: See **2 Kgs 20:17**.

> **2 KINGS 25:14**
>
> וְאֶת־הַסִּירֹת וְאֶת־הַיָּעִים וְאֶת־הַמְזַמְּרוֹת וְאֶת־הַכַּפּוֹת וְאֵת כָּל־כְּלֵי הַנְּחֹשֶׁת אֲשֶׁר יְשָׁרְתוּ־בָם לָקָחוּ׃

25:14   הַסִּירֹת

Twice written like this   ב׳ כת׳ כן   Mp

Exod 38:3; **2 Kgs 25:14**

הַסִּירֹת *twice* written like this   הסירת ב׳ כת כן   Mm

All the Torah (Exod 38:3)	כל אוריתא
וְאֶת־הַסִּירֹת וְאֶת־הַיָּעִים	ואת הסירת ואת (העם) [היעים]
of Kings (2 Kgs 25:14)	דמלכים
And *once* written הַסִּרוֹת	וחד כת׳ (הסירת) [הסרות]
in its *first occurrence in Jeremiah* (Jer 52:18)	קדמיה דירמיה
And in the rest it is הַסִּירוֹת *doubly plene*	ושארא הסירות שלמ׳ דשלמ

Com.: The Masorah notes the *two* occurrences of this lemma written plene י but defective ו, to distinguish them from its *sole* occurrence written defective י and plene ו (הַסִּרוֹת) at Jer 52:18.

This distinction is implied in the additional notation *of Kings* to the 2 Kgs 25:14 reference, which distinguishes it from its parallel passage in Jer 52:18, where the lemma occurs as הַסִּרוֹת.

The additional notation of *and once written* הַסִּרוֹת *in its first occurrence in Jeremiah*, is to contrast the *first* occurrence of this lemma in Jeremiah with its *second* occurrence (in the next verse, Jer 52:19), where the lemma occurs differently as הַסִּירוֹת (doubly plene with both plene י and plene ו).

The Masorah also notes that the form that occurs in the rest of the Bible is the doubly plene one הַסִּירוֹת.

25:14   יְשָׁרְתוּ־בָם

Three times   גׄ   Mp

Num 4:12; 2 Kgs 25:14; Ezek 44:19 (מְשָׁרְתָם בָּם)

Com.: The Masorah notes the *three* occurrences of the verb שָׁרֵת in various forms with בָּם, to distinguish them from the *two* occurrences of this verb with בָּהֶם (יְשָׁרְתוּ בָהֶם) at Num 3:31 and Jer 52:18.

---

2 KINGS 25:16

הָעַמּוּדִים ׀ שְׁנַיִם הַיָּם הָאֶחָד וְהַמְּכֹנוֹת אֲשֶׁר־עָשָׂה שְׁלֹמֹה לְבֵית יְהוָה לֹא־הָיָה מִשְׁקָל לִנְחֹשֶׁת כָּל־הַכֵּלִים הָאֵלֶּה:

25:16   הַיָּם הָאֶחָד

Twice   בׄ   Mp

Com.: See 1 Kgs 7:44.

25:16   כָּל־הַכֵּלִים הָאֵלֶּה

Four times   דׄ   Mp

1–5   Exod 25:39; 1 Kgs 7:45; 2 Kgs 4:4; **25:16; Jer 52:20**
6   **2 Chr 4:18**

כָּל־הַכֵּלִים הָאֵלֶּה *four times*, and their references   כל הכלים האלה ד׳ וסימנהון   Mm

2 Kgs 25:16   לנחשת כל
Jer 52:20   לנחשתם
1 Kgs 7:45   ואת הסירות
וַיַּעַשׂ שְׁלֹמֹה *of Chronicles* (2 Chr 4:18)   (וינח) [ויעש] שלמה דדברי הימים

Com.: Both the Mp and Mm headings here and at Jer 52:20 of *four times*, and the Mm list here and at Jer 52:20 of *four* references for this lemma, are incorrect since the phrase כָּל־הַכֵּלִים הָאֵלֶּה occurs *six* times.

From the information given in the headings of the Mp and Mm at 2 Chr 4:18 of *three times lacking* אֶת, it seems that this note has to do with cases where the phrase כָּל־הַכֵּלִים הָאֵלֶּה is *not* preceded by the accusative sign אֶת. This situation occurs *three times* at 2 Kgs 25:16, Jer 52:20, and 2 Chr 4:18, and these *three* references are listed in the Mm at 2 Chr 4:18.

The intent of the note is further implied in the additional notation in the Mm here *of Chronicles* to the catchwords of the 2 Chr 4:18 reference, which distinguishes itself from its parallel in 1 Kgs 7:48, which does have the phrase כָּל־הַכֵּלִים preceded by an אֵת.

However, if this is the intent of the note, the placement in the Mm list of the catchwords for 1 Kgs 7:45 constitutes a problem because כָּל־הַכֵּלִים הָאֵלֶּה in that verse is preceded by וְאֵת.

Neither M^C nor M^A has a note on this lemma here.

> ### 2 KINGS 25:17
> שְׁמֹנֶה עֶשְׂרֵה אַמָּה קוֹמַת ׀ הָעַמּוּד הָאֶחָד וְכֹתֶרֶת עָלָיו ׀ נְחֹשֶׁת וְקוֹמַת הַכֹּתֶרֶת שָׁלֹשׁ אַמּוֹת וּשְׂבָכָה וְרִמֹּנִים עַל־הַכֹּתֶרֶת סָבִיב הַכֹּל נְחֹשֶׁת וְכָאֵלֶּה לַעַמּוּד הַשֵּׁנִי עַל־הַשְּׂבָכָה:

25:17   אמה

Read אַמּוֹת   אמות ק   Mp

Com.: The *katîb* (אמה), and the *qərê* (אַמּוֹת) represent examples where the *katîb* and the *qərê* fluctuate between cstr. and absol. forms; see Gordis, *The Biblical Text*, 143.

This lemma is featured in a Masoretic list of words where a ת that is not written is read; see the Mm to Cant 4:9 *sub* בְּאַחַד, Frensdorff, *Ochlah*, §162, and Díaz-Esteban, *Sefer Oklah we-Oklah*, §148.

25:17   וְכָאֵלֶּה לַעַמּוּד

Twice   ב֗   Mp

2 Kgs 25:17; Jer 52:22

Com.: The Masorah notes the *two* occurrences of this lemma in the parallel passages of 2 Kings and Jeremiah.

> ### 2 KINGS 25:18
> וַיִּקַּח רַב־טַבָּחִים אֶת־שְׂרָיָה כֹּהֵן הָרֹאשׁ וְאֶת־צְפַנְיָהוּ כֹּהֵן מִשְׁנֶה וְאֶת־שְׁלֹשֶׁת שֹׁמְרֵי הַסַּף:

25:18   צְפַנְיָהוּ

Twice   ב֗   Mp

2 Kgs 25:18; Jer 37:3

| צְפַנְיָהוּ *twice* | צפניהו בׄ | Mm |

Jer 37:3   וישלח המלך (צדקיה) [צדקיהו]
2 Kgs 25:18   כהן משנה

Com.: The Masorah notes the *two* occurrences of this lemma with the divine element יָהוּ, to distinguish them from its more numerous occurrences (9x) of this name written with the divine element יָה (צְפַנְיָה).

2 KINGS 25:19

וּמִן־הָעִיר לָקַח סָרִיס אֶחָד אֲשֶׁר־הוּא פָקִיד ׀ עַל־אַנְשֵׁי הַמִּלְחָמָה וַחֲמִשָּׁה אֲנָשִׁים מֵרֹאֵי פְנֵי־הַמֶּלֶךְ אֲשֶׁר נִמְצְאוּ בָעִיר וְאֵת הַסֹּפֵר שַׂר הַצָּבָא הַמַּצְבִּא אֶת־עַם הָאָרֶץ וְשִׁשִּׁים אִישׁ מֵעַם הָאָרֶץ הַנִּמְצְאִים בָּעִיר:

25:19   עַל־אַנְשֵׁי

Four times   דׄ   Mp

1 Sam 18:5; **2 Kgs 25:19**; **Jer 11:21**; **52:25**

| עַל־אַנְשֵׁי *four times* | על אנשי דׄ | Mm |

1 Sam 18:5   (וישמהו) [וישימהו] שאול
2 Kgs 25:19   ומן העיר לקח
And its companion (Jer 52:25)   (וחב׳) [וחבירו]
Jer 11:21   לכן כה אמר יהוה

Com.: The Masorah notes the *four* occurrences of אַנְשֵׁי with עַל, to distinguish them from its more numerous occurrences (8x) with אֶל.

25:19   וְאֵת הַסֹּפֵר

Unique   לׄ   Mp

Com.: The Masorah notes the *sole* occurrence of וְאֵת with הַסֹּפֵר, to distinguish it from its *sole* occurrence with סֹפֵר (וְאֵת סֹפֵר) in the parallel text at Jer 52:25; see Ognibeni, *'Oklah*, §117Q.

25:19   הַמַּצְבִּא

Twice   בׄ   Mp

2 Kgs 25:19; Jer 52:25

> **2 Kings 25:20**
>
> וַיִּקַּ֣ח אֹתָ֗ם נְבוּזַרְאֲדָן֙ רַב־טַבָּחִ֔ים וַיֹּ֧לֶךְ אֹתָ֛ם עַל־מֶ֥לֶךְ בָּבֶ֖ל רִבְלָֽתָה׃

25:20   וַיֹּ֧לֶךְ

Four times   ד   Mp

Com.: See 2 Kgs 6:19.

> **2 Kings 25:21**
>
> וַיַּ֣ךְ אֹתָ֠ם מֶ֣לֶךְ בָּבֶ֧ל וַיְמִיתֵ֛ם בְּרִבְלָ֖ה בְּאֶ֣רֶץ חֲמָ֑ת וַיִּ֥גֶל יְהוּדָ֖ה מֵעַ֥ל אַדְמָתֽוֹ׃

25:21   וַיִּ֥גֶל

וַיִּ֥גֶל *four times*   ויגל ד   Mm

2 Kgs 17:23   מעל אדמתו
2 Kgs 25:21   מעל אדמתו
Jer 52:27   ויגל יהודה
Job 36:10   ויגל אזנם למוסר

Com.: The Masorah notes the *four* occurrences of this lemma with a ו consec., to distinguish them from its *sole* occurrence with a ו cj. (וְיִ֥גֶל) at Job 36:15.

> **2 Kings 25:22**
>
> וְהָעָ֗ם הַנִּשְׁאָר֙ בְּאֶ֣רֶץ יְהוּדָ֔ה אֲשֶׁ֣ר הִשְׁאִ֔יר נְבֽוּכַדְנֶאצַּ֖ר מֶ֣לֶךְ בָּבֶ֑ל וַיַּפְקֵ֣ד עֲלֵיהֶ֗ם אֶת־גְּדַלְיָ֙הוּ֙ בֶּן־אֲחִיקָ֖ם בֶּן־שָׁפָֽן׃ פ

25:22   נְבֽוּכַדְנֶאצַּ֖ר

Unique plene in the book   ל מל בסיפ   Mp

Com.: The Masorah notes the *sole* occurrence in the book of this lemma written plene ו, to distinguish it from its *five* occurrences in the book written defective ו (נְבֻכַדְנֶאצַּ֖ר), *two* of which are in this chapter in vv. 1 and 8.

M^L, contrary to M (נְבֻכַדְנֶאצַּ֖ר), has another occurrence of this lemma at 2 Kgs 24:11 (נְבוּכַדְנֶאצַּ֖ר); see Breuer, *The Biblical Text*, 136. However, the Mp heading here supports the enumeration inherent in the text of M.

2 Kings 25:23

וַיִּשְׁמְע֣וּ כָל־שָׂרֵ֣י הַחֲיָלִ֡ים הֵ֣מָּה וְהָאֲנָשִׁים֩ כִּֽי־הִפְקִ֨יד מֶֽלֶךְ־בָּבֶ֜ל אֶת־גְּדַלְיָ֗הוּ וַיָּבֹ֤אוּ אֶל־גְּדַלְיָ֙הוּ֙ הַמִּצְפָּ֔ה וְיִשְׁמָעֵ֣אל בֶּן־נְתַנְיָ֡ה וְיוֹחָנָ֣ן בֶּן־קָ֠רֵחַ וּשְׂרָיָ֨ה בֶן־תַּנְחֻ֜מֶת הַנְּטֹפָתִ֗י וְיַֽאֲזַנְיָ֙הוּ֙ בֶּן־הַמַּ֣עֲכָתִ֔י הֵ֖מָּה וְאַנְשֵׁיהֶֽם׃

25:23   תַּנְחֻמֶת

Twice   בׄ   Mp

2 Kgs 25:23; Jer 40:8

Com.: The Masorah notes the *two* occurrences of this lemma, *one* here and *one* in the parallel passage at Jer 40:8.

25:23   וְיַאֲזַנְיָהוּ

Twice   בׄ   Mp

2 Kgs 25:23; Ezek 8:11

Com.: The Masorah notes the *two* occurrences of this lemma written with an א, to distinguish them from its *sole* occurrence without this א (וְיֵזַנְיָהוּ) in the parallel passage at Jer 40:8.

Com.: The circellus has mistakenly been placed on the preceding word הַנְּטֹפָתִי which occurs *five* times. It is thus most likely that, as with both M^A and M^C, the note belongs here since this lemma does occur *twice*.

25:23   הֵמָּה וְאַנְשֵׁיהֶם

Three times   גׄ   Mp

2 Kgs 25:23; Jer 40:7; **40:8**

Com.: The Masorah notes the *three* occurrences of הֵמָּה with וְאַנְשֵׁיהֶם, to distinguish them from its occurrence with (הֵמָּה וְהָאֲנָשִׁים) in the same verse.

25:23   וְאַנְשֵׁיהֶם

Four times   דׄ   Mp

2 Kgs 25:23; Jer 18:21; 40:7; **40:8**

Mm	ואנשיהם ד	וְאַנְשֵׁיהֶם *four times*

<u>2 Kgs 25:23</u> ויבאו אל גדליהו
Jer 18:21 לכן תן את בניהם
Jer 40:7 וישמעו כל שרי
Jer 40:8 ויבאו אל גדליה

Com.: The Masorah notes the *four* occurrences of this lemma without the prep. ל, to distinguish them from its *two* occurrences with the prep. ל (וּלְאַנְשֵׁיהֶם) at 2 Kgs 25:24 and Jer 40:9.

---

2 KINGS 25:24

וַיִּשָּׁבַ֨ע לָהֶ֤ם גְּדַלְיָ֙הוּ֙ וּלְאַנְשֵׁיהֶ֔ם וַיֹּ֣אמֶר לָהֶ֗ם אַל־תִּֽירְאוּ֙ מֵעַבְדֵ֣י הַכַּשְׂדִּ֔ים שְׁב֣וּ בָאָ֔רֶץ וְעִבְד֥וּ אֶת־מֶ֖לֶךְ בָּבֶ֑ל וְיִטַ֥ב לָכֶֽם׃ ס

25:24   וְיִטַב

Mp   ג֟ חס   *Three times* defective

Com.: See **1 Sam 24:5**.

---

2 KINGS 25:25

וַיְהִ֣י ׀ בַּחֹ֣דֶשׁ הַשְּׁבִיעִ֗י בָּ֣א יִשְׁמָעֵ֣אל בֶּן־נְ֠תַנְיָה בֶּן־אֱלִישָׁמָ֨ע מִזֶּ֤רַע הַמְּלוּכָה֙ וַעֲשָׂרָ֤ה אֲנָשִׁים֙ אִתּ֔וֹ וַיַּכּ֣וּ אֶת־גְּדַלְיָ֖הוּ וַיָּמֹ֑ת וְאֶת־הַיְּהוּדִים֙ וְאֶת־הַכַּשְׂדִּ֔ים אֲשֶׁר־הָי֥וּ אִתּ֖וֹ בַּמִּצְפָּֽה׃

25:25   הַמְּלוּכָה

Mp   כ֟   *Twenty times*

Com.: See **1 Sam 10:25**.

25:25   וְאֶת־הַיְּהוּדִים

Mp   ג֟   *Three times*

Com.: The Mp heading here of *three times* is incorrect since this is the *only* occurrence of this lemma. Both M^C and M^A correctly read here *unique*.

| 25:25 | וְאֶת־הַכַּשְׂדִּים |

| Three times | ג֗ | Mp |

2 Kgs 25:25; Jer 21:4; 41:3

| Mm | ואת הכשדים ג֗ | *three times* | וְאֶת הַכַּשְׂדִּים |

הנני מסב את כלי	Jer 21:4
ואת כל היהודים אשר היו	Jer 41:3
ויהי בחדש השביעי (דמלכי) [דמלכים]	וַיְהִי בַּחֹדֶשׁ הַשְּׁבִיעִי *of Kings* (2 Kgs 25:25)

Com.: The Masorah notes the *three* occurrences of this lemma with a ו cj., to distinguish them from its *three* occurrences without a cj.

The addition *of Kings* to the catchwords of the 2 Kgs 25:25 reference is simply to distinguish that verse from its parallel in Jer 41:3 which is also in the list.

2 KINGS 25:26

וַיָּקֻמוּ כָל־הָעָם מִקָּטֹן וְעַד־גָּדוֹל וְשָׂרֵי הַחֲיָלִים וַיָּבֹאוּ מִצְרָיִם כִּי יָרְאוּ מִפְּנֵי כַשְׂדִּים: פ

| 25:26 | מִפְּנֵי כַשְׂדִּים |

| Unique | ל֗ | Mp |

Com.: The Masorah notes the *sole* occurrence of מִפְּנֵי with כַשְׂדִּים, to distinguish it from its occurrence with הַכַּשְׂדִּים (מִפְּנֵי הַכַּשְׂדִּים) in the parallel text at Jer 41:18.

2 KINGS 25:27

וַיְהִי בִשְׁלֹשִׁים וָשֶׁבַע שָׁנָה לְגָלוּת יְהוֹיָכִין מֶלֶךְ־יְהוּדָה בִּשְׁנֵים עָשָׂר חֹדֶשׁ בְּעֶשְׂרִים וְשִׁבְעָה לַחֹדֶשׁ נָשָׂא אֱוִיל מְרֹדַךְ מֶלֶךְ בָּבֶל בִּשְׁנַת מָלְכוֹ אֶת־רֹאשׁ יְהוֹיָכִין מֶלֶךְ־יְהוּדָה מִבֵּית כֶּלֶא:

| 25:27 | נָשָׂא אֱוִיל |

| Twice | ב֗ | Mp |

2 Kgs 25:27; Jer 52:31

Com.: The Masorah notes the *two* occurrences of this lemma, *one* here and *one* in the parallel passage at Jer 52:31.

25:27 מִבֵּית כֶּלֶא

Three times   ג׳   Mp

Com.: See **2 Kgs 17:4**.

---

2 KINGS 25:28

וַיְדַבֵּר אִתּוֹ טֹבוֹת וַיִּתֵּן אֶת־כִּסְאוֹ מֵעַל כִּסֵּא הַמְּלָכִים אֲשֶׁר אִתּוֹ בְּבָבֶל׃

25:28   בְּבָבֶל

Eight times   ח׳   Mp

1–5 **2 Kgs 25:28**; Isa 48:14; **Jer 29:22**; 51:44; 52:32
6–8 **Ezra 5:17**; 6:1; 2 Chr 36:7

בְּבָבֶל *eight times*   בבבל ח׳   Mm

1–5   2 Kgs 25:28   וידבר
      And its companion (Jer 52:32)   וחבירו
      Isa 48:14   אהבו
      Jer 29:22   ולקח
      Jer 51:44   ופקדתי
6–8   2 Chr 36:7   [ומכלי] (ומכליו)
      Ezra 5:17   [וכען] (כען)
      Ezra 6:1   באדין

Com.: The Masorah notes the *eight* occurrences of this lemma with the prep. בּ, to distinguish them from its more numerous occurrences (200+) without this preposition.

---

2 KINGS 25:29

וְשִׁנָּא אֵת בִּגְדֵי כִלְאוֹ וְאָכַל לֶחֶם תָּמִיד לְפָנָיו כָּל־יְמֵי חַיָּיו׃

25:29   וְשִׁנָּא

Twice, *once* written with א and *once* written with ה   ב׳ חד כת׳ א׳ וחד כת׳ ה׳   Mp

2 Kgs 25:29; **Jer 52:33** (וְשִׁנָּה)

Com.: The Masorah notes the *two* occurrences of this lemma, *one* written with א (here) and *one* written with ה in the parallel passage at Jer 52:33.

This lemma is featured in two Masoretic lists. One is in a Mm list of various forms with an א ending; see Qoh 8:1 *sub* יֵשְׁנָא. The other is in a list of doublets that end once with א and once with ה; see Frensdorff, *Ochlah*, §95, and Díaz-Esteban, *Sefer Oklah we-Oklah*, §78.

2 KINGS 25:30

וַאֲרֻחָתוֹ אֲרֻחַת תָּמִיד נִתְּנָה־לּוֹ מֵאֵת הַמֶּלֶךְ דְּבַר־יוֹם בְּיוֹמוֹ כֹּל יְמֵי חַיָּו׃

25:30   וַאֲרֻחָתוֹ

Twice and defective: תָּמִיד   ב׳ וחס׳ תמיד   Mp

2 Kgs 25:30; Jer 52:34

Com.: By noting that this lemma occurs *twice* and both times written defective ו, the Masorah is also implying (correctly) that this lemma does not occur elsewhere written plene ו.

The catchword תָּמִיד added to the Mp heading here refers the reader back to the parallel passage in Jer 52:34.

25:30   חַיָּו

Four times defective   ד׳ חס׳   Mp

2 Sam 18:18 (בְּחַיָּו); **2 Kgs 25:30**; Jer 52:33; Qoh 5:17

חַיָּו *four times* defective   חיו ד׳ חסירין   Mm

2 Sam 18:18	(ואבשלום) [ואבשלם] לקח
וַאֲרֻחָתוֹ *of Kings* (2 Kgs 25:30)	וארחתו דמלכים
וְשָׁנָה *of Jeremiah* (Jer 52:33)	ושנה דירמיה
Qoh 5:17	הנה אשר (ואותי) [ראיתי] אני

Com.: The Masorah notes the *four* occurrences of this lemma written defective second י, to distinguish them from its more numerous occurrences (17x) written plene second י (חַיָּיו/בְּחַיָּיו).

This distinction is implied in the additional notation *of Kings* to the 2 Kgs 25:30 reference, which distinguishes it from its parallel passage in Jer 52:34, where the lemma is written plene as חַיָּו, and in the additional notation *of Jeremiah* to the Jer 52:33 reference, which distinguishes it from its parallel in 2 Kgs 25:29, where the lemma is written plene as חַיָּו.

This lemma occurs in the ms. in folio 220v, but the Mm note appears on the bottom right of the preceding folio 220r.

| The number of the verses in the book is *one thousand, five-hundred* and *thirty-four* | סכום הפסוקים של ספר אלף וחמש מאות ושלשים וארבעה | Mf |